A WORLD MADE SEXY:
FREUD TO MADONNA

The cult of eroticism is a pervasive force in modern society, affecting almost every aspect of our daily lives. In this book, Paul Rutherford argues that this phenomenon is a product of one of the major commercial and political enterprises of the twentieth and twenty-first centuries: the creation of desire – for sex, for wealth, and for entertainment.

A World Made Sexy examines museum exhibitions, art, books, magazines, films, and television to explore the popular rise of eroticism in America and across the developed world. Starting with a brief foray into the history of pornography, Rutherford goes on to explore a sexual liberation movement shaped by the ideas of Marx and Freud, the erotic styles of Salvador Dalí and pop art, the pioneering use of publicity as erotica by *Playboy* and other media, and the growing concerns of cultural critics over the emergence of a regime of stimulation. In one case study, Rutherford pairs James Bond and Madonna in order to examine the link between sex and aggression. He details how television advertising after 1980 constructed a theatre of the libido to entice the buying public, and concludes by situating the cultivation of eroticism in the wider context of Michel Foucault's views on social power and governmentality, and specifically how they relate to sexuality, during the modern era.

A World Made Sexy is about power and pleasure, emancipation and domination, and the relationship between the personal passions and social controls that have crafted desire.

PAUL RUTHERFORD is a professor in the Department of History at the University of Toronto.

PAUL RUTHERFORD

A World Made Sexy

Freud to Madonna

UNIVERSITY OF TORONTO PRESS
Toronto Buffalo London

© University of Toronto Press Incorporated 2007
Toronto Buffalo London
Printed in Canada

ISBN 978-0-8020-9256-4 (cloth)
ISBN 978-0-8020-9466-7 (paper)

Printed on acid-free paper

Library and Archives Canada Cataloguing in Publication

Rutherford, Paul, 1944–
A world made sexy : Freud to Madonna / Paul Rutherford.

Includes bibliographical references and index.
ISBN 978-0-8020-9256-4 (bound)
ISBN 978-0-8020-9466-7 (pbk.)

1. Erotica – History.   2. Sex in advertising – History.   3. Sex in popular
culture – History.   4. Sex in mass media – History.   5. Sex – Social aspects.
I. Title.

HQ21.R975 2007   306.7   C2007-901374-0

This book has been published with the help of a grant from the Canadian
Federation for the Humanities and Social Sciences, through the Aid to
Scholarly Publications Programme, using funds provided by the Social
Sciences and Humanities Research Council of Canada.

University of Toronto Press acknowledges the financial assistance to its
publishing program of the Canada Council for the Arts and the Ontario
Arts Council.

University of Toronto Press acknowledges the financial support for its
publishing activities of the Government of Canada through the Book
Publishing Industry Development Program (BPIDP).

Contents

Acknowledgments

A supporting grant from the Social Sciences and Humanities Research Council of Canada made possible much of the research for this book. Additional research monies, some also derived from the SSHRC but administered by the University of Toronto, assisted a number of forays to places outside Canada. I would like to thank Maxine Iversen and Jennifer Ellison, both past students, who acted as research assistants on particular aspects of the project. I am grateful to my daughter, Stephanie Rutherford, who took time away from her own research labours to assist me in reading through the entire manuscript. And I would like to thank Jane Abray, Chair of the Department of History at the University of Toronto, who kindly allowed me to rearrange my teaching schedule so as to speed the completion of the book. My thanks, as well, to the two anonymous reviewers who provided criticisms of the manuscript that served to sharpen the arguments of the book. Once again it has been a pleasure to work with Virgil Duff, my editor at the University of Toronto Press. As always, my deepest gratitude is to my wife, Margarita Orszag, who lived with this project, at home and abroad, through all the research and the writing.

Paul Rutherford
October 2006

A WORLD MADE SEXY:
FREUD TO MADONNA

Introduction

This is the story of the building of a modern utopia of Eros where just about everyone (who was affluent, that is) might dream, play, and, above all, shop.

I have set out to explore the significance of some chance remarks the philosopher and historian Michel Foucault made many years ago. Just before the publication of his introductory volume on the history of sexuality in 1976, Foucault gave an interview in which he speculated about how things had changed during the course of the twentieth century.[1] He recognized the emergence of 'the revolt of the sexual body' against all the rules and regulations and prohibitions that had organized sex, the legacy of the so-called Victorian order. But authority had swiftly responded to this resistance, he mused, by shifting from coercion to provocation. The past practice of 'heavy, ponderous, meticulous and constant' discipline over the body no longer suited the type of capitalist society that had emerged by the 1960s. 'Then it was discovered that control of sexuality could be attenuated and given new forms.' All of which led to a novel process of governance – specifically, a reworking of the power of the erotic and the erotics of power. 'We find a new mode of investment [in the body] which presents itself no longer in the form of control by repression but that of control by stimulation.' Witness the 'economic (and perhaps also ideological) exploitation of eroticization, from sun-tan products to pornographic films. "Get undressed – but be slim, good-looking, tanned!"'[2]

The new regime of stimulation would soon prove a much more pleasing mode of governance than the earlier brand of repression, in large part because it did allow room for play and pleasure, even a modicum of rebellion. Its rise occurred over the course of the twentieth century, but mostly after 1950, and in the affluent world, especially in North America. Of course, like other structures of authority, the regime of stimulation had a normalizing effect whose practices worked to determine subjectivity and behaviour, which meant it had an impact on the wider culture, even outside the First World. No one actually set out to build a regime of stimulation or to render the world sexy, the two dimensions of what I will call the Eros project. This is the history of a largely unwitting 'conspiracy,' in which some individuals and certain businesses played a leadership role. The resulting 'apparatus,' to borrow again from Foucault, was an unexpected ensemble of beliefs, conventions, institutions, mechanisms, and operations that responded to 'an urgent need' – chiefly the need to discipline consumption.[3] The overall advance of the project explains how and why things got sexy – 'this general eroticization of the material world,' as one art historian has called it.[4] The purpose of all the attention was to organize the economic conduct of each and every person as well as to ensure 'the right disposition of things.'[5] Sex was not free, whatever the rhetoric to the contrary in the age of liberation.[6] Desire might well be a biological force, productive and inventive, the result of innate drives.[7] People did resist and subvert the effects of the new regime. But desire was conditioned, shaped, focused, and channelled by a plethora of images and the products that these images touted.[8] Mammon was wedded to Eros.

Consider a few of the results that made the news around the year 2000.

- *the pornography boom:* According to the *New York Times* (23 October 2000), the 'annual adult market' led by erotic magazines, video porn, pay-per-view sex, and Internet sex sites ran to an estimate of $10 billion. Some of the most profitable ventures were now subsidiaries of major American corporations. 'The 8.7 million Americans who subscribe to DirecTV, a General Motors subsidiary, buy nearly $200 million a year in pay-per-view sex films from satellite ...' It had become commonplace to wonder whether people were watching more sex than they were having.
- *the voyeur's gaze:* A British study, reported in the *Toronto Star* (17 November 1999), argued the 'food is porn' theory, that people derived an erotic charge from looking at glossy images of sensual dishes. 'It is the images of food as it is prepared and presented in magazines, TV shows and in books that leave us weak in the knees.' The thought was that many people would rather look at the food

than make it (too time consuming) or even eat it (because they were on a diet).

- *the display of flesh*: 'Women's power dressing now means less is less, and that's O.K. So the argument goes.' Jenny Lynn Bader in the *New York Times* (2 July 2000) reported that over the previous decade 'cleavages became more pronounced, shorts became shorter,' and even longer skirts had become 'so sheer, they're almost transparent.' That phenomenon she linked to the recent mauling of women by an assortment of males at a Puerto Rican Day parade in the city's Central Park.
- *the tyranny of looks*: An article in *EnRoute* magazine (October 2000) focused on the fascination of young women in the Orient with 'jiggly prosthetic breasts,' the shelves 'dedicated to breast care and development' in discount cosmetic supermarkets, and the popularity of 'saline breast implants' in the 'beauty "saloons"' of Shanghai. Apparently East Asian women had decided that bigger was indeed better, rejecting the traditional slim physique still valued a decade earlier.
- *the success of Viagra*: All sorts of Canadian men, not unlike men everywhere else, were fascinated by the little blue pills that promised harder and better erections, claimed a report in the *Globe and Mail* of Toronto (8 March 2000). 'One full year after it was approved, Canadians have lapped up more than 534,700 prescriptions of Viagra making it one of 1999's most successful new drug launches, even among those who don't really need it.' Young men were trying the brand 'for kicks.' So were some women. Sales reached more than $40 million for the maker, Pfizer Canada.
- *the Armani exhibition*: Late in 2000 the Solomon R. Guggenheim Museum of New York mounted an exhibition of the fashions designed by Giorgio Armani, who had specialized in a cool version of the erotic (unlike, say, his compatriot Gianni Versace, the champion of overheated sex). The display of dress was treated with all the pomp and ceremony devoted to painting or photography, complete with a high-quality Harry N. Abrams book memorializing the exhibition.[9] At least in the beginning, the exhibition attracted a host of the usual collection of museum and gallery visitors, apparently ready to accept that erotic and elegant fashion was indeed a fine art.

All of which were signs of the arrival of a 'libidinal economy,' to misappropriate a phrase used by J.-F. Lyotard.[10] That involved a double operation: a portion of the economy was eroticized, a portion of the libido was commódified. The result was a marketplace organized around exploiting and satisfying the erotic dimensions of the body situated in its various social settings. The sexual energies were most intense at the core of this economy where a combination of theatrics and aesthetics fostered volatility in two distinct but overlapping systems. The first, the fashion system, encompassed products that clothed or embellished the body, whether jeans,. sweaters, shorts, dresses, jewellery, perfumes, cosmetics, or the like.[11] The second, the entertainment system, encompassed in addition (for it was also deeply implicated in the marketing of fashion) products that pleased or diverted the mind, notably movies, some television, and music videos. Brand competition could be fierce here, and fads and fancies swept through these systems at a dizzying pace, making them sites of constant innovation. All of which occurred in a cultural environment dominated by the communications industry: the necessary condition for the libidinal economy was a state of being that approximated Marshall McLuhan's vision of the media as 'the extensions of man,' or rather of people's senses.[12] That enabled signals to move with extraordinary rapidity from their sources to huge numbers of individuals, thereby building the regime of stimulation.

The very form of the commodity changed in the process. The meaning and utility of that commodity was informed by an aura of sensual excitement or its role as an instrument of sexual desire or its function as a catalyst for some erotic narrative. The commodity became an object of 'total design,' requiring 'a conflation of the aesthetic and the utilitarian' and producing 'a datum to be manipulated – to be designed and redesigned, consumed and re-consumed.'[13] Aesthetics, or more specifically spectacle, determined the fate of this commodity, now a unit of the knowledge created, distributed, and altered by publicity as erotica. Consider the case of haute couture, a fine example of the new form of commodity. That kind of fashion was ever changing, each garment a prototype that could be altered dramatically to suit the desires of a buyer rich enough to demand the most sensational outfit. Or the item might become a 'knock-off': after superstar Jennifer Lopez wore a clinging and diaphanous Versace outfit at the Grammy Awards night in 2000, it was not long before a similar gown – seemingly in leather, though – turned up on the body of a Toronto socialite. Such was the alliance of entertainment and fashion. But the real significance of haute couture lay elsewhere. For it served first and foremost as a promotional vehicle: the hoopla and the hype of the various fashion shows, usually in the spring and fall, sought to create a sensation in the media that would boom the designer's name, his or her house, and the growing collection of branded goods that the house marketed to a huge constituency of consumers.[14]

Anne Hollander has emphasized the crucial importance of photography in the dissemination of fashion. 'The deep aesthetic pleasure they [the actual clothes] can give, the sparks of visual delight they can strike, are always largely in debt to the ideal fictions the lens has created, the vivid images that give fashion its true life.'[15] So too with most other eroticized products. Consequently my focus is first on signs – words, sounds, especially images, and occasionally artefacts – and second on practice, what people did with the signs. Theory, art, literature, pornography, advertising, entertainment, celebrity, fashion – all played some part in the grand story of the sexual century. They amounted to a kind of publicity for the Eros project. Whatever the intentions of its makers, whatever the products or dreams they touted, a series of motifs were repeated time and again in what served as a campaign to promote the emerging ideology of eroticism.[16] That ideology celebrated a sex drive liberated from the constraints of reproduction and family, even the softer bonds of love, so that the individual might realize unhindered the most exquisite of pleasures, the delights of the flesh.[17] Listed below are its main attributes.

(i) *transgression*: Ideologies extol particular actions – say, worship or marriage or working. One of the most striking attributes of eroticism was its penchant for 'sin.' The past seemed a time of repression, its baneful legacy the source of present unhappiness. Sigmund Freud, who must count as the reluctant founder of the Eros project, asserted that desire, caged in the unconscious, was fundamentally transgressive, and thus dangerous to the social order.[18] Georges Bataille, a theorist and pornographer, argued that the breaking of taboos was fundamental to eroticism because it produced the most intense brand of pleasure.[19] Admakers urged consumers to challenge convention, to enjoy indulgence, whatever the dictates of tradition or morality.

(ii) *the hedonist*: Ideologies create subjectivities, narratives of the self that serve to build an identity and a self.[20] Eroticism valued a different kind of subject. The appropriate citizens were the woman and the man who knew their desires, commanded their environ-

ment, and realized their will. In short they were hedonists, sometimes the sensualist or libertine but always devoted to the pursuit
of pleasure. Such a person was a variation on the prevailing model
of the modern or sovereign self: a calculating creature, a risk-taker,
coherent, autonomous, and imperial.[21] Except that, in the utopia
of Eros, this person was ruled by passions as much as by reason.

(iii) *the streamlined body*: Ideologies shape the image of the body. What
eroticism promoted was a body perfected as stimulus, a body that
looked so good because it was smoothed, symmetrical, flawless,
ordered, elevated, indeed processed by fitness and fashion and
photography. It could take the form, for example, of a Barbie or a
Bond. In many ways the resulting body seems just a modern version of the long-standing classical ideal.[22] Except that the erotic
body was committed to lust and indulgence.

(iv) *assemblages*: Ideologies organize ways of living in the world. The
regime of stimulation rested upon the multiplication of networks
and connections, or rather 'assemblages,' to borrow from the
vocabulary of Gilles Deleuze and Félix Guattari.[23] One set of these
were aggressive and avaricious agents called 'desiring machines,'
composed of various body parts like a mouth or a breast or an
anus, always coupled to some other object. 'We' (that is, every person) were an amalgam of these desiring machines (and, one might
add, 'fearing' machines as well), organized in a series of chains
that linked us with people and things outside our skins.[24] On a
broader scale were the 'libidinal assemblages,' much more complicated and extensive formations of bodies, technologies, and signs
designed to achieve certain ends. So eroticism worked through the
purposeful connections of bodies or body parts, objects and products, spaces and moments, behaviours and intensities, most especially the intensity of lust.[25] The body became 'an unfinished
project' and 'a relational "thing"' that was 'created' and 'sus-
tained' by such assemblages.[26] Put another way, the self was
extended in space and in time to connect with a material world of
goods that was in turn eroticized.[27] That was how the modern
utopia of Eros was assembled.

(v) *the carnival of sex*: Ideologies generate utopias and dystopias.[28] It
was Paul Ricoeur who argued the significance of utopia in contemporary life, utopia as 'fancy,' as 'an alternate to the present
power,' as 'the exploration of the possible.'[29] The term 'carnivalesque' came out of the work of Mikhail Bakhtin where he posi-

tioned carnival against the medieval church, the festivals of the people against the dictates of the official order. [30] The carnival of sex referred to an erotic paradise ruled by the priority of appetite, a place fascinated with sin and excess, committed to play and indulgence. It was mostly a happy place, at least according to advertising, but it had a dark side as well, brought out in the work of Georges Bataille, who linked eroticism both to religious ecstasy and to violence and death. In any case, the carnival of sex was presented as an alternative realm of existence where people might escape the trials and tribulations of the workaday world.

A World Made Sexy is about both power and pleasure. It is not just another entry in the bleak story of an always triumphant authority. The Eros project was an agent of modernity, meaning it was committed to those twin goals of emancipation and domination: in this case the liberation of individual desire as well as the social mastery of the wants and passions that liberation encouraged.[31] But the project employed mechanisms of seduction rather than coercion, which placed it in the camp of what might best be called the second wave of modernity.[32] It was transnational, oriented around consumption rather than production, fascinated with images, committed to the freeing of the body, using the 'soft power' of communications to organize desire. Mass eroticism was linked to the ongoing marketing 'revolution' that gathered speed during the course of the twentieth century. The techniques of surveillance were seconded to the technologies of spectacle in order to construct a world made sexy. Perhaps most striking, the Eros project served, like so much of pop culture, to re-enchant a lifeworld rendered prosaic and dull by the rise of logic and industry.[33]

I have not attempted a general survey of what happened in the twentieth century. Instead I have employed a case-study approach, which means that a lot of issues and events (notably the very recent story of sex on the Web) have been left out of this account. The argument proceeds via a series of 'jumps,' focusing attention on theory or art, a book or a creed, a brand or a campaign, a genre of mass culture, a person or some institution, at various points in time, using these to reveal the trajectory of the Eros project. These cases are presented as separate sections, of varying size, grouped within much grander chapters that cover a specific domain of activity. My focus is mostly (but not exclusively) on things American, reflecting the importance of the United States as the source of so much of the mass culture of the twentieth century. The first chapter explores the story of pornography in times past, both its European and American expressions, though from the perspective of recent exhibitions of erotic materials and the collections of sex museums. The second explores various designs for the liberation of sexuality, authored by radicals on the Left and by an apologist for capitalism, during the years between 1930 and 1965. It also serves to highlight the significance of Freud, whose ideas remained important throughout the history of the Eros project. The next two chapters concentrate on pioneering examples of publicity as erotica in the United States, such as the early *Playboy*, and the intellectual concerns that the erotic sell produced in the minds of various critics, American and otherwise, between 1950 and 1980. Chapter 5 uses two case studies, of Bond and Madonna, to show the linkage of eroticism and aggression in the late twentieth century. The final chapter probes how television advertising in particular made eroticism so commonplace in the homes of the affluent world of North America, western Europe, and the capitalist East by the 1990s. The conclusion not only summarizes the findings of these case studies but puts the Eros project in the context of Michel Foucault's history of modern sexuality.

1 Exhibiting Eros

The model building designed to house America's first sex museum was certainly different. The concept of 'a spatial solution that is open, gestural, revealing, and sexy' won an award in 1999 from an architectural magazine. The 'solution' was intended for the corner of Fifth Avenue and East Twenty-seventh Street in the Flatiron District of New York city. Built out from an existing block, the seven-story structure of some 30,000 square feet would stand above the sidewalk on stilts. 'The extremely narrow floor plan of the site suggested the use of a layered organizational device,' noted the architects, 'and the generative concepts of organic form, tactile expression, and exposure and concealment led to thinking of this device as "skin."' The skin was to be composed of layers of opaque and translucent material, both plastic and glass, attached to steel frames, to act as walls 'that recede, like epidermal layers, from the street to the back of the site,' added William Hamilton of the *New York Times* (11 March 1999), and thereby shape the interior of galleries, halls, and stairways that visitors would experience as if they were walking through a fluid, enticing 'body.' Light, more properly 'the play of dim and bright, of suggestion and sight, between the skins,' might thus deliver 'an architectural encounter that the designers hope will mimic a sexual one.' The 'transparent and translucent panels ... will undulate like a torso in motion, seductively silhouetting the galleries for the street and creating flirtatious shadows and light for visitors inside.' Outside, the building would seem to 'blush' when a cloud passed by or the evening lights went on.[1] Altogether, the building would 'perform like sexuality,' argued Gregg Pasquarelli, one of the architects. More to the point, it would perform eroticism, not just for the visitors inside but for passers-by on the street, hailing both as voyeurs eager to be aroused. 'Take me, Twenty-seventh Street, take me!' Such was the wry response of Anthony Lane, writing in the *New Yorker* (31 January 2000).

The building was designed as the permanent home for a novel institution, a special place embodying the purpose and ethos of New York's forthcoming Museum of Sex, then known as MoSEX (an abbreviation shed when it actually opened). The ambition was to turn MoSEX into one of the city's leading museums, receiving at least 100,000 visitors and, it was hoped, many more each year (although the Guggenheim Museum SoHo only attracted around 120,000 in 1998).[2] The two co-founders of the project, Daniel Gluck, a onetime software entrepreneur, and Alison Maddex, a radical artist noted for her celebration of the phallus, had gone public with the idea in 1998. They assembled a team of supporters drawn from the worlds of celebrity (including Maddex's long-time companion, Camille Paglia), fashion, entertainment, academe, and even pornography (notably Candida Royalle and Annie Sprinkle, ex-porn stars, the latter now a performance artist). The news was all the more enticing to the press because Rudy Giuliani, the city's aggressive mayor, was waging a very public crusade against vice, meaning strippers, burlesque theatres, porn shops, even drag queens. Indeed a spokesperson for the mayor's office later warned that the city would shut MoSEX down 'if it made a wrong move.'[3] Initial efforts to win state approval as a regular museum ran afoul of the New York Board of Regents, which apparently thought MoSEX 'made a mockery of the institution of the museum.'[4] That was why the promoters had decided to create a for-profit institution, which would also avoid the sorts of difficulties the Brooklyn Museum of Art had suffered in 1999 when Giuliani took umbrage at their 'Sensation' exhibition.[5] By the summer of 2000 MoSEX boasted a classy black-and-white website, complete with undulating lines, the sounds of water, a gentle, vaguely New Age melody, and lots of text (though no pictures).[6]

The MoSEX project was promoted as a cleansed version of sex, not a 'lewd, cheesy, T&A tourist trap,' said Gluck, where 'T&A' was a euphemistic way of sneering at the 'tit and ass' motifs of so much pornography. What the promoters liked to call their 'Smithsonian of Sex' would be a cultural institution, offering education as well as sensation. 'It's for Joe Construction Worker and a Harvard emeritus professor,' in the words of Maddex. So MoSEX would sponsor the scholarly study of sex, collect an archive of pertinent documents and artefacts, offer changing exhibits on the history of sex in New York and America, and display such curiosities as a bundling board from colonial America, designed to keep sleeping couples apart, or an orgone box of the mid-twentieth century, an invention of Wilhelm Reich that was supposed to rejuvenate the sexual faculties. Gluck claimed he would be especially happy to get hold of the infamous 'stained dress' of Monica Lewinsky that had played some part in the failed impeachment proceedings against President Bill Clinton. Thought had been given to a multimedia auditorium for performances by guest stars such as Glenda Orgasm, a local drag queen. Or a visitor might relish the menu of a special cafe, serving up 'aphrodisiac-oriented food.' Even though the media repeated the publicity line, still they could not resist invoking the inherited notion of sex, more properly public images of sex, as somehow dirty, a brand of pornography. That did not provoke overt expressions of disgust anymore, but it did foster doubt, mirth, even the sneer. Consider the assorted words used to title some of the columns: 'Exhibition for Exhibitionists' or simply 'Exhibitionism,' 'The Lewd?,' 'Sexcitement,' or 'XXX-hibits.' 'Just when Mayor Giuliani thought he made New York safe from sex,' announced Mary Jane Fine in the *New York Daily News* (19 January 2000), 'along comes an upstart museum devoted to doing The Nasty.'

The journalist had a point: whatever else MoSEX offered, the mainstay of any collection was bound to be erotic images and objects and texts, especially from the remote and recent pasts, the very kind of stuff that was not usually on public display despite the massive growth of the pornographic industry during the late twentieth century. Public institutions had long collected pornographic material, such as 'The Private Case' of the British Library or the 'Collection de l'Enfer' of the Bibliothèque Nationale, the latter dating from 1836[7] and also kept largely out of sight – the British Library apparently decided to begin listing its erotic works in the general catalogue only in the mid-1960s. The enormous holdings of art, photography, books, films, and the like at the Kinsey Institute for Research in Sex, Gender and Reproduction at Indiana University remained open only to qualified researchers, estimated at 400 to 600 individuals a year.[8] Alison Maddex admitted that MoSEX was after the extensive and uncatalogued collection of the Institute for Advanced Study of Human Sexuality, which, its president Ted McIlvenna asserted, contained 3 million items locked away in nine warehouses in San Francisco.[9] The raison d'être of the sex museum was to reveal that which had remained hidden, the secret history of lust.

MoSEX and like institutions were promoters of an eroticism now deemed by many people, though not by all officials, fit for public consumption. They provide an invaluable entry into the wider world of erotica and pornography, past and present. Understanding that world is crucial to understanding the nature of the Eros project. First of all, pornography amounted to a discourse on sex and sensuality that was a predecessor to the project. Second, pornography constituted, as it were, the raw material out of which admakers and entertainers would fashion the imagery employed to such great effect by the regime of stimulation. Finally, the responses people had to such exhibits demonstrates the source of the power, the appeal and the repulsion, such images exercised, and still exercise, over the imagination of the public.

1 The Sex Museum

When the Museum of Sex opened late in 2002 – and, by the way, not in the imagined building whose design was so erotic – it was actually a latecomer. The public exhibition of erotic material had become something of a craze at the beginning of the new millennium, in New York and elsewhere. In 1999 Barcelona's *jardín de eros* had encompassed paintings and sketches, mostly European, mostly twentieth century, many of them lewd. In 2001 *Picasso Érotique* had focused only on the sizable body of images Picasso had authored, many of these representations of the vulva and the vagina, more graphic than sensual, from the beginnings of his career right up to the end. In 2002 New York's Metropolitan Museum of Art hosted a scaled-down version of *Surrealism: Desire Unbound*, organized by the Tate Modern in London, to show how much the force of desire – for sex, for women, for sensation – had excited the passions of so many surrealists, women and men. That same year Brooklyn's Museum of Art carried *Exposed: The Victorian Nude*, another British import, which demonstrated the celebration of the nude in English art in the nineteenth century. This was in addition to erotic or sexual displays found in broader exhibits such as *Moral Fibre* on dress (Textile Museum of Canada, Toronto, 2002), the nudes of Die Brücke (Thyssen Museum, Madrid, 2005), or some of Picasso's erotic prints in *Tres Grandes de España* (Centro Cultural Estación Mapoche, Santiago, Chile, 2006). The popularity of these shows suggested how acceptable erotic art was among the generally upscale audience of museumgoers.

But this was only one sign of the acceptance of a public eroticism. Aside from a few slighting comments about peep shows and the like, the participants in the MoSEX debate had failed to recognize that the sex museum, albeit in a much less grandiose fashion, was already an established presence in western Europe by the end of the 1990s.[10] Amsterdam boasted two sites, a proper Seksmuseum (and Venustempel), near the train station, that had purportedly launched in 1985, making it the first successful such enterprise, and the smaller Erotisch Museum in the city's red light district. Hamburg had a large Erotic Art Museum (opened in another location in 1992) on the infamous Reeperbahn, the most notorious sex street in the city, full of prostitutes, police, and exotic parlours. Since 1997 Paris had sported a Musée de l'érotisme on the boulevard de Clichy, near the Moulin Rouge, in the quartier Pigalle, surrounded by 'girlie' shows and sex shops. The Museum Erotica (1994), by contrast, overlooked a busy pedestrian walkway in the commercial district of Copenhagen, full of stores and restaurants. The Beate Uhse Erotik-Museum in Berlin (1996) was located very near the heavy traffic zone of Joachimstaler Strasse and Kurfürstendamm, where daytime shoppers and night folk congregated in a downtown centre of what had been the western portion of the city. Barcelona's Museu de l'Eròtica, opened in 1997, fronted on La Rambla, that most extraordinary street full of stores, trees, pedestrians, and cars in the centre of the city. The even more recent Museo Erótico de Madrid (2000) was situated downtown, not far from the famous Plaza Mayor, in a commercial zone, some sex shops and a sex show within walking distance. The last four institutions also had a presence on the Web where they not only displayed some of their offerings but sold books, videos, artefacts, and sometimes much more (indeed modest, independent online museums had also sprung up on the Web). All the European sites were featured in tourist guides, print and online, especially those geared to singles and youth seeking something out of the ordinary.

Shanghai's Museum of Ancient Chinese Sex Culture was not so easy to find, certainly not in the official guides to the city's offerings. It was one of the very few non-European sites (although there was, briefly, a museum in Canberra, Australia, and reported sex collections attached to temples in Japan).[11] The museum was the work of Liu Dalin, a retired professor of Shanghai University, who had begun to display his collection of research material overseas in the 1990s. In 1999 he established China's only sex museum in association with a department store in the downtown area of the city. That found favour with the foreign media, who gave the museum considerable publicity – its appearance was taken as a sign that the sexual revolution had begun to eat away at the prudery of communist China.[12] The welcome was in stark contrast to the attitude of the municipal authorities, who still regarded the public display of sex with suspicion and forbade any advertising of the museum's presence. Indeed, visiting the museum proved at least as popular with tourists as with locals: half of the 40,000 people who took in the collection were foreigners. Twenty months later the department store ended its sponsorship, purportedly costing at least $200,000 U.S., because the museum did not generate sufficient traffic.[13] Dalin swiftly reopened the museum at a new, more modest site in a residential area, though again he was not allowed to attract attention through advertising.[14]

Each of the erotic museums was the result of private initiative, although some of the founders enjoyed a greater share of public support than did Liu Dalin. According to one report, authorities in Paris welcomed the addition of such a potential tourist attraction as the Musée de l'érotisme. New York's Museum of Sex was able to work closely with the well-established Kinsey Institute to assist in mounting exhibitions. Claus Becker, a local property developer, started Hamburg's museum, which he stocked with a large collection of erotic prints produced in western Europe since the eighteenth century. Ole Ege, a porn pioneer and filmmaker, was the moving force behind Copenhagen's Museum Erotica. The most colourful personality, however, was the founder of Berlin's institution, named after one of the country's more notorious figures. Sometimes called 'Germany's Queen of Porn,' Beate Uhse was ranked among those erotic entrepreneurs, of whom Hugh Hefner was probably the most famous, who in the last half of the twentieth century had mined lust to produce legal and very popular commodities.[15] She began just after the Second World War to dispense birth-control information to married women, shortly moved into retailing sex aids, and established her first Sex Institute for Marital Hygiene in 1962. Although constantly harried by the state under the obscenity laws, or so the story goes, she created a chain of sex stores and blue movie cinemas throughout West Germany where consumers might purchase quality goods in a friendly, clean environment. 'She has tried to take the sleaze out of sex,' reported *Time* (13 April 1981), thereby confirming her own publicity. Right after the Berlin Wall fell in late 1989, she moved swiftly to market her catalogues to the porn-deprived denizens of East Berlin and East Germany, eventually finding some two million customers there, about the same as in the west. Establishing the museum, presumably out of her own personal collection, was one of her 'gifts' to the country.

According to an online report, surveys of Asian travellers (the actual places of origin were never specified) cited the Beate Uhse Erotik-Museum as 'the best known tourist destination in the whole city,' attracting altogether an incredible (and likely wildly inflated) figure of 'a quarter million visitors annually.'[16] In June 2000 the museum was located in an undistinguished office building that also housed a sex shop cluttered with all manner of aids and toys and, upstairs, a small bar and video cinema. The collection amounted to roughly 5,000 erotic artefacts, displayed on three floors.[17] The tour started on the third floor in a large, slightly darkened room full of spotlights, display cases, and wall hangings, some dioramas, and the occasional vaguely phallic column. That room, in fact the three rooms, contained a jumble of all sorts of items. The third floor featured mostly Asian material, both paintings and artefacts, as well as a Marilyn Monroe corner, a sadomasochistic scene of life-sized men and women posing in a pleasure room, and a section devoted to the life of Beate Uhse. Although the Asian theme continued into the second floor, many of the special exhibits were drawn from the Western experience: a collection of paintings and a diorama entitled 'Sodom Berlin,' a bland display of corsets, and a circulating portrayal of Rudolph Valentino dancing with a bare-breasted partner – strangely, his exposed penis was flaccid. The room on the first floor was much smaller, since so much space was taken up by the bar and the cinema. Still, there was a section devoted to the sexologist Magnus Hirschfeld as well as a closed-off area showing a continuous series of short porn films from Europe and the United States, both in addition to assorted paintings, prints, and erotic objects. A tape of semi-classical and New Age music played softly and continuously, a distinct contrast to the rap or rock music that greeted anyone who wandered into the bar and cinema area at night. On the ground floor visitors could purchase two pamphlets of highlights from the museum, a more substantial booklet on 'Sodom Berlin,' and a videotape of the porn films shown on the first floor.

Each of the establishments had different specialties. Shanghai's museum was very much a site of learning: the visitor first saw some wall plaques attesting to the acclaim Dalin's collection had won from foreigners plus a table display of his major books. On one floor, divided into a number of sections, the museum provided a chronological tour of artefacts and images about sex in China dating from before the emergence of the Han dynasty. The various exhibits were carefully ordered, always tasteful, and supported by wall texts describing, for example, the marriage system, prostitution, or 'sexual pleasure in life.' The much-better funded Museum of Sex was even more of an academic establishment, opening with a fine exhibition entitled *NYCSex: How New York City Transformed Sex in America* (and a book of the same title). The exhibition looked broadly at the story of the sexual underground in New York from the early nineteenth century through to the end of the twentieth century. It covered prostitution and white slavery, sex scandals and the media, the porn industry and anti-porn campaigns, burlesque and the like, the rise of a gay and lesbian lifestyle as well as a sado-masochism (S/M) subculture, culminating with considerable material on the 'sexual revolution' and its aftermath. All of the displays were carefully annotated, and visitors could secure an audiotape to help explain all the various mysteries.[18] There was no doubt that the museum had delivered on its original promise to treat sex seriously.

Which may be why one visitor deemed the exhibition 'antiseptic.' She had seen the European sites, which were usually much less learned. Indeed, Amsterdam's Erotisch Museum was very much a funhouse, where visitors might try out a love analyser, rest their heads on the figure of either a 'hunk' or a 'babe' (for the requisite photograph), or sit in a bondage chair. Similarly its rival, the Seksmuseum, had a series of gags: a sailor who ejaculated water against a window, a flasher who attracted attention with a 'hey' and a 'psst,' a vibrating seat, and, on the wall of one of the stairs, a farting ass, complete with sound and odour. But that museum also contained an extensive collection of much more serious displays on three floors, including a 'Photo Gallery 1860–1960,' the largest array of erotic photographs presented by any site. Hamburg's museum, called an 'art-brothel' by one wag, was a large concrete structure of four floors devoted to past and present erotic art, paintings, photographs, pin-ups, and the like. You could purchase a small book of pictures from the museum in its book store, postcards, and all kinds of art and pornographic literature. The Paris museum, in an old but refurbished house, had three floors of mixed art and sculpture, three more floors devoted to selling contemporary paintings, plus an elegant gift shop. Copenhagen's Museum Erotica boasted a video wall that continuously played porn films. This site also fashioned the most overt political message: its focus on past struggles over pornography and prostitution, much of this in Denmark, explicitly developed the narrative of sexual liberation. Although the smaller Museu de l'Eròtica in Barcelona filled only one floor of an old house divided into many rooms, it offered the widest variety of art, displays, films, and artefacts from around the world. It also featured the most graphic photographs of S/M and fetish. The Madrid site provided an assortment of quotations from theorists, including Georges Bataille, Jean Baudrillard, Roland Barthes, even Gilles Deleuze and Félix Guattari, as well as various learned, sometimes humorous commentaries, making it the most thoughtful of all the European museums.

Even so, the European establishments had much in common. They were geared particularly to the tourist trade: indeed, when I visited Amsterdam's Seksmuseum in September 2001, it was clear that the place was one of the regular sites for groups of foreigners, who poured in during the late morning and mid-afternoon. The cost of entry at these museums was low, the equivalent of a few Euros or U.S. dollars.[19] They were open from roughly ten in the morning to midnight, though the Museo Erótico in Madrid did cater to local sensibilities with a siesta from 2:00 to 4:00 p.m. The captions and descriptions were usually in three languages, one of which was always English – Shanghai's museum also offered English translations of descriptions and commentaries. Surveillance was minimal: there were never attendants in any of the rooms, and although some sites had installed video cameras, the clerk at the front desk did not actually watch what was happening. Visitors were free to wander through the exhibits, to linger over some choice morsel, and to take photographs of whatever they wanted. All that was true in New York as well, though photographs were not allowed in Shanghai. (Only in one site was I ever accosted, the Erotisch Museum in Amsterdam, and then not because I was taking pictures but because I was taking notes, apparently an unusual activity that might betoken some unwelcome exposure – one of the attendants eventually asked me to leave.) That was quite unlike the situation in the erotic art exhibitions of regular galleries, where the behaviour of people was constantly monitored by room attendants and taking pictures was strictly forbidden.

The sex museum belonged to a special class of sites labelled 'heterotopias' by Michel Foucault in a playful lecture entitled 'Different Spaces.'[20] His attention focused on places that juxtaposed scattered points in the vast social network of knowledges and practices, points that would otherwise appear either incompatible or contradictory. Like utopias and dystopias, these places staged 'a kind of contestation, both mythical and real, of the space in which we live.' But unlike those fictions, the heterotopias did exist: they constituted sites where 'all the other real emplacements that can be found within the culture are, at the same time, represented, contested and reversed, sorts of places that are outside all places, although they are actually localizable.' These heterotopias took different, partial forms in various cultures and at various times. Foucault applied his description almost casually to gardens, cemeteries, festivals, idealized colonies, even old people's homes. Three designations stood out in this hodgepodge of institutions.

1 Concentrations of time: institutions that accumulated and preserved time indefinitely, notably museums and libraries, which constituted general archives of fashions, ideas, forms, and so on, from the cultures of the past.
2 Centres of deviance: places that warehoused individuals who had broken with norms and conventions, such as psychiatric hospitals or prisons. That same designation could readily apply to any site that collected the objects and instruments of deviance.
3 Houses of illusion: sites creating a space of fantasy which explicitly or implicitly dishonoured all other emplacements that normally partition the lifeworld into separate domains. Foucault cited here the brothel, or rather he said, mysteriously and mischievously, 'those famous brothels which we are now deprived of.'

The sex museum juxtaposed artefacts and representations of sex from a wide variety of places and domains so that they could be viewed almost simultaneously by any visitor. Consider this very partial list of items that referenced particular kinds of places: photographs of the performers at El Molino (the reference here to a music hall) and the prostitutes of 'Barrio Chino' (the zone of brothels), both in Barcelona; sexological works and erotic books (the library); a poster of a leather-clad, youthful Marlon Brando (the cinema); phallic mountains and vaginal clefts (an eroticized nature), these shown through large photographs in Shanghai; S/M accoutrements and displays (the pleasure/torture room); ads for erotic telephone conversations (the private home); pornographic films (the peep show) and an Internet room (the World Wide Web); or a diorama of a painter in action (the artist's studio). Consider as well this equally partial list of displays that referenced separate domains: an exhibit of corsets, lotus shoes, and foot binding or a series of fetish photographs (the domain of fashion); the covers of innumerable magazines or a series of erotic postcards (the domain of communications); bottles of aphrodisiacs and potency drugs (the discipline of medicine); prints from the *Kama Sutra* (referencing a lost past); a sensual Buddha, locked in an embrace, or a satire of St Theresa de Avila, caught up in an orgasm (religion); matchboxes and Zippo lighters (examples of kitsch); pin-ups and calendars (the so-called low erotica) as well as lithographs from special, limited editions (its high-class rival); paintings and photographs galore (the world of art); a castration knife, chastity belts, or a vibrator (sexual technology); a vagina doll and such like aberrations (kid's toys). Altogether, they spoke of the extraordinary diversity and persistence of the sexual underworld throughout the course of history.[21]

2 History as Past Pornography

The exhibitions, and particularly the sex museums, linked the viewer to the virtual realm of sex, a realm that otherwise remained largely invisible and distant, at least in its totality, to much of the public.[22] In some ways the sex museum was akin to the so-called premodern cabinet of curiosities that had attempted to provoke surprise and wonder.[23] The desire to entertain visitors led to efforts to display objects that were unusual and exceptional, indeed singular rather than typical. So the Erotisch Museum in Amsterdam showed an image of the first vibrator, called Le Pulsoconn, a cumbersome assemblage of wheels and bars that made a metal plate pulsate. The Museum of Sex had a display from the so-called anatomy museums of the nineteenth century that showcased the results of bad sex, meaning diseased organs and the like. The basement floor of the Paris museum boasted a collection of all sorts of sensational items, among the most startling a set of twisted objects called simply 'anal jewellery,' that were presented without any detailed explanation. That museum and the one in Copenhagen both featured a large and bizarre piece of sculpture, the Erotik-Robotik aka the Terminator. According to the Danish museum, the original was among the private holdings assembled by Sylvester Stallone: it was, so the caption read, 'sculptured in Thailand from collected and recast ammunition casings from the Vietnam war.' The sculpture was composed of two intertwined figures, a male android giving oral sex to a nude female he held erect in his powerful arms, while the female, though caught up in the passion of the moment, was still managing to caress the android's erect penis with one of her feet. Just about all the museums featured a picture or model of a sex machine, more often looking like a torture machine but nonetheless supposed to excite various parts of the body and, presumably, to penetrate the vagina or anus. The model in Barcelona was based on a chair, plus manacles, pulleys, and a dildo, complete with a button to activate the weird construction (not in working condition at the time I visited). Such strange amalgams of technology and sexuality were in themselves marvels of deviance, evidence of a crazed ingenuity that sought to maximize passion.

Still, most of the collections conformed to that ordered system of show and tell that characterized the style and purposes of the modern museum. The aim of such exhibits was educational, to use objects considered either typical or important to deliver a precise cluster of meanings to the visitor.[24] That required captions and descriptions, sometimes elaborate commentaries, especially common in Barcelona's Museu de l'Eròtica, where small essays told visitors about the culture of sex in prehistoric times, ancient Greece, and premodern India and Asia.[25] Madrid had a special History and Anthropology Hall, where it laid out a range of items to show what different societies had done with and to the body. *Jardín de eros* offered a special section on 'el universo de la prostitución,' full of photographs and some paintings of women, brothels, activities, and even a pair of pants. Indeed the establishments became history machines spinning tales about lust and life in times and places both far distant and contemporary.[26]

Not everywhere, of course: there was no attention to the world of Islam or medieval Europe, no *Decameron*, for instance. And not everything: missing was much reference to venereal disease, except for one anti-syphilis poster in Paris, a graphic display of diseased genitals at the Erotisch Museum, and some of the exhibits in New York. There was surprisingly little about prostitution in the sex museums, though both the Museum of Sex and the Museum Erotica had some notable displays. None of the sites, however, paid close attention to the extraordinary wave of moral and medical hysteria over the act of masturbation that reigned in Europe (and America) for about two and a half centuries after 1700. Still one section of the catalogue of *jardín de eros* was devoted to the styles and mechanisms of 'autoerotismos.'

But what was present did work to inform. Displays of Etruscan or Incan pottery, African sculpture, or Indonesian penis cases might demonstrate how eternal and universal was the erotic imperative: right from the beginning of 'civilization' – in fact, even before the birth of civilization – humanity had paid homage to the powers of lust. The wealth of Indian prints or Chinese roll pictures purportedly proved how 'direct and sophisticated' was the Asian attitude towards 'eroticism and sex': unlike the West, so the argument went, sex in the orient had always been a source of happiness and health.[27] That much vilified creed of orientalism still flourished in the European sex museum, where the myth of a sensual and exotic East was a lesson on how natural the culture of sex was when not encumbered by the guilt and fear of the Christian order. (When the Museum of Sex mounted an exhibition on China's erotic obsession, however, it avoided drawing such conclusions or championing the virtues of oriental ways.)[28] The extensive collection of erotic paintings and drawings from early modern and nineteenth-century Europe in Hamburg's Erotic Art Museum indicated how artists had struggled to evade the moral censure of church and state to produce a graphic display of sex in action. The Museu de l'Eròtica drew on the rhetoric of the avant-garde to justify its aesthetic credentials: 'Yes, art is dangerous,' Picasso claimed. 'If it's chaste, then it's not ART.'[29]

All of which fed into a gospel of sexual liberation. The Erotic Art Museum in Hamburg was Claus Becker's 'personal answer to what he perceived as the "unholy renaissance" of puritans and moralists – not to mention the "state managed culture sector" – all of whom[,] he was convinced, preferred keeping erotic art out of the public eye.'[30] The Copenhagen site detailed the various efforts to free sex from the restrictions of local puritans in the city and in Denmark during the twentieth century. The Beate Uhse Erotik-Museum celebrated the career of the sexologist Magnus Hirschfeld, who was persecuted by the Nazis. Its kindred institution in Barcelona showed a still shot from the first commercial ever on TVE to feature a naked woman; that came long after the death of the moralistic dictator Francisco Franco, though the caption suggested it was somehow related. Even the Museum of Sex presumed, and sometimes celebrated (especially in the exhibition book), the merits of liberation in its study of the trajectory of sex in New York. Given the dubious propriety of the institution, the Shanghai museum was more circumspect: it touted the virtues of balance and of knowledge, a liberation from ignorance, but eschewed making any statements about the contemporary scene – indeed, the museum avoided covering any event after the fall of the Chinese Empire in 1911, containing not even a mention of Shanghai's once-sordid past as the whorehouse of Asia before the communist takeover.

The erotic art exhibitions were more emphatic in this commitment to liberation. Their curators were consciously engaged in a battle to enlighten the public. The more reserved style of Sir Nicholas Serota, the director of Tate Modern, meant he simply explained how *Surrealism:*

Desire Unbound demonstrated a central theme of the movement, namely that desire was 'an expression of the sexual instinct and, in sublimated form, the impulse behind love.'[31] What motivated the character of *jardín de eros*, according to Victoria Combalía, the chief organizer, was the need to reveal 'the way that certain images, archetypes, and fantasies recur down through different ages and in different civilizations.' She took aim at the timidity of other museums, in particular in the United States, 'where a new puritanism attempts to conceal from view everything that might be considered too daring for conventional morality.'[32] Likewise, the three directors of the museums behind *Picasso Érotique* proclaimed their worry, and so perhaps their bravery, in the face of a new plot against knowledge and freedom, 'the return of a moralist order on the Western shores of the Atlantic.'[33] Their exhibition, it seemed, exploited what might be only a fleeting moment in which it was permissible to devote significant public space to the display of the erotic.

In short the museums and the exhibitions employed a trinity of narratives about human nature, artistic expression, and sexual liberation to legitimate and promote their brands of eroticism. The signs of this ideological operation were reasonably clear. But that was hardly the total package of meanings the sex museums delivered. The staple of the sex museum, excepting those in Shanghai and New York (which nonetheless did have a display of 'smut'), was history as past pornography. Not that the various institutions, outside of the Museum of Sex, ever admitted they dealt in pornography: rather, they spoke of art, sexuality, and the erotic, perhaps aware that a blunt declaration might scare off supporters and visitors. But the evidence of their fascination was blatant. It was striking how often pornographic films were on display. In Copenhagen there was a video wall devoted to such, in Madrid a darkened room with eight monitors, at the Erotisch Museum some special booths plus a showing of 'filthy funnies' (the adult version of kid's cartoons). The Museum of Sex showed four American 'stag' films, including the earliest extant example, entitled 'A Free Ride' (circa 1915–19). The porn films made for King Alfonso XIII of Spain were run in Paris, Barcelona, Madrid, and at the *jardín de eros*. One of the first things a visitor to *Picasso Érotique* in Montreal might spot was a video monitor playing repeatedly an old pornographic movie. *Jardín de eros* ran a lusty film in which a performer played out the kind of display of the vulva so notoriously celebrated in Gustave Courbet's painting *The Origin of the World*. Even *Exposed: The Victorian Nude* had three silent French films, dating around 1900, showing women undressing.[34] All of these films were in addition to large quantities of photographs, books, magazines, paintings, sculptures, and artefacts that could easily fall within the definition of pornography, especially the broadened definition that highlighted the pleasures derived from viewing indignities done to the human body.

The significance of this view of history as past pornography requires some exploration of the meaning of the eroticism the institutions promoted. *Webster's Unabridged Dictionary* offers a serviceable definition of one form of eroticism widely accepted in the domain of the arts: 'the arousal of or the attempt to arouse sexual feeling by means of suggestion, symbolism, or allusion in an art form.' That identifies eroticism as a discourse, a way of 'talking' about sex, a special repertoire of words and images that seek to provoke desire. So seemingly simple a definition, however, masks what to many people remains a fundamental distinction between a legitimate kind of material, namely erotica in the form of art or literature, and an immoral if not dangerous brand of material, pornography, and especially the hardcore or violent type.[35] Consequently, one academic commentator distinguished erotic art from pornography by claiming that the latter lacked 'any artistic intent' and worked not only 'to stimulate the spectator sexually but to degrade, dominate and depersonalize its subject, usually women.'[36] The distinction common in the press was often simpler: erotica was refined and cerebral, pornography was crude and physical. Witness this claim: 'Porn goes straight to the groin, but erotica goes to the head first.'[37]

Such a formulation constituted a double evasion. First, it hid the fact that erotica was in practice merely acceptable porn, thus a political category determined by the tastes and morals of the speaker or the times. Its application eliminated the shame attached to making and using pornography. But in fact all manner of twentieth-century artists, not just the infamous George Grosz or Salvador Dalí, but Gustav Klimt, Francis Picabia, nearly all of the surrealists, and above all Pablo Picasso, had produced images too obscene to be widely shown in their own day. Times changed. The successful exhibition in Paris, Montreal, and Barcelona of *Picasso Érotique*, devoted to exposing these once-hidden paintings and sketches by that esteemed artist, demonstrated that fact. Second, the formulation presumed that pornography was only a crude kind of sex aid, or at least that porn was designed just to awaken sexual desire. On the contrary, pornography could be cerebral as well as emotional; it did seek to excite a person's libido, but it could also work to disgust, frighten, warn, subvert, honour, and dishonour.[38] Simply put, pornography was and is the graphic display or description of sex designed to arouse the body and the mind: it encompasses all those vehicles, whether words or images, sounds or artefacts, that construct 'the spectacle of sex.'[39] Pornography as 'a category of understanding' is a European invention, roughly 200 years old – the word first appeared in the *Oxford English Dictionary* in 1857, where it referenced 'a description of prostitutes or of prostitution, as a matter of public hygiene' – although that category encompassed an earlier grouping of obscene prints, pictures, and artefacts that had a much longer history. (So, for example, an exhibition of art in the time of Hieronymus Bosch displayed a series of erotic badges worn to signify, maybe elicit, sexual pleasure.)[40] During the 1920s and 1930s, according to one historian, the term 'pornography' acquired an even broader meaning as any symbolic practice that violated the dignity of the human body, which was why, for example, films of Holocaust victims or news photos of starving Africans have been deemed 'pornographic.'[41]

In time eroticism became as well an ethical discourse, albeit a perverse one. More precisely, pornography and its tamer cousin, erotica, were a species of anti-morality that advocated the triumph of desire.[42] They put the rights of lust, the imperative of indulgence, before every other moral stricture. In 1957 the French theorist Georges Bataille, who had already written some pornographic classics, said as much in a peculiar work of advocacy entitled *L'Erotisme*. He linked eroticism, which he considered a universal condition of human existence, both to religious ecstasy and to violence and death, arguing that the source of eroticism lay in the dialectic of taboo and transgression. Humanity established prohibitions about sex and death that set people apart from animals; yet people swiftly sought to evade these controls, to rediscover a kind of animality, an intensity of emotion, by indulging in forbidden acts. Erotic conduct was the denial of normal conduct, an expression of the natural sadism of man – violation, violence, was 'the core of eroticism.'[43] This was a dark vision indeed, since Bataille espoused the virtues of a kind of personal sovereignty that owed much to the writings of the Marquis de Sade, making *L'Erotisme* both misogynistic and cruel.[44] Others recognized this quality of eroticism: pornography soon required, in the words of Susan Sontag, 'the exploration of extremes,'[45] which involved not only the display of sex but issues of power and the terror of violence. 'Eroticism is a realm stalked by ghosts,' observed one of its great champions, Camille Paglia.[46] That was why erotic expression had always pushed against the rules and regulations society erected to protect itself against the force of desire. That was also why first obscenity and later pornography had been an object of official displeasure throughout the history of the West (and sometimes in the East, as well), though authority might target different kinds of pornography – in the late twentieth century, for example, the main villain became what was called 'kiddie porn.' Eroticism mixed obscenity and subversion, and therein lay its ability to shock, shame, and fascinate.

From this standpoint the sex museum was not just a celebration of the passions but a school for scandal as well. It taught the visitor how to achieve the pleasures of transgression; it demonstrated the mechanics of the erotic pursuit. That was obvious in the case of the *Kama Sutra*, virtually a sacred text in the European museums, which amounted to a manual of positions. But it applied as well to all the offerings: the visitor was exposed to a diversity of sexual deviations well beyond the range of most people's experience. The expected response was, 'So that's how they do it,' which has always been part of the appeal of pornography. The most common images showed men and women fornicating. Such intercourse could involve a wide variety of positions: man on top, woman on top, from the rear, seated, two people on a swing, and other sorts of gymnastics. What added a bit of sin to these get-togethers were the practices of fellatio and cunnilingus, buggery or sodomy, some coprophilia and coprophagia (meaning a taste for fecal matter), and occasionally interracial unions, notably between black males and white females. Of course all of the classic 'perversions' were present: voyeurism and exhibitionism, narcissism (most obviously images of masturbation), homosexuality, bestiality, fetishism, sadism and masochism, even suggestions of necrophilia and paedophilia. That last aberration, of course, had to be dealt with very carefully because of the laws against child pornography and the sensibilities of the public; but it was represented in some of the paintings of George Grosz at Hamburg and Madrid, in Hans Bellmer's second doll series in *Surrealism: Desire Unbound*, and in an assortment of images at other museums.[47] By contrast, voyeurism, the first of the 'perversions,' was constantly on display: children watched parents, a mother watched her daughter in bed with a husband, a stranger peered into the boudoir of a woman, and on and on. The pictures affirmed the very kind of prurient curiosity that the museum visitor was expected to indulge.

Particularly striking was the mixing of violence and sex, which might take the form of entrapment or bondage, whipping and other tortures, outright rape, and in one instance murder: a drawing, published in 1918 by Michel Fingesten, and presented in the Beate Uhse Erotik-Museum, showed a large naked male, his penis erect, about to swing an axe down upon a nude female bent over a chopping block. Such dark imagery was a twentieth-century specialty, marking the eroticization of violence, now a persistent motif in the pornographic repertoire. Madrid's museum offered visitors a double room devoted to S/M, complete with masks, chains, a special bed and chair, looking very surgical, and all kinds of instruments: a clinic of pain meant to produce pleasure. The 'Photo Gallery' of the Seksmuseum showed a range of early punishment pictures of the 1890s and early 1900s in which women were bound up and whipped. Hamburg's gallery featured an artist who juxtaposed the soft and the hard – highly sexed women with sharp spikes either pressing into their flesh or driving out of their bodies. The Museu de l'Eròtica devoted considerable wall space to the work of Gary and Pierre Silva, who specialized in depicting S/M. Two of their black-and-white photographs were particularly sinister because they featured bloodied figures – as if someone had attacked the genitals of a man and a woman. These disturbing pictures were only the most outrageous among a series of images in the collections that suggested or celebrated the joys of violation: a tutor thrashing his female students, a mother whipping and then molesting her daughter, one lesbian spanking another. Pleasure and pain were twins here, both promising that intense experience that was the goal of eroticism. The threat and the thrill of violation was best captured by a famous photograph of Robert Mapplethorpe, simply and appropriately entitled 'Cock & Gun' (1982), on prominent display in the Museu de l'Eròtica, where sex, violence, and power were inextricably linked. It was all confirmation of the argument Bataille had made about the 'true' nature of eroticism.

Even the act of violation was not the most extreme of the deviations, however. Sexual frenzy reached its highest point, its true pitch, in the orgy, a claim again that Bataille had advanced in L'Erotisme. This turbulent parody of the social bond, a bizarre community of sex, where people broke free from the normal constraints to seek the most exquisite pleasure – this was the grand transgression that could subsume, or better yet deploy, all other kinds of sins. (Liu Dalin specifically denigrated one version of this, the communal or group marriage, in displays and a video compact disc available at the Shanghai museum.) In fact, there were only a few scenes of wild orgies in the collections of the sex museums, although the Seksmuseum did feature a revolving exhibit, entitled 'Sex through the Ages,' that left an impression of the history of civilization as really one massive orgy. But there were many more depictions, in paintings, drawings, photographs, and film, of group sex – that is, where three or more people were engaged in some species of sexual activity. A series of drawings in the Musée de l'érotisme demonstrated the complicated pleasuring of two men and two women, who eventually created a column of bottoms, penises, and mouths as they sought gratification, much like the elaborated scenes of many bodies that graced the pages of the Marquis de Sade's *Juliette*. In an undated French film shown in the Beate Uhse Erotik-Museum, a man, his wife, and his mistress indulged in a series of games: straight heterosexual intercourse, oral and anal sex, bondage and whipping, and lesbian play. The mini-orgies allowed pornographers to display all manner of deviations in one tableau, so signifying the presence of sexual frenzy.

These scenes bring us into that Rabelaisian domain of excess revealed many years ago by Mikhail Bakhtin.[48] Bakhtin used *Gargantua and Pantagruel*, the masterpiece of the sixteenth-century French novelist François Rabelais, to celebrate the folk culture of medieval and Renaissance Europe, whose legacy, albeit in a degraded form, had persisted well into the modern period. Bakhtin placed this culture in opposition to the official world, initially of the church and the feudal state and much later of bourgeois society and its politics. The folk culture had found expression in the ritual spectacle of the carnival and the indulgence and abundance of the feast, the bawdy life of the marketplace, a vigorous and abusive style of speech he termed billingsgate, and, above all, in parody, ridicule, satire, and comedy. The carnival emerged as a brief time of utopia, a place where hierarchy, prohibitions, and norms were subverted, energies were renewed, and the life of the ordinary people was set free. This was the site of a topsy-turvy world. The carnival and the marketplace celebrated a 'material bodily principle,' as Bakhtin put it, a fascination with food, drink, defecation, birth and death, and, naturally, sex, thereby linking humanity to its collective existence as part of the material world. That led to another dialectic, this between the high or 'classical' body of the individual – symmetrical, finished, closed, contained, self-sufficient, cerebral – and the low or 'grotesque' body of the people – disproportioned, fleshy, open, clamorous, needy, emotional. The classical body spoke of reason, its rival of appetite. The grotesque body had no centre; it did not value the head, that which commanded the actions of the ideal bourgeois, but emphasized instead the gaping mouth, the big belly, the anus, and the genitals, always seeking gratification. Crucial to the story of carnival and the low body was the reality of struggle: authority constantly endeavoured to restrict and suppress that which constituted the great Other. How ironic, then, that the repressed always returned, since the loathing for the Other was eventually transformed into longing for what was denied or abjected.[49]

Bakhtin's insights suggest two different kinds of inquiries into the nature of erotic imagery.[50] First, the museum collections construct twin biographies of the high and the low bodies, or rather of their sexual histories. They follow very different trajectories, which, I must emphasize, reflect only what was made available in the museums and the exhibitions, not necessarily the whole realm of pornography. The grotesque, or variants thereof, was the favoured shape in much of the 'primitive' and traditional art. Many of the examples of pottery and sculpture from the Americas, Asia, and Africa, some of them authored in the recent past, featured enlarged genitals, buttocks, or breasts that spoke of the extraordinary sexual appetites, as well as the potency or fertility, of these figures. The image of the satyr, the classic sexual predator, a mix of male and goat, appeared in replicas of Greek pottery as well as in the paintings of early modern Europe and right into the nineteenth century: for instance, in the work of the painter Félicien Rops at Hamburg's museum. In his later paintings, Picasso refashioned that image as the Minotaur, some samples of which were on display at *Picasso Érotique*. Some of the Japanese works on display wildly exaggerated the size of the penis and, to a lesser extent, the vulva. The fashion of displaying a low body consumed by appetite survived right through the nineteenth and twentieth centuries, eventually becoming the degraded forms of 'fat porn' where large women exhibited their lushness and what I will call 'penis porn' where men, often African males, displayed huge, always erect members. 'Sodom Berlin' featured a series of drawings (1935–50) by Hildebrandt of effeminate young men, dressed as women yet sporting prominent erections. The hermaphrodite or the androgyne or the woman with a dildo, who thus encompassed both sexes, appeared in images and scenes throughout the museums and in *jardín de eros* and *Surrealism: Desire Unbound*. So the low body persisted as a signifier of the primacy of lust. But it had become either vulgar or bizarre, the Other that personified strange passions.

The high body made its first appearance in the replicas of Greek pottery and sculpture – the Museu de l'Eròtica, for example, featured a replica of the Doriforo, a huge statue of a naked, symmetrical, male athlete, which the caption declared was 'the model of ideal perfection.' Thereafter, such smooth, muscular male bodies were rare indeed in the collections of the sex museums until the twentieth century and the arrival of gay art. Although the stylized prints of India, China, and Japan featured clothed figures that did not fit Bakhtin's distinctions, which after all were based on the European experience, still the richly decorated and colourful dress of the Shunga prints of Japan, a form of art developed in the eighteenth and nineteenth centuries, suggested the closed body of the aristocrat, at least to contemporary Western eyes. Well-proportioned females did proliferate in the genre of the nude so apparent in European oil paintings, a genre that reached into the nineteenth century – but that was not well represented in the sex museums outside of Hamburg. The one site that did celebrate the idealized types of the nineteenth century, male as well as female, painted and sculpted, was *Exposed: The Victorian Nude*. Even there, however, most of these distanced figures, especially those produced in England, were marked by a certain prudery, appearing as symbols of beauty rather than creatures of lust.[51]

The invention of photography swung the balance decisively in favour of an eroticized version of the classical body: so many of the photographs, including the early daguerreotypes, focused on beautiful females, objects of desire, whose willing demeanour, flawless skin, long hair, pretty faces, perfect breasts, shapely legs, and rounded forms were all meant to arouse the voyeur, assumed here to be a heterosexual male. The American tradition of the pin-up, so common from the 1920s into the 1950s, shown in the museums of Copenhagen, Barcelona, and especially Hamburg, illustrated idealized and available young females, always posing, in various states of undress. Out of that tradition came one of the most famous portrayals of a sex symbol, albeit in the shape of a photograph, the depiction of a provocative Marilyn Monroe reproduced on a 1954 calendar. Images of her body, including some life-size replicas, were featured in Amsterdam's Seksmuseum, the Beate Uhse Erotik-Museum, and the Museu de l'Eròtica in Barcelona. The perfected woman had also become the model for lesbian and sado-masochistic imagery: one intriguing variation was the woman as fetish, encased in rubber, totally closed to the world outside except through guarded points of access. The erotic body of the twentieth century, if fashioned on the classical model, had incorporated or rather 'cleansed' elements of the low, notably abundant sexual attributes, designed to capture (mostly) the fancy of heterosexual males.

The second line of inquiry probes the carnivalesque elements of the collections. Now the focus shifts away from the body itself to how that body performs. Was the sexual underworld a part of a Rabelaisian domain, full of a harsh joy and gruff laughter? Consider some of the performances on display in the various sex museums and erotic exhibitions, here arranged as examples of the behaviours that Bakhtin extolled in his work.

(i) *vulgar pleasures*: Everywhere you looked the sexual underworld was a site of those vulgar pleasures, the affronts to convention and normality, that Bakhtin cherished. A woman fondled a man's penis in a what looked like a lively cafe, oblivious to the other customers and the waiters all around them (Museum Erotica). A woman sat astride a satyr, obviously relishing the experience, in one 1925 painting by Gerda Wegener (Beate Uhse Erotik-Museum). Two beautiful, intertwined, nude lesbians exchanged a passionate kiss in an exotic, vaguely oriental room full of couples apparently resting after some marvellous debauch (Musée de l'érotisme).

(ii) *bacchanal*: Perhaps the best expression of these vulgar pleasures, though, were the assorted scenes of orgy, broadly defined, where the participants gave themselves over to 'perversion' in its many forms. In a huge mural by Jon Mikel Euba, a host of nude people were gathered in copulating columns, à la Sade, as if carrying out some bizarre ceremony of mass desire (Museo Erótico de Madrid). In a sketch of the harem, often a site of Western fantasy, three men watched intently as two mostly naked women, boasting huge breasts, were locked together in a genital kiss (Erotic Art Museum). Yet another sketch showed an elegant room where one man, his penis erect, and a host of women, some exhausted, some engaged, were caught up in a mood of wild abandon. These bacchanals, of course, were not quite the feasts of Bakhtin – or Bacchus: the same indulgence was present, the same abundance was celebrated, but the appetite was not for food or wine but for unlimited sex.

(iii) *parody*: A similar kind of excess was manifest in the scenes of mockery. The Chinese roll picture 'Satire on the Strength of Men'

(Beate Uhse Erotik-Museum), a work modelled on an eighteenth- or nineteenth-century original purportedly found in a monastery, depicted anxious men trying to do impossible things with their enormous penises. A group of semi-nude American stars, including Jean Harlow, Raquel Welch, and, of course, Marilyn Monroe, displayed their bodies to please a gaggle of fans, who appear as happy but pudgy penises in a 1976 spoof (Erotic Art Museum). Laughter, joyous or ribald, was always a part of the underworld: one short American porn film showed how a bevy of women fooled an overheated male into entering a pig, through a hole in a wooden fence, when he thought he was giving pleasure to one of the beauties.

(iv) *acts of degradation*: During the ancien régime in Europe, pornography had often served as a vehicle to dishonour the high and mighty or to question the social order.[52] Although commercial and aesthetic priorities won out after 1800, nonetheless degradation remained a persistent theme. So an undated exhibit (Musée de l'érotisme) indulged in some anti-religious satire: a mock Russian icon showed a robed figure – an unnamed saint, presumably – who held the sacred text in one hand while he fondled his erect and leaking penis in the other. An early twentieth-century wall painting depicted a voluptuous, naked demon attempting to seduce a still resisting monk (Museum of Ancient Chinese Sex Culture). One of the old porn films (Beate Uhse Erotik-Museum) told the story of a nun, very much the classical body, slim and elegant, who disrobed, masturbated, and engaged in a wild bout of sex with a passing male, only to return to her habit after passion was spent. *Moral Fibre* contrasted a promotional image of the famous Canadian Mountie with a mannequin dressed in a leather suit, making him the wearer of a brand of fetish gear. A Hildebrandt sketch in the 'Sodom Berlin' exhibit depicted two American soldiers, their penises exposed, who together held a young, largely naked, and very 'Aryan' teenager. His body was spread open, his member in the grasp of one soldier, his anus exposed, ready to receive their attentions. The date scribbled in the corner of the picture was 1945.

(v) *the topsy-turvy world*: The Hildebrandt sketch might easily be read as a wry commentary on what war and occupation had really done to Germany. For the act of degradation often formed part of a second theme – namely, a world turned upside down.

The gynaecologist's office had become a site of pain and pleasure at the Erotisch Museum: there a partially clad doctor, his
penis encased in a metal shaft, assisted by a nurse in a transparent outfit, prepared to 'operate' on a naked, willing woman, her
legs spread apart. Another artist in the 'Sodom Berlin' exhibit, S.
Vigny, produced a series of drawings around 1930 in which, as
the caption put it, 'almost all the perversions are represented.'
But what was most striking was the way his work inverted and
laughed at convention: a naked woman led two policemen away
by their erect penises, a nun fondled an enormous penis, two
waiters replenished their bowls from the urine and excrement
flowing out of the bared posterior of a woman, a young girl
sucked the penis of an old man, and so on. Still a third artist in
the exhibit, Michel Fingesten, explored partly in a humorous
fashion the well-established motif of the femme fatale. In a port-
folio published in 1918 he purported to show how man was
actually enslaved by woman: his sketches illustrated men, or
rather their penises, serving women's lusts. By contrast a series
of recent works (Musée de l'érotisme) by Michel Ange and Damnation, informed by feminism, featured bits of female bodies as
wall plaques and a huge statue of an anguished black woman,
entitled 'Le sans Papier.' The moral? That woman was enslaved
to man's lusts. Both of these were examples of unmasking, à la
Foucault, using sex to compel people to see the world as it actually was.

(vi) *ambiguous rituals*: Bakhtin celebrated the virtues of comic or subversive rituals attached to carnival pageants, the so-called feasts
of fools and of the ass, or the comic spectacles of the marketplace
that marked the entry of the medieval subject into the world of
laughter. The ritual unique to the sexual underworld was the
opening of the body, almost invariably the female body. The collections were full of scenes of women, their legs spread or their
bottoms revealed – 'La Belle Fanny' in one French print of *jardín
de eros*. The diorama of a happy Marilyn Monroe (Beate Uhse
Erotik-Museum) offered all voyeurs an open-mouthed greeting,
her dress was cut to disclose her cleavage, and a gust of wind
blew up her skirt whenever anyone passed by. More bizarre was
a contemporary painting (Musée de l'érotisme) in which a man
had actually pushed his head right into a woman's vagina and
her breasts spouted out two joyous streams of milk in response.
But the most striking example of this ritual of the opening was a

Japanese print (Beate Uhse Erotik-Museum) entitled 'Geisha
with Gynaecologist': a woman lolls on a chair, her clothes in disarray, her breasts naked, her legs spread and the lips of her
vagina apart; a seated male inserts his erect penis plus a wafer,
raising up her flesh, so that the white fluid flowing out of her
body can be collected in a small cup resting on a stool. Such
openings signalled both the escape from the realm of the ordinary and the entry into the site of pleasure.

(vii) *hybridization*: The grotesque has found expression in weird, temporary combinations of bodies or strange mixtures of sexual
parts. The phallic woman, a woman with a penis, was on display
in both of the Amsterdam museums, as was a large red hermaphrodite in Paris. The Seksmuseum had pictures of voluptuous transsexuals in its de Sade room. In *Clover Leaf*, a mid-
twentieth-century painting from India (Beate Uhse Erotik-
Museum), the man in the centre, naturally boasting an erection,
pleasured four different women with his hands and his feet,
each woman at one of the points of the compass. Hans Bulmer,
an artist in the 'Sodom Berlin' display, unravelled and reconsti-
tuted the body, turning an eye into a vagina or mixing a woman
and a bicycle or enfolding a daughter in a mother that was little
more than a huge vagina with arms, legs, and hair. The later surrealist Pierre Molinier cut up photographs to provide the elements to reassemble women as creatures of many legs, objects of
lust that catered to his leg fetish (*Surrealism: Desire Unbound*).
The contemporary artist Richard Fand at the Museu de l'Eròtica
simply dispensed with the outline of the body altogether, building, in one instance, a compacted feminine thing of breasts, buttocks, and vagina. All these images are prototypes of the
obscene 'desiring-machines' made notorious in the classic work
Anti-Oedipus of Gilles Deleuze and Félix Guattari: that is, assemblages of body parts, in this case often copulating, forever lust-
ing and forever indulging.

(viii) *demonization*: The grotesque and the hybrid might also take on a
sinister cast, reflecting masculine fears and, at times, misogyny.
Victor Brauner's *The Complete Woman (Anatomy of Desire)* was a
horror (from 1936) of red pupils, wings, tubes from nipples to
naval, a web at the back of her legs, a beard but no arms, seemingly a creature of monstrous lusts (*Surrealism: Desire Unbound*).
Eulàloa Valldosera offered a more recent impression of the age-
old nightmare of the vagina dentate, this a photo-collage (1990)

that showed, literally, an opened vagina with teeth (*jardín de eros*). A different version of the same nightmare, on the stairwell of Hamburg's Erotic Art Museum, was a poster of a naked woman whose vulva was a menacing face complete with a mouth full of teeth.

So, yes, the sexual underworld was a carnival of sex, though the laughter and the joy celebrated by Bakhtin were sometimes in short supply, especially among children and women. If the Rabelaisian world had waned, not so the carnival of sex.[53] It had found new vigour and new customers in the nineteenth century as communications discovered, or rather the media built, a mass audience. Indeed, it had enjoyed a spectacular expansion during the twentieth century, using all the new forms of technology, and most recently the Internet, to flood the private sphere and eventually the public stage with erotic images. Copenhagen's Museum Erotica offered the most compelling evidence of this phenomenon of colonization: postcards, magazine covers, movie posters, advertisements, its video wall – all charted the escalating significance and the growing acceptance of the pornographic empire. The carnival of sex was a place of mockery, resistance, and renewal, meaning in this context the stimulation, the excitement, of the libido.[54] There, bourgeois morality was contested, but the authority, especially the authority of the white, male, heterosexual, was also affirmed.

The sexual underworld had remained a zone of privilege where, even though hierarchies might be overturned, inequalities persisted. (By the way, that was also true of the historical carnival, which had a dark side that Bakhtin's apologia neglected.) History as past pornography was about power as well as sex, most obviously in the many displays of sado-masochism. Stereotypes of race or ethnicity, class, and especially gender were everywhere. Consider race first. On its website Barcelona's museum repeated that old chestnut about the variable lengths of the average European, Asian, and African penises, this in a long discussion of phallic symbolism and the efforts to lengthen the penis. Non-white peoples figured as exotics: primitive tribes were noted for their sexual exuberance, ancient India for its sexual sophistication, present-day Africans for their sexual potency. Both Barcelona and Madrid offered what amounted to 'imperial erotica': photographs taken by whites in the early twentieth century of nude or semi-nude young men and women native to the colonized lands outside of Europe. A small exhibit in the Beate Uhse Erotik-Museum (and a series of photographs in Madrid) focused attention on the cult of the phallus, still extant in the 1950s, supposedly a part of the Shinto religion of old Japan. The exhibit featured a replica of a phallus shrine, a pilgrim robe, a phallic flag, and a detailed description of the annual phallic procession. 'The possessor of the flag gives it to the Shinto holy shrine and wishes such a splendid [member?] as the one portrayed.' The sacred and the profane were rendered as one. Yet further proof, perhaps, of how different was the culture of sex in the orient? But the imperative and the priority of sex was deemed universal, meaning that lust reigned over the lives of all peoples whatever their race or nationality.

The signs of class were most evident in the pornography authored by Europeans and Americans. The ordinary person, the common man or woman, was usually the hero of any porn drama, if hero there was. Such, for example, was the case with America's 'Tijuana Bibles,' adult comics that featured acts of hectic sex, at the Museum of Sex. The tenor of pornography was decidedly anti-establishment. First the effete aristocrat or the sour priest, later the fat businessman or perhaps the general – these were often sources of mockery. So a cover illustration on 'The Satyrical' (Museu de l'Eròtica) showed a large, aged male, smoking a cigar, whose nose was a penis and whose jowls were his testicles.[55] Elegant women commonly served as the target of some sort of degradation: a victim of sexual frenzy, a lesbian encounter, or even a rape. Except, that is, for the dominatrix, always stylish, always arrogant, the new version of the classical body as the object of admiration, if not fear. But she, and the S/M world in general, were a challenge to bourgeois convention and morality.

Above all, the sexual underworld was represented as a gendered zone: it operated almost always under the sign of the phallus. By now it should be obvious that the underworld conjured up by the erotic exhibitions and sex museums was the abode of what were deemed eternal male fantasies. There were, here and there, a few images made by women: Tina Cohen's 'Pornage' series of natural images, for example, at Barcelona's Museu de l'Eròtica. There were, occasionally, images of powerful women, sometimes aggressive lesbians or a dominatrix. There were, much more often, pictures of women silenced, restrained, abused, or submissive. *Surrealism: Desire Unbound*, for example, carried that horrifying painting *The Rape* by René Magritte, where he transformed a women's face into a body, making of the pubic hair a goatee that covered her mouth. But there were a lot more women willing, inviting, worshipping, loved, enjoyed, and enjoying – this was no exclusive preserve, and women certainly found pleasure here. There was joy for everyone in this site of constant transgression. Still, the active principle was normally male: the museums were filled with images of the erect penis, penetrating, spurting, sometimes demanding or threatening, but very rarely flaccid. Everywhere were the signs of this phallic obsession. Even the much more staid Shanghai site featured in its display and its pamphlet a double dildo, a penis on each side, purportedly used by lesbians in the sixteenth or seventeenth century. What greeted the visitor as he entered the Museo Erótico de Madrid was a large sculpture of a bent penis. Barcelona sported in one room a huge, huggable, wooden penis, plus a lengthy commentary on the importance of the phallus. Paris was replete with erect, enlarged, and engorged penises, forever penetrating one orifice or another. The carnival of sex served first the lusts, the anxieties, the desires of adult men, gay as well as straight.

All histories teach lessons about the human condition. History as past pornography was no exception. Indeed it was more didactic than most. The museums and the exhibitions told visitors that sex and desire were natural, universal, and eternal – the argument that sexuality was a construct of culture, as Foucault had argued elsewhere, found no support here.[56] The sex museum identified the man as the active agent: a man's eyes, his hands, his penis – these instruments activated the game of sex. It identified the woman as the object of desire: she controlled access to sex, to the source of pleasure that was her body. (Obviously I have left aside the minority traditions of feminine, gay, and lesbian porn.) And it posited the existence of a sexual underworld, which, in the West at least, had always been subversive, at odds with authority, secular and religious, though the intensity of the war against the erotic varied according to the times and the place. There was much evidence of separate narratives, notably the different experience of the orient or the recent growth of S/M or the slow rise of sexual liberation and the spread of pornography into the mainstream. But the sex museum as an institution propagated a brand of history that was monolithic rather than multifarious, where what was eternal trumped what was particular. Anatomy really was destiny, it seems.

3 The Voyeur's Gaze

'Islam is wise to drape women in black,' mused Camille Paglia, 'for the eye is the avenue of eros.'[57] And again: 'A pornographic image is worth a thousand erotic words,' wrote the Cuban novelist Guillermo Cabrera Infante.[58] That might stand as the credo of the voyeur. Usually images did a far better job of arousing a person than could mere words. Images have the capacity to stun the mind, to overwhelm reason, to provoke a response. In particular images, and especially realistic ones, evoke the presence of the person that they represent; or, as David Freedberg put it, the sign becomes 'the living embodiment of what it signifies.'[59] The image and its prototype are fused. This may be an illusion, but it is an illusion rooted in the psychology of humanity.

From its beginnings in the sixteenth century pornography had mostly meant writings, and these were usually aimed at a highly literate public of gentlemen.[60] There were many salacious paintings, illustrations, and engravings produced in the seventeenth and eighteenth centuries, but again mostly for a very small market of elite buyers. So the invention of photography, roughly speaking after 1840, an invention that soon allowed for the infinite reproduction of images, enormously expanded the potential market for pornography. The Amsterdam Seksmuseum contains an extensive collection of 'dirty pictures' dating from the 1860s, mostly studio photographs though supplemented by some amateur efforts. The photographs of the 1890s and early 1900s showed not only beautiful young women in various states of undress but scenes of all kinds of intercourse (in many different positions), oral and anal sex, some lesbian couplings (though none of gay men), plus what was called 'erotic punishment,' usually whippings but sometimes other forms of sexual torture as well. At some point early in the twentieth century 'dirty pictures' became a common part of male culture in western Europe and North America, especially in young men's lives, where it served, among other needs, to introduce them to the mechanics of sex play.

This kind of imagery, albeit more often the milder varieties, was sold cheaply to a widening audience of people in the form of erotic postcards.[61] That was a part of the general postcard craze of the times, after these had been accepted by mail services: it has been estimated that around 140 billion postcards were sent in the world between 1894 and 1919. The popularity of erotic postcards was so great that they swiftly became the most widely distributed brand of commercial pornography. Paris's Musée de l'érotisme displayed a series of French examples from the early decades of the twentieth century, many of which caught women showing off some forbidden flesh, a breast, a thigh, the crotch. The much larger Milford Haven collection at London's Victoria and

Albert Museum favoured images of the exotic, including lots of semi-nude colonial women; shots of available and sexualized white women and girls; and comic cards that poked fun at the aristocracy and the clergy, a legacy of the time when pornography had been part of the literature of social and political protest. The more outrageous cards were never actually mailed, of course, since the authorities were soon on the lookout for this kind of porn. But they were widely available, sold in variety stores, news shops, tobacconists, and the like: in 1904 the police found one London vendor who had 2,287 'problematic cards' in his total collection of nearly 6,000.

The rapid spread of such pornographic images ushered in the era of the voyeur in the realm of mass culture. Voyeurism in its milder forms means no more than taking visual pleasure from looking at other people's flesh or sex play.[62] But it has a double, even a triple, nature. First of all, the erotic fascinates many people. In evidence I cite this anecdote of visiting one museum. It was a hot day, inside and outside the museum. Still the temperature did not stop people from pouring into the exhibition to see a myriad of sights, mostly paintings but also some films, photographs, and artefacts. The topic, after all, was sex. Not just men but lots of women, in couples and groups, appeared eager to see the exhibition.[63] Visitors were especially taken by the showing of a selection of old pornographic films – silent movies, in fact – quaint because they seemed so coy, at least by comparison with what was available nowadays, films that had initially been made for the pleasure of the king of Spain in the 1920s. The place was Barcelona's Palau de la Virreina, the time summer 1999, and the exhibition was called *jardín de eros*. 'In all times and in all cultures,' Joan Clos, the mayor of Barcelona, claimed, 'the expression of erotism has been one of the most creative and at the same time most closely guarded facets of human culture.'[64] But not that day, not in Barcelona at least, when people could pull back the veil on the world of the erotic.

Sex pleases. Look at these notes on an exhibition, written in the visitors' book of *Exposed: The Victorian Nude*.

'The pieces are wonderful. We flew from Florida to see this.'
'Worth the trip from Texas.'
'We need more shows like this!!!!'
'Once again I leave a museum wishing I were a woman.'
'So different from the nudes on the Internet.'
'The human figure is pure beauty.'
'Titillating.'

That visitors' book was not the place for profound comments, obviously. Yet the people who left their thoughts, or most of them, felt that they had witnessed something unusual, out of the ordinary, indeed exciting. One dissenter was unhappy – the exhibition 'sucks' – because he (presumably a man) wanted more 'pussies,' in short a greater display of sex. Likewise another disgruntled soul who decided the museum was just 'playing it safe.'

But sex also disturbs. Its images sometimes stare back at us, and so upset our equilibrium or even repel our view.[65] They can exercise a kind of power over our eyes and our psyche, compelling a response. Here the spectacle threatens to control the viewer. That was why both *Picasso Érotique* and *Moral Fibre* prominently displayed a warning that the material might offend people (and one older woman did find the exhibition of dress, or a least of the fetish Mountie, 'gross, shocking'). Witness the effects of the material in Room 9 of the exhibition *Surrealism: Desire Unbound*. It was an unusual place. How puzzling that there was no reference to the room in the audio guide, which otherwise had led visitors to particular paintings in the twelve rooms of the exhibition. Perhaps that was because the site served as a showcase for a variety of raw images? The room made people uneasy. On the two days I visited the exhibition – and both times there were crowds of people at the site – this was the one room that sometimes was empty: many people moved past its images quickly. One woman was obviously troubled and ready for the end of the exhibition. A nervous older man sneered and snickered to his companions about some of the representations. A father found all this 'crap,' though his son replied that it was 'great.' A group of young women laughed when they looked at the blatantly sexual portrayals of the Czech surrealist Jindrich Styrsky. A young woman found Marcel Duchamp's *Study for 'Given'* 'gross.' (The strange image showed a naked and headless woman apparently attempting to straddle a rock.) Another exclaimed, 'Oh God ... that's terrible,' and moved away swiftly, when she spotted Victor Brauner's *The Complete Woman (Anatomy of Desire)*. An older woman told her companion, 'I think some of these people are sick,' echoing the comment of a female teen at the end of the exhibition: 'Are these done by psycho people?'

Of all the sex museums, only Amsterdam's Seksmuseum was equally crowded. Here the visitors were much more vocal, and they moved through the exhibits much more rapidly. Except, that is, in the case of the de Sade room: a small, hot, darkened space, full of lewd and bizarre colour photographs of sexual performers that held the interest of all sorts of people. Many more of the visitors were young than at the *Sur-*

realism exhibition, or for that matter the other erotic art exhibitions, which were also well attended. The most boisterous were groups of males, some of whom were clearly excited by the succession of erotic sights and by the various gags. Noisiest were clusters of Englishmen, especially if women were present. Typically, the groups and couples took pictures of a companion in front of some display that caught their fancy. There were some signs of disgust. One series of watercolours, entitled 'The Affectionate Dog,' showed the erotic play between a dog and her mistress. A group of young women found this a bit noxious, though as one of them exclaimed, 'I reckon that really happened.' Often the single most important determinant of any response was grounded in gender. Witness the behaviour of one Japanese couple in front of the 'Photo Gallery': he was absorbed and kept talking about one photograph or another, but she was not interested; indeed, she looked distressed and remained silent, eventually sitting to one side to wait until he was finished.

The other museums attracted all kinds of people, many couples, some groups of men and women, single men, and less often single women, of all ages, except for children (though in the case of Shanghai one loud kid disturbed the peace of the museum) and early teens, who may have been excluded. Men predominated, especially in Berlin. Once again, with a few noticeable exceptions, and those at the Hamburg site, most people moved through the exhibits quickly, pausing at only a few sights. The fact is that so much sex, especially the older prints from Asia and Europe, or the assorted African and South American figures, could become boring to anyone other than an aficionado. The 'woman's calm, otherworldly gaze' in 'those exquisite Indian miniatures' suggested to the columnist Anthony Lane (*New Yorker*, 31 January 2000) 'not that she is nearing climax but that she is trying to remember where she put the keys to the elephant.'[66] But there was the opposite reaction: one woman, part of a family, let out a yelp of surprise in front of a series of Japanese photographs in Hamburg. Recent items often proved the most interesting: for example, unusual photographs of lesbian play, fetish dress, or S/M practices; a giant wooden phallus or a huge red hermaphrodite and other such curiosities; and the short films, where the people shown really did seem engaged in some sort of passionate activity. In an early porn drama made for Spain's King Alfonso XIII, a young woman was compelled by her mother to satisfy the desires of an older client: the film was on display in three sites and always attracted attention. At the Museum of Sex (in my visit of 2004) men hogged the few decent spots available for watching the porn films. Some of the exhibits provoked embarrassed laughter, both giggles and guffaws, at least when the observer was with a group. Usually people kept their voices low, talking briefly and only with their companions. In Shanghai the presence of a European woman watching a video on ancient sex culture (not pornographic at all) clearly made a group of Chinese men uncomfortable, so much so that at times they averted their eyes from the screen.

There was an aura of sin about these sites and their wares that appeared to deter visitors from approaching, or even recognizing, any stranger. People were acting as voyeurs – indeed, that is exactly how the museums hailed visitors – and it was not always possible for an observer to maintain the traditional posture of detachment or distance when looking at photographs or films of exotic or attractive bodies rendered naked to the eye. They could stimulate, perhaps arouse a sexual interest, perhaps disgust. But more important they represented an invasion of privacy, a somehow illicit look at the intimate body of another.[67] Hence the laughter, a way of dispelling this tension, that was the most common response in all of the sex museums.

The way people act in the domain of the erotic is a consequence of 'the civilizing process.' The phrase was coined many years ago by Norbert Elias, a social scientist, in his study of the tyranny of manners in Europe.[68] He took a very long view of history, going back roughly 500 years to trace the emergence and the expansion of a new kind of control over 'the expression of drives and impulses' that fostered a 'split between an intimate and a public sphere, between private and public behaviour.'[69] There was a lot of Freud in this argument: Elias saw the civilizing process as a denial of pleasure and the imposition of restraint upon the body, as a result of the growing dominion of the superego, itself a social conscience and a moral agent that operated on the individual through shame, embarrassment, repugnance, and fear. One consequence was a change in the very significance of the senses: the civilizing process emphasized the eye, or what Elias called 'spectating,' over the hand, so as to avoid the intense emotions of 'direct action.'[70] He charted the civilizing process in descriptions of table manners, codes of speech, the regulation of bodily functions (such as blowing one's nose or going to the bathroom), the disciplining of aggression, and, of course, the practice of sex. So he talked about the avoidance of nudity, even in the home; the segregation of sexuality, away from the public eye, behind closed doors; the effort to restrict sex to marriage and then to regulate that sex as well. A thicket of prohibitions and regulations served to condition the behaviour of the modern person, and the discipline was especially harsh on the young.

Allow me to extrapolate from Elias's argument. The result of the civilizing process was that the erotic became a largely secret domain, full of injunctions and taboos. And, as a consequence, it also became a domain of escape, a place where people went to seek out the very pleasures denied them by the disciplines of life.[71] Viewing the images of 'perversions,' of orgies, of sadism, and of the vulgar pleasures or the strange rituals of wild sex – again this was a case of 'spectating' – might cause shame or foster guilt, especially if the voyeur was discovered looking at the illicit. It might disgust, as well – witness some of the responses to the surrealist exhibition. 'But disgust always bears the imprint of desire,' as Peter Stallybrass and Allon White put it.[72] What was suppressed by the prevailing bourgeois order returned to haunt and excite the imagination of people. Read that as the social dimension of Freud's classic warning about the return of the repressed.[73] The carnival of sex was a site where lots of men and women wanted to play, at least some of the time.

The voyeur's gaze involves an obvious but unstable relationship of power between the one who looks and the one who displays. Consider this hypothetical comment, one woman to another: 'It felt like he stripped me with his eyes.' She was a victim of the voyeur's gaze. 'The gaze is the erection of the eye,' claimed Jean Clair, later the chief curator of the *Picasso Érotique* exhibition, a comment that emphasized the gendered nature of this way of looking.[74] A voyeur, normally male, turned a woman into a sexual object. His action amounted to an exercise of power, an invasion of privacy, nowadays something of a transgression. His was an illicit pleasure, the cause of her pain. The scenario seems age old, a consequence of male dominance and female submission, manifested in the long tradition of European oil painting. 'Men look at women. Women watch themselves being looked at,' claimed John Berger, an art critic, in an analysis of how people see, written just as a new wave of feminism had begun to attack such conventions. 'This determines not only most relations between men and women but also the relation of women to themselves. The surveyor of woman in herself is male; the surveyed female.' She is, in short, colonized. 'Thus she turns herself into an object – and most particularly an object of vision: a sight.'[75] Here was a classic statement of the power of surveillance, the ability of the gaze to dominate and control another person.[76]

Consider, by contrast, a second hypothetical comment: 'He couldn't take his eyes off me.' Now she was the master of the erotic spectacle. A person, normally female, had constructed an image of desire that captivated the watcher. This time she was the subject; she exercised the power – less coercive than seductive, to be sure – to which he submitted. But her pleasure, if not at his expense, was also illicit, because it too involved a submission of his will. 'REGARDEZ-MOI DANS LES YEUX ...' ordered a beautiful young woman. Then again: 'J'AI DIT LES YEUX.' The object of these commands was unseen – she was looking directly at us. But experience suggested that her target was yet another dazzled male, dazzled because the woman was wearing a revealing black bra whose effect was accentuated by her body language. Presumably he could not raise his eyes from her bosom. Les yeux was aimed at women, not men: the late 1990s ad represented Wonderbra as an instrument of romance able to so enhance the physical charms of its user that she might overwhelm any male. Here was an example of the power of spectacle, the way an image could work to dominate the mind of another and determine his behaviour.[77]

Yet in a way I have cheated with this example. Les yeux was an example of commercial, rather than personal, spectacle. The power lay not so much with the model in the tableau as with its creator, whether a man or woman, who constructed her look to suggest her erotic power. In short the admaker exploited the nature of voyeurism to sell a particular good, that Wonderbra, which now was positioned as an erotic instrument. Put another way, commerce worked to refashion the voyeur, turning that kind of self into someone who saw sex throughout the world, especially the world of commodities. The success of the effort was one crucial reason for the failure of the Left's vision of sexual liberation.

2 Liberation Theory

'They don't realize we're bringing them the plague.' Sigmund Freud supposedly made this comment to his two colleagues, Carl Jung and Sándor Ferenczi, on board a ship in the New York harbour in 1909, on the eve of their visit to deliver the messages of psychoanalysis to America at Clark University. A good story, except it is probably not true. The source was Jacques Lacan, that notorious trickster, the man who would mastermind a reinterpretation of Freud (though he called this a return to Freud) after 1950 to suit the new and French fascination with language. Lacan told the story in a speech he gave in Vienna in 1955, claiming that at a recent visit Jung had repeated Freud's words. But Jung never 'repeated' this sentence again, especially not the crucial word 'plague,' not even in his *Memoirs*. Nor did Ferenczi or Freud, or any of Freud's biographers.[1]

Yet Lacan's story had merit. It highlighted the existence of what might be called 'the radical Freud.' For Freud's effect was subversive. The good doctor did deliver a shock to the prevailing bourgeois society of his times. Not that Freud consistently or loudly warred against bourgeois laws, even though at one point in his life he clearly was an enemy of what he once termed 'modern sexual morality.'[2] Rather it was the force and the novelty of his doctrines. The signature of psychoanalysis was its obsession with sex, more particularly with the power of the sex drive and the intensity of sexual desire, as the key to understanding the psyche and behaviour of men and women. That fascinated and repelled many people. According to one recollection of America in the 1910s, 'young women all over the country were reading Freud and attempting to lose their inhibitions.' An ad in an American magazine of the 1920s touted the virtues of his teachings: 'Are you shackled by repressed desires? Psychoanalysis, the new miracle science, proves that most people live only half-power lives because of repressed sex instincts.'[3] Writing in the early 1960s, and a fierce critic of Freud's view of women, Betty Friedan nonetheless admitted the virtues of his creed: 'Freudian psychology, with its emphasis on freedom from a repressive morality to achieve sexual fulfillment, was part of the ideology of women's emancipation.'[4] Even at the end of the century, Freud was widely remembered as the liberator of sex: so, for example, a plaque in Barcelona's Museu de l'Eròtica claimed that Freud demanded 'a free sexual life without hindrance or taboos.'

Psychoanalysis was not only comprehensive but protean: at once a total theory of the psyche, a therapeutic style, a reputed medical science, and an ideology, 'the new truth' as one of his followers put it.[5] It was always evolving, always unfinished. Freud kept reworking his ideas, and these were open to various interpretations, to a conservative as well as a progressive twist, to suit the needs of the place, the times, or the individual.[6] Lacan, for example, employed his apocryphal anecdote to support an assault on the conservative brand of psychoanalysis dominant in the United States.

In fact Freud, perhaps grown cranky with age, thought liberation a recipe for disaster. Supposedly he told one colleague, Ernest Jones, 'that he had been half-converted to Bolshevism. A Bolshevik predicted great carnage followed by universal happiness. Freud said he believed the first half.'[7] Three of his successors, nonetheless, all of them Jewish and German or Austrian émigrés to the United States, proved eager to take up the cry of liberation.

Two were on the Left. Wilhelm Reich and Herbert Marcuse carried the ideas of 'the radical Freud' much farther than the master himself: they fashioned an amalgam of psychoanalysis and socialism that promised a transformation of human society. Reich foresaw sexual liberation as an end in itself, the key to permanent happiness; Marcuse thought liberation a means to an end, the arrival of the socialist utopia. So was born 'Freudo-Marxism,' rightly called 'a hybrid for the times' suited to a century obsessed by the psychic needs of humanity.[8] Reich and Marcuse designed a route never taken: the 'radical Freud' became the avatar of a revolution that did not occur, at least not as expected. The lasting significance of Freudo-Marxism lay elsewhere, as a doctrine of criticism, initially of the repressive order that prevailed early in the century and later of the regime of stimulation that emerged after the middle of the century.[9]

The last of the émigrés was on the Right. Dr Ernest Dichter sought not so much a social as a psychological revolution, the spread of a new, exuberant hedonism among the populace. He did not advocate sexual liberation as either a goal or a means. Rather, he urged an affluent America to find freedom and happiness in the endless consumption of the marvellous array of goods now so widely available. He fashioned what amounted to a Freudian brand of capitalism in which liberation was bound up in the erotic nature of products and of the marketplace. Here was a gospel meant for a consumer society.

I will discuss these different versions of liberation through a close reading of a few key texts written by Freud, Reich, Marcuse, and Dichter. None of the accounts are meant as complete assessments of an author's ideas. In each case I will focus on the discussions of sexuality. That thrust is especially fitting in the case of Reich, who wrote about little else. But it does work an injustice to Marcuse, whose book dealt with a lot of other material as well. The purpose of these accounts, though, is to identify the intellectual substance of the Eros project.

1 The Radical Freud

The first text is Freud's own *Civilization and Its Discontents* (1930), supplemented by material drawn from the rest of his oeuvre. I have read *Civilization and Its Discontents* through the prism of two articles, one by a young Wilhelm Reich (meaning before he recanted his socialist views) and the second by another young psychoanalyst and Marxist, Erich Fromm (before he turned away from Freud's libido theory).[10] The aim is to bring out 'the radical Freud' in the context of the early 1930s: that is, to present the interpretation of the master's views that suited the demands of what became Freudo-Marxism.[11]

According to Peter Gay, one of Freud's biographers, *Civilization and Its Discontents* was 'a briefly stated psychoanalytic theory of politics.'[12] Freud had long tried to put society on the couch, to employ his findings to assess both the past and the present of culture, and that mission had become more pronounced as he grew older. This extended essay, less than a hundred pages long, was his definitive statement on the nature of civilization.[13] Freud designed his polemic for a broad audience of literate readers, and so he wrote in a conversational style. Freud always had a knack for engaging his readers. This time he definitely succeeded: the essay enjoyed, again according to Gay, an 'astonishing popularity,' its first edition of 12,000 copies selling out within a year.[14]

That was all the more remarkable because *Civilization and Its Discontents* argued such a dismal hypothesis. It asserted the inevitability of discontent, a severe psychological malady that must afflict everyone in every time. Freud argued that what people sought was pleasure, and that pleasure depended upon satisfying desires. These desires were rooted in the instincts, most especially the two powerful drives of sex and aggression (or death), which furnished humanity with the psychic energy that fuelled creativity and achievement in all their many forms. Freud employed an economic model of the human mind, using, for instance, a term like 'libido-economy' (13), to argue that the individual had only a limited quantity of energy to invest in certain endeavours. Effort in one area of life meant neglect in another. So the pleasure principle, as Freud termed the imperative of desire, could never be allowed free rein to seek gratification and avoid pain. Instead humanity had to submit to the reality principle, especially 'the compulsion to work, created by external necessity' (30), to secure the wherewithal to live, whether in comfort or hardship. And that was not the only misfortune. The 'primal instincts' (67) were constantly at war: Eros favoured procreation and union while aggression inspired strife and destruction. No wonder men and women were always the victims of ambivalence, unable to resolve an opposition that defined their humanity. There was no way out of their dilemma, except the remedies of work, intoxication, and fantasy.

The argument might seem very unpromising material from a Marxist standpoint. Neither Reich nor Fromm much cared for the book, and Fromm actually disposed of it in a footnote, emphasizing instead earlier texts. But here, as elsewhere, there was a double Freud at work. The key to making Freud progressive was to disentangle the views of the pessimist from the findings of a supposed scientist who had established a materialist explanation of human psychology. Progressives accepted the fundamental truth-claim of psychoanalysis: namely, that it was a proper science, a natural science, based upon hard fact in the form of clinical evidence.[15] That this evidence was no more than the result of encounters between patients and analysts, plus Freud's introspection, and so inherently subjective, did not faze the believers.

The outstanding value of Freud's instinct theory to a Marxist was the way it grounded the psyche in the body, not the mind or the soul where bourgeois psychologists might locate the source of human activity. The instincts were defined as physiological phenomena that generated stimuli, a kind of chemistry, driving humanity to act.[16] This instinctual apparatus existed in a dialectical relationship with the world outside so that what a man or a woman might do depended in part on both their physical constitution and their social environment.[17] *Civilization and Its Discontents*, in fact, was full of all manner of opposites: not just Eros/death, but pleasure/pain or pleasure/reality, morality/desire, egoism/altruism, and so on. Freud had designed a conflict theory of human action similar in shape to the Marxian notion of sociology (except that Freud's war of the instincts was eternal, whereas Marx's class war might end with the triumph of the proletariat). Likewise these opposites could generate all kinds of contradictions, reversals, and transformations in human ideas and behaviour. That was why the early Reich, for one, could make the excited declaration that psychoanalysis was a dialectical science like Marxism.

The tragedy of human existence reflected Freud's mapping of the human psyche. He employed two distinct, though related, topographies of the mind. The original formulation had divided our psyches into an infernal unconscious, the abode of all manner of desires, and a beleaguered conscious, the abode of reason. The second topography, a more recent invention, and one featured in *Civilization and Its Discontents*, posited a fragile ego, where resided our sense of self; the id, almost a biological entity, the realm of the instincts and their demands; and the superego, the conscience, a tyrant of the mind designed by the culture.[18] The ego was buffeted by stimuli, by demands, from outside and inside, from the world and the body, from the superego and the id. Much of the life of the mind was really lived in the unconscious where we as self-aware, logical creatures could never go, at least not directly. The result was to dethrone reason: we thought and did why we knew not. Men and women were fundamentally irrational.[19]

History demanded the constant sacrifice of desire. Love and aggression fostered desires – to fornicate, to own, to rule, to rape – that could only endanger the fabric of the community. These suppressed desires released instinctual energies that were channelled to serve culture. Civilization had to employ a transformed libido, meaning sexual energy, to build families and states, monuments and literature, ties of affection and harmony, a process that required the restriction and regulation of sexuality. Likewise, that same civilization redirected the energy of aggression to conquer nature and discipline humanity. Two key psychic processes determined just how individual desire was suppressed, deferred, or redirected. Sublimation involved the transfer of psychic energy to socially useful aims: the 'anal erotism' of children, consequently, was changed into such traits as 'thriftiness, orderliness, and cleanliness' (27–8). Repression involved the denial of 'an instinctual trend,' so that 'its libidinal elements are transformed into symptoms and its aggressive components into a sense of guilt' (65). In any case suppression was never sure, never complete. All the wishes, the desires, the cravings, however forbidden, remained in the unconscious, the id, forever seeking gratification. It was against this return of the repressed that the superego waged its harsh war.

How and why the superego operated so ferociously reflected the twisted logic of the death instinct. The discovery of the death instinct, sometimes called an instinct of destruction or aggression, had proved especially controversial, even in psychoanalytic circles, as Freud himself noted. Reich first accepted and later denied the idea. Fromm had distinct reservations, preferring instead to work with an earlier formulation of instinct theory. Nonetheless, the notion served to simplify Freud's theory, establishing a pleasing symmetry between thesis (Eros) and antithesis (Thanatos). The death instinct obviously constituted 'the most powerful obstacle to culture' (49) because aggression would destroy the community. Yet even here civilization could master the energy of instinct, turning aggression into a weapon the superego deployed to discipline the wayward ego. The superego monitored desire, for nothing – no wish, no need – could ever be completely hidden from the mind's censor. It also fashioned a sense of guilt to punish any self that indulged in dreams of the forbidden. The Oedipus complex was the foundation of the system: the fundamental trinity of 'daddy, mummy, and me,' operating in and through the family, served to program morality into the mind of every child. The complex rested on the primal act of patricide that lay at the base of civilization: the remorseful sons had re-established the law of the dead father in the form of a superego to prevent any repetition of such aggressive and dangerous desires.[20] This process, Freud believed, was played out in all historical epochs to design what amounted to a 'cultural super-ego,' which 'sets up high ideals and standards' and punishes 'the failure to fulfil them ... with *anxiety of conscience*' (67).

But sex still ruled. An early charge against psychoanalysis was its pansexualism, its belief that underlying virtually every trait or action or ideal was a sexual cause. The legacy of this pansexualism remained even after the discovery of the death instinct: not even psychoanalysis could escape its origins.[21] Certainly both Reich and Fromm presumed the centrality of the sex drive. Freud had split lust away from its earlier entanglement with procreation. The sex drive now was the chief source of desire, because the act was the ultimate source of pleasure, the 'prototype for our strivings after happiness' (31). Desire he rooted in childhood: boys and girls were identified as sexual beings, who found pleasure in playing with their own bodies and hungered after the love of one of their parents. Elsewhere Freud had proposed that the developing child moved through various stages of sexual development: the oral, the anal and the sadistic, and eventually the genital.[22] The initial site of sexual discipline was the family, and the basic mechanism again the Oedipus complex, where boys and girls learned to reject their incestuous longings and so to deny and control desire. That first disciplining became the foundation for an elaborate apparatus of moral control and sexual prohibition over the life of adults. Therein lay the source of the neuroses that disturbed the sex lives of so many people: they were compelled to suppress their desires, to seek some 'substitutive gratifications for unfulfilled sexual wishes' (65).

Freud's observations highlighted the allure of transgression, and most especially of the so-called perversions. In one of his earlier, seminal works, *Three Essays on the Theory of Sexuality*, Freud had argued that perverse impulses were built into humanity: the sexual instinct in children was, as he famously put it, 'polymorphously perverse.' Successive waves of repression and sublimation, the rigours of shame and disgust, strove to subdue the forbidden passions in adolescents and adults. But victory was never complete: the innate 'disposition to perversions' must persist – we were all perverts, in fact or in our dreams.[23] Women might have a propensity for exhibitionism and men for voyeurism; bisexuality and fetishism plus sadism and masochism were commonplace in the mental make-up of populations. So men and women always yearned to escape the force of the moral law. What he called the pleasure principle still determined the 'programme of life's purposes' (11) even when, as must happen, the decent citizen submitted to the demands of the reality principle, the requirements of living in the world at large. 'The feeling of happiness produced by indulgence of a wild, untamed craving is incomparably more intense than is the satisfying of a curbed desire,' he theorized. 'The irresistibility of perverted impulses, perhaps the charm of forbidden things generally, may in this way be explained economically' (13).

Did any sin have priority? One might argue that sadism and masochism were the signature 'perversions' of the twentieth century. Both derived pleasure from pain: they worked a fusion of the erotic and the aggressive that repudiated the whole apparatus of moral control. Freud never made such a claim. Not quite, anyway: in the *Three Essays* he did single out the special position of sadism and masochism among the 'perversions' because they embodied that contrast between 'activity and passivity' that characterized all sexual life.[24] In *Civilization and Its Discontents* he further suggested that a masochistic ego could develop an 'erotic attachment' to a sadistic superego, thus placing this 'perversion' at the core of the human personality (63). Arguing from a more radical perspective, Fromm considered sadism a tool employed eagerly by the ruling classes to bolster their authority, an insight that forecast the later emergence of the regime of stimulation.[25] The point was that power could be eroticized.

One way that might happen was through the workings of ideology. Freud put a lot of store in fantasy as a mode of reconciling humanity to its sad lot. Apparently we all lived a large part of our lives in a world of illusions where desire might claim sovereignty.[26] That attribute was a result of yet another psychic mechanism at work. What Freud called 'the life of phantasy' had been 'expressly exempted from the demands of the reality-test and set apart for the purpose of fulfilling wishes which would be very hard to realize' (14). In an article written much earlier, Freud had emphasized how fantasies were an extension of child's play into the realm of the adult, one reason why people were often ashamed of their fantasies as childish. 'The motive forces of phantasies are unsatisfied wishes, and every single phantasy is the fulfilment of a wish, a correction of unsatisfying reality.'[27] Two varieties predominated: 'ambitious wishes' or 'erotic ones,' the latter especially common among young women.[28] Popular writers (and here Freud was concerned with novelists who reached the masses much more than he was with those who pleased the critics) worked with this raw material to construct what amounted to acceptable illusions that soothed the unconscious. 'Our actual enjoyment of an imaginative work proceeds from a liberation of tensions in our minds.'[29] The term 'writers,' of course, could encompass anyone who worked with words or images to fashion fantasies for the masses, whether preachers, politicians, or admakers.

So Freud posited a human psychology in which the symbolic played a major role in determining the stability as well as the transformations of civilization. The escape into fantasy might mean no more than an addiction to art or literature, but it could extend to neuroses and psychoses or even mass delusions, such as 'the religions of humanity' (15).

Here was an entry point for any Leftist because it helped to explain the development and the persistence of unfortunate ideologies.[30] The very people who placed their trust in capitalism or who sought solace in fascism, it could now be argued, were living out a mass delusion inimical to their own interests. That was a finding of some importance: it should be recalled that Freudo-Marxism was developed in a place, Weimar Germany, and at a time, the 1920s and 1930s, when the leading political questions were the persistence of authoritarianism and the emergence of fascism.

It was crucial to shift Freud's emphasis from the biological to the social plane, and thereby to bring Freud into history, if psychoanalysis were ever to realize its revolutionary potential. Freud himself gave licence to such a translation in a number of passages in *Civilization and Its Discontents* (and even more elsewhere) where he criticized the excess of sexual restrictions. He wrote of a 'cultural super-ego' and of 'collective neuroses': 'many systems of civilization – or epochs of it – possibly even the whole of humanity – have become *neurotic* under the pressure of the civilizing trends' (69). A greedy culture would slake its appetite for psychic energy by restricting too severely the passions of sex. That practice, he feared, had reached its 'high-water mark ... in our Western European civilization' (33). Both Reich and Fromm, in different ways, drew out the obvious conclusion, at least from a radical perspective, that the ruling classes had imposed a rigorous form of sexual repression upon Europe and America during the rise of capitalism.[31] The initial purpose was to take command of the bourgeois body, to ensure that psychic energy was sublimated in production and acquisition. Later that discipline was extended to the proletariat, indeed to the whole of society, in order to strengthen the rule of Capital. So was born the repressive hypothesis, or a version of it, linking class, sex, and power into an unholy trinity.

The hypothesis required one more addition, the identity of the site where the crucial work of repression was always reproduced: the answer was the family. Reich and Fromm described the family, respectively, as 'the ideological nucleus of society' and 'the psychological agency of society.'[32] The family that exercised both men was the bourgeois or patriarchal family (the two adjectives sometimes seemed interchangeable), a class institution organized by capitalism and reflecting the material conditions of life. It was here that the Oedipal mechanism worked its awful magic on the vulnerable soul of the child to fashion a brand of sexual oppression that served class rule.[33] The reign of Oedipus, in short, was not eternal, as Freud had mistakenly presumed, but very much historical, and only likely to disappear when socialism triumphed. 'In short, Oedipus arrives: it is born in the capitalist system,' wrote Gilles Deleuze and Félix Guattari many years later. 'It is our intimate colonial formation that corresponds to the form of social sovereignty. We are all little colonies and it is Oedipus that colonizes us.' Thus there had emerged what would prove one of the recurring maxims of Freudo-Marxism.[34]

2 Reich's Sexual Revolution

The career of Wilhelm Reich (1897–1957) amounted to a long, slow descent into the realm of the absurd. He seemed intent on replaying Freud – that is, on becoming one of the century's presiding geniuses. Instead he became a parody of Freud, ending his days as an embarrassment to the medical and scientific establishments, though not to a few devoted disciples who saw him as a guru. Even so, he has been remembered as the man who first preached that extraordinary event in the life of the twentieth century, the so-called sexual revolution.[35] A display in Copenhagen's Museum Erotica, for instance, celebrated Reich's attempt to bring his gospel of liberation to Denmark in the mid-1930s.[36]

Reich's career began full of promise. He came to Vienna after the First World War where he swiftly established himself as among the most innovative of psychoanalysts, developing a noted expertise in the realm of analysis. His clinical endeavours gave rise to two important monographs: first, *The Function of the Orgasm* and much later, *Character Analysis*. He became fascinated with social problems, working in a free clinic, work that led him towards activism and eventually to communism. In 1929 he and some like-minded associates established a series of clinics to dispense sex education and socialist wisdom to working-class youth in Vienna. He briefly visited the Soviet Union to see the new society in operation. After a move to Berlin in 1930, he participated in the general and already well-established sex reform movement in that city and attempted to organize what he called Sex-Pol, a united front of existing reform associations linked to the Communist Party in a common effort to bring about both a sexual revolution and the proletarian revolution. The Sex-Pol program called for a massive campaign of sex education, the free distribution of contraceptives, free abortions, easy divorce and the abolition of adultery, and other such unlikely measures, given the prevailing morality of the times.[37] Reich himself lectured widely to youth and working-class audiences to spread the revolutionary messages.

Meanwhile he tried to wed Freud and Marx. The effort to synthesize those two grand ideologies of science, psychoanalysis and Marxism, intrigued a number of German thinkers during the 1930s, particularly those attached to the Frankfurt Institute of Social Research. But Reich acted independently, and his work preceded that of Erich Fromm, who introduced the institute to the Freudian oeuvre.[38] Reich's most substantial theoretical contribution was an essay, published in Russian and German editions, entitled 'Dialectical Materialism and Psychoanalysis' (1929) where he argued, and argued very cleverly, that the two were 'auxiliary sciences,' one treating 'psychological phenomena' and the other 'social phenomena' from a common standpoint of dialectical materialism, the golden phrase among Marxists of the day.[39] Here, and even more in other works, notably *The Mass Psychology of Fascism* (1934), he pushed the significance of sex, the sex drive and sex repression, as a key to understanding the course of history. The term 'Freudo-Marxism' itself may have originated with the French translator of a collection of essays (*La Crise Sexuelle*, 1934), authored by Reich, which, in a changed form, were later published as part of his book *The Sexual Revolution*. That translator doubted the Marxist credentials of the synthesis.[40] So did others: a few years earlier a Communist Party leader had told Reich and Sex-Pol as much. 'Your starting point is consumption, ours is production; therefore you are not Marxists.'[41] Certainly there was much more Freud than Marx in Reich's mix.

Disaster struck in the mid-1930s. The victory of Adolf Hitler early in 1933 turned Reich into a refugee: he had to leave Germany to escape arrest. Even worse, he and his ideas were rejected by his two 'parents,' communism (the 'father') and psychoanalysis (his 'mother').[42] Freudo-Marxism was anathema to the orthodox in both camps: in 1933 the party expelled him, supposedly because it deemed Sex-Pol a dangerous distraction and, a year later, the International Psychoanalytical Association dropped him from the official list of members. According to Charles Rycroft, the German branch hoped to make peace with the National Socialists, and Reich, given his red past, was a definite liability.[43] It is tempting to argue that an Oedipal drama of such intensity and tragedy unhinged Reich, except that he had already earned a reputation as 'a difficult, argumentative, "crazy" colleague.'[44] In any case he began to shift his energies from politics and psychology towards a brand of 'weird science,' in his case a search for the physical nature of libido. First in Norway, later in the United States (where he moved in 1939), he conducted experiments in psychosomatic research that gave birth to his particular nostrum of orgonomy. He measured electrical impulses in the erogenous zones, looked for signs of radiation, and found what he deemed were important temperature differentials indicating that a new form of energy was everywhere in the atmosphere. Reich came to believe that he had discovered cosmic orgone energy, 'the very stuff of life' according to one critic, imbued with 'a "bluish-green" colour, flickering and vibrant, as if it were vitality itself.'[45] The energy could be gathered in special accumulators (the notorious orgone boxes), reminiscent of a telephone booth, in which patients would sit, all to cure a wide assortment of ills, including neuroses and cancer.

Even so, Reich had not given up his mission to proselytize the masses. Whence came *The Sexual Revolution* of 1945. This book was the English translation of a collection of essays on bourgeois morality and sex education, initially published in German (1930), plus an investigation of sexual reform and reaction in the Soviet Union, that had been brought together in 1936 as *Die Sexualität im Kulturkampf*. The essays were full of detail, sometimes anecdotes or case studies, sometimes closely reasoned critiques of the arguments of others (mostly sexologists), occasionally sets of statistics. The selection of the new title proved particularly inspired: it made the book seem up to date, despite the fact that much of its research came from the 1920s. Reich took the opportunity to add prefaces (there were eventually three of these, dated 1936, 1945, and 1949) and, as he put it, 'to make many changes in terminology' (xv).[46] The revisions, and even more the prefaces, served to distance Reich from some of his past enthusiasms. In the actual text there remained many signs of Marxism: the mention of ruling classes or the means of production, the constant use of the word 'ideology' (a sin, of course), a lingering belief in base and superstructure, the search for contradictions, and so on. But the name of Marx hardly appeared in the text. The few references in the index to Marx were, with one exception, to the essay on Russia. The preface to the second edition (1945) celebrated some vague, ideal state of happiness known as 'work democracy,' free of all relations of power. The preface to the third edition (1949) specifically denied the significance of class as a factor in the struggle for sexual freedom. Revolution now meant not violence and subversion but 'an open and public warning directed to human conscience' (xviii–xix). Reich disdained politics, calling instead for the rule of science and, presumably, of scientists. The final preface talked not of a social or psychological transformation but of an ongoing 'biological revolution' (xii), which, so it seemed, was most advanced in his new love, America. Here, he observed, 'the negation of life is being confronted by the affirmation of life' (xiii). That last comment signalled the decay of Reich's theoretical skills. Fortunately, most of the argument in *The Sexual Revolution* was superior, presumably because he had not tampered with the original text.

Reich could not so easily erase Freud, even if in places he did substitute his own terminology of character analysis and what he called 'sex-economy.' For Reich had remained a sex determinist whose views were rooted in the understandings of psychoanalysis. Where he differed was that he was also a sex enthusiast. Near the beginning of *The Sexual Revolution*, Reich took issue with the theory of culture outlined in *Civilization and Its Discontents*. He much preferred the early Freud who had sketched 'a revolutionary sexual critique of culture' (10). Unfortunately, the later Freud had lost his nerve, elaborating the necessity of renunciation to mollify a bourgeois establishment alarmed by the prospect of unleashed desire. Reich set out to realize Freud's lost opportunity.

Reich could be equally doleful. One would be hard put to find a happy person in Reich's version of the world. He filled the book with stories of troubled souls and failed rebellions. Everywhere he found sickness: neuroses galore, 'perversions,' crimes, violence, alienation, misery. The average person was emotionally ill, subject to confusion, self-doubts, resignation, misguided faith, and on and on. Marriages were almost never happy. Childhoods were nearly always oppressive. Youth was forever anguished. Each individual harboured an infernal unconscious, full of seething and demonic desires. Reich even outlined these horrifying fantasies: boys who wished to murder the father and possess the mother; women seized with 'violent urges to castrate the man and acquire his penis'; men who yearned to injure, stab, or pierce the woman; people of all classes troubled by 'impulses to eat their own or others' feces' (11). What was the reason for this wave of mental sickness? Simply the repression of sexuality, which blocked the natural drives of children and adolescents, men and women. No aspect of life was untouched, especially not the unconscious.[47] The culture had made people ill.

The crucial agents of disease were an authoritarian ideology and the social order that ideology buttressed. Here were shades of Marx: Reich admitted that 'the ideological superstructure of society' was, in one way or another, rooted in 'economic interests' (34, 37). But he did not pursue this argument very far. Rather he was obsessed by the workings of the mechanisms of repression, and thus that Freudian villain the Oedipus complex entered the stage once more, in what Reich variously called the 'authoritarian,' 'compulsory,' or even 'lower- middle-class' family. There, a patriarchal father ruled supreme, his dominance at home compensation for his subservience at work. There, a frustrated mother transformed her children into 'house pets which can be loved but also tortured at will' (80). The enforced monogamy served to thwart desire – especially the woman's because she lacked the opportunity, and the financial means, to escape its rigours. Fidelity was often the result of 'an atrophy of sexuality,' itself 'resulting from premarital abstinence' (149). The chief victim was as always the child: 'He is crushed by parental authority ...' (79). His incestuous desire, his genital impulses were all suppressed. 'From this repression most of the sexual disturbances of later life are derived' (78). The adolescent was no better off, perhaps worse because of the intensity of the sex drive, subject to 'an unconscious fear of castration' or a deep-seated 'pleasure anxiety' (107). Altogether, an insistence on abstinence and obedience, no matter what the cost, a network of prohibitions and inhibitions – on masturbation, on sex play, on adultery – all this repression drove desire into the unconscious, permanently crippled sexuality, and fostered hatred, if not sadism and other 'perversions.' That hatred too could be repressed, more properly processed, at least in many individuals, to produce 'the authority-fearing, life-fearing vassal' (82) who endorsed fascism. In short the family, however defined, was 'the factory of authoritarian ideologies and conservative structures' (75). It would have to disintegrate in the course of any effective social revolution.

This was raw stuff. Yet Reich's argument still did not stray far beyond the boundaries of psychoanalysis. Where Reich escaped Freud was in the prescription of the cure – indeed, in the belief that there was a cure. That cure was orgasm, lots of orgasms, and better orgasms, the total release of pent-up sexual energies. Reich was a firm believer in the imperative of genital satisfaction. What he advocated was that most traditional form of sex, namely heterosexual intercourse in which the man's complete ejaculation and the woman's vaginal excitation (he was no booster of the clitoris) produced a burst of mutual pleasure. All alternative forms, including anal or oral sex, masturbation, and homosexuality, were less worthy, less able to realize his ideal of the total orgasm. He was nothing less than a genital chauvinist.

The brand of liberation Reich touted was an elaborated form of sexual hygiene reigning over a society so ordered that people could readily fulfil their 'natural sexual needs' (68). Unlike Freud, Reich did not worry about a death instinct because he had found the source of aggression in sexual repression.[48] Nor did he think that civilization required all forms of desexualized energy to progress: what needed sublimation was 'the gratification of pregenital, not genital, needs,' by which he meant infantile, notably oral and anal, sexual desires (19). Most important, he believed that Eros was always benign if allowed free expression. Marriage would be replaced by what Reich called 'an enduring sexual relationship' (122), though men and women could indulge their need for sexual variety, no longer troubled by the insistence on fidelity or the ban on adultery. The harsh discipline of the Oedipal mechanism would wither away should the boy 'be allowed to masturbate and play genital games with children of his age' (78). The 'perversions' would disappear in the new atmosphere of freedom. Even the sex murderer would relinquish 'his pathological sexual goals ... if a biologically normal sexual life is opened to him' (16). All sorts of good things would happen – people would be healthier and happier – and all sorts of bad things would end, such as aggression and fascism, if desire were unleashed and people could determine their own sexuality. It was this sort of claim that made Reich seem a hopeless romantic who promoted, in the words of Herbert Marcuse, 'a sweeping primitivism' wild beyond belief, at least beyond rational belief.[49]

In other moments, however, Reich made clear that his utopia was not quite so free of control as the passage above might suggest. He might champion the self as hedonist, but the pleasures he allowed were restricted and regulated. Reich was no fan of either excess or transgression. (At the end of his life, he feared that his ideas would be used to justify 'a free-for-all fucking epidemic.')[50] The liberation of sexuality had to be gradual to prevent the sexual explosion that could occur if the apparatus of repression were removed immediately. Sex experts had to be tested and if necessary re-educated to ensure right thinking. Pornography would have to go – 'all literature which produces sexual anxiety should be prohibited' (276). Mass culture must be reformed: 'The reactionary, patriarchal kind of love culture will be replaced by a life-affirmative one in literature, film, etc.' (278). Sex education had to train the masses in the principles of 'sex-economy.' A network of Sex-Pol organizations would discuss 'the life problems of the masses and return to the masses with their solutions' (279). A variety of institutions would research and teach the virtues of sexual wisdom.[51] Harmony and health, it seemed, would be imposed through propaganda.

There are ways in which Reich's utopia looks a lot like the dystopia outlined by one of his contemporaries, Aldous Huxley, in *Brave New World* (1932). 'Our Freud' was the master of psychological lore in this disturbed paradise. Huxley imagined a future where people were no longer born but hatched in a series of state-run nurseries and then brought up in this collective setting. That eliminated the need for families – no more daddy, mummy, me. 'Our Freud had been the first to reveal the appalling dangers of family life,' the narrator recalled. 'The world was full of fathers – was therefore full of misery; full of mothers – therefore of every kind of perversion from sadism to chastity; full of brothers, sisters, uncles, aunts – full of madness and suicide.'[52] References to fathers and mothers, brothers and sisters, were now the new form of smut. The bottle-babies were programmed via drugs and the hatched children indoctrinated via sleep conditioning to accept their lot in life. At an early age children were directed to play erotic games. The adults were likewise encouraged to form temporary liaisons with a wide variety of partners to relieve their sexual tensions. Sex was thus channelled to ensure the stability of a totalitarian state. 'As political and economic freedom diminishes,' noted Huxley in a later foreword (1946), 'sexual freedom tends compensatingly to increase ... It will help to reconcile his [the dictator's] subjects to the servitude which is their fate.'[53] Nowhere was there any place for transgression. The hero of this tale, a 'savage' called John, could not stand a world in which love and poetry and morality had been banished. His only way out was suicide.

None of which is evidence of any sinister intent on Reich's part. He was a sincere anti-authoritarian. But the juxtaposition of the two works does highlight the origins of Reich's version of sexual liberation. Although so much of Huxley's novel extrapolated trends he saw to be most advanced in America (Henry Ford, after all, was the god of the Brave New World), the work also bore the mark of Lenin. Likewise much of the description of the shape of the new society in *The Sexual Revolution* came near the end in Reich's discussion of the failure of the Soviet experiment of a new society. The body of this essay was a long lament about how the real promise of a sexual and social liberation in Russia was eventually destroyed by the ignorance and arrogance of so-called experts and state bureaucrats. They had not perceived either the wisdom or the necessity of Sex-Pol in the task of social transformation. Nonetheless Reich's blueprint for a utopia reflected the initiatives taken in the attempted reforms of moral and family law, abortion, the education of children, and the attitude towards youth that briefly flourished in the Soviet Union of the 1920s. His dream of liberation was shaped by the early practices of communism.

The publication of *The Sexual Revolution* in 1945 was by no means the end of Reich's story. He conducted more experiments, further developed his orgone therapy, and produced a series of books promoting orgonomy. He worked without the support or sanction of existing medical or scientific bodies, of course. Indeed he came to feel that his labours were opposed by all kinds of forces. This increasing paranoia was not unjustified. His endeavours came under the close scrutiny of the American government. Not surprisingly, the FBI had launched an investigation, in 1940, to discover whether this ex-communist was engaged in anything subversive. Although after ten years the FBI concluded that the orgone project was not a threat to national security, the file on Reich kept growing until it reached 789 pages, much of this bulk because of a flurry of letters and the like from the Reich Foundation about the efforts of purported enemies of the United States to subvert the efforts of the project.[54] During the 1950s Reich had become a ferocious Cold War warrior who believed 'red fascists' were determined to destroy him in the effort to destroy America.

Meanwhile another agency, the Food and Drug Administration, moved to investigate the therapeutic promise of orgonomy, possibly inspired by press and medical pressure to protect the public against what seemed yet another brand of quackery. The association of orgonomy and sexuality, the suspicion that Reich was a sexual anarchist, likely contributed to the inquisition. The eventual charge was not moral or political subversion but commercial fraud. In 1954 the attorney general filed an injunction against the interstate distribution of both the orgone boxes and promotional literature by Reich and his foundation. That Reich ignored. He and some associates were then tried on contempt of court charges two years later. He was sentenced to two years in prison. A collection of orgone accumulators was seized and destroyed. Worse yet, a lot of Reich's books, including *The Sexual Revolution*, were collected and burned. After imprisonment Reich was initially diagnosed as paranoid, sent off to a penitentiary with psychiatric facilities, and then deemed sane. No matter: he died in jail of a heart attack late in 1957.

3 Marcuse's Utopia of Eros

The career of Herbert Marcuse (1898–1979) was far different. Reich and Marcuse shared some attributes: the German-Jewish background, a common Marxism (though Marcuse never recanted his faith), and eventual residence in the United States. But Marcuse was a theorist rather than an activist, trained at university to be a philosopher, and had no experience as a psychoanalyst. During the 1930s he was an important member of the Frankfurt Institute of Social Research, and in 1934 he moved to New York where he worked in the home established for the institute by Columbia University. During the 1940s he served the American government, engaged in the war against fascism, as he later suggested, at the Office of Strategic Services and the Office of Intelligence Research. He did not return to Germany after the war, unlike some other leading members of the institute. Instead in the early 1950s he sought an academic position, eventually becoming a professor of politics and philosophy at Brandeis University. During the 1960s, really at the end of the decade, he became very famous indeed, both reviled and admired, as the philosopher of choice of the New Left, especially in the United States, though his reputation and the influence of his works extended into Europe as well. In 1968, for example, placards appeared in the streets of Rome bearing the names of the gods of revolution, 'MARX MAO MARCUSE.'[55] Marcuse's great cause was liberation, such an appealing goal to the youth of the sixties: he wrote to free humanity from the repressive structures of advanced industrial civilization, especially its capitalist variant in the United States and western Europe.

Marcuse came to Freud late in his intellectual progress. Marcuse had already worked through an intensive study of Hegel and Marx, especially the early Marx, to fashion a distinctive understanding of critical theory, particularly a distaste for empiricism and 'a fascination with negation' as a tool of analysis.[56] In the late 1930s he began to read Freud carefully, and he took up the task of actually analysing Freud in depth in the early 1950s. According to Douglas Kellner, his biographer, Marcuse was searching for a way out of the radical despair that afflicted other theorists of the Left, notably Max Horkheimer and Theodor Adorno, his former colleagues at the Frankfurt Institute, during the era of the Cold War.[57] Marcuse found a new source of optimism in 'the radical Freud.' That interpretation of Freud he defended in an appendix to *Eros and Civilization*, where he fiercely attacked the psychoanalytic establishment and assorted revisionists, including another one-time colleague, Erich Fromm, who now, in America, argued a much more restrained brand of Freudianism.[58] The Freud that Marcuse championed was an intellectual figure seen through a Marxian lens, a ploy that Marcuse hid by never actually mentioning the name of Marx in the text, likely because of the prevailing anticommunism in the America of the 1950s.[59]

Eros and Civilization (1955) was very much a 'philosophical inquiry' into Freud's theory, as the subtitle indicated. It was not easy to read. It lacked the wealth of empirical data and concrete studies that had characterized *The Sexual Revolution*. Instead *Eros and Civilization* was full of the ideas of such (named) luminaries as Plato, Kant, Hegel, and Nietzsche. Reich, by the way, hardly appeared at all, but for a brief mention in the appendix as a pioneer of 'the radical Freud,' a pioneer whose thought, unfortunately, proved too shallow to advance the cause of liberation. The theorists Marcuse favoured served to explore and buttress his own set of priorities: so Schiller was deployed to rescue the erotic aspects of 'the aesthetic function' and 'the play impulse' (182) in order to free humanity of toil and repression. Marcuse was forever playing his game of negation, writing of 'the negation of unfreedom' (144) or celebrating what he called the 'Great Refusal,' 'the protest against unnecessary repression' (149). The Marxist obsessions with conflict, domination, alienation, contradiction, and dialectics underpinned the whole structure of Marcuse's argument. But that argument worked with the vocabulary and the theory of Freud: *Eros and Civilization* began with reflections on *Civilization and Its Discontents* and thereafter employed an extraordinary range of claims and terms from the Freudian oeuvre. Marcuse accepted the import of instincts, and of repression and sublimation in the work of civilization, the distinction between the pleasure and the reality principles, the primacy of sexuality as well as the existence of a death instinct, and so the all-encompassing war of Eros and Thanatos. These concepts, however, he cleverly reworked to historicize Freud, meaning to bring the ideology of psychoanalysis into accord with a fundamentally Marxist vision of the course of history.

Marcuse focused his attention first on the material base of civilization. He did not deny the implacable force of a scarcity that compelled the restriction of instincts. The death instinct, for example, had been 'brought into the service of Eros; the aggressive impulses provide energy for the continuous alteration, mastery, and exploitation of nature to the advantage of mankind' (52). But he argued that scarcity had been 'organized' (36) to suit the needs of those in authority, and so to doom much of humanity to a state of 'alienated labour' (46), 'painful and miserable' (85), never properly gratifying the individual. Indeed the advance of technology had now made possible the freeing of humanity from a life of unremitting toil. There was abundance enough to enable, in advanced countries, the 'painless gratification of needs' (153), though Marcuse here meant only basic needs and not the manufactured wants of the affluent society.

The problem lay not with the nature of civilization but with the structure of society. Marcuse converted Freud's notion of an always oppressive civilization resting upon a kind of biological determinism into a system of domination, a sociological concept, by fashioning two new tools of analysis, namely 'surplus-repression' and the 'performance principle.' Surplus-repression encompassed 'the restrictions necessitated by social domination' (35), an additional weight of repression beyond whatever was necessary to the work of civilization. From that followed the performance principle as 'the prevailing historical form of the *reality principle*' (35) – 'under its rule society is stratified according to the competitive economic performances of its members' (44). In this cunning fashion Marcuse could explain how people had been, and still were, subjected to a fierce regimen of control as well as programmed to obey in ways that served to perpetuate the dominion of a few.

Enter sexuality, or rather 'the repressive *organization of sexuality*' (40). Marcuse was never much interested in the family, Reich's bête noire, as a tool of domination. His few comments suggested that in recent times the family, and particularly the father, had lost social significance to the media, experts, and peer groups – in short, outside authorities. Rather, Marcuse focused on the search for pleasure. He posited an ideal time (in infancy, in history?) of polymorphous perversity when all the erogenous zones (the genitals, the anus, the mouth, the nose, and so on) were engaged, vital, flourishing under the regime of the pleasure principle. The memory of that golden age when the instincts reigned supreme lingered on in the unconscious, becoming not only the fount of art and fantasy but the seedbed of rebellion. For the pleasure principle had been suppressed: civilization 'as organized domination' (34) demanded not only the drastic reduction in the intensity of sexual pleasure but the desexualizing of much of the body itself. What was deemed proper sex was confined to the genital zone, harnessed to the task of procreation, restricted by monogamy, limited to leisure time.

That left most of the body 'free for use as the instrument of labor' (48). That also released a flood of libidinal energy to serve 'socially useful performances' (45). 'The restrictions on the libido appear as the more rational, the more universal they become, the more they permeate the whole society' (46). Before long, 'the individual lives his repression "freely" as his own life: he desires what he is supposed to desire; his gratifications are profitable to him and to others; he is reasonably and often even exuberantly happy' (46). All of which conjured up the image of a great, dumb beast, most of its body numbed, much of its life spent on the treadmill of work, allowed only occasional and restricted moments of pleasure.

This reasoning led Marcuse to celebrate the 'perversions' as harbingers of utopia, the answer to a 'repressive ego.'[60] Like Freud, Marcuse was struck by the seductive appeal of sexual transgression. 'The perversions seem to give a *promesse de bonheur* greater than that of "normal" sexuality' (49). Again like Freud, Marcuse appeared to believe that sado-masochism was the signature 'perversion' because it eroticized aggression.[61] What intrigued him even more, however, was the subversive character of the alternative sexualities. The 'perversions' embraced desire and disdained repression, becoming the instrument not of a dominated culture but of the passionate id. Fantasy, their ally, not only played 'a constitutive role in the perverse manifestations of sexuality' but, as art, linked 'the perversions with images of integral freedom and gratification' (50), a perceptive claim about the work of erotica. Transgression in fancy and in fact acted out those seething desires repressed in the unconscious that yearned for a release, a pleasure that was always denied by the system of domination. It harked back to the time of a polymorphous sexuality before genitality had been granted its sovereign power over Eros. That was the reason the taboo was so strict: authority deemed the 'perversions' 'monstrous and terrifying' because they expressed a 'rebellion against the subjugation of sexuality under the order of procreation' (49). So the pervert, whatever his or her passion, became a political warrior who had raised the banner of freedom and happiness and challenged the foundations of domination.

Marcuse presumed that the careful release of sexuality from the weight of surplus-repression and the undoing of the performance principle would usher in a kind of socialist utopia where toil was banished and people were served according to their needs. He posited 'a non-repressive mode of sublimation which results from an extension rather than from a constraining deflection of the libido' (169–70). How this could come into being remained unclear: Marcuse was no tactician. [62] In one passage he suggested that the very workings of the repressive order might produce conditions of such alienation that domination would collapse, and collapse into freedom, a line of argument reminiscent of the old Marxist dream that the contradictions of capitalism made inevitable the coming of the revolution.[63] That would have been a triumph of negation. In other passages he left the impression that the performance principle had produced the necessary abundance and fostered social and psychological changes of such importance as to arrange its own dissolution or replacement.[64] Still the purpose was clear: to resexualize the whole body, to re-establish a polymorphous sexuality, to reintegrate work and play – in short, to resurrect that barely remembered paradise of gratification now possible for all because of technological progress. 'The body in its entirety would become an object of cathexis, a thing to be enjoyed – an instrument of pleasure' (201). In the process, however, sexuality was transformed into something apparently much grander, a life-affirming force able to overcome all obstacles, even tame the destructive energies of the death instinct. He waxed poetic about a sensuous reason, the conquest of time, the mythical reign of a homosexual Orpheus and a self-absorbed Narcissus, two Greek archetypes who lived a different sexuality.[65] 'The opposition between man and nature, subject and object, is overcome' (166): in other words the old ideal of utopian harmony would finally be achieved. Even Eros and Thanatos would ultimately converge in this marvellous state of a desire both reasoned and realized.

What Marcuse wanted, it seems obvious, was a very genteel brand of sexual liberation. He advocated 'a spread rather than explosion of libido' (201). Marcuse never thought to unleash this destructive energy to work its will upon civilization. 'A society of sex maniacs,' he warned, meant 'no society' at all (201). He was well aware of the hideous forms of transgression, and he cited 'the sadistic and masochistic orgies of desperate masses, of "society elites," of starved bands of mercenaries, of prison and concentration-camp guards' (202), which, so he claimed, were the results of a repressed sexuality. Ironically, Marcuse did not foresee a very happy future for the 'perversions' once their role as vehicles of resistance had passed. Rather he hoped that the 'instinctual substance' (203) of the 'perversions' would somehow take on a better expression in a non-repressive society, though he did not specify what the expression might be. Indeed Marcuse presumed that there was a pure kind of 'libidinal morality' that would reign in the non-repressive society (228). 'Is there perhaps a "natural" self-restraint to Eros so that its genuine gratification would call for delay, detour, and arrest?' (226). No more than Reich could Marcuse endorse excess. In the end *Eros and Civilization* was a very unsexy tome, and in more ways than one, certainly not a ringing celebration of the flesh.

The appearance of a new edition of *Eros and Civilization* in 1966 brought an additional 'Political Preface.' Marcuse was very angry. His optimism about the advent of liberation was long gone.[66] 'Today the fight for life,' he intoned, 'the fight for Eros, is the *political* fight' (xxv). His 'Political Preface' was a call to arms. What explained the surge of militancy? One answer was the American South and Vietnam, the civil rights and antiwar protests, uproar on the campus, altogether the beginnings of that whole eruption that would make the late 1960s such a time of contention. But Marcuse was especially upset because he had misjudged the resources and the capabilities of the enemy. Or, to put this another way, he had come to recognize anew the formidable imperialism of the market. The master class had designed new methods for reproducing domination, notably a massive publicity machine and the attendant science of marketing, which constantly manipulated the minds of the affluent populace. He had already named the favourite technique of authority in his recently published *One-Dimensional Man* (1964): that was 'repressive desublimation,' a perversion of his vision of sexual release and sexual freedom.[67] The technique referred to the ways in which authority now managed sex, no longer through overt repression but via an illusion of liberty, offering a modicum of erotic gratification: alluring sights, sexy goods, or lurid entertainments channelled libidinal energy towards the support of the status quo. The result was the transformation of Eros as life, the total and sensual enjoyment of the body and the world, into Eros as sexuality, the obsession with the sexual encounter. He was particularly incensed by the ability of capitalism to appropriate the cry of sexual freedom in its constant efforts to sell brands: 'merchandise which has to be bought and used is made into objects of the libido ...' (xii). Marcuse never understood the appeal of mass consumption; he always saw affluence as obscene in a wider world of want and inequality.[68] But he realized that the success of admakers, public relations professionals, and other practitioners of the propaganda arts had made a mockery of the radical cause of sexual liberation.[69]

4 The Wisdom of Ernest Dichter

In the 1950s a brand of promoters won a lot of notoriety by trying to manipulate the unconscious of Americans. These were the experts in the great marketing fad of the decade, what was called motivational (or sometimes just motivation) research, which sought to apply techniques drawn from psychology, anthropology, and sociology to answer the question 'Why do people buy?' That question was crucial because of the central importance of consumption in a postwar economy of abundance, where profit and prosperity depended on a high and increasing level of purchases by the average American family. Corporations were willing to pay all kinds of money to social scientists able to explain the habits, moods, fears, and hopes of their customers, as well as how these might be triggered to heighten sales. *Fortune* guessed that advertisers and agencies were spending nearly $1 billion on such research in the mid-1950s.[70] For what was soon shortened to the acronym 'MR' promised to enable clients to manage desire.

There were many different individuals and firms involved in motivational research. Louis Cheskin, head of the Color Research Institute in Chicago, asserted that he had started doing commercial work in the mid-1930s. His greatest claim to fame was to shape the sex change of Marlboro cigarettes twenty years later, when Philip Morris relaunched this woman's brand in a new, manly flip-top box via an ad campaign featuring weathered males puffing away at the macho smoke, now meant for the real man.[71] James Vicary, a psychologist, ran a New York operation that tested the meaning of words and trademarks.[72] He became infamous at the end of the 1950s when he reported how he had successfully used the hidden commands 'Eat Popcorn' and 'Drink Coke,' flashed on a cinema screen too quickly to register on the conscious mind, to boost sales of these products at the concession stands of a movie house, a promotion that produced the first great scare over subliminal advertising. Vicary later admitted that his report of the experiment was a hoax, designed to generate business.[73] Pierre Martineau, the research director at the *Chicago Tribune*, though not a psychologist himself, proved one of the most noted promoters of MR, even writing a book on the topic.[74] Quite different was Social Research Incorporated (SRI), another Chicago firm, started in 1946 by the noted sociologist Lloyd Warner, managed by Burleigh Gardner, an anthropologist, assisted by William Henry, an expert in psychological testing, and staffed by graduate students in the social sciences at the University of Chicago, who produced reports for a range of corporate clients, including General Mills and United Airlines – reports that usually emphasized the significance of social class as a determinant of consumer behaviour.[75] The Psychological Corporation was similarly linked to academe, boasting on its board of directors in 1953 professors from Columbia University, the chairman of the department of psychology from the University of Michigan, and another professor of psychology from Yale.[76] A directory of firms produced by an advertising association in the mid-1950s listed eighty-two organizations ready to carry out MR studies for a fee.[77] It was all a sign of how closely the social sciences in America wedded themselves to business during the postwar years.

Advertising agencies increasingly welcomed this brand of applied science, although there were always advertising executives who doubted the more outlandish expressions of MR. Burleigh Gardner of SRI spoke to the American Marketing Association about the proper use of stereotypes and prejudices in effective advertising. Weiss and Geller, a Chicago advertising company, held regular meetings where psychologists addressed its staff.[78] McCann-Erickson, Leo Burnett, and Foote, Cone and Belding, all major ad agencies, employed in-house teams of psychological researchers. Young and Rubicam and Ruthrauff and Ryan, also big names in the industry, acknowledged carrying out or sponsoring and then using MR studies. Grey Advertising used motivational research to design a new campaign for Greyhound buses, just as Weiss and Geller used reports from the Institute of Psychoanalysis to fashion a campaign for Wrigley chewing gum that exploited the public's sense of frustration over the hardships of life.[79]

Marketing journals and the like had begun discussing the promise of MR from the early years of the decade, and it was not long before the message got out to mainstream business periodicals and then to the public. Finally, in 1957, Vance Packard published his first and most successful work of social criticism, *The Hidden Persuaders*, which exposed 'the large-scale efforts being made, often with impressive success, to channel our unthinking habits, our purchasing decisions, and our thought processes by the use of insights gleaned from psychiatry and the social sciences.'[80] This investigation amounted to an attack on motivational research, not advertising per se, as an insidious tool of manipulation, a threat to the psychic health of America – an attack that took much too seriously the claims of success put out by its practitioners.

The book stayed near the top of the list of non-fiction bestsellers for roughly a year, proof that it had struck a chord with readers, who clearly were worried by the prospect of being 'brain-washed' by the admakers.[81]

Packard's star villain, and the source of many of his most interesting tales, was also one of the most renowned and controversial figures in the advertising community, Dr Ernest Dichter (1907–91).[82] A few years later he would figure again as a villain when Betty Friedan used his files and his words in *The Feminine Mystique* to explore how 'the sexual sell' had disciplined the minds and actions of American women.[83] Like Cheskin, and probably with more reason, Dichter considered himself the founder of motivational research in America. He had first come to public notice in 1940 when he figured in a story in *Time* (25 March) about the need to apply psychology to advertising. By the end of the 1950s, his was certainly a name to conjure with: he was billed as something of a magician who always had an answer to solve the troubles of any corporation having difficulties in the marketplace. According to Martin Mayer, a contemporary writer who explored the mores of Madison Avenue, he was 'widely regarded as the greatest copy idea man of our times – a veritable Claude Hopkins of the world of repressed symbolism.'[84] He was not especially well-liked in the community, however, perhaps because he was considered a braggart, certainly because rivals doubted the veracity of his findings.[85] For Dichter gained his stature in part because of aggressive self-promotion: he had a knack for winning corporate clients and pleasing journalists, particularly with some sensational comment that could be quoted ad nauseum.

Like Reich and Marcuse, Dichter was one of those Jewish refugees from Hitler's Europe who had become so important in the intellectual life of America after the war. Born in Vienna, educated there and at the Sorbonne, he earned a doctorate in psychology in 1934 and began the study of psychoanalysis, undergoing the requisite analysis himself, whence came his attachment to Freudian ideas, though he would later deny he was a Freudian. He set up practice as a lay psychoanalyst across the street from Freud and dabbled in some market research, until leaving Vienna for Paris in 1937, after he had been arrested and briefly jailed by the authorities and then labelled as a subversive by the Nazi party. He emigrated to New York a year later, purportedly after telling the vice-consul in Paris how he would use psychology to transform commerce in America – that legend emphasized his skills as a master of persuasion. Dichter worked for a time with Paul Lazarsfeld of Columbia University, a key figure in the application of the social sciences to manage American affairs. He also found employment in advertising and market research, where he began to advise corporate America on the better way to sell its wares: indeed he considered the study he did for Ivory soap in 1939 the first exercise in motivational research in the United States.

But Dichter was too much a maverick to work happily under the aegis of anyone else. In 1946 he set up what became the Institute for Motivational Research, eventually located in an impressive and isolated mansion, atop a hill overlooking the river, near Croton-on-Hudson in New York, a fitting site for 'a mad genius.'[86] He published a book, *The Psychology of Everyday Living*, in 1947, in which he offered up the findings of motivational research in a novel form, as 'mass therapy to a sick nation,' troubled by feelings of 'impotence, chaos, and futility.'[87] He started a monthly newsletter called *Motivations* where for $100 a year interested people could read regularly about his research and insights. He steadily built up the business, estimated at around $750,000 a year in the mid-1950s, until he employed a full-time staff of sixty at the institute and hundreds of part-time interviewers there and across the country.

Dichter utilized a variety of unusual techniques, often derived from clinical practice and psychoanalysis, to plumb the unconscious of consumers. He was most famous for his depth interviews, an intensive but unstructured exploration of one person's views that was modelled upon the classic patterns of analysis, except here the subject confessed his or her recollections of life with affluence. He was particularly interested in the first experience his subjects had with a product or brand, since he deemed this had a formative effect on their later preferences – that was reminiscent of the way Freudians privileged the experience of childhood. By 1963 he claimed that his institute had 300,000 interviews with individuals on file, presumably some large portion of these derived from group discussions. He experimented with psychodramas built around a product or brand in which people played out various roles, enacting fantasies of consumption and possession. He sent investigators out to observe how women used make-up, and he filmed how people, again mostly women because they were the normal household buyers, actually handled soap. Once Dichter himself played the role of car salesman and then car buyer to discover the routines of purchasing a new automobile. He was one of the innovators who organized the first focus groups, for instance, gathering a collection of people – this started in 1957 – to watch a commercial and discuss their responses.[88] He maintained a 'psycho-panel' of several hundred people, local to the institute, whose emotional character was already evaluated, so that their responses to particular advertising ploys could furnish useful test data.

Always he reiterated the importance of starting with a hypothesis that might change as a result of findings, though it seemed the hypothesis was more often a frame used to interpret these findings. Always he dismissed the virtues of statistical and survey work, touted by more traditional market researchers, though he did admit that such work might yield useful results after the qualitative research was completed. All of which meant that his research could not be replicated: everything depended on the ability of the master to weave a narrative of explanation to guide the client to market success. Critics were unconvinced. Charles Adams of McManus, John and James, writing in *Advertising Age* in 1958, expressed this disdain clearly: 'All the motivational mumbo-jumbo, all the Freud-happy figures assembled since Her Doktor Dichter was knee-high to a couch cannot make the public's taste buds tingle nor its ego pant for a new car.'[89] Even less acerbic types scoffed at Dichter's efforts. Witness the comment from Richard Lessler, also a psychologist, employed by Grey Advertising: 'I tell our clients use this guy. Use his ideas. Milk him. But for Christ sake don't tell me it's research, because it isn't research as I understand the word.'[90]

Not that any of this doubt hurt business. Dichter claimed 500 completed studies by 1956, 1,000 by 1963, all in the interests of some brand, company, or industry. He actually sent a letter of thanks to Vance Packard in 1958 because the success of *The Hidden Persuaders* had produced new clients: it was like an advertisement for motivational research, at least in Dichter's mind. Perhaps Dichter's very notoriety fascinated businessmen. Certainly his association with Freud helped him win custom, since the 1950s were the highpoint of the influence and fame of psychoanalysis in elite circles in the United States. He was most famous for his findings about brands that, in some way, highlighted the importance of the sex drive. In an early study, much remarked on then and later, he had told Chrysler that American men regarded convertibles as mistresses, sedans as wives, which was why they admired the former but bought the latter. This meant that featuring the convertible in ads and showrooms had the virtue of attracting males, even if they ultimately bought a more staid automobile. He explained to Ronson that fire was a sexual symbol, rooted in humanity's past, so the company ought to show the potency of its flame-producing mechanism in its efforts to promote its lighters. A study for Procter and Gamble's Ivory soap revealed that bathing was something of an erotic encounter, where otherwise restrained Americans enjoyed the opportunity to caress their own bodies, a fact that advertisements could then exploit. Standard Oil (later called Exxon) learned that it should promise to 'Put a Tiger in Your Tank' to exploit the meanings of virility and power attached to this animal. Because males thought donating blood meant a loss of vigour, the American Red Cross was told to prepare posters that showed donors leaving centres surrounded by beautiful women. Likewise, investing in life insurance was a way in which a man might reassure himself of his virility, or even boast of his sexual prowess, especially the more money he invested in a policy. Virtually any good or service, in short, could become an erotic brand.

Eventually Dichter decided to propagate his gospel by publishing two further books, *The Strategy of Desire* (1960) and *Handbook of Consumer Motivations* (1964).[91] Both of these texts drew on the research studies of his institute and reflected the views he had developed and elaborated over the past two decades of work. The *Strategy* avoided repeating too many of the outlandish claims for which Dichter had become so notorious. The *Handbook* was less restrained. The *Strategy* was aimed at a broad audience of readers and sought to justify his brand of motivational research as a means of saving America, thus answering the strictures of a critic like Packard. The much longer *Handbook* was intended for people in the communications business: it amounted to a dictionary of objects, services, activities, occupations, representations, even psychic phenomena, each meriting a separate essay in which Dichter explored the meaning of things. Together these books have a lasting significance because they established Dichter as the chief theoretician of the erotic sell in America.

Dichter grounded his arguments in Freudian psychology, especially that powerful notion of a dynamic unconscious, though as always Dichter was unorthodox. Motivations were just a modified form of the basic drives of sex, hunger, and security that underlay most kinds of behaviour; indeed, motivations were 'drives aroused by outside influences' (HCM 346). Rationality was largely a myth: people were saturated with unfulfilled longings, subject to waves of emotion, and moved by impulses of which they were unaware. He could write, for instance, of an 'animal residue ... the dark forces, the invisible enemies, within ourselves' that threatened peace and progress, an entity that

sounded very much like Freud's id (SD 208). Dichter posited the existence of a quantity of 'psychic energy' – in effect, libido, though he did
not use that term – that could be allocated to loving the self (narcissism), wanting another (homosexual or heterosexual attraction), or
desiring an object (consumption) (HCM 399). Virtually every encounter
with a person or an object had an erotic dimension, and in the *Handbook*
he constantly referred to folklore and mythology to show how universal and eternal was this dimension. The trouble was that a legacy of
puritanism worked to thwart America's enjoyment of affluence, and
that sickness – not materialism – lay at the root of so much grief. The
burden of guilt, the weight of sin, blocked the force of 'constructive discontent' that led people to buy, to welcome change, to progress (SD 21).
Just as bad, the traditional morality dictated 'the way we feel in our
modern world about sex, considering it as an animalistic, undesirable,
dirty emotional business that one has to live with but should be controlled as much as possible' (SD 112). Dichter called instead for a new
kind of hedonism in which Americans would receive the 'moral permission to enjoy life' (SD 186). Put another way, he had translated that
old bogey of repression into his preferred term of puritanism. And he
had outlined a new conception of the self, not as producer but as consumer, the hedonist who bought his or her way to happiness. The
answer remained the same as for the Freudo-Marxists, the liberation of
Eros, except now the agent was commerce not revolution.

   That was because of how we lived with and in a material world.
'Objects have a soul' (SD 86). Dichter might well have added that they
had sex as well. We invested them with personalities, with gender, with
an assortment of meanings, so that they shaped the way our lives were
organized.[92] Although Dichter recognized that possessions could fulfil
a variety of needs, particularly the need for security, he constantly
returned to the erotic significance of things, especially in the *Handbook*.
Dichter, in other words, played out the role of the voyeur, forever seeing the sexy in the surrounding world. Consider this very partial list of
ordinary objects: the shape of cigars made them obviously phallic;
leather was 'strongly sexualized'; silk was 'sexually exciting – for many
men, almost as exciting as the woman in the flesh'; sugar symbolized
'adult love'; the red of lipstick reminded 'one of blood and, probably,
unconsciously, of menstruation'; there was both 'moral and immoral
furniture,' even 'voluptuous furniture'; huge machinery was intrinsically erotic, because it evoked a sense of boundless power; the orange,
so round, so textured, stimulated the 'tactile sense' and evoked visions

of a lush and fertile nature; evaporated milk suggested 'mother's milk,' which is why it both pleased and disgusted.[93]

Much the same kind of reasoning, or perhaps 'ascription' is the better term, operated when he discussed the meanings evoked by what people did with things. Smoking was so prevalent in part because it activated 'the powerful erotic sensitivity of the oral zone.' (Did he mean to suggest a surrogate for oral sex?) Lighting another person's cigarette was an act full of 'erotic significance, especially when the other sex is concerned. Match and cigarette are contact points.' (Was this a reference to intercourse?) Likewise eating ice cream, filling the mouth with that smooth and sweet concoction, was called 'orgastic' (meaning what? perhaps a sublimated form of sexual climax?) and, later on, 'orgiastic' (this a reference to some fantasized orgy?), particularly when the ice cream ran down a person's chin. Indeed any foods that required licking, and notably sweets, were akin to 'forbidden sexual pleasures.' (Back to oral sex?) Shaving was a more ambivalent practice, a form of masochism that both robbed the man of 'a masculinity symbol' (castration?) and yet reaffirmed the manhood he acquired, at least symbolically, when he first used a razor. The symbolic properties of skiing were especially plentiful. That sport was akin to flying, which in Freudian lore suggested sexual potency. Yet it also expressed 'a sort of defloration – a raping of virgin snow.' (Violation?) Not to discount the fact that the excitement of swooping down the slopes had 'a relationship to orgasm,' spiced with 'an unconscious desire for self-destruction.' (Sado-masochism?) Dichter even drew a parallel between the role of the skiing instructor and 'traditional voyeurdom. It is almost as if you are taking a public course in sexual intercourse, the skiing instructor giving you lessons and everybody watching.' (Exhibitionism as well?) Obviously the sex drive, in one way or another, often a way that hinted at 'perversion,' nearly always hidden from the conscious mind of the individual, lay at the bottom of an extraordinary range of ordinary activities.[94]

The task was to unlock this Pandora's box of hidden meanings and repressed urges. The tools were readily at hand. Motivational research offered the kinds of information about how men, women, and children eroticized their material world. That explained, for instance, the spectacular failure of the Edsel: the design of this new Ford car simply did not suit the symbolic significance of the front end of an automobile (where the Edsel in 1958 and 1959 had an oval), which signified it was 'a penetrating instrument. It symbolizes speed and power, it has, furthermore, in a psychological sense, considerable significance as a phallic symbol' (SD 116). Ordinary market research had overlooked this fact.[95]

Psychology supplied the concepts necessary to fashion the erotic sell. Dichter referred, for example, to the Freudian notion of 'cathexis,' the channelling or investment of libidinal energies: 'Your product, your stores, your logotype, your slogan must become the focal point of much cathected psychic energy, love energy' (HCM 399). The mass media provided the requisite technology to deliver a constant stream of these messages to specific targets. 'Movie producers, novelists, and good copywriters' had known for years how to craft an 'erotic drama' that could captivate an audience: how exciting it was to see a woman slowly remove a long glove because that stimulated the senses and simulated the opening up of the whole body (HCM 426). Admakers were learning how to overcome guilt by 'offering absolution and giving the subject the permission to indulge' – advertising, in short, could sanction transgression (HCM 420). The elitist thrust of Dichter's argument was obvious: he foresaw a range of experts acting as moralists, social engineers, and sex therapists to guide Americans into a new Garden of Eden.

Dichter's effort to persuade had only modest results. The *Strategy* neither won a large audience nor convinced readers that MR was the solution to the world's troubles. The *Handbook* languished because it was such a strange hodgepodge of bizarre claims, quite unlike the normal run of marketing textbooks, which were full of logical argument and heavy with statistics.[96] This despite the merit of much of Dichter's analysis: things were sexy, if not by nature then because of the culture. The voyeur's gaze was an existing resource, a particular way of seeing, that capitalism could use, indeed already did use, eventually to render erotic virtually all objects and activities. The social or political merit of motivation research, of course, was not so obvious, given the intent to manipulate and control, as Vance Packard and other critics made clear. Besides, although a hedonistic outlook clearly was on the rise in the postwar United States, puritanism remained a powerful counter-force, then and later, especially among fundamentalist Christian communities, for whom Dichter's celebration of a sexy world was anathema.

Dichter laboured on, claiming more than 5,000 studies in a 1977 interview, by which time he had also produced a few more books of wisdom. But his moment of public fame had passed: Dichter's credo fitted the business mood of the 1950s when clients were ready to apply Freud to the task of selling. Dichter's star had begun to wane by the mid-1960s, even if he remained a person of some significance until the end of his life.[97] Indeed motivational research had lost its sheen in the marketing business, partly because its brand of analysis was too subjective. It would shortly be replaced by a new and more lasting type of research, 'psychographics,' which used the very kind of quantitative methods Dichter had disdained to generate apparently objective results about people's psychological states. Also, business simply got tired of the exotic reasoning so fashionable in the MR field. 'Is it better to sell a man a pair of suspenders as a means of holding up his pants or as a "reaction to castration anxiety"?' asked two doubters. 'Is it easier to persuade a woman to buy a garden hose to water her lawn or as a symbol of the "futility of genital competition for the female"?'[98] Not until the late 1990s, another boom time, would American business seem once more willing to listen to a new crew of depth boys and girls who explored 'the consumer unconscious to sell soap.'[99]

3 The Erotic Sell

They were both young, and no doubt very fashionable. The pretty woman appeared so demure, dressed in some sort of finery, holding roses in one hand, and looking off into the distance. The handsome man seemed a bit anxious, perhaps because he was indulging in a small act of intimacy. She had presented one of her dainty hands, and that object of loveliness he now held very gently while he brushed her soft skin with his lips. The tableau spoke of romance, even sex.[1] The slogan read 'A hand you love to touch,' and the copy told women to protect their skin with Woodbury's Facial Soap against the ravages of life. This ad first appeared in 1911, and it shocked some readers of the *Ladies Home Journal* so much that they cancelled their subscriptions. The ad had been created by Helen Lansdowne, one of the few female copywriters in the business. Apparently she knew her business, because the campaign continued for many more years to sell the virtues of Woodbury's, and dreams of romance, to a nation of women. The slogan was still used in a Woodbury ad in 1949.[2]

This famous campaign was hardly the first time advertisers had used sex to sell goods.[3] The photograph of what looked like 'a slut for sale' – young, languid, complete with a tight tunic on her upper body, her skirt spread open, legs slightly apart, arms bare, breasts apparent – appeared on one cigarette card circa 1900, a mild version of the pornographic print and meant for collectors.[4] A series of beauties, some in revealing or suggestive diaphanous gowns, graced illustrated ads for Lux and Swan soaps in English magazines during the 1890s. [5] Shapely and ample women had been commonplace as a symbol of abundance in mid-nineteenth-century advertising in America.[6] Perhaps what startled consumers about the Woodbury's ad was the appearance of a man and a woman together in an erotic setting. Later ads offered pictures of other romantic couples exchanging intimacies in public places such as a dance or a theatre.[7] In any case the Woodbury campaign is remembered, rightly or wrongly, as the first successful effort by a major advertiser to eroticize its brand in the United States in the twentieth century.

In the years after 1910 the advertising profession in the United States slowly moved towards an understanding of consumer motivations that encouraged the growth of the erotic sell. Before, most admakers had usually assumed (which is not to say that they always acted on the assumption) that an advertisement was chiefly a form of information, a mode of education, this idea sanctified by the Victorian belief that a person was, or should be, fundamentally a rational being. Later, admakers came increasingly under the sway of psychology and admitted that they were engaged in a game of persuasion where the consumer, now defined as a woman, was fundamentally an emotional being.[8] One of the most prominent ad executives of the 1920s was John B. Watson, a behavioural psychologist employed by J. Walter Thompson, a major American agency, who thought that the individual could be easily conditioned if the admaker only found the right trigger. According to Watson, people were moved by the basic stimuli of fear, rage, or love, the last a code word for sex.[9] The recognition of the potency of the 'sex appeal,' as it was commonly called, was widely accepted in advertising textbooks of the 1930s authored by psychologists, some of the texts clearly influenced by psychoanalysis. Consider, for example, the comment of Albert Poffenberger, a professor of psychology at Columbia University: 'Man is probably sensitive to the sex appeal at all times and as frequently responds to it in [a] sublimated form. Not only persons of the opposite sex, but objects, pictures, statements, ideas may arouse these desires that may manifest themselves in the purchase of handsome garments, jewellery, books, face powder, automobiles, furniture, and decorations,' he claimed. 'In fact, this desire in its sublimated form is so widespread that it may, under skilful hands, be made to furnish the drive toward the purchase of almost any kind of object.'[10] By the end of the 1930s admakers were using all manner of sex appeals to attract the eyes of readers, including occasional nudity – tradition has it that Woodbury pioneered again, employing a photograph of a female nude sitting with her back to the camera in 1936 in one soap ad.[11]

The erotic sell, however, evolved into much more than just a display of sexy images of women. Its practitioners sought to evoke the libidinal energies manifest in the 'perversions' and like taboos, from the orgy to the rape, the appeal here not just of sex as such but of forbidden sex. The resulting techniques suited the Freudian paradigm, where the sex drive and the repressed unconscious were crucial to behaviour. Indeed, after the Second World War, the influence of psychoanalysis on the practices of admakers did grow, because of the huge influence of Freud in the wider society, and the work of his followers, notably Ernest Dichter, in the marketing industry.[12] But even more important, I suspect, was the impact of mass culture, most especially erotica in literature and film and the growing volume of pornography.[13] Admakers have not left behind records indicating how they drew their ideas from sexual material – understandably, given the fact that owning pornography was deemed both immoral and illegal in most jurisdictions. But we can assume that admakers, like most men, were exposed to examples of erotica and pornography as they matured, since it was so much a part of male culture.[14] Sometimes the influence was even more direct: according to one report, Bertram Brooker, a well-known admaker of the 1930s and 1940s attached to McLaren Advertising, a major Canadian agency, kept in his lower desk drawer a large collection that was open to younger associates to view.[15] Although the influence of porn may not always have been conscious, its example certainly was apparent in the eventual advertising. Admakers employed the kinds of images evident in the porn repertoire to circulate what would become one of the most public varieties of erotica in affluent societies.

What follows looks first at an artist who discovered the virtue of employing sex and 'perversion' to promote himself as a distinct brand. Then I consider three pioneering efforts to use eroticism to market new brands to different target audiences of women, men, and children during the 1950s and 1960s. In each case the makers of these campaigns sought to cleanse this eroticism by packaging the sex in another discourse and/or aesthetic that enjoyed a greater degree of acceptance, even respectability, in the mainstream. The purpose was to retain the arousal of sex but to filter out the sleaze of porn. The answer was to employ additives, such as a bit of humour or the mystique of fashion, that provided a licence to 'sin,' or at least to show sin. Tactics varied. The how, the actual performances, mattered: the overall strategy had to be tailored to suit the product and the different audiences. The last section shows how another group of artists portrayed the visual surround created by the advance of the erotic sell.

1 *The Secret Life of Salvador Dalí* (1942)

'It is a book that stinks,' wrote George Orwell in 1944. 'If it were possible for a book to give a physical stink off its pages, this one would ...' The work in question was a fictionalized autobiography, entitled *The Secret Life of Salvador Dalí*, first published in New York two years before. Orwell called the famed artist 'a diseased intelligence' and 'a disgusting human being,' whose autobiography, 'simply a strip-tease act,' was 'an assault on sanity and decency.' Ironically, the taint spread from the book to the review: Orwell's essay was deemed obscene in its own right by the initial publishers, who actually cut the essay out of each copy of their collection.[16]

What most interested Orwell was the significance of the Dalí phenomenon in the broader context of something he called 'the decay of capitalist civilization.' There, Orwell revealed his adherence to that crippling conceit of the Left, the conviction that capitalism was a system bound to end up soon in history's dustbin. Orwell, after all, was still a socialist, and something of a puritan. That aside, Orwell's argument was undeniably perceptive. The autobiography, he declared, made clear how Dalí had succeeded by being wicked. 'Always do the thing that will shock and wound people.' This was a sure route to fame and fortune in pre-war Europe and now in wartime America. He got away with acting like 'a dirty little scoundrel' simply because he was an artist. 'The artist is to be exempt from the moral laws that are binding on ordinary people,' Orwell lamented. Dalí had discovered, 'If you threw dead donkeys at people,' a reference to one of Dalí's affectations, 'they threw money back.' Orwell did not know 'why it should be so easy to "sell" such horrors as rotting corpses to a sophisticated public.' Dalí's success was 'a symptom of the world's illness,' he decided.

Whatever else his autobiography was, and biographers and scholars have found it a source of all kinds of puzzlement and inspiration,[17] *The Secret Life* can also be labelled an extended advertisement for the 'Dalí brand,' a new kind of product that embodied the name and the style of one of the most notorious painters of the day. The 400–page book was written by Dalí in French, translated, apparently with some difficulty, by Haakon Chevalier into English, and published by the distinguished New York house Dial Press (facilitated by Caresse Crosby, a socialite and Dalí's American host).[18] The autobiography was divided into an extended treatment of Dalí's childhood, more than 100 pages long; another even longer chunk on his adolescence, education, and entry into the art world; and a final section detailing his years in the surrealist movement, mostly centred in Paris, his growing fame among the public and high society, and his eventual move to the United States to escape Hitler's armies as well as to tap the wealth of that land of abundance. Sufficient images were scattered throughout the text to give the reader a good notion of the Dalí style: sketches he drew to illustrate his comments; clusters of photographs to represent his life and ideas, including some shots of his famous paintings; and two colour plates that featured one of his self-portraits and a picture of the face of Gala, his beloved wife. Dalí's account of his life was full of declarations, anecdotes, reflections, exaggerations, imaginings, evasions, betrayals, outright lies, and much humour.[19] He played games with his readers, offering them what he called 'false memories' and 'true memories,' revealing all manner of neuroses and 'perversions,' but never all his indiscretions or secrets because, as he put it, these might prove useful later to publicize a 'corrected and augmented' (201) version of his *Secret Life*. He also used the opportunity to distance himself from his revolutionary past, to tout his new-found zeal for Catholicism, and to praise America. All this made for superb story telling, but hardly for truth telling. The book was an instant hit, though the many reviewers gave it a decidedly 'mixed reception.'[20]

The autobiography was both a method of self-promotion, where Dalí explained how he was the most sensational genius of his times, and an exercise in self-fashioning, where he constructed his own myth out of the raw material of his experiences. Such a narrative required the description of an 'other,' that which was not Dalí. The 'very rich' and the 'very poor,' they impressed him – but never 'average people' (339). He would not be a part of the crowd. Throughout he showed the deepest contempt for the dull and the ordinary. What he disdained was the bourgeois dominion, its emphasis on respectability, its devotion to order, its respect for authority, its love of progress. 'Our epoch is dying of moral skepticism and spiritual nothingness' (303). Scrap convention: Dalí depicted himself as a flamboyant rebel, devoted to the return of tradition, a reinvigorated 'Classicism' (354) that was really his version of an aristocratic dominion. His was the life of colour, in dress and in performance, a life devoted to shock and excitement in the pursuit of pleasure. Call him the joker. In short, Dalí had imagined himself in the preferred mode of the Eros project, a self who knew his own desires, eventually commanded his situation, and so realized his ambitions.

Behind the text was a not-so-hidden master, none other than Sigmund Freud. Dalí had discovered Freud early on at school and remained a constant reader throughout the 1920s and 1930s, particularly impressed by *The Interpretation of Dreams*, which he treated as a never-ending source of bizarre imagery. At the end of the 1930s he actually met the great man, who supposedly exclaimed, 'I have never seen a more complete example of a Spaniard. What a fanatic!' (25). That Dalí took as a compliment. And Dalí also read other Freudians who figured in the autobiography: both Jacques Lacan, then best known for his thesis on paranoia, and Otto Rank, who wrote about the trauma of birth. Dalí filled his pages with Freudian bits and pieces, words, symbols, scenarios, and concepts. He spent so much time detailing his childhood, even claiming some 'intra-uterine memories' of the womb, because Freud had emphasized how infancy predetermined a person's adulthood. Above all, Dalí wrote a life that presumed psychoanalysis was correct, that the sex drive determined the course and personality of the individual. Right at the beginning he admitted that the key to his story was the phenomenon of regression, for he was a person who had never forgotten that state of infantile paradise Freud called 'polymorphous perversity' (2). That explained why, as an adult, he was always at odds with his world, a soul in anguish, consumed by uncontrollable passions, bedevilled by narcissism, paranoia, hysteria, and megalomania, a victim of the Oedipus complex, complete with castration anxieties. His troubled sexuality meant he boasted an extraordinary range of 'perversions': you could find somewhere in *The Secret Life* references to both oral and anal eroticism, hints of incest, lots of masturbation, voyeurism and exhibitionism, sadism and masochism, a fascination with fetishes (he even displayed some of his favourites), signs of necrophilia and coprophilia and bestiality, cross-dressing and homosexuality (although he emphatically denied he was a homosexual) – all that was missing from the roster, it seemed, was paedophilia. Especially pronounced was his taste for mixing pain and pleasure, at least in fantasy: so he recalled daydreams where he crushed one girlfriend (108–9), forced another to cry because of his cruelty (143–6, 150–3), and played an elaborate game of erotic coupling and torture with adolescent chums (53–62). Supposedly he had been saved from this seething stew of sexual obsessions by the arrival of his Gala, at first the wife of a fellow surrealist, Paul Eluard. Gala became after 1929 Dalí's ideal woman or 'Gradiva,' that too a reference to one of Freud's literary analyses, which dealt with a woman who cured her man of his repression and delusions.[21] But the legacy of these 'perversions' constituted the raw material out of which came his art: Dalí recorded his unconscious, painting the signs and symbols of the irrational, which resided in that psychoanalytic realm. *The Secret Life*, in short, played out all manner of Freudian scripts.

What was not so obvious, either in the autobiography or in later biographies, was the influence of pornography on Dalí's life and art. There are fragments of information suggesting that Dalí was very familiar with the repertoire of pornography. There may be more than coincidence to the similarity of the title of his autobiography and that of *My Secret Life*, a Victorian classic of erotica. His diary indicates he was reading erotic novels in his mid-teens; apparently he found the French ones more sensual than their Spanish equivalents.[22] One of his favourite works, so he claimed much later, was Georges Bataille's pornographic classic *The Story of the Eye*.[23] But he derived the greatest pleasure from visual stimuli: 'sometimes it's enough for me just to look in order to have an orgasm.'[24] Dalí did admit that at an early age he was fascinated by pictures of the nudes he found in a collection of art books his father had given him (71). He certainly collected erotic photographs, which he wrote he 'pinned up on the walls of my studio' at one point in his life (364). In an article in 1930, Dalí extolled the virtues of the erotic postcard 'as the document that is the most alive of modern popular thought.'[25] He also produced pornographic images for private collectors, according to one of his patrons, who thought this a result of Gala's efforts to sublimate Dalí's innate homosexuality.[26] The exhibition *jardín de eros* in 1999 in Barcelona carried three of his erotic tableaux, one a sketch of a couple engaged in a variety of sexual acts and suggestively entitled *Paul y Gala* (1932).[27]

In any case Dalí filled *The Secret Life* with signs of the voyeur's gaze. It was a source of great pleasure and sometimes of shame, at least when he thought he had been caught out, which must have been often if his claims about all this peeping were at all accurate. He was forever gazing at a woman's arms or breasts or lips or hips, able so he said to focus his gaze in a way that blotted out the rest of the world. No matter whether he looked at people or animals, plants or rock, everything he could and did sexualize. So on a small excursion by row-boat along the coast of his beloved Catalan neighbourhood, he spotted a formation that 'was exactly like a woman's two breasts ...' (305). The skyscrapers of New York became at night gigantic shapes 'ready to perform the sexual act and to devour one another' (334). Keys, crutches, candles,

towers, swords, arrows – all became phallic objects. The lion represented the libido; steps and stairs suggested intercourse; the grasshopper evoked the horror of sexual contact; an opened drawer stood for a
woman's vagina; ripe melons took the place of women's breasts; the
decaying donkey meant sexual inadequacy. And he filled his paintings
and sketches with many of these symbols. No wonder a prude like
Orwell could charge that 'some of Dali's pictures would tend to poison
the imagination like a pornographic postcard.'[28]

What most fascinated Dalí, then, was the grotesque body that
Mikhail Bakhtin would posit as one of the extreme poles of the representation of the human shape.[29] Sometimes the figures appeared elongated and androgynous, a style that suited his own taste in women –
Gala, he pointed out, had 'a build like a boy's' (276). But Dalí's most
startling version of the grotesque was a figure often incomplete and
ambiguous, sometimes in fragments, perhaps boasting an exaggerated
appendage, or melded with some extraneous object, marred by its own
blood or excrement, softened or twisted into a gruesome shape.

Consider one of his most famous pictures, The Lugubrious Game
(1929), reproduced in a small black-and-white photograph in The Secret
Life. He painted this, he claimed, in a frenzy of delirium that allowed
his unconscious to record its strange images directly on the canvas.
One of the figures, standing on a pedestal, had a huge, elongated hand
that signified the masturbator, whose sexual aberration caused shame,
since his other hand hid his face, a reflection of Dalí's own guilty
addiction to this act. Another male, watching from the steps, had his
shorts spattered with excrement – it was this figure, he recalled, that
had led the surrealist leader André Breton to worry that Dalí was
coprophagic. Not so, Dalí told Gala, acting here as Breton's representative: 'I consider scatology as a terrorizing element, just as I do blood, or
my phobia for grasshoppers' (231). The prevailing image, however,
was an amorphous collection of things, shaped but not enclosed, in the
centre of the painting: a bizarre assemblage of soft and hard objects,
such as faces (including Dali's?), hands, shells, a grasshopper or an
umbrella, symbols signifying his sexual desires and fears, all linked to
the tortured lower body of some androgynous creature. Here was a
desiring machine that seemingly did not, could not, work. In all,
Bataille thought, and with some cause, that this painting was really
about castration.[30]

Which, by the way, was one of Dalí's persistent worries. Paranoia
served as his guiding philosophy; indeed, he would turn this psycho-

sis into an aesthetic and critical technique. The grotesque body, for him, expressed anxiety, representing the sexual worries and obsessions that were harboured in the psyches of all individuals. In Dalí's hands the grotesque was more often the creature of nightmares than a celebration of the people that it represented in Bakhtin's cosmology. One of Dalí's purposes, as he loved to tell his listeners, was to stupefy and confuse, to produce 'the systematic cretinization of the masses' (309). It was this type of bizarre and sinister imagery, an imagery both fascinating and repellent, that made Dalí into a figure of such significance by the end of the 1930s.

In retrospect *The Secret Life* looked like the culmination of a long campaign of events and stunts – parties, exhibitions, special displays (one of these at the New York World's Fair), public announcements, and press conferences – all meant to boom the Dalí brand in the virgin market of America. While still in Europe, Dalí had cultivated the friendship of the wealthy, and he would always enjoy the company of rich people, celebrities, the fashion set, and the like. But in America he was especially attentive to the needs of the press. He admitted outright that he loved publicity, which, he explained characteristically, was a sign of his honesty by comparison with the hypocrisy of other artists.[31] Perhaps so, but it also reflected his recognition of the importance of the media, the way their attention could be used to construct his public persona as a flamboyant genius.

He recounted one coup in *The Secret Life*. Hired in 1939 to design two display windows for Bonwit Teller, then a famed department store on Fifth Avenue in New York city, he produced two startling images, one of 'Day' and the other of 'Night,' supposedly to evoke 'the Narcissus myth,' featuring some eroticized mannequins in surrealist settings. The displays certainly attracted public attention – too much, it seemed, since the store quickly changed the look, substituting different figures for Dalí's mannequins. He claimed that he had tried to get management to change its mind. When that failed, Dalí took direct action: he trashed the display personally, in the process smashing a plate-glass window. Although picked up by the police, he was vindicated when the judge accepted his right to protect his original vision, getting off with a suspended sentence for disorderly conduct and payment of damages to Bonwit Teller. This gave the press a sensational story that worked to reaffirm Dalí's own self-image as an artist and rebel.

Here and elsewhere Dalí offered public displays of sin and sex. That was apparently the reason another of his escapades in 1939 was so popular, this too recounted in *The Secret Life*. Dalí gleefully accepted another commission, to create a pavilion entitled 'The Dream of Venus' at the New York World's Fair. He filled it with surrealist imagery, including the famous sofa in the shape of Greta Garbo's lips. The highlight was a show of female swimmers dancing underwater in order to express the dream itself. Once more, Dalí found dealing with management a trial – the whole affair became 'a frightful nightmare' (376) – and he left before the fair opened. Even so, the pavilion won the favour of the press and the public, mostly it seemed because the swimmers were nude to the waist. 'It is the scantly clad, live and very normal-looking mermaids who cavort in these morbid surroundings that hold the attention of the crowd, which still likes its Dalí spelled "Dolly,"' claimed the Cleveland *Press* (18 July 1939).[32] Dalí had discovered that the recognized artist could indeed sell a bit of wickedness to the American public.

The purpose of Dalí's efforts was to win fame and make money. And the campaign worked. After the opening of a solo exhibition in New York in 1939, where according to *Life* magazine crowds 'gaped open-mouthed' at his wild pictures, Dalí managed to sell twenty-one works to collectors for roughly $25,000.[33] Equally popular with the public was a joint Miró-Dalí retrospective at the Museum of Modern Art, opening in late 1941, and afterwards sent on a tour to eight other American cities. Dalí's work proved the big draw and generated yet another wave of free publicity. 'If Americans like to rebel they also like to be shocked,' claimed one critic, 'and Señor Dalí has shocked them more deeply than any other artist of modern times.'[34]

Showing and selling pictures was only one way that Dalí and Gala hoped to get rich, however. Like previous artists, he designed sets and costumes for ballet, notably *Labyrinth* (1941), where he brought his brand of surrealist imagery onto a still traditional stage. He worked on two projects for the filmmakers Alfred Hitchcock and Walt Disney in 1945. He repeated his trademark clichés, ants and crutches and keys and the like, in a whole series of illustrations he produced for all sorts of specialty books, such as *Macbeth* and *Don Quixote* in 1946. Dalí also took to painting portraits of wealthy folk, especially society women, on commission, the fee around $5,000.[35] His unusual if not risqué style was sufficient to attract such notables as Lady Louis Mountbatten and Helena Rubinstein. He put his subjects in a 'Dalínian' landscape, the head emerging from a rock, say, and sometimes he eroticized slightly the image of the woman. Nothing grotesque here, of course; indeed some of the portraits took on the appearance of the finished, smooth, and symmetrical shapes of the classical body.[36]

But what was much more interesting, and certainly more controversial, was Dalí's move into the realm of advertising. Dalí was always fascinated by pop culture, the liveliness of ordinary or low art (like the erotic postcard), though now his interest may well have been chiefly mercenary because that was where the money was. In 1943 he undertook a commission from Elsa Schiaparelli, a friend, to promote her new 'Shocking Radiance' oils in which, á la Botticelli, a cherub poured oil 'over the breasts of a naked, conch-borne Venus engaged in admiring her face in a mirror.'[37] The same year he produced a fashion ad for Bergdorf Goodman, appearing in *Vogue*, that used a series of willowy androgynes to set off a fashionable scarf and handbag.[38] A year later appeared an advertisement for Bryan's Hosiery, in which he foregrounded a woman's leg, clad in nylon, atop a table held up by three legs marked by hieroglyphics, and set off by a variety of weird, dismembered body parts and humanoid characters.[39] The list of sponsors ready to buy the Dalí brand would steadily grow over the next few years: De Beers' diamonds, Gunther's furs, Ford cars, Wrigley's chewing gum, Gruen watches, Abbott Laboratories products, the Container Corporation of America. By 1947 he was receiving roughly $2,500 for each advertisement and $600 for a magazine cover.[40] Dalí and Gala were well on their way to a life of comfort and pleasure.

All of this commercial work appeared to purists to be a form of prostitution. In 1942 a disgusted André Breton had coined the fitting anagram Avida Dollars (eager for dollars) from Dalí's name. But in fact Breton and his ilk had set the stage for this renegade. Surrealism as an artistic movement had won so much fame because it consistently produced sexual images that intrigued and scandalized. Breton himself had declared, in 1937, that desire was 'the sole motivating principle of the world, the only master that humans must recognize.'[41] The surrealists had worked very hard to rehabilitate the reputation of the Marquis de Sade and so of his pornography. They had also touted the virtues of Freud as the champion of the irrational and the unconscious. Dalí's determination to reveal on canvas his own demons and 'perversions' had made him a major force in the success of surrealism during the 1930s. His invention of the surrealist object, for example, that bizarre juxtaposition of the ordinary and the erotic, had given the movement a new frontier of shock to exploit.[42] In some ways Dalí was the consummate surrealist, as he imagined in *The Secret Life*, his every action in public a working out of the desires harboured in his unconscious.

Looking at his career in a wider context, Dalí was clearly the beneficiary of the past work of the avant-garde, an artistic formation that had emerged after the mid-nineteenth century in Paris. The avant-garde was an ever-changing collection of artists and intellectuals, and particularly painters, who challenged the prevailing conventions of the art world. They were famous for producing images that startled and confounded the bourgeoisie. Yet, ironically, their success and their livelihood depended upon the readiness of some portion of this same bourgeoisie to purchase their paintings. So Dalí in 1942 stood at the end of a long line of rebels that included Monet, Van Gogh, Klimt, Picasso, and Miró, to name but a few. Where Dalí innovated was in transforming his 'perversions,' the sexual imagery that troubled his own psyche, into a distinctive kind of high art. The acceptance of this work by the art world was crucial: naming the image 'art' cleansed the obscene, making out of what was once deemed dirty something exciting, even enticing, at least in the minds of those who were counted the fans of the avant-garde. There was an obvious commercial potential here because any signs of moral subversion retained the power to capture attention and to mobilize desire. That Dalí and Gala realized. Dalí had pioneered the technique of selling the thrill of sexual transgression to American business and to the American public.

2 The Maidenform Woman

In 1999 one wall of a room in Copenhagen's Museum Erotica was devoted to an impressive piece of nostalgia, an exhibition of images and artefacts that celebrated a mid-twentieth-century and mostly American addition to the repertoire of pornography, the famous 'pin-up.' Here was work by both Alberto Vargas and George Petty, two of the leading erotic illustrators of the 1930s and 1940s, the high point of the craze. Other sex museums boasted their own examples – indeed Barcelona, Berlin, and the Seksmuseum of Amsterdam all offered displays of a naked Marilyn Monroe, who had posed for the most famous of all calendar pin-ups (though in this case a photograph) in 1949. Typically the pin-up was an illustration of a sexy, beautiful young woman, usually semi-clad, and carefully designed to reveal her physical charms, especially her breasts and her legs, to the lustful eyes of the male voyeur. Like Lady Godiva, the archetypal model of this style of exhibitionism, she was on public display. But she was nearly always alone in the picture, except possibly for a dog or cat and the necessary props – no man was present to suggest ownership. In some cases the treatment was frankly erotic, in others a bit comic, but always the woman was inviting. She was awesomely popular, called a 'pin-up' because so many men used the images to decorate their rooms, lockers, cars, offices, restrooms – in short, their lives. She appeared in magazines, on posters, calendars, matchbook covers, notepads, lighters, and on and on. And, eventually, she spread to sites far removed from her place of origin: American soldiers carried her image throughout the world during and after the Second World War. Aside from the visual pleasure of gazing at such enticing beauties, the practice was one way of signifying masculinity and marking the male domain.

Advertising did not escape the craze. Milder versions of the pin-up, used in ads for Old Gold cigarettes and Coca-Cola, were on display in Copenhagen. Barcelona's Museu de l'Eròtica exhibited a collection of matchbook covers (1954–66) where local enterprises, a restaurant or bar or garage, advertised their services next to the image of a seductive woman, usually portrayed in a comic setting. But none of the sex museums carried samples of what was arguably the most famous use of the tradition of the pin-up in advertising history, namely the post-war 'Dream' campaign for Maidenform bras, which lasted twenty years, from 1949 to 1969.

The first tagline was 'I dreamed I went shopping in my Maidenform bra,' perhaps an inevitable theme, though swiftly Maidenform's 'pin-up' would enjoy more unusual adventures. The campaign used more than 100 different themes, and even more distinct 'dreams,' because sometimes a theme was replayed. By 1960 the company was spending close to $2 million to purchase space, more than any rival manufacturer.[43] The ads ran chiefly in women's magazines such as *Harper's Bazaar, Ladies' Home Journal, Vogue,* and *Women's Day,* sometimes in less gendered publications such as the *New Yorker.* They also appeared around the world, in 115 countries by 1963 according to one account.[44] Indeed Maidenform was apparently the first American company to use television commercials to sell its intimates.[45] Increasingly the print campaign had colour photography rather than drawings (common in the first years) or black-and-white pictures to heighten the 'realism' of the fantasy. Once the campaign became familiar, Maidenform sometimes dispensed with much text to highlight just the image of the dream, though the label of what that dream might be always remained. Crucial to each ad was the display of a young woman, supposedly caught up in a dream, who exposed her bra-encased breasts, and much of her upper body, in some social place to an unseen audience. Underwear became outerwear. The private was now the public. Here a male brand of erotica was transformed into a message designed to capture the fancy of hordes of female consumers in order to sell a lot more product.[46]

The brassiere business was only about twenty-five years old when Maidenform launched the campaign. Bras that separated and lifted the breasts were a recent innovation, introduced largely after 1900. The company itself was a pioneer, founded back in 1923 by Ida Rosenthal and Enid Bissett, two dressmakers, and Rosenthal's husband, William, listed as a designer. He filed a U.S. patent in 1926 for the first 'uplift' bra. The company's name, 'Maiden Form,' was chosen to emphasize how the product accentuated the femininity of its wearers. Business expanded rapidly during the 1930s – Maidenform grew prosperous in the Depression[47] – when fashion moved away from the boyish style of the twenties. Equally important was the development of nylon and similar materials, which made it possible to produce bras that were more comfortable, stylish, and lasting.

By this time bras were already an item of erotic excitement because of their ability to hide and to reveal, to accentuate and to suggest. Certainly other manufacturers had played with the sexual connotations of underwear before: a 1934 cinema ad for Scandale, a French company, showed a woman clad only in her one-piece sheath and nylons who displayed her form admirably in a series of exercises at a gymnasium.[48] In the next decade the look of the bra was hyped by the popularity of full-figured movie stars such as Jane Russell, her bosom made famous and controversial by the movie *The Outlaw* (1943), and Lana Turner, called the 'Sweater Girl.' Big breasts symbolized sexual potency in postwar America. The bras that suited this obsession were formidable affairs: the breasts were contained, separated, raised, and exaggerated by two cone-shaped cups that produced a 'pointy' effect, supposedly realizing the aim of an enhanced femininity made famous by the arrival of Christian Dior's 'New Look' in 1947.[49] Two years later Maidenform introduced the Chansonette, a 'cotton broadcloth basic' with a 'circle-stitched cup to accentuate and round the bust,' soon labelled the 'bullet bra.'[50] Indeed the conical bra looked engineered, already streamlined, a veritable symbol of modernity for the new femininity of the postwar era.[51] The Chansonette would prove the main beneficiary of the novel advertising strategy the company had adopted, becoming the top seller during the 1950s – some 60 million items were purchased in the next fourteen years.[52]

The exact origins of successful advertising are often difficult to trace because all sorts of people and actions are involved in the first and later designs. Legend has it that Mary Fillius, a copywriter at William H. Weintraub, the company's ad agency, got the inspiration that led to the 'Dream' campaign, of some significance because it identified a woman as the key creative. One adman, however, recalled that Herman Davis, an art director at another agency, had earlier conceived the idea to sell slips made by Seamprufe, which turned down the initiative.[53] That put a man as the author. Fillius, then an associate of Davis, moved to Weintraub where she resurrected the notion, except now the fantasy was about a bra, not a slip, in itself an important change because the exposure of a bra was a much bolder move. Certainly Fillius sold the idea to the agency and to an initially reluctant Maidenform, including Ida Rosenthal, who was very doubtful. Thereafter Dr Joseph Coleman, Rosenthal's son-in-law, was in charge of Maidenform's publicity. As time went on the actual dreams were determined twice a year by a committee made up, among others, of Coleman and his wife, Beatrice. On one occasion the company also solicited scenarios from the public: '*Your* dream can WIN $10,000!'[54] Normally the agency submitted themes, up to forty or fifty, from which only a few were selected.[55] Men and women, in short, bore a responsibility for the final design of the campaign.

Did Freud, or at least his shadow, also bear some responsibility? Certainly later commentators thought so. Norman B. Norman, the key man at the presiding agency, NCK, was trained as a social psychologist and something of a Freudian with a passion for finding sex behind desire.[56] The 'Dream' campaign exploited the energies psychoanalysis associated with 'perversion.' According to Freud, fantasies of being naked in public were not only commonplace but freighted with moral and sexual significance because they were, above all, 'dreams of exhibiting' that usually but not always evoked feelings of shame.[57] Such dreamers, it seemed, flirted vicariously with the forbidden pleasures of exhibitionism, based upon memories of childhood when infants could and did realize the desire to appear naked. As a result, mused one adman in 1952, the headline 'I dreamed ...' was 'likely to hit some readers with haymaker force,' though he was not sure that impact would produce increased sales because the experience of being unclad was inherently unpleasant.[58] A few years later, when the campaign was an obvious success, Vance Packard suggested that the agency had consulted psychologists, at least some of whom had argued that 'the ad was sound because the wish to appear naked or scantily clad in a crowd is "present in most of us" and "represents a beautiful example of wish fulfillment."'[59] The key, apparently, was the claim that the woman in the ad was dreaming, an admission that was also a licence, allowing readers to relish the transgression. 'Everybody dreams, many people dream of running around naked; but they can't talk about it,' mused Norman B. Norman. 'We *make* our copywriters talk about it.'[60] The initial public response, Joseph Coleman recalled, was mixed, some critics finding the ads 'corny' but not 'violations of good taste.' A survey of fashion ads by a rival agency, Leo Burnett, actually found that women gave the Maidenform ads the lowest ranking of three examples. The fashion director at NCK claimed she was delighted: 'Housewives should think those ads are shocking. That's the point.'[61] In any case the agency and the company worked to mute the campaign's 'Freudian appeal. The sight of these very active dreams might not be good for teen-age girls. Even fifty-year-old women might get ideas ... We made the approach lighter and more discreet.' Beatrice Coleman added, 'We don't mind double meanings, so long as they are in good taste.'[62] The comic touch served to ease the tension the sight of public sex might evoke.

Such attitudes explain, in part, why the campaign sketched a world of escape that had some of the properties of carnival: at first a bit of the grotesque, always inversions and reversals, signs of abundance, bold appetites, strange hybrids, humour and parody, and much joy. There was even a touch of subversion, at least a challenge to bourgeois norms of conduct. Consider first the dreams where women fled their lives of drudgery and constraint, able to indulge in all sorts of fantasies of independence and power and pleasure. Sometimes they boasted unusual occupations, at least for the 1950s: a 'Lady Ambassador' or a 'Lady Editor,' a toreador, a private eye, a boxer, a window washer, or a winning politician. Always such women remained feminine, according to the standards of the times. That 'Lady Ambassador' rested lightly against a marble column, her eyes closed, as she held out her hand to be kissed.[63] There was no sense here, or in most of the parodies that featured an occupation, that the woman actually worked for a living. She was, in short, posing, pretending to be whatever. The 'Lady Fireman,' one of the most famous of the series, was dressed in glossy black boots, red short shorts, silver gloves, a red fire hat, and of course the white bra.[64] She did not so much hang on the side of the fire engine as thrust herself out from the engine, her arm outstretched as if to greet her many admirers. There was, then, a distinct air of mockery about such scenarios. Women, it was assumed, were ready to laugh at such impossible dreams.

Sometimes the dreamers were just at play, enjoying life to the fullest. That all started with two of the first ads, which displayed women caught up in the abandon of shopping, one in a fairy-tale supermarket and the other in a plush hat shop. In later ads the Maidenform woman could be found doing the Charleston, going to a theatre, on a cruise, acting the part of Cleopatra, riding a balloon, even walking a tightrope. A final group of dreams were completely absurd: a woman who was sawn in half, two women who dreamed they were bookends, a brave soul who had literally grasped the bull by the horns (now there was some phallic symbolism). In the 'Egyptian Woman,' for example, she became a marvellous exotic: her lower body clothed in a magnificent blue dress, her blonde tresses topped by a golden crown, she sat upon a plush divan, surrounded by the accoutrements of majesty, once again her arm outstretched to signal she was on display.[65] These may not have been the 'vulgar pleasures' Mikhail Bakhtin had esteemed but they were certainly extraordinary.

Whatever the scenario, the dreamer remained the focus of attraction. Many of the scenarios featured women whose bodies seemed weightless, sometimes floating or gliding, sometimes propelled forward, sometimes suspended in a moment of freedom.[66] That expressed the motif of the dream. It also signified the comfort of the bra, a means of control that nonetheless promised a liberated body. No crowd of others, in particular no man (though in one ad a man's hand was shown, in another a man was shown 'making-over' the beautiful dreamer), appeared to share the spotlight. At times the text of the ad emphasized how the Maidenform woman had enthralled the unseen audience: 'I'm the center of attention ...'[67] 'Every little star is winking – even the man in the moon is carrying a torch! They're enchanted, entranced by a magic someone.'[68] They were enthralled, of course, because her charms were enhanced by her Maidenform bra. 'No wonder I'm the people's choice for the figure of the year!'[69] Often the copy of the ads promised that the bra would shape and control, make the most of a woman's curves, mould the wearer into something stunning. 'It curves me, moulds me, makes me such a star attraction that all the other dolls wish they were me,' exclaimed the 'jack-in-the box' who announced the virtues of Maidenform's new Prelude bra.[70] The images and the words worked to define the bra as an erotic instrument, making its owner striking and happy – in any case, a person of significance. Consequently the ads played on the age-old notion of competition embedded in the prevailing beauty culture to assure the Maidenform woman that she would outshine any friends or rivals.

Then consider the looks of the campaign. Rarely did any of the dreamers look directly at the reader in the 1950s – after all, they were supposed to be caught up in their own reveries. During the next decade, though, they did become more and more bold, they did often gaze outward to show how proud they were of their appearance, indicative of the more aggressive femininity of the 1960s. At any time the Maidenform woman might appear haughty and aloof, playful or indulgent, sometimes surprised or even innocent. On occasion she was 'clowned,' drawn or photographed in ways that made her look silly or giddy, perhaps a too-literal rendering of the dream motif. But as the campaign persisted, beginning in the early 1950s, she became increasingly sexy and glamorous. That last quality grew out of the repertoire of fashion where the cut of the clothes, the quality of the fabric, the style of the design, elaborate hair-dos, careful poses, the skill of the photographer, all served to enhance the allure of the body. The Maidenform woman was clad in beautiful dresses, furs and silks and satin, fine scarves, fancy slacks, gorgeous jackets and coats (but always open to reveal the bra). She was, in other words, an assemblage of flesh, cosmetics, dress, body language, and the bra. A pamphlet the company released much later emphasized how its advertising agency had employed leading fashion designers, such as John Frederics and Arnold Scaasi, and fashion photographers, naming Irving Penn and Richard Avedon, to produce visions of elegance.[71] Maidenform had discovered one of the crucial mechanisms of the erotic sell: the use of fashion as a filter to reduce the shock of the sexual. It was a lesson many later admakers would employ to good effect.

So the feminine 'pin-up' was very much a sophisticated clothes-horse. But the contrast, the baring of the bra, was no less essential to signify her sexual potency. A voluptuous woman stood in a classical setting, positioned to emphasize her curves, her sensuality, and clad in a long gown and a tight-fitting corset, Maidenform's new Prelude, dreaming 'I was Venus de Milo ...' (1955). Two stylish twins, each wearing tight black skirts and matching jackets, presumably out shopping, complete with hat boxes and Dalmatians, stared boldly at the camera and proudly held open their jackets to reveal their strapless bras, right in the middle of the street (1956). Another elegant twosome, both blondes, enjoying 'Tea for Two,' coyly wore their wraps off their shoulders and presented long legs clad in tight satin pants (1957). Also in satin pants, enhanced by two flares attached to her waist, again blonde, the Maidenform woman, this time her top completely bare but for the bra, walked carefully on a tightrope – her expression suggesting a state of ecstasy (1961). What was missing, naturally, was the exposure of the breast: only rather late, in 1965, was a woman shown wearing a bra 'with a balcony' and so displaying some cleavage.[72] Otherwise, all sorts of gestures and poses and dress or undress that serve to sexualize the body cropped up in the course of the campaign: an exposed midriff, naked arms and legs, inviting eyes, flowing hair, mesh nylons and high heels, a chest thrust forward, a leg turned to accentuate its curves, a well-fitted skirt, short-shorts, an opened mouth, the pout.

Obviously the Maidenform woman did not fit the prevailing image of the suburban housewife. She was more often akin to an imagined sex goddess out of Hollywood. At the campaign's height, in the late 1950s and early 1960s, the women fitted best the stereotype of the classical body, albeit modified to suit the presumed taste of American males: ample bosoms, long and slender legs, a slim waist, a harmony of curves, a poreless and unblemished appearance. One report claimed that the model had to be 'healthy, unmarried, 26 years old and apparently more fulsome than the 34B of the average American woman'[73] – in addition, though this was not mentioned, she had to be white. Then they were subjected to a process of streamlining by fashion experts and photographers to render them erotic, sometimes exotic. Like some of the more artistic pin-ups, a few became commanding figures, elegantly clad, who boldly announced their sexual charms. Such spectacles of erotic power must always have seemed a bit strange, outside of the movies and magazines, at a time when sexual life was encumbered by a thicket of moral sanctions and the cult of domesticity weighed heavily upon the female consciousness. Their appeal lay in their illusion – they were, in a word, fun, not to be taken too seriously. That said, the campaign did in effect urge suburban housewives to become 'glamour girls' for their husbands, echoing a message evident in leading women's magazines, especially during the 1950s.[74]

In 1963 *Printer's Ink*, a trade journal for the ad industry, decided that the 'Dream' campaign must be counted among the 'Greatest Advertisements of All Time.' No wonder: a poll two years earlier had revealed that 37 per cent of female respondents could recall an actual Maidenform ad, double the number of any of its competitors.[75] Another sign of success was the way in which it had captured the fancy of all sorts of different folk. A different marketing journal, *Sales Management* (5 April 1963), published a series of gags that parodied the campaign. A female comedian on the popular *Garry Moore Show*, a television program, told how she had invented the 'Maidenform money belt: it has two compartments – for cash and cheques.' A greeting card featuring a naked woman said 'I dreamed of you without ...'; another carried the line, 'I dreamed I was in your Maidenform bra.' A Key West retailer displayed a photograph of a Fidel Castro look-a-like who 'dreamed I ruled Cuba in my Maidenform bra ...' Some fraternity houses in a New York state college had painted various satires on the walls: so 'a buxomy woman in bustles "dreamed I shot McKinley ..."' Much later the campaign was remembered as the vehicle of a kind of proto-feminist message, even though such a view masked the erotic character of so much of the advertising. The ads 'showed women wearing bras in the real world [sic!] and then made that world so absurd that it was completely non-threatening,' recalled one writer in the 1980s. 'Underwear had been both brought out of the bedroom and kept private.'[76] A few years later, the psychologist Carol Moog in her book compared the campaign favourably to later efforts by Maidenform since 'I dreamed ...' gave voice to unspoken yearnings for freedom and power. She called the advertising 'a kind of emotional road map for the women's lib activities that came to the surface in the seventies.'[77] The 'Dream' campaign had not only affected popular culture but become a part of that culture.

The question of the campaign's impact on the market was more complicated, however. Certainly the marketing industry thought the advertising a success. Indeed the volume of sales did increase substantially, from around $14 million in 1949 to $43 million in 1963, and an estimated 30 per cent of American women, by the company's own reckoning, owned a Maidenform bra. But competitors' sales also grew. In 1950 Maidenform was already the leading national manufacturer of brassieres in the United States, with an estimated tenth of the total business. But ten years later it still sold only about 10 per cent of all the bras purchased by American women.[78] So the campaign did no more than keep Maidenform ahead of the pack. Thereafter the impact of the advertising began to wane: its imagery appeared more and more dated, especially now that a softer style of bra and a more natural look had won increasing favour with younger women. After trying to update the images, ironically by making its models more playful and active and thus less arrogant or fashionable, Maidenform eventually brought the campaign to a close at the end of the decade. International Playtex was by far the leader in the huge bra market of $460 million in

1976.[79] In later years Maidenform did try to revive the dream motif in one form or another, though it never had the success it enjoyed in the 1950s and early 1960s. Indeed the company's fortunes sank so low that it sought bankruptcy protection in 1997, emerging two years later with additional financing.

Yet the 'Dream' campaign left a lasting mark on the underwear industry by exploiting the image of the bra as a thoroughly erotic commodity. That 'discovery,' of course, had been made by pornographers well before 1949. But Maidenform brought a cleansed version into the realm of the marketplace, using images of sex and power (or the illusion of power) to sell directly to the fantasies, the presumed unconscious, of millions of American women. The brilliance of this innovation was certified by imitation. By the mid- and late 1960s rival companies were sponsoring even more sexy ads to win the custom of the bra-buying public.[80] So it was fitting that Advertising Age (3 August 1999) would still list the 'Dream' theme among the top 100 campaigns (at no. 28) of the twentieth century.

3 The Early Playboy

In December 1964 Playboy published a short, congratulatory letter from a reader in Hungary. In passing he noted that the local press was always hostile to what its masters deemed a pornographic magazine, a charge he personally found ridiculous. The editors were hardly surprised by the animosity of the communist press: 'for Playboy is, after all, an elegant, full-color promotion on the benefits of a capitalist economy.' Indeed it was. Glossy, fat, flashy, and sassy, full of fiction, humour, pictures, opinion, letters, an interview, all meant to please men. At nearly 300 pages, roughly half of the space was devoted to selling product, via reviews and guides as well as ads, and more than 50 of these took a full page or more. Which was not an answer to the initial charge, of course. Rather, Playboy was so full of editorial and advertising content because it was pornographic, or rather because it offered a particular ensemble of sex and sophistication that had made it one of the best promotional vehicles in the land. What Playboy 'sold' was not just products but a lifestyle of hedonism and consumption, a special and obviously gendered version of the pleasures of affluence. That is why, at one level, the whole magazine seems to be a piece of propaganda. I will use this edition of December 1964 as my chief example of the Playboy phenomenon of the 1950s and 1960s.

Playboy realized the dreams, better yet the fantasies, of its founder,

Hugh Hefner (1926–), though by 1964 the magazine's commercial success depended on the efforts of a platoon of talent. Legend has it that Hefner endured a strict, moral upbringing in the American Midwest, living a youth where all kinds of pleasures, including sex, fell under the category of sin, at least at home, an experience that only served to enhance their allure. After the war, at the University of Illinois, where he majored in psychology, he discovered Sigmund Freud and, above all, Alfred Kinsey, whose 1948 blockbuster on the diverse and vigorous sex life of the American male served not only to justify Hefner's own sensual nature but to provide Hefner with a mission to liberate that male. He saw a major contradiction between what men said and what they did, between the structure of sexual repression and the reality of sexual obsession. His genius was to recognize the commercial possibilities of exploiting the wellsprings of lust. At some point, perhaps while he worked for the upscale and once risqué *Esquire*, a men's magazine now seeking to distance itself from its bawdy past, he started to plan his own, more daring effort (his initial title was 'Stag Party') to cater to the urban and urbane young male.

The result was one of the most successful postwar launches in the American magazine industry. The first *Playboy*, founded on little money and lots of credit, hit the newsstands in December 1953, boasting an exclusive, the already famous nude photograph of Marilyn Monroe that had once graced a pin-up calendar, the rights to which Hefner managed to purchase for a few hundred dollars. The press run rapidly sold out, enabling Hefner to finance other issues, which also sold out, generating a continuing and ever-increasing revenue stream. But not much profit, according to *Fortune* (May 1957): HMH Publishing still had a $25,000 deficit at the end of 1954. Early in the next year, Hefner strove to clean up his magazine by moving away from total nudity and pictures of professional models, finding his first real Playmate, Janet Pilgrim, a beautiful and wholesome blonde employee working in the subscription department, who appeared as Miss July. At the same time he sought to improve the quality of the fiction, humour, and commentary. This revamping was crucial because it distinguished *Playboy* from the legion of 'girlie' magazines of times past and present: the stigma went, and respectability beckoned.[81]

Although most businesses still remained leery of associating with a sex magazine, advertising did become increasingly significant after the fall of 1956, lured by reports that *Playboy* had captured the eyes of so many young men, especially on campuses across the nation: the

November 1956 edition, for example, boasted full-page ads for Marlboro and Salem cigarettes, Canadian Club whisky, and a Grundig hi-fi
system. By the end of the 1950s *Playboy*'s circulation had exceeded a
million, surpassing *Esquire*'s figures, though this circulation was still
largely the result of newsstand sales rather than subscriptions, proof
that *Playboy* had a doubtful reputation in the home.[82] And there were
some problems with advertisers over content, especially in 1962 when
one of the short stories sexualized rape.[83] But sales really boomed in
the decade of the sixties, especially after 1963, buoyed up no doubt by
the onset of the sexual revolution, and advertisers jumped on board.
According to *Forbes* (1 March 1971), the circulation of *Playboy* had
reached roughly 6 million copies a month and ad revenues approached
$34 million a year.

Some of the millions he earned Hefner invested in the creation of the
famous Playboy Clubs (the first opened in Chicago in 1960), a series of
nightclubs where young and shapely waitresses served members and
their guests. The licence to leer was obvious: the waitress, known as a
bunny, was dressed in a version of the corset that pushed her bosom
out and up, sucked in her waist, and displayed a lot of hip and bottom,
the outfit completed by rabbit ears and a 'tail,' 'a grapefruit-sized
hemisphere of white fluff' that hooked on to 'the costume's rear-most
point.'[84] Later Hefner also put his profits into leisure resorts, even a
hotel, as well as a model agency, a movie theatre, a television program
and motion pictures, a publishing house, and Playboy Products, sellers
of jewellery and the like. The result was to make him the wealthy
master of a huge Playboy empire, mostly to cater to the male taste in
entertainment.

Even more fabulous, or so it seemed to male reporters, Hefner lived
an almost scandalous life of luxury and indulgence in his notorious
Playboy Mansion in Chicago, sometimes referred to as a 'love temple,'
surrounded by Playmates and Bunnies, where he could work and play
as he wished. Happily ensconced in 'the house that flesh built,' mused
Time (24 March 1961), 'Hefner is actually a living promotion stunt, the
most conspicuous playboy in the Middle-Western world.' He was, so
he claimed years later, just living out the dreams he invented 'in his
teens.'[85] This was one 'revolutionary' who had done very well out of
the cause he espoused.

The key to *Playboy*'s success was sex (obviously!), something Hefner
never forgot, and he always resisted efforts to downplay the erotic by
associates who wished to emphasize the sophisticated side of the pub-

lication. If the cover art might be sexy or spicy, the covers rarely revealed much, an act of restraint necessary to avoid harassment by the authorities, something that in the early years did occasionally trouble Hefner. Rather, the erotica was reserved for the inside, especially the famous centrefold, the large colour photo of a semi-nude but always beautiful young woman, called the Playmate of the Month. In the mid-1950s, at least, finding high-quality colour photographs of a desirable woman unveiled was no easy matter for the average American male. So *Playboy* was, first and foremost, as the actor Burt Reynolds (who in 1972 posed for a nude picture in the women's magazine *Cosmopolitan*) once put it, 'a masturbatory magazine': a man bought it to imagine what sex would be like with the Playmate, to fantasize about touching and feeling her body, perhaps to 'go to his john and jerk off.'[86]

In the America of the 1950s, masturbation was still regarded as a sin, a dirty practice that fouled young men and one that parents must strive to stamp out. That was the legacy of a wave of moral hysteria, especially in the late nineteenth century, that had condemned this form of 'self-abuse' as the cause of all manner of physical and mental ills. But the practice was nonetheless widespread among adolescents and adults, or so Kinsey claimed, especially at a time when repression and enticement coexisted. These men could see nude photographs of women in art and sunbathing magazines that were often sold, 'under the counter,' at newsstands and the like in the 1940s and 1950s. The first chapter of Gay Talese's exploration of the sexual revolution in America, *Thy Neighbor's Wife*, contained a striking reminiscence of the use to which the needy male might put such pictures. Harold Rubin, the owner of a massage parlour, recalled how as a teenager in 1957 he once positioned the photograph of his favourite woman between his naked legs and created a fantasy in which he approached and penetrated her on the beach, all the while manipulating his penis until the inevitable release.[87] Masturbation was obviously much safer and cheaper than other ways of seeking pleasure. All that this sexual practice required was privacy (Rubin masturbated in his bedroom and the bathroom), a healthy imagination, a degree of skill, some sort of lotion or oil or even soap, and a visual aid. That last is what *Playboy* always supplied.

Hefner personally vetted the photographs of potential Playmates: a journalist in 1962 reported how he watched Hefner going through portfolios, muttering '"Too flat," or "Too big in the rear." The scene had all the warmth of a restaurant proprietor selecting sides of beef for his establishment.'[88] Perhaps so, but Hefner was always searching for the right look, the so-called girl-next-door, a vivacious person with a fresh and wholesome appearance, well-rounded and, usually, well-endowed, who did not look like a showgirl, a fashion model, or a femme fatale. Such an image appealed to his own taste in women. At least in the early years Hefner, his hand or his torso, his pipe, or a piece of his clothing, might actually appear in the picture, itself a cue that invited the male reader into the fantasy of the centrefold. To enhance the illusion of avail-ability, Playmates rarely had acknowledged boyfriends or husbands, even when they were in fact married.[89] Hefner, of course, became noto-rious for dating Playmates, and later the Playboy Bunnies of his clubs, living out the dreams he conjured up in the minds of his readers.

Consequently the best entry point to any *Playboy* were the pages devoted to the Playmate of the Month where in every issue some nubile, young body of a fresh female would be 'opened,' in that classic ritual of pornography. In December 1964 that was Jo Collins, identified as a nineteen-year-old 'aspiring film starlet' of simple tastes, a hard worker, ambitious but content. She was, of course, white: the first black Playmate did not arrive until ten years after the start of *Playboy*, and non-white bodies remained rare in its mix of erotica.[90] The feature included a series of photographs, one a close-up of her face, some showing her semi-naked, some clothed, playing on a roller coaster at Pacific Ocean Park. 'Jo's wide-eyed exuberance,' we are told, 'proves that she's "still just a kid at heart. On days when I model chic fashions, I can't wait to get home and jump into a pair of jeans."' The point was to build the illusion of a decent, ordinary woman, the kind a reader might meet, or rather might want to meet, at work or at play. A centrefold of three pages presented the whole body of Collins, clad only in an open, wet, man's dress shirt and elegant sandals, sporting a stiletto heel, her hand grasping the cloth in front of her genitals. The voyeur's gaze was directed first to her ample breasts, the nipples erect, excited, outlined beneath the wet shirt, then to her bared, tanned legs, spread slightly apart, displayed to accentuate their curves. She looked directly at the camera, or rather the observer, her head slightly down but her eyes sparkling and her smile bright, suggesting a willingness to play. It was a coy and inviting pose of a person proud of her body and aware of her allure, making her a sexual object both 'pliant and obedient,' to borrow the language of an earlier centrefold.[91] She was, however contradictory that might seem, both wanton and unspoiled – a good girl unveiled, a 'camera virgin' in the words of Gay Talese.[92] The description merely underlined her friendliness, and her availability. 'Sailboats – and the fellows who own them – are my weakness,' Jo confessed. 'But I'll settle for something less fancy, like surfing at Malibu: just as long as I'm near the water.' The tableau captured the '"seduction-is-imminent" look' that Hefner always wanted.[93] The formula had varied little over the years, at least since early 1955, although in the late 1950s the Playmates had usually showed less flesh than Ms Collins displayed.[94]

What Collins lacked were any flaws. There were no blemishes, no pimples, no unwanted hair, no unsightly fat, not really any pores, nothing to mar the picture. Critics of the Playmates made much of the fact that the pin-ups were airbrushed. They weren't real women.[95] But this was all a part of the process of streamlining, which worked to produce a body perfect for viewing. The aim was to capture an idealized version of a real body, something rendered tangible by the technology of colour photography and rendered sensual by the skill of the editors. 'The Playmates have always been rooted in a tradition of American "good girl" art,' Hefner argued in an interview much later. 'The pin-up photography of World War Two – the glamour girls, the movie stars, the Betty Grables: that's the origin of the Playmate centerfolds.'[96] The Playmate was yet another expression of the classical body: she was well-ordered, symmetrical, finished, smoothed, contained, a distinct and self-sufficient individual. But she was above all an object for the male voyeur, akin to the innumerable nudes that were so commonplace in the annals of European art. Collins's look, her bright eyes, her open smile, her erect nipples, her carefully positioned hand were as much a part of her dress as her clinging shirt and fashionable shoes.[97]

There were more visual delights in this edition, of course. One pictorial showed Carroll Baker, identified as 'Hollywood's hottest sexpot,' in an assortment of sensual poses, though the photographs (one excepted) hid as much as they revealed. 'Man at his Leisure' offered words, illustrations, and photographs of the women at the Paris Lido, on stage and off stage. That sort of fare was commonplace: earlier editions had taken readers to Chicago's Gaslight Club (November 1956) or allowed them to ogle the showgirls at Vegas (April 1958). A two-page spread was devoted to one of Alberto Vargas's pin-ups, a regular in Playboy, in this case showing a voluptuous redhead who had just removed her blouse to reveal enormous breasts, and now told a 'Mr. Dinkler: If we don't go to bed, Santa will never arrive.' But the most exciting feature was 'Readers' Choice,' a pictorial devoted to the ten favourite Playmates of Playboy's first decade. Each of the women received a page made up of three or more colour photographs, at least one of which displayed her breasts, usually from the side, occasionally on an angle, normally thrust forward. All but one of the women had large bosoms, the signature of that first generation of Playmates. Two of the women also bared well-rounded bottoms. None of the photos showed the vulva, however, which would not often appear in *Playboy* spreads until the so-called 'pubic wars' of the early 1970s when *Playboy* and the rival *Penthouse* battled for sensation and circulation. So the breasts had to bear the brunt of the voyeur's desire. A brief commentary told readers more about these women, emphasizing where possible their success or their joy since being featured as a Playmate of the Month.

The *Playboy* look sought to purify the sexy, to subtract the dirt but preserve the sensation, and thus to convert the pornography into the more acceptable erotica. A man might still 'sin' by reading *Playboy*, but he did not 'sin' too much. What was important as a kind of negative sign, especially in the first decade of publication, was what was usually absent: no total nudity, no coupling, no touching, certainly not the infamous 'money shot,' which would become a staple of hard-core porn. Nowhere was the bared or aroused male body on display, no lusty eyes or wet lips or groping hands, never mind an erection. These the reader's imagination had to supply. As the years passed, of course, Hefner and company pushed the envelope to ensure that the sex remained exciting at a time when erotic imagery was rapidly become much more common in public. The Playmate of May 1969, for example, adopted a more raunchy pose than her 'sisters' of the previous decade: standing in front of the camera, her prominent breasts fully exposed and her thumbs poised to pull down the bottom of her bathing suit – though her face still registered happiness rather than desire. Likewise the story in that issue about a new European film, *Camille 2000*, did feature glossy images of bondage, a whipping, lesbian sex play, and heterosexual intercourse, but always in surroundings that spoke of wealth and order – the film, so the review stated, was 'an erotic comment on the decadent trend of contemporary high society.' The images were reminiscent of those bacchanals of sex so esteemed in the world of porn. But the very elegance of the performance, supposedly drawn from the work of Alexandre Dumas, served to distance the stilted images of indulgence from that world.

This attribute signalled another method *Playboy* used so effectively to cleanse its sex: the magazine loudly announced both its elegance and its sophistication, notably in the 'Playbill' where the month's authors and offerings were touted, to make clear that it always spoke to the man who was a lot more than just his 'private parts.'[98] Hefner sought to attract quality fiction and intelligent commentary to balance the visual display of semi-nude women. In 1956 he hired Auguste Spectorsky, a noted author and cosmopolitan, first as an assistant and later as an associate publisher and editorial director, 'to bring a touch of class and New York urbanity to Playboy.'[99] The prosperity of Playboy enabled Spectorsky to offer much larger fees than normal to noted authors willing to publish their material alongside the naughty pictorials. One coup in 1957 was a story of a man obsessed with Picasso by the famed science-fiction writer Ray Bradbury and illustrated by none other than Picasso himself.[100] The December 1964 edition carried fiction by Lawrence Durrell, a 'soliloquy' from James Baldwin, some opinion by Bertrand Russell, and a lengthy interview with Ian Fleming. The attachment to literary celebrity gave Playboy status. It became a standing joke to claim, 'I buy it for the articles':[101] a joke because the centrefold always remained the key to circulation, but a 'joke' that also registered the success of the effort to identify Playboy as an upscale magazine that might be read because it provided so much food for thought. Besides, the presence of celebrity, like the label of art in the world of painting, rendered all the bosoms and bottoms more acceptable.

You might also read Playboy because it offered all kinds of sophisticated and spicy humour, yet another way of shedding the stigma of sleaze. In December 1964, the 'Ribald Classic,' a staple from the early days of the magazine when funds were low, was a tale of the deflowering of a virgin drawn from Hungarian folklore. Much newer were the ongoing travails of 'Little Annie Fanny,' clearly a takeoff on the famous Orphan Annie cartoon strip because the scrapes the Playboy gal was always getting into resulted in some man eventually ripping her top off to unleash her swollen breasts. Here was very definitely a kind of bawdy humour, reminiscent of what had long been commonplace in the pornographic repertoire. But most famous were always the Playboy jokes, especially the full-colour illustrated jokes, noted for their novelty and their wit. One never-ending source of mirth, for example, was the desire of old men for young women: a lascivious Santa locks the door to the boudoir of a scantily clad ingénue ('I understand you've been a bad little girl ...!'); two older men stare raptly at the huge bare breasts of a woman serving appetizers at a nudist party ('Either of you gentlemen care for something to nibble on?'). Hefner told an interviewer for Cosmopolitan (May 1966) that all this humour served to 'decontaminate' sex, necessary because it constituted 'the single biggest bugaboo, the most important taboo, in America.' 'Levity lets the fresh air and sunshine in,' where before all was dank and dark,' he said on another occasion.[102]

It was here that humour played its part in the first grand cause of *Playboy*, what Barbara Ehrenreich has called the 'male rebellion' against the togetherness and domesticity of the 1950s.[103] She argued that Hefner's enterprise exploited a growing desire among men to escape 'the bondage of breadwinning.' Not that *Playboy* opposed the work ethic. Indeed the magazine celebrated success in the worlds of business and the arts; but it urged men to play hard as well and to use their income to enjoy life. This was how Hefner inverted things, how he built a topsy-turvy world, in the realm of fantasy, where the disciplines of marriage, family, and home no longer served to restrain male desires.

In the first issue *Playboy* asserted that one purpose was to reclaim the indoors, celebrated as the domain of women, as a site of male pleasure: the home, better yet the apartment downtown, became the man's lair where he wined, dined, and seduced women. Wives, it seemed, were the enemy. Nearly half of the men who read *Playboy*, the magazine boasted (April 1958), were 'free men,' meaning single, 'and the other half are free in spirit only,' which telegraphed what the editors thought of marriage. The very first issue contained a polemic, entitled 'Miss Gold-Digger of 1953,' against alimony and the greedy wives who enslaved husbands, actual or ex, to ensure their security. The November 1956 edition featured 'The Abdicating Male,' an article by Philip Wylie, a popular writer noted for his denunciations of marriage and moms.[104] 'Why,' he wondered, 'have American men built a civilization for women, then sweated themselves into early graves to sell it to women, and finally willed their earnings to women?' The short answer was advertising, which suggested that American men had been betrayed by their own kind. That was followed by a bit of satire on 'Selecting Your Second Wife,' where readers were told to wear out the old one and then choose a newer model, youthful, softer, more curvaceous, and above all good-natured.

The spectre of the emasculating female continued to haunt the pages of *Playboy* even into the next decade, evident for example in Jules Feiffer's 'Hostileman,' a cartoon introduced in December 1964, which featured the adventures of a submissive male who could be transformed, when he uttered the magic word 'hurt,' into a superhero ready to defend a downtrodden mankind. Elsewhere in the same issue Hefner admitted that much of the success of *Playboy* came about because it had sought to reassert the masculinity of men in the face of an entrenched matriarchy.[105] Ironically, this admission came just before a new wave of feminism made a more compelling case against patriarchy, that power lay not with the mothers of the nation, or the wives who spent the money, but with the men who earned that money and occupied the seats of power in society.

By this time, however, the spirit of rebellion had found a new and in some ways much better target, not so obviously infected by misogyny, namely the whole structure of moral repression, or what was more often referred to as 'puritanism.' Here Hefner began to play out that role of sex radical envisioned by Wilhelm Reich. 'This society's traditional concept of sex is sick,' he told *Cosmopolitan* (May 1966). 'We've taken the fun out of it by making it either sacred or obscene.' His purpose was to liberate pleasure. 'I think that life can be a great adventure – something more than a vale of tears.' Hefner started writing a long – some critics thought interminable – column called 'The Playboy Philosophy' to proselytize America. He launched 'The Playboy Forum' where readers might write in to express their views on the matters raised in his editorials, particularly, so it seemed, to recount clashes with the police or churchmen or schoolteachers over moral issues. The magazine carried occasional features on the sexual revolution, such as a story on Denmark (October 1970) that cited statistics to show how sex crimes had dropped dramatically after the Danes eliminated all censorship. And the new Playboy Foundation actually provided funds to help some of the victims of puritanism with legal costs and the like, an action signalled to readers by letters of thanks.

The December 1964 instalment of 'The Playboy Philosophy' was especially revealing. It ostensibly focused on sex and religion, opening with a quotation from Alfred Kinsey, the patron saint of *Playboy*, followed by a few words about Christianity, and filled with an edited transcript of a debate broadcast on the radio that Hefner had had with three clerics. According to Hefner, the problem was not sexual behaviour but moral attitudes. The 'raw sex drive' could not be easily denied, else it would find expression in some other form dangerous to society: 'it is precisely because what is involved here is an attempt to control a natural instinct,' he warned, echoing the sentiments of 'the radical Freud,' 'that excessive sex suppression wreaks such havoc.'[106] Instead Hefner argued that sexual freedom allowed, even encouraged, the individual to seek and express his personal identity, serving the social good by countering the conformity and impersonality of contemporary life. Sex became, in short, one vital key to the persistence of a free society. All of which justified *Playboy*'s brand of negation, an opposition to censorship, to restrictions on sexual conduct, at least between consenting adults, and to the barrage of moral assertions that crippled the pursuit of pleasure.

During the course of this debate, Hefner went to great pains to argue both the merits of 'the playboy life' and the virtues of his magazine as its advocate. Almost 'everyone' could share some piece of this life because of the prosperity of postwar America, though Hefner's examples of 'everyone' were 'a successful business executive, a man of the arts, a college professor, an architect or an engineer,' in short, the haves in society. According to one survey, about half the readers of *Playboy* did earn more than $10,000 a year. The typical reader was around twenty-nine, lived in a big city, 'and drinks more, smokes more, and travels more than his fellow citizens.'[107] What defined the playboy was 'his point of view':

> He must see life not as a vale of tears [in a phrase Hefner obviously relished], but as a happy time: he must find pleasure in his work, without regarding it as the end and all of living; he should be an alert man, an aware man, a man of taste, a man sensitive to pleasure, who – without acquiring the stigma of the voluptuary or the dilettante – can live life to the hilt. That, we said, is the sort of man we mean when we use the word *playboy*.

The issue of December 1964 had a two-page section entitled 'On the Scene,' where three males who had earned some sort of acclaim were photographed and described. It even offered readers a self-image of a handsome, mature, and stylish person, dressed in a suit, very much the gentleman, engaged in some sort of activity, in this case choosing a perfume, and, naturally, the object of admiring glances from various women.[108] Here, in words and images, were representations of the self as hedonist, men who commanded themselves and their situation and so won the favour of beautiful women.

In fact readers were not always so assured or so secure, especially those who were adolescents and university students – fully a quarter of all the magazines were sold on college campuses.[109] *Playboy* was designed, consequently, as a kind of 'operating manual,' 'a tutor in manners and desires,' that might explain how to live the good life as a man.[110] 'Playboy after Hours,' an early and continuing feature, told readers where to go and what to see or read or listen to, as if these men were always in search of the right entertainment. A later addition, 'The Playboy Advisor,' answered readers' questions about sexual behaviour and social etiquette, how to dress, what to say, what to order at a restaurant, and on and on. Thomas Mario, the longtime food and drink editor, explained in many a lushly illustrated article just what to serve and how to prepare all kinds of delicacies when entertaining at home.[111] He made much of the adventure of cooking, how it required particular skills, thus emphasizing why this supposedly feminine art was suitable to the magazine's masculine hero.[112] Occasional articles identified the attire and the accoutrements necessary to be a winner – 'There's nothing so immediately revealing of class and caste as luggage,' argued one such piece.[113]

But, again, the most interesting features were the glossy, full-colour pictorials, displaying a range of branded goods, each briefly described, complete with price, and assembled to please the discriminating buyer. So, for example, one two-page ensemble of Christmas gifts (December 1964) included an 'earthenware cooking vessel,' a golf set and leather bag, a wooden butcher's block from France, an English wicker basket, a terry robe from Dunhill Tailors, a stereo system (pricey at $1,600), even a spectacular barometer, all posed together in a fashion reminiscent of the stylized portrayals of the Playmates. The consumer was positioned as a voyeur again. Not only did these presentations provide evidence of exactly what *Playboy* meant by the good life and good taste, they also worked to arouse desire in the reader, to provoke dreams of indulgence and luxury, dreams that could be realized so easily by acquiring just the right goods. Indeed by the 1960s *Playboy* had become one of the crucial agents bent on making the American male into as fervent a consumer as the woman. Just as Hefner had sought to masculinize the home, so his magazine worked to masculinize shopping as well.

The commodity displays fitted well with all the advertising that had been attracted by the success of the *Playboy* formula. Thirty per cent of the magazine (again December 1964) contained ads. Ford Mustang, Van Heusen shirts, J&B Scotch whisky, Winston cigarettes, and Chanel No. 5 perfume had all bought a full page. What was missing was also significant. There were no ads for hair restorers or diets, nothing that might remind the reader about his flaws or warn him of what he might lose. Nor were there any ads for stag films and other sleazy items that might shatter the illusion of a cleansed sexuality. The most prominent advertisers were the makers of alcohol, clothes, and, because of the season, perfumes – products designed, in short, to pleasure the body and enhance its appeal.

Some of the ads were specially prepared for *Playboy*. Budget Rent A Car offered a credit card as a 'status symbol for playboys.' Sony talked about 'Perfect Playmates,' referring to 'your record player' and its new tape recorder. Sultry or dreamy women of one sort or another graced the pages of some of the big ads. A Van Heusen page, the most sensual example, boasted the sharp image of a mature, handsome, and rugged man buttoning up his shirt over a hairy chest, a faint knowing smile on his face, this image superimposed on a much softer picture of an enlarged woman's face, who clearly admired the show: 'I love watching him get dressed in the morning ...' Everything Jack did, so the copy claimed, was 'exciting.' The ad went on to celebrate his – or was it the shirt's? – masculinity: 'Sass. Spirit. Red blood.' What made this spiel unusual was that the man, rather than the woman, was presented as the object of desire. Still this motif of male sex appeal and male self-assertion was also noticeable in ads for cosmetics such as By George ('a very persuasive fragrance for men'), Mark II (toiletries 'for the Male Animal'), and Brut for Men ('If you have any doubts about yourself, try something else'). Old Spice After Shave Lotion simply attached the rouge imprint of a woman's lips to its bottle.

These were not the only kinds of messages. A two-page, black-and-white spread for Goodyear Tires showed NASCAR racers in action: here was competition and excitement aplenty. Viceroy cigarettes placed its two smokers in a different kind of adventure, off by a lake somewhere, hunting ducks. The ads for whisky, bourbon, or Scotch, by contrast, suggested class and style: White & McKay's, for instance, set its tableau of an older man and a younger attractive woman against the background of a jazz trio. Even Schlitz advertised the exclusivity of its beer by drawing attention to the five special employees who had a key to the 'yeast room,' an obvious reference to Playboy's own key clubs. Sylvania claimed 'a flair for elegance' with a set of stereo components that performed so well it was 'like putting a handle on Carnegie Hall.' Much of the advertising, in other words, suited the *Playboy* milieu because the messages evoked the different identities of the playboy: the male as satyr, as adventurer, as gentleman, and as connoisseur.

A report in *Business Week* (28 June 1969) made abundantly clear how the attitudes of advertisers and agencies had changed towards *Playboy*. 'Ten years ago,' claimed a media buyer for J. Walter Thompson, then the world's largest agency, 'none of our clients would have dared use

Playboy. Today it's a routine buy.' According to a colleague at Young and Rubicam, *Playboy* 'is one of the easiest books to sell our client,' referring specifically to Goodyear Tires. But perhaps the media director at Wells, Rich, Greene, one of the new, hotshot agencies of the decade, put it best. 'The book delivers what it promises: millions of men between 18 and 34. It gets them with an editorial formula that suits the young man of today. God help us.' It was even better than television, reaching more of this audience than the hit comedy *Laugh-In* and the regular NFL football games, both considered male pleasers.

Hefner had managed to make *Playboy* almost respectable: one critic, a college activist, proclaimed it was 'practically the voice of the establishment.'[114] Yet the magazine nonetheless retained the allure of transgression – it was still a tool of masturbation, its centrefold something a heterosexual male could use to arouse and even satisfy his libido. So it provided an excellent environment to market all manner of goods: here was a site where an advertiser might expect readers were already aroused, as it were, where their desire could be channelled into the purchase of some part of the so-called playboy lifestyle. One lust begat another?

The success could not last. The profits of the over-extended Playboy empire sagged in the mid-1970s. Even after some cost cutting, when the famous 'Big Bunny,' Hefner's own personal DC-9, was sold off, profits fell once again in the early 1980s, especially following the loss of his British casinos due to infractions of the gaming laws. The last company-owned Playboy Clubs closed in 1986. No doubt part of the trouble had to do with the management of the business. But the environment as well was changing. Witness what happened to the flagship enterprise: the circulation of *Playboy* slowly decayed, reaching 3.4 million in 1985.[115] Put the company's decline down to too much competition, whether that meant the challenge of more explicit magazines such as *Penthouse* and *Hustler*, or the boom in porn films and eventually videos, or the spread of new sites and forms of male entertainment. In a way Hefner, a pioneer of the Eros project, was also its victim, though of course he retained his millions plus a scaled-down version of his once swollen empire.

4 Fetish Barbie

The small collection of bizarre photographs was tucked away in a corner of one of the rooms in Barcelona's Museu de l'Eròtica. The pictures displayed a series of dolls, some in bondage, either dressed to expose their breasts and their genitals or garbed in rubber and masks. One of the figures was presented as a nun, albeit sporting a white miniskirt, who pushed up her ample breasts, both topped by prominent rouged nipples and surrounded by a tight-fitting habit. The only attribution attached to this collection was the name 'Carmen' and the brand 'Bar-bitch.' The reference, obviously, was to Mattel's famous Barbie doll.

Such pornographic caricatures were not at all uncommon. One artist had turned Barbie into the replica of Edouard Manet's bold woman, the one who had so notoriously challenged the male gaze, featured in his classic nineteenth-century painting *Olympia*.[116] *Urban Desires*, an online magazine in the mid-nineties, offered a series of stylish and glossy photographs of Barbie engaged in erotic play.[117] Adult collectors fashioned displays that showed Barbie indulging in lesbian fun, or put her into orgies, or locked her up in a pleasure dungeon where she could enjoy the erotic thrills of sado-masochism. The many strange things people did and do to Barbie was revealed in a documentary called *Barbie Nation* made by El Rio Productions in 1998. Not that this pleased Mattel, Barbie's maker, which threatened and even sued some of the purveyors of degraded and 'perverted' images. But the pornography of Barbie was a sign of just how popular the doll and her friends and family had become by the end of the twentieth century: it was esti-mated that Mattel had sold roughly 1 billion dolls since releasing the first Barbie back in 1959. Barbie had become an icon, familiar through-out much of the world, and an icon not just of childhood but recog-nized by all generations, which made her an attractive target for imaginative souls bent on seeking publicity and presenting sex.

The pornographic imagery was also a sign of an attribute of Barbie that Mattel had never admitted, namely her status as a sexual fetish designed to win the hearts of American girls. This attribute reached back to the origins of Barbie. Legend has it that the key person, Barbie's 'mother,' so to speak, was Ruth Handler, then a co-owner and the man-ager of Mattel, a small but successful toymaker. She had noted that her daughter (named Barbara, whence came Barbie) loved to play for hours with paper dolls and cut-out fashions. Handler thought, and rightly so, that there was a market for a three-dimensional fashion doll because in America most dolls were babies or infants that did not allow such play. On a trip to Switzerland she spotted an adult-sized doll in a store win-dow. She brought this doll back to the Mattel's male designers, whom she persuaded, over some resistance, to develop what became Barbie.[118]

The prototype, however, was a German sex toy, representing an imagined femme fatale, glamorous and sexy, meant not for children but for men. Lilli, as she was called, had been born on the pages of the racy tabloid *Bild Zeitung* in 1952 as a cartoon figure noted for her good looks, loose morals, and expensive tastes. She was turned into a doll in 1955, offered in two sizes (eleven and a half inches and seven inches), and sold to men in bars and the like as a novelty, a car ornament, perhaps a joke gift for their girlfriends. Lilli boasted blonde hair, big eyes, a distinctive pout, painted earrings and red lips, large breasts, long legs, and high heels or laced-up boots. She looked very much like one of those Nordic 'ice maidens' often featured in the world of pornography. Over the years she acquired a variety of exotic and fashionable costumes, fancy hats, a swing, even her own poodle. No wonder she was promoted as a symbol of joyful and illicit sex.[119]

If never so overtly wanton, Barbie shared a lot with her older German sister. The faces of the first Barbies had a sultry look, 'bitchy with pouted lips and an icy stare,'[120] though that did not last because Mattel soon sought to attach an air of innocence and eventually of friendliness – the Malibu Barbies of the early seventies even sported a half-smile. The new 'Barbie Look,' to borrow an ad slogan, suggested an idealized version of the all-American, teenage beauty queen. Always Barbie had lustrous hair, in a variety of colours, and different styles, that gave the doll a special, sensual feel. The most striking similarity was in the body, however. Barbie, too, was eleven and a half inches tall. She was made of hard plastic, smooth to the touch: in other words she came streamlined. She boasted the style of the classical body: elongated, an extended neck, a tiny waist, extremely long and slim legs, arched feet, no pores, and no openings of any kind (not even the hint of a navel). She had jutting breasts but no nipples, broad shoulders but narrow hips, well-rounded buttocks but no genitals. Barbie's breasts, of course, broke with the classical pattern: her protruding bosom suggested a creature of appetites, at least in the context of the 1950s. Had she been translated to human size, her 'vital measurements' were variously estimated at an impossible 39-21-33, perhaps 40-18-32, and thus lacking sufficient 'body fat to menstruate regularly,' according to one acerbic critic.[121] This body did not change, even when the new 'Twist 'n Turn' version appeared in 1967: Barbie got eyelashes and a rotating waist but retained her curves. Barbie was one shapely doll whose sexiness was a consequence of an implausible anatomy, a fact that never prevented her from becoming a model and a metaphor of femininity in the United States and elsewhere.[122]

Mattel argued that this anatomy enabled Barbie to wear clothes that looked stylish, a crucial attribute since Mattel planned that the purchase of Barbie would lead consumers to buy a whole range of accessories. The doll always was, above all, a platform for marvellous clothes. When introduced she cost three dollars, two dollars less than the price of her 'Wedding Day' ensemble. Many of the fashions were drawn from the haute couture of Europe, the styles of Dior or Balenciaga, elegant and elaborate and glamorous. If you did let her into your home, the *Nation* (27 April 1964) warned parents, you might find yourself spending $150 to dress her. And that was only the beginning. Barbie herself was joined by boyfriend Ken (1961),[123] an exceptionally bland doll, lacking much sex appeal (really a eunuch, though he did have a slight 'bump' at the crotch);[124] a girl friend called Midge (1963), considered definitely lesser; and Ken's more sexy friend Allan and Barbie's younger sister Skipper (both in 1964). All of these dolls had outfits: according to the *Saturday Evening Post* (12 December 1964), there were '54 different costumes for Barbie and Midge, 36 for Ken and Allan, and 10 for Skipper – which is 100 right there, or roughly $200 worth.' Besides, the obliging parent could buy a dream house, a barbecue kit and a baby-sitting kit, a college campus, and a fashion shop. Then there was a Barbie record and Barbie stories, a special game, a magazine, even a Barbie line of clothes for real girls. Buying Barbie also meant buying into an ever-expanding world of commodities.

The task of selling Barbie posed some difficulties. Mothers, who were most likely to get the toy for their daughters, felt uneasy about a doll with breasts, especially a doll that was also obviously erotic. A preliminary six-month study carried out by Ernest Dichter in 1958 revealed this liability.[125] Dichter discovered, not surprisingly, that girls loved the doll, particularly because of her looks. He also learned that mothers found her sexuality much too blatant, also because of her looks. 'I call them "daddy dolls" – they are so sexy,' exclaimed one mother, a comment that harked back to the persisting shadow of Lilli.[126] Upset by this sexiness, or so the legend goes, the Sears buyer actually refused to take Barbie for the company's catalogue when she debuted at a New York toy fair in 1959.[127] Much later a woman recalled how her mother had eventually baulked at the prospect of buying a Barbie, even though she had taken her daughter down to the store to buy the toy. '"I couldn't buy that Barbie doll for my three year old," I heard Mom tell Grandma on the phone, "– why, that girl has a ... a ... a ... full bust!"'[128] Another woman mused about a similar reluctance on the part of her mother: 'I feel that she had an innate sense of Barbie as being somehow illicit, an object that should be kept out of our home if at all possible.' So she was given instead Barbie's sister, Skipper, 'a less-threatening, presexual version of Barbie.'[129] Barbie, in short, was inherently dangerous, a view that reflected the sexual unease of the late fifties and early sixties, and likely (or so some women thought) to undermine the moral order of the home.

One way around this dilemma, Dichter claimed, was to advertise Barbie as a toy that would encourage good grooming. Mothers could be persuaded that Barbie would help refine a problematic daughter, perhaps making her an attractive product in the marketplace of romance that she must eventually enter. In sum, Dichter cleverly reversed his normal line, showing how the brand could be imagined as a teaching toy, so that its intrinsic erotic appeal was masked, at least from the mothers who would buy the doll.

Mattel used television to reach girls directly to create an excitement that would overwhelm the reluctance of parents.[130] The company mounted what was later remembered as 'the most intensive (and expensive) TV promotional campaign in doll history.'[131] A list of Mattel's ad expenditures revealed how it concentrated on network television, buying $1.3 million of time in 1960, or more than half of what the whole toy industry spent.[132] When the girls and their mothers reached the stores, they discovered that Mattel had also arranged special displays at retail counters, a colour catalogue of fashions, even a diorama of the dressed dolls on a turntable, all to show the assorted costumes to best effect. (An additional reason for such colourful displays was to offset the liability of black-and-white television, which could never show the sensual quality of fashion effectively.) The response was astonishing. Mattel's revenues doubled in the first two years of the doll.[133] Barbie magazine, started in 1961, had roughly 100,000 subscribers four years later.[134] A commercial inviting girls to join a Barbie Fan Club produced an extraordinary response, far beyond what was expected or normal.[135] Barbie became a bigger celebrity than most movie stars, and Mattel received on average 10,000 letters a week addressed to the doll.[136] By 1965 the company blanketed all the networks with 'wall-to-wall daytime and night-time television commercials,' purportedly at a cost of $12 million.[137] The Barbie Fan Club had around a million members by 1966.[138] A survey of girls the same year revealed that more than nine out of ten recognized the Barbie name.[139] By 1969 Mattel was the largest toymaker in the United States, chiefly because of Barbie sales. Altogether, Mattel's innovations revolution-ized the practice of selling toys to children, because they revealed how television advertising could pre-sell children before their mothers entered the toy store.

The messages television conveyed were carefully crafted to provoke desire and avoid offence, and they were tested on child audiences to ensure their impact. Mattel fashioned a rhetoric of unending possibilities to seduce the girls of America. Barbie was presented as if she were an actual person who lived in a child's fantasy of adolescence. The commercials often featured enthusiastic girls admiring Barbie or playing Barbies or yearning for her clothes, treating her as an older companion. Consider this snippet from an early ad: 'Someday I'm gonna be exactly like you, till then ... Barbie, beautiful Barbie, I'll make believe that I am you.' Children learned little about her from television, though a bit more if they wrote to Mattel or read the Barbie books:[140] she might go to school, though she had no obvious parents; she was called a teenager, but she often dressed and looked much older. The idea was to enhance her play value not to restrict the imagination of her owner, allowing girls to make up their own roles and narratives.[141] Barbie might be identified as a 'career girl,' at first a teenage fashion model, later a nurse or stewardess, and even briefly an astronaut (in 1965!). But she did not work, and certainly she did not do housework or produce children; indeed, according to one commentator, Barbie was 'an early rebel from the domesticity that dominated the lives of baby-boom mothers.'[142] Instead she met friends, went to fashion shows, visited the beach, travelled around the world (one ad put her in the Olympics), and seemed to party incessantly. She lived, in short, in a kind of teenage utopia.

But Barbie had to pay a high price for this life of leisure. Mattel overtly suppressed her sexuality. Those threatening breasts were always fully covered, even when she was shown in the standard swimsuit that came with the basic model of the doll. Not until a 'Living Barbie' ad of 1970 did she reveal any cleavage. Sex became glamour: one of the introductory ads focused attention on all the beautiful garments Barbie might wear to a party or a ball or night-club to impress onlookers. Publicly Mattel liked to boast, as Dichter had suggested, that parents loved Barbie because she was an educational toy that taught girls the virtues of good grooming.[143] Sex was translated into romance: in a 1961 ad, at a fateful dance, Barbie and Ken embarked on their long journey together, and though Mattel suggested they just might end up married, the relationship was never consummated – in Mattel's advertising anyway. Mostly sex was transformed into a different kind of lust. Barbie was always surrounded by beautiful things: shoes, gowns, cars, a house. Two girls ogled the wide selection of clothes Mattel made for Barbie in a commercial about a fashion show. When asked, 'Which ones would you like?,' the inevitable reply was 'All of them.' A woman who owned the doll in the sixties still marvelled over the quality and the design of Barbie's original wardrobe. 'The clothes lust they triggered in my brain has never subsided, and like my mother, I am an avid sale shopper.'[144] When 'Talking Barbie' arrived, one of the first things she asked, according to the ad, was, naturally, 'Would you like to go shopping?' Barbie, in short, was a victim of sublimation, her sex drive converted into a desire to consume.

Years later Barbie almost achieved a sexual release, of sorts, in a television commercial made to promote a Norwegian soft drink called Solo. The parody opened when a girl exited her playroom suddenly because of a storm, leaving the 'Ken' and 'Barbie' clones seated at a table in a doll's house. Ken noticed how the vigour of the storm had spilled a drop of her drink onto her chest, which then slowly rolled down between her swelling breasts – the camera supplied the close-up shot. That sparked desire: he pushed 'Barbie' against the wall and, to her surprise, began to strip off her clothes. The music was now loud, raunchy. 'Barbie' got into the right spirit and stripped off her top. 'Ken' cleaned off the table. 'Barbie' lay back on the table, her legs up and apart. 'Ken' took down his pants and then ... he discovered he had nothing but a bulge. Swiftly he put back on his pants and shrugged. On screen came the message: 'The only soft drink that cures nothing but thirst. Solo.' 'Barbie' was left on her back, her legs apart, her desire still unconsummated.[145]

It was up to the girls, the people who consumed Barbie and her meanings, to free her sexuality.[146] Indeed that act of recuperation was intrinsic to the appeal of Barbie because it released her potential as a toy that enabled owners to explore the erotic. The initial wave of Barbie owners were likely pre-teens, say between eight and twelve years old, although swiftly the potential market expanded to include much younger children.[147] Understandably, these pre-teens were intrigued by the mysteries of sex. The evidence that girls liberated Barbie comes from their recollections later on as mature women reflecting on the experiences of playing Barbie – not the most reliable source of information since memory can be so easily tainted by invention. Yet report after report suggests that one of the first things girls did to a Barbie was to take off her clothes and fondle her body, especially her breasts. 'We weren't interested in any other part of the anatomy but Barbie's breasts,' exclaimed one woman. 'They were perfect. None of us had ever seen perfect breasts.'[148] 'Wow! I could hardly wait to have a pair of my very own,' remembered another.[149] Some girls enhanced Barbie's sexuality: one obsessive owner would paint nipples on her doll, using a red magic marker, only to rub them off, and paint them back on again.[150] Others posed their naked Barbies, like a *Playboy* centrefold. Even more admitted to playing sex with Barbie and Ken and the rest of the crew, sometimes co-opting a brother's G.I. Joe, the macho action figure introduced by Hasbro in 1964, to spice up the erotic games. By age twelve, Joyce Maynard claims, she had dreamed up 'thrillingly bizarre punishments in which Barbie was chained to her bed, or made to go naked.'[151] Heterosexuality and homosexuality, intimacy and orgy, bondage and even torture, all sorts of sex were enacted in the privacy of bedrooms and playrooms. Sometimes the toy failed, of course: upset by an incident at school, where all the other girls were white 'Barbies,' one black girl destroyed her Barbie, dragging its head on the stairs till that popped off, then tearing off each limb, leaving only the torso intact.[152] Less dramatic but more common was the loss of the supernatural quality that made Barbie so compelling: many girls simply left behind their Barbies after reaching puberty and becoming teenagers, finding other means and other tools to explore or sample the pleasures of sexuality.

The case of Barbie pointed to the inherent power of television commercials as a vehicle of culture and a means of persuasion. More than other forms of advertising, the commercial could perform much like the dreams that Freud had charted so many years before.[153] That was because commercials could talk and show: they offered packages of moving images, sounds, and music that were intrinsically more exciting to a wider range of individuals than the static pictures of print or the sightless messages of radio. The Barbie stories were condensed and edited collections of an assortment of images, compiled into apparently coherent narratives that embodied the fulfilment of wishes. Like Freud's dreams, they were full of symbolic content, especially suggestions of sex, always illicit because the target audience was children. The ads too had a 'manifest' and a 'latent' content, a style of organization that masked some of their meanings – call that their subversive intent – to evade the veto of a censor, which in the case of the Barbie stories constituted the prevailing standards of morality at home and in society. Informing the public was only part of their purpose, since they were obviously designed to awaken desire in the hearts and minds of viewers, to make girls fantasize about growing up sexy. Instead of being messages from the unconscious, as Freud had labelled dreams, however, the television commercials were messages to the psyche. Indeed it was the girls who were expected to retrieve the 'latent' content, to recognize and to use the sexiness of Barbie. The sales and the success of Barbie suggest that this is exactly what many of the girls of America did.

There is a well-known irony about Barbie: ideologies have stuck to her body better than her own clothes.[154] Advocates of the New Left began the attack on the Barbie craze: 'Both boys and girls are introduced to a precocious, joyless sexuality, to fantasies of seduction and to conspicuous consumption' – this from a director of a mental health unit, cited in a muckraking article in *Ramparts*.[155] Especially after 1980, when Barbie's popularity actually increased, critics of all sorts lamented Barbie's influence on a whole generation of American girls. She was blamed, for example, for encouraging a deep-seated anxiety about body image: 'Barbie's basic problem – her bland homogeneity of feature and anatomy – reinforces the American epidemic of unnecessary face lifts, tummy tucks, breast reduction surgery, breast augmentation surgery, as well as anorexia, bulimia, and diet fanaticism.'[156] So Barbie had made all women want to be streamlined? Feminists worried that playing Barbies trained girls to exhibit their bodies, not their brains.[157] 'Her posture showed us that being sexual meant being immobile,' asserted Naomi Wolfe. 'It meant: walk on your toes, bust out, limbs rigid.'[158] Some women decided to take direct action against so sexist a toy. According to the *Economist* (5 February 1994), the so-called 'Barbie Liberation Organization bought Barbies and swapped their female voice boxes for those from G.I. Joe ... before replacing both toys on shop shelves. The returned Barbies spit phrases such as "Eat lead, Cobra."' Anti-racists feared that Barbie's whiteness contributed to the social and personal difficulties that African-American girls had growing up non-white. 'She is an icon – perhaps the icon – of true white womanhood and femininity,' fumed Ann Ducille, 'a symbol of the far from innocent ideological stuff of which the (Miss) American dream and other mystiques of race and gender are made.'[159] Lesbians charged Barbie with privileging the straight world. Child experts thought Barbie had programmed play and corrupted the imagination of girls.[160] Critics of all stripes, naturally, condemned Barbie the shopper who taught girls that the chief meaning of life was to consume and possess. So Barbie emerged as the tool of authority, an especially clever instrument of class, race, and gender domination that transformed girls into subordinated women: Barbie, it seemed, was no less than an agent of hegemony.

There was certainly some merit to the assorted charges, especially the complaint about Barbie's obsession with commodities. But the litany of damnation fails to comprehend how Barbie assumed, particularly in the early years when sexual repression was so common, the character of a fetish. By one definition the fetish is an uncanny object that enables its possessor to negotiate differences and solve contradictions.[161] It works as a surrogate or substitute, in this case for sexual activity, enjoying some of the attributes of the phallus. According to Freud, what makes a fetish is a mix of expectation, absence, and fear, all of which were present in the interaction of doll and owner.[162] The girl hoped for the perfect bodies that neither she nor her mom had (those firm and dangerous breasts again); she imagined a sexual life obscured by adult prohibitions but suggested in movies and books; and she feared what might happen, how she might never be beautiful, not have sex, never be a proper woman. Barbie as fetish could work wonders to relieve that stress and to experiment with what sex might involve, away from the prying eyes of parents, always in a realm of make-believe. This Barbie exercised power. Witness the comment from another breed of feminist: 'Our Barbies had jobs and sex lives and friends. We weren't staring at their plastic figures and Dynel tresses hoping to someday attain their pneumatic measurements.'[163] Even Wolfe admitted to 'doing bad things to Barbie.'[164] Indeed many boys, gay and straight, had fun playing sex with Barbie.[165] What was so important was the discovery of a sinful pleasure in performing some erotic game. Fetish Barbie, the doll Mattel made but never named, the object the girls fashioned and used, was very much an agent of 'wicked' play.

There is, however, an intriguing footnote to this story. Over forty years after the initial release of the doll came 'Palm Beach Barbie.' Why she stood out was because she was 'Always Dressed.' Her two-piece swimsuit was painted on her body. 'Many young children tend to take off a doll's clothes without putting them back on,' commented one observer. 'This can result in a house full of naked dolls or a child dragging around a naked doll, which can be quite embarrassing and unsightly.'[166] Indeed – but why introduce such a line now? To please parents, to suit a demand, to meet some prudish criticism? Or, put another way, it raises the question of why Barbie was not so bounded in the beginning, why Mattel did not submit to the moral rumblings of the fifties by covering those dangerous breasts in some painted outfit? The introduction of the new line seemed a betrayal of the initial design, which had emphasized how Barbie was a toy intended to encourage girls to fantasize freely. Only time will tell, when the new generation of users grows up, whether we will have reminiscences of how girls scratched the paint off their 'Always Dressed' Barbies.

5 The Imagery of Pop Art

In 1956 the British artist Richard Hamilton produced a collage of images depicting the inside of a modern home as a poster advertising an exhibition called 'This Is Tomorrow.' Although not displayed in its own right until later, that work, entitled *Just what is it that makes today's homes so different, so appealing?*, was soon designated a classic of early pop art, constantly reproduced in art surveys and the like, especially studies of advertising.[167] For 'publicity' was one answer to the question that Hamilton had posed. Another answer, however, might well have been eroticism, since his depiction of domestic space was clearly influenced by the growing emphasis on the display of sex.

In *Collected Words* Hamilton recalled that the collage was assembled according to a particular script dictating the 'interests' that had to appear: man and woman, humanity and history, newspapers and cinema, naturally television, household appliances, cars, comics, and, though this seemed a trifle strange, space as well.[168] There were a lot of oddities here: a traditional portrait of an unhappy Victorian hanging on a wall, a tumultuous carpet underfoot, and a glowering planet as ceiling.[169] Featured as well were an assortment of commonplace objects, one of the distinctive markers of pop art: a can of ham and a vacuum cleaner with a very long hose (signifying convenience?), a tape player and a television set and a huge cover of a comic book hanging on a wall (signifying easy leisure?), plus some tacky furniture (a sign of mass production).

But the focus of attention was on two oversexed bodies, carefully posed to display their physical attributes. The muscular husband, clad only in white underpants, stood in the foreground, just off the centre of the collage, looking very much like a Charles Atlas clone, 'the world's most perfectly developed man.'[170] Atlas had won fame through a con-

stant stream of American comic-book ads showing how he, once a piti-
ful ninety-seven pound weakling, had been converted into a sexy and
potent lover, able to wow the girls and crush rivals, because of a special
course of physical training now available to every anxious young man.
'Atlas' looked strange in Hamilton's tableau because he carried a strategically placed and gigantic Tootsie Pop, both his club and his phallus,
signifying his virility and infancy. By contrast the buxom young wife
was naked, lounging on a sofa, her eyes closed, her lips pouted, one
hand behind her head, on which was perched what looked like a hair-
dryer, the other hand seeming to hold, and to offer, a large breast to
whomever was watching. Even more bizarre were her huge nipples,
painted or possibly enamelled to accentuate the lust of the onlooker.
These two specimens, in short, were commodities, designed for sexual
pleasure, surrounded by other commodities, by the words and images
of a media-saturated environment, while in the background was a
corporate insignia, the Ford emblem as a lampshade. This collage
expressed one slightly ironic response to the hype, the materialism, the
excitement, and the eroticism of a mass culture made in the United
States.

Although pop art may first have appeared in Great Britain, it became
the dominant art movement in the late 1950s and early 1960s in the
United States because that was the centre of affluence and communications in the world. There, a collection of young men turned away from
the abstraction and the individuality valued previously to reproduce
found images as art. They appropriated pictures and styles, the more
ordinary the better, from advertising, news, and entertainment, the
very sources that daily bombarded the public with signs and signals.
From the mid-1950s Jasper Johns and Robert Rauschenberg deified the
simple artefacts of life, whether the American flag or the Coca-Cola bottle. Roy Lichtenstein copied typical scenes, albeit much enlarged, from
the comics, using the same techniques of presentation to render an
authentic representation. James Rosenquist, once a painter of billboards, juxtaposed images of jeans, a car, a hot dog, President Kennedy,
whatever was prevalent, to produce strange assemblages that suggested some kind of weird conjunction of objects. Claes Oldenburg
came to specialize in huge sculptures, some hard, some soft, of ham-
burgers, telephones, and so on. The most famous of them all, Andy
Warhol, a one-time ad designer, employed mass-production techniques
to fashion works full of repeated, ubiquitous images, dollar bills,
Campbell's Soup cans, and the like. The critics by and large loathed pop

art, rightly seeing the work as a reaction against prevailing aesthetic standards, most especially the previous moment of abstract expressionism. But dealers, collectors, journalists, the managers of galleries, and the public marvelled, and enough of them clearly loved the results to make pop art very profitable.

Not surprisingly the exploration of the new eroticism was a staple of pop art, inside and outside the United States. Hamilton himself had identified 'sexy' and 'glamorous,' plus 'mass produced' and 'big business,' as leading characteristics of the new art.[171] Warhol, for one, admitted to a lifelong addiction to pornography, 'the really dirty, exciting stuff,' and he was fascinated with the widespread phenomenon of voyeurism.[172] Like so many artists before, so too with American pop artists: theirs was a gendered vision. They were fixated on the look of the female body, rarely probing the sexiness of masculinity (with the notable exception of some treatments of male stars such as James Dean and Elvis Presley). Hamilton's work was unusual in this regard because it drew such an explicit equation between the lush figure of the woman and the muscular shape of the man. But otherwise pop art diverged from the well-established European tradition of the nude because the purpose was not just to fashion yet another variety of erotica, a succession of beautiful and available young women designed to please the eye of the male voyeur. Indeed their pictures sometimes lacked any overt sexiness. Rather they amounted to comments on what had happened to eroticism in the modern world of brands.

The art works exposed, better yet emphasized, two aspects of the new imagescape. First, they captured the prevalence of the streamlined body, a body designed according to a kind of 'machine aesthetic,' a body smoothed so it lacked flaws like wrinkles or pimples or even pores, styled and glamorized so it lost 'the idiosyncrasies of character,' and thus perfected so it embodied some male and heterosexual ideal of beauty.[173] Second, they highlighted the libidinal assemblages constructed by the linkage of these bodies, or parts of the bodies, to objects, especially branded commodities, sometimes in situations that suggested consumption.[174]

Each of the artists played the voyeur in a different way, however. Hamilton produced some of the most sensuous images in later years, say *Hers is a lush situation* (1957), which melded the forms of driver and car, or *Pin-up* (1961), in which the almost liquid shape of a woman, full of curves, marked by full breasts, held out a finally detailed bra. Lichtenstein stuck to comic-book-style blondes, their faces flattened and simplified, involved in some romantic upheaval (as in *Engagement Ring*

1961 or *Hopeless* 1963). Oldenburg fashioned giant phallic symbols in the form of huge lipsticks, inflatable as well as solid, one actually fixed on tank treads (*Lipstick, Ascending, on Caterpillar Tracks*, 1969), that suggested how one common object was endowed with erotic power. His notebooks contained a British ad, dated 1965, in which a young woman was clasped to the top of a giant lipstick.[175] Rosenquist linked cars, sex, and food in collages denoting the promise of satisfaction such as *I Love You with My Ford* and *Lanai*, both from 1964. The latter featured a Buick Skylark, shiny and new, flanked on one side by glistening canned peaches and on the other by a shapely nude woman, also luminous, kneeling over the side of a swimming pool – commodities all? Tom Wesselmann embarked on an extended series called the *Great American Nude*, borrowing from the style of Matisse, to produce spare images of naked and nearly faceless women, whose sensual body parts, notably lips and nipples, sometimes a bared vulva, were enhanced, the way ads highlighted the special attributes of their brands. These he might surround with other objects, such as a television set or a telephone, ice cream or Coca-Cola, a radiator or a sofa.

Rosenquist, Wesselmann, and in particular Warhol were all intrigued by the place of celebrity in America. Andy Warhol manufactured a striking assemblage of images of the face of Marilyn Monroe, using a publicity photograph shorn of detail and presented in different colours, sometimes in heightened, sometimes in smudged shades, an allusion (so one historian has put it) 'to the painted faces of Hollywood.'[176] *Marilyn Diptych* (1962), as Warhol titled the assemblage, spoke of the bombardment of the American public by the slightly changing images of popular icons. One separate reproduction of her face from 1964 (simply called *Marilyn*) was reminiscent of Barbie: Warhol used glossy, rich colours, notably blonde and pink, to transform Monroe's face into that of a doll. She had been rendered as the epitome of beauty, the consequence of mass publicity.[177]

Mel Ramos, a west coast painter born in 1935, drew the most direct connection between sex and consumption. His work was also the most consistently sensual of all the pop artists. He began in the early 1960s to play with the genre of pin-ups, and in 1965 developed his own signature that mixed blatant images of female nudes with an assortment of branded goods, cigarettes, drinks, fruit, candy bars, toothpaste, and on and on. His nudes were hard-edged, full-coloured, unmarred, perfect creatures, the attention focused on a smiling face, abundant hair, large breasts, and lots of curves. These sirens mimicked poses common in girlie magazines. The scenarios were humorous, perhaps an ironic statement on the vulgarity of lust, whether for the body or for the brand. That product was invariably enlarged, giving it a status equal to the nude. The woman might be found lounging behind a huge Coca-Cola bottle, resting on a Hunt's Catsup bottle, hugging a life-sized AC battery, emerging from a Milky Way or Babe Ruth chocolate bar, even embracing a giant package of Life Savers – in each case the product had a definite phallic character. You could take such pictures as mockery of the claims of the vigour and virility of branded goods. Then again, the woman might be seated on a pack of Vantage or Kent cigarettes, looking out expectantly to the missing viewer; bent over the wheel of a Firestone tire, her untanned bottom and breasts on display; emerging out of an empty can of Valvoline Motor Oil, her large breasts hanging down to one side; or perched inside a Coca-Cola emblem, here her ample buttocks, shapely back, and a cascade of blonde hair the source of visual pleasure. Each of these pictures linked the brand to the male, heterosexual dream of an available playgirl. Some like *Chiquita* (1964), *Miss Fruit Salad* (1965), or *Babe Ruth* (1965) emphasized the prospect of consuming the girl with the brand. Other titles suggested advertising slogans, such as *You Like It, It Likes You* (7–Up), *Lucky Lulu Blonde* (Lucky Strike), or *The Pause That Refreshes* (Coca-Cola).

The blatant sexuality of his work overwhelmed the ironic message: Ramos was labelled an erotic painter, hence the appearance of his work in Hamburg's Erotic Art Museum and on innumerable websites devoted to erotica of one form or other. But that designation was not the full story: for Ramos had carried the technique of the erotic sell into the realm of the absurd, well beyond the boundaries of good taste, something admakers always tried to avoid, exaggerating the link between the sexy and the brand to the point where the fabrication was patently obvious and sometimes offensive. It was all supposed to demonstrate how artificial, calculated, and shallow were these desiring machines, according to one of his apologists.[178]

In fact, like all of the pop artists, you never could be sure whether Ramos's imagery was meant to be ironic or accepting. These men were not critics of what they had found, and often their personal responses seemed ambiguous or ambivalent.[179] Had they not betrayed the traditions of fine art, certainly of that avant-garde where art always challenged the bourgeois dominion? Pop art was a bit like Dada without the bite, a kind of banal anti-art that was more an adjunct of advertising. The artists were consummate voyeurs who had produced works that embodied the practices and effects of the Eros project.

4 Signs of Angst

Advertising had boomed in the 1950s and 1960s in the United States. Total billings went from $1.3 billion in 1950 to $10.6 billion twenty years later.[1] The boom was driven in part by the spread of television (by 1960 television reached 87.1 per cent of all homes), which swiftly proved the best medium for delivering ads. It was also fuelled by a 'youthquake' (around 57 per cent of the population was under the age of thirty in 1960, roughly one in five made up of teens and youth), which expanded the market for all sorts of goods.[2] But the reputation of advertising was poor. Indeed, on the eve of the boom, Frederic Wakeman published the hit novel *The Hucksters* (1946), which depicted advertising as immoral and manipulative. Stephen Fox has pointed out that this set the tone for a series of novels on the industry and the profession that were written through the forties and fifties.[3] Seemingly, as Fox noted, this minor genre reflected public doubts about the worth and veracity of advertising, or so the occasional poll indicated. That was the reason Vance Packard struck gold when he published his famous *The Hidden Persuaders* in 1957.

The abiding suspicion of advertising was the foundation for an increasing upset over the regime of stimulation that I will explore by analysing a few key texts. The signs of this upset emerged around the mid-century in the first major work of Marshall McLuhan. McLuhan, perhaps, was too much a pioneer since his arguments were largely neglected by the public and the academy until after he won fame for his later books on the media. In the late sixties and in the seventies, after the erotic sell had proved its success, a group of foreign and domestic critics – Jean Baudrillard, Wilson Bryan Key, and Jean Kilbourne – resurrected the attack, although in very different ways. Like McLuhan, whose work was now considered a classic of the genre of cultural criticism, each of these critiques (though Key's was the least appropriate, even if one of the most popular) offered insights into the character of the new regime, both its mechanisms and its effects. Besides, they gave voice and focus to a wider stream of public concern over the consequences of the marriage of Mammon and Eros.

1 *The Mechanical Bride* (1951)

'Ours is the first age in which thousands of the best trained individual minds have made it a full-time business to get inside the collective public mind. To get inside in order to manipulate, exploit, control is the object now. And to generate heat not light is the intention. To keep everybody in the helpless state engendered by prolonged mental rutting is the effect of many ads and much entertainment alike.'[4] Here was the erotic metaphor at work, meaning the application of the language of sex to characterize or explain personal and social phenomena. That paragraph was the opening blast in *The Mechanical Bride*, the first book written by Marshall McLuhan (1911–80), originally published in 1951, in which he assessed the mass culture of America.

The book was not a great success in its day.[5] It appeared well before McLuhan had become a media guru, when he was just another upset highbrow who hammered away at the words and images manufactured by Madison Avenue and Hollywood – in other words, part of a general uprising of literary intellectuals in North America against the presence and power of mass culture. The reviewer at the *New York Times* (21 October 1951) told him to lighten up, to drop some of his 'righteous anger,' and recognize how funny much of advertising really was.[6] McLuhan himself came close to repudiating the book a few years later after he had begun to develop his own philosophy of communications.[7]

In fact *The Mechanical Bride* was a witty, perceptive, and original work in its own right. Nor was it without a sense of humour, since McLuhan did recognize the ironies of 'adspeak,' although his amusement was always shadowed by his conviction that a crisis of the soul afflicted North American life. The book had been years in the making. McLuhan was an English professor, already labelled a bit odd, who after 1946 taught at St Michael's College, a Catholic university associated with the University of Toronto.[8] One sign of his oddness was a passion for collecting all sorts of ephemera – ads, comics and cartoons, front pages, and occasional photographs – which he used to illustrate talks he gave about the debauched culture of the times. *The Mechanical Bride* was a printed version of his slide and lecture performances.[9] Although the manuscript began as a huge box of examples plus hundreds of pages of text, it was much edited and eventually published as a large-format book of 157 pages, composed of fifty-nine separate essays, about the same number of reprinted illustrations, these mostly ads, and a series of small quips and commands in the form of questions to provoke the reader that appeared at the beginning of each of the short chapters. It had a brief preface but not a conclusion because the book had no single, overt hypothesis – supposedly. In the preface McLuhan adopted the pose of the detached observer who said that he wished to place the reader at the centre of the 'whirling phantasmagoria' (v) concocted by newspapers, movies, radio, and publicity, so that people might understand their plight, and how things worked, in order to design their own strategies to bring salvation.[10] Each of the chapters used its example to probe some aspect of culture or character – how an ad for an iron displayed the American obsession with 'know-how,' for instance; and the essay often became a delirium of imaginative, intriguing, and occasionally silly speculation backed up with a dazzling (and not always appropriate) array of quotations and citations from all sorts of twentieth-century novelists and writers. McLuhan did alert readers to the fact that all he wrote was just 'provisional,' his concepts valuable 'in the grip they provide' to comprehend life (vi). But it was hard to take such a claim seriously. In reality McLuhan's distaste for mass culture, excepting Al Capp and his Li'l Abner cartoon strip, was all too clear, as the reviewer of the *New York Times* pointed out. McLuhan had tried to mask his polemic in the guise of a dispassionate inquiry.

Although he never cited the good doctor (Siegfried Giedion and Margaret Mead were his declared guides), he was actually replaying Freud: McLuhan had set out to psychoanalyse America, putting its popular culture on the couch. He talked of 'a sort of collective dream' (v) and of 'a wish-fulfillment on a huge scale' (50), both of which were manifest in the kinds of examples he presented to his readers. He peppered his accounts with terms and phrases drawn from the language of psychology, such as 'sado-masochist' (10), 'the human ego' (33), 'anal-erotic obsession' (62), 'a phallic relationship' and 'a deep psychic wound' (84), the 'unconscious' (97), 'a narcissistic quality' (99). He made reference to penis envy. He cited the views of Wilhelm Reich. But most telling was McLuhan's fascination with sex, or rather with the ways in which sex was represented and manipulated in the media. Everywhere in the visual surround he found 'a dominant pattern composed of sex and technology,' commonly associated with 'images of hectic speed, mayhem, violence and sudden death' (98), an unholy mix that marked the death of sex as it once was, or at least that signified a mechanized brand of sex previously unknown to humanity. The focus on sex and death, and especially the convergence of these drives, placed *The Mechanical Bride* firmly within the Freudian universe.

The book might seem on first reading an instance of conspiracy theory. Like most of the highbrow breed, McLuhan regarded commerce as the modern ogre, responsible for all manner of social and moral ills. 'For the first time in history,' he lamented, 'there exists an unofficial program of public instruction carried on by commerce through the press, radio, movies' (43) variously seeking 'to stimulate a constant readiness to discard habits and possessions alike' (112) and 'to release the unconscious pressures and desires of the mind' (90). Elsewhere he referred to this as 'the mechanism of mass delirium and collective irrationalism' (144) because it sought to bypass the rational faculties of the public. Note the worry about the fate of reason, a sure sign of his commitment to that rival of Eros, the empire of logic.

McLuhan assigned an important place to entertainment – comics, movies, radio sitcoms – and to celebrity, as associates, secondary villains if you like, in the campaign to debauch humanity. He also made reference to the role of fashion, for men as well as women, as a tool of discipline that encouraged the constant turnover of goods. But he laid the blame for the doleful state of the American imagination chiefly on the shoulders of admakers. They produced a never-ending stream of messages to 'wallop the subconscious' of people (10): that is, they worked to impose their dreams on the minds of the unwary. 'The ad agencies flood the daytime world of conscious purpose and control with erotic imagery from the night world in order to drown, by suggestion, all sales resistance' (97). They targeted both sexes, usually in different ways: women were programmed, taught how to behave and how to look, while men were seduced, promised an experience. The most obvious offenders were the messages promoting products for the care and clothing of the body, though McLuhan also singled out ads for Buick, Kodak, Coke, and Ivory Flakes as vehicles of the erotic sell, evidence of how far the virus had spread.

What made the harangue intriguing was McLuhan's explanation of the design of this erotic sell. The admakers, he was convinced, had deployed the aesthetic innovations championed by the 'Moderns' – the poet/critic Baudelaire, the artist Picasso, a poet such as Mallarmé, novelists like James Joyce and Scott Fitzgerald, even a mathematician and philosopher like A.N. Whitehead – all of whom (and more) were mentioned in the text of *The Mechanical Bride*. Perhaps the copywriters or layout men had never actually studied these 'Moderns,' though McLuhan neither affirmed nor denied that possibility. Certainly the agency creatives had responded to the same kinds of cultural trends first discovered by the avant-garde. McLuhan was especially taken with the way admakers had employed complex symbols that overflowed with contradictory meanings. So he wrote about the wholesome but sexual Coca-Cola girl, who fed the oral obsessions of America, and the popularity of the drum majorette, a 'goose-stepping combination of military mechanism and jack-booted eroticism' (121).

The most striking example of this imitation of the avant-garde was a 1947 ad for Berkshire nylons that McLuhan assessed under the heading 'Woman in a Mirror,' apparently an allusion to Picasso's painting *Woman at a Mirror* (1934). The crucial figures were a rearing stallion, a symbol of 'raging animality,' placed in the background and facing a stylish young woman, whom McLuhan called 'classical,' leaning against a post, her face turned outward, looking beyond the ad tableau towards some unseen object. The two figures were joined by the word 'palomino,' which thrust out from the stallion's rear legs toward the woman's bottom. The ostensible purpose of the word was to describe the colour of the nylons. But the actual purpose was to suggest the 'brutal violation' of a woman who was 'gentle, refined, aloof, and innocent' (82). According to McLuhan, this juxtaposition debased the technique Picasso had used to produce 'a single image of great intensity' in his painting. As to the ad, 'the opposition of the cool elements' – which he termed, a bit mysteriously, 'phallic and ambrosial' – triggered a set of responses, the equivalent of a 'chain reaction,' in the psyche of the beholder (80). There was a grudging admiration for such artistry here, enough that Jonathan Miller, a later commentator, found disturbing because it seemed to celebrate skill rather than to critique intent.[11] In any case this imaginative reading did not really explain why a woman intent on buying nylons might find the ad persuasive, indeed why she might not find the hidden message repulsive. Unless, that is, one accepted the notion à la Freud that ads, like dreams, could evade the censorship of the superego and so excite the libido.

Much the same caveat applied to McLuhan's next foray, entitled

'Husband's Choice,' which probed the style of car ads, using a 1949 ad for a Buick Roadmaster designed to capture the fancy of a male buyer. McLuhan noted in passing the convention of linking the picture of a beautiful woman to the glistening image of a new automobile. But he was interested in something more complex. The Buick ad did not feature any woman, though it did offer the shiny convertible parked outside a house of obvious refinement, the car boasting a shark-like grill and a streamlined splendour that suggested speed and power and excitement. McLuhan was equally taken with the copy of the ad: first the title, 'Ready, Willing – and Waiting,' then the pledge of a 'Dynaflow Drive,' 'quiet-voice life,' 'satiny smoothness,' 'big billowy tires,' and 'under its bonnet, 150 Fireball horsepower wait the touch of a toe ...' (84). One might easily translate the 'smoothness' into a reference to soft skin, the 'tires' into ample breasts, and the 'horsepower' into a waiting passion. This time the juxtaposition, the contrast of image and words, had produced a paradox, an apparently impossible mix: the car was represented both as 'a womb symbol' and 'a phallic power symbol,' thus appealing to the masculine psyche in two very different ways. The promise of Mother and Lover? Once again, unfortunately, McLuhan never addressed the issue of response, why the unconscious would respond to such a cluster of meanings. That was one of the signal weaknesses of his overall investigation: he had simply presumed the existence of a Freudian unconscious, never explaining how these complicated and contradictory symbols worked their magic. Still, McLuhan had 'discovered' the emerging grammar of the new eroticism, a grammar that was both visual and verbal: the juxtaposition of images, the deployment of contrasts and associations, the use of symbols and stereotypes, the practice of innuendo, word play, and allusions.

McLuhan did try to show how the Buick ad manifested a deeper paradox often present in publicity, the way it so readily fused sex and technology: 'The body as a living machine is now correlative with cars as vibrant and attractive organisms' (84). No wonder one of his opening quips to the reader was to ask whether the automobile, perhaps most especially a muscle car like this Buick, had 'taken up the burden of sex in an increasingly neuter world?' (82). That exemplified the prevailing creed of advertising, though McLuhan preferred the term 'myth': the mechanization of sex, something he explored everywhere and at considerable length in two linked essays, 'Love-Goddess Assembly Line' and 'The Mechanical Bride.' In the world of publicity women were transformed into standardized and processed machines – 'Maxfactorized, streamlined, synthetic blondes' (96) – whose legs, hair, lips, look, walk, and so on, were all objects that commodities might enhance to engender the sexual excitement of male victims. Men were made into superhumans (or maybe subhumans) of toughness, the results of '"scientific" muscle-building' and '"scientific" character-building' (143) or of wearing the right clothes, obedient to 'The Law of the Jungle' (122) where the most brutal was also the most effective. In this world sex was less about affection and more about power, the sexual experience reduced 'to a problem in mechanics and hygiene' (99). McLuhan found plenty of signs of 'sex weariness and sex sluggishness' (99) engendered by all the ad campaigns. The admakers and their associates worked to reanimate the passions of sex by associating eroticism with danger or violence à la the Marquis de Sade. Indeed, McLuhan feared that the ideology had awakened unnatural appetites among more and more people: a hunger for thrills, for novelty, an unending desire for sensations that would offset the prevailing emphasis upon conformity – these encouraged a new kind of sadism, a 'cult of violence' (99). At the core of publicity, and of mass culture in general, McLuhan had discerned something very sinister: 'the widely occurring cluster image of sex, technology, and death which constitutes the mystery of the mechanical bride' (101). Put another way, McLuhan had perceived how advertising exploited the appeal of transgression, and he worried that it must therefore encourage 'perversion' (including, as he put it, a bit obliquely, 'the case for homosexuality' [99]).

In the end, McLuhan qualified his own polemic. The conspiracy, it turned out, was not the root cause of the sexual blight. The ad agencies were only responding to the popular mood. Their success was the result of their particular skill, the ability to plumb the psyche of consumers. They gave 'spatial form to hidden impulse,' expressing 'for the collective society that which dreams and uncensored behavior do in individuals' (97). Which meant that the culture had sponsored the very imagery cursing the popular imagination. It could not be otherwise because no culture would nourish myths that were 'alien to its dominant impulses and aspirations' (96). So the amalgam of sex and technology was 'born of a hungry curiosity to explore and enlarge the domain of sex by mechanical technique, on the one hand, and, on the other, to *possess* machines in a sexually gratifying way' (94). In short, McLuhan had recognized that the Eros project was rooted in the particular nature of a self moulded by the ethos and the practices of modernity. A clampdown on advertising was no solution. Recognition was.

Which brings us back to McLuhan's announced purpose, to reveal hidden truths in order that individuals might fashion their own course of action. In passing, though, he did suggest a strategy of salvation. One way out of the trap, he mused, was via the liberating power of 'wild laughter,' sufficient to shatter the illusions of the man and woman as love machines. Why? Because the 'person who thinks, works, or dreams himself into the role of a machine is as funny an object as the world provides' (100).

2 *The System of Objects* (1968)

As the 1960s closed, there was a new wave of interest among Left intellectuals in Europe in the formidable capacity of capitalism to order the life of everyone in the affluent West. Some of the resulting commentary drew upon the tradition of Freudo-Marxism, although now its proponents (like the chastened Marcuse of 1966) were much more pessimistic about the prospects of liberation. *Le Système des objets*, written by Jean Baudrillard (1929–2007) and first published in 1968, stood out from the rest of the studies because the book constituted the most sophisticated and extended investigation of how the regime of stimulation operated, especially the crucial role played by advertising in conditioning the public psyche and the governing culture.[12]

Verso published an English translation of *The System of Objects* in 1996, at a time when Baudrillard was famous as one of the most prolific and interesting explorers of the postmodern condition.[13] The cover art of this edition was particularly fitting: a reproduction of James Rosenquist's pop classic, *I Love You with My Ford* (1961). The painting confronted the viewer with three separate images: the front end of a Ford, a close-up of canned spaghetti, and, sandwiched between these, another close-up of an erotic scene, this of a woman's face pressed against the side of a man's face, her lips near his ear. As usual, such a tableau might provoke a number of different readings. But on the cover of this book it suggested the equivalence of all three images as representations of desirable objects, and it signalled the eroticization of ordinary products. The picture had captured two of the themes of Baudrillard's work.

In 1968 Baudrillard had just begun teaching sociology at Nanterres in France. *The System of Objects* followed in the footsteps of Roland Barthes, who authored *The Fashion System* (1967), which would become a classic in the field of semiotics. Baudrillard had set out to classify all the possible categories of objects as well as to explore the import of ideology, especially of advertising: this was a kind of cultural critique, and a very earnest one, unlike his later writings where he could play the comic. His chief subject was the nature and importance of the commodity in contemporary life. He was then a Marxist of sorts, though much influenced by the views of Freud and Saussure, both of whom had become very trendy in intellectual circles in Paris during the 1960s. The uneasy mix of conflicting theories was one reason the arguments in the book appeared inconsistent and even contradictory. The other reason was Baudrillard's own style of expression: already he showed a liking for aphorisms, all sorts of binaries, and opaque, if bold, declarations that made his arguments both striking and puzzling. Whatever its flaws, however, *The System of Objects* was an imaginative work, full of insight about matters trivial or significant in the make-up of the consumer society.

Among much else, the book constituted a response to the philosophy laid out earlier by Ernest Dichter. Dichter was cited in a number of places, though only *The Strategy of Desire* was mentioned, which suggests that Baudrillard was not aware of the even more revealing *Handbook of Consumer Motivations*. Where Dichter was a great champion of American business, Baudrillard was equally the critic of American and any other form of capitalism. Baudrillard included an actual example of Dichter's musings where he had proclaimed the need to promote a new hedonism so that America could progress.[14] That provoked a nice outburst, with Baudrillard mixing Freud and Marx, about how Dichter's way meant giving consumers only the freedom to act irrationally, to regress, to become like children, all in the interests of 'a specific social organization of production' (186). This was neither hedonism nor liberation but a new form of slavery, a shoring up of authority figures – re-establishing the strength of 'the images of the Father and the Mother' – that would exercise a strict control over the behaviour of the consumers who were its victims (187). The Oedipus complex had returned in a new form to discipline humanity.

Still, Dichter and Baudrillard shared a common intellectual heritage: they accepted Freud's understanding of the psyche, including his fascination with the sex drive. Most important, like Dichter, Baudrillard ascribed an erotic significance to ordinary objects, that significance evident in fantasy, or what he called 'the discourse of the unconscious' (60). Throughout, Baudrillard sprinkled such phrases as a 'phallic order' and a 'faecal order' (29), 'fetishized objects' (79), 'symbolic castration' (89), possession as 'perversion' (99), and 'a libidinal instrumentality' (117) in his discussions of the various categories of objects. His most extended example was the imagining of the automobile:

> Think of the 'erotic' significance of the car and of speed: by lifting social taboos and at the same time releasing us from immediate responsibility, the mobility of the car removes a whole set of resistances concerning ourselves and others: dynamism, brio, infatuation, daring – all flow from the freedom of the driver's situation, a situation which also fosters the erotic relationship by bringing into play a dual narcissistic projection onto a single phallic object (the car) or a single objectified phallic function (speed). The eroticism of the car is therefore not that of an active sexual approach but, rather, the passive eroticism of narcissistic seductiveness in both partners, or of a shared narcissistic communing in the same object. The erotic significance of the object here plays the same role as the image (real or mental) in masturbation. (68)

He specifically doubted the wisdom of admakers' efforts to feminize the automobile because fantasy had demonstrated that the car was 'experienced – and by everyone, men, women and children – as a phallus, as an object of manipulation, care, and fascination' (69). You could not argue with the unconscious, apparently.

Not that Baudrillard doubted the importance of advertising in modern culture. The victory of technology, it seemed, had destroyed a traditional phallic symbolism rooted in the actual use of handheld tools, even encouraging a kind of passionless sexuality. No order could survive without a symbolic foundation, however, and advertising had soon moved to fill the resulting void. He was particularly taken by the capacity of advertising to gender any object, making the commodity a woman ready 'to be bought,' 'the woman-object being the advertising world's most effective persuasive device and social myth' (69). But Baudrillard did not subscribe to the common view that advertising had the capacity to sell any kind of good to anyone. Indeed, he thought that the welter of ads led consumers to doubt the specific virtues of one brand or another. That discount, however, did not operate at the level of ideology: advertising confirmed a way of life organized around the seductions of consumption and the realities of capitalism. Whatever our proclivities, whether we avoided or noticed an ad, we now lived in a world of constant stimulation where advertising always had abundance on display. The generality of advertising worked to sexualize the very act of consumption in a way that smacked of the peep show:

By virtue of advertising, too, the product exposes itself to our view and invites us to handle it; it is, in fact, eroticized – not just because of the explicitly sexual themes evoked but also because the purchase itself, simple appropriation, is transformed into a manoeuvre, a scenario, a complicated dance which endows a purely practical transaction with all the traits of amorous dalliance: advances, rivalry, obscenity, flirtation, prostitution – even irony. The mechanics of buying (which is already libidinally charged) gives way to a complete eroticization of choosing and spending. (172–3)

Such was the modern brand of carnival – soulless and empty, established everywhere in the lands of affluence, but most especially in America – that Baudrillard feared was the future for humanity. Neither escape nor resistance was possible in this kind of erotic encounter.

The advertisement had become, in its own right, an object of consumption. It had won acceptance – no-one really wanted to do away with advertising – because it satisfied a need to feel looked after, cared for, and it provided an opportunity to play, to daydream, something Baudrillard thought lacking in modern life. That last observation was a crucial insight into why people paid attention to ads. Baudrillard went one step farther, drawing an analogy between the dream and the advertisement and emphasizing that both had 'an essential regulatory function':

Like the dream, advertising defines and redirects an imaginary potentiality. Like the dream's, its practical character is strictly subjective and individual. And, like the dream, advertising is devoid of all negativity and relativity: with never a sign too many nor a sign too few, it is essentially superlative and totally immanent in nature. Our night-time dreams are uncaptioned, whereas the one that we live in our waking hours via the city's hoardings, in our newspapers and on our screens, is covered with captions, with multiple subtitling. Both, however, weave the most colourful of narratives from the most impoverished of raw materials, and just as the function of nocturnal dreams is to protect sleep, so likewise the prestige of advertising and consumption serves to ensure the spontaneous absorption of ambient social values and the regression of the individual into a social consensus. (173)

The ad appeared to satisfy desire while actually managing desire: its hidden purpose was not so much to sell a brand, which was no more than a 'cover' (166) to mask the really important job, namely to promote the social order. 'True, we do not buy potato crisps *just because* they are connoted by a woman with blonde hair and a sexy bottom,' Baudrillard declared. 'What is certain, though, is that the brief moment when the libido is thus mobilized by an image offers a sufficient opportunity for society as an agency of control to invade us in its entirety, complete with its customary armamentarium, namely the mechanisms of repression, sublimation and transference' (180).

Advertising worked according to a Freudian script. Baudrillard tried to explain just how the ad disciplined the psyche in a short, closely reasoned discussion of the complex agency of advertising. Ads took on the character of a fantasy, as Freud had defined that term, except that here the fantasy was planned by an external authority. The advertisement itself was a closed text, the image impoverished and any words disciplined to ensure that all the signs were carefully orchestrated to produce a directed reading. It offered the promise of satisfaction, gratifying a desire, but it evaded reality, more properly absented what was real, inevitably leading to eventual frustration, a frustration that was essential to perpetuate the work of ideology. The single ad operated first through a process of deception, focusing on the brand rather than the product, to encourage desire and to invest that desire in the possession of the celebrated object, which was immediately, and perhaps often eventually, impossible for consumers unless they had a lot of disposable cash. In the process the individual was hailed as a consumer, given an identity as a passive kind of citizen whose chief task was to choose from the offer of goods. What the deception produced was 'dashed hopes: unfinished actions, continual initiatives followed by continual abandonments thereof, false dawnings of objects, false dawnings of desires' (176–7). One could never gratify this desire, most especially because one ad led not to a purchase but to another ad. 'In actuality, the sheer profusion of images works at the same time to counter any shift in the direction of reality, subtly to fuel feelings of guilt by means of continual frustration, and to arrest consciousness at the level of a phantasy of satisfaction' (177). The constant awakening and repression of desire dazzled and overwhelmed the bemused consumers, who found themselves always enticed but never satisfied by the spectacle of abundance, their attention and desire constantly focused on a succession of brands. They were caught up in 'a continual mental orgy, but one which is stage-managed, a controlled regression in which all perversity is resolved in favour of order' (178). Advertising naturalized the plethora of goods, excluded any kind of criticism, evaded social reality, and thereby legitimated the social order. Or, as Baudrillard concluded, it served to 'activate the repressive reality principle at the very heart of the pleasure principle' (178).

Whatever the merit of that last sinister comment, Baudrillard's overall explanation had captured one of the defining properties of the erotic sell: sexual desire was always deferred and redirected in the world of consumption; or rather, that was the intent. An ad awakened the voyeur's libido but only to excite the lust for a commodity. The very images that might provoke the libido were meant to tease, never to satisfy, consumers. They were normally presented with attractive or elegant, and usually young, persons as objects of desire imagined in some sort of erotic drama that promised extraordinary pleasure. But the consumers were also distanced from this drama, watchers not participants. The narrative climaxed with the celebration of the product, shifting the object of desire from a sexy body to a sexy brand. How this process worked was, or rather would be, most obvious in the case of television commercials, where the narrative could be elaborated and performed, though it was apparent in other forms of publicity as well. Even here, however, the signals of eroticism might always be appropriated and transformed into a tool of play by consumers uninterested in the brand or the magazine or the movie. Which is why Baudrillard's final comment presupposed a level of success that business might dream of but could never realize.

3 *Subliminal Seduction* (1973)

Wilson Bryan Key (1925–) made the discovery of his life while teaching at the University of Western Ontario in 1970. Then a professor of journalism, he was lecturing to his class about an article in the magazine *Esquire*. 'I happened to walk around the desk,' he remembered, 'and looked at the illustration for the article upside down. "Wow!" I thought. "Who put that there?" It was a phallus on a bookshelf! That was the first one.' This, at least, was the story he told a journalist writing in *Forbes* twenty years later.[15]

That moment of epiphany proved extraordinarily profitable. Key went in search of more signs, and he found all manner of sexual references embedded in advertisements: phallic and vaginal symbols, words like SEX or FUCK, images of orgies, adultery, bestiality, or fellatio. During the next two decades he published four books detailing his discoveries, selling by various estimates well over a million copies.[16]

Although Key soon left the university, his books remained behind, even appearing on course reading lists where students might learn from the new master. He went on the lecture circuit and performed on television to please audiences ready to be scandalized by the immoral doings of admakers. In the process he made the whole notion of 'subliminal seduction,' the title of his first book, immensely popular and more than a bit frightening.[17] The Federal Communications Commission in 1974 actually warned stations that knowingly broadcasting an ad spiked with subliminals was 'contrary to the public interest.'[18] Although neither academic researchers nor ad executives were impressed with his arguments or his proof, the public was: one survey published in 1983 found that around 80 per cent of respondents knew about subliminal advertising, most believing it was effective, a level of acceptance that persisted in later surveys.[19] Key and the spectre of subliminal seduction just would not disappear. 'He's figured out a way to make large sums of money using his imagination,' admitted one slightly envious professor. 'I kind of wish I thought of it 20 years ago.'[20]

Subliminal Seduction, the most successful of his works, earned its notoriety because Key detailed how advertising agencies sought to program the unconscious of consumers.[21] One crucial selling point was the inclusion of sixteen pages of photographs that seemed to demonstrate the ubiquity and the style of subliminals. That enabled readers, as it were, to see for themselves: in short, to engage in a new kind of parlour game – to discover the sexual 'embeds' not only in his samples but then in ads on television or in their magazines. Another reason the book caught on was its reworking of the old notion of a conspiracy – the leitmotif was invisibility, the claim that a secret cabal of corporate sponsors and their admakers were delivering hidden, powerful, and immoral messages that victimized Americans – this at a time when the public doubted the wisdom and the practices of all sorts of elites.

No less important was the way in which Key dressed his work in the robes of science. The book jacket noted his PhD degree and his wide experience teaching in a variety of North American universities. He referred to various authorities in the book itself, sometimes attaching a footnote. He devoted considerable space to a potted survey of theory, especially theories of the mind, leaving the impression that he was an expert on psychology. He recounted assorted experiments he had carried out to demonstrate the responses of students to subliminals, though never in sufficient detail to allow an independent evaluation of the rigour of these experiments. Best of all, his book opened with an introduction by Marshall McLuhan, by now very much a popular star, who thus extended his reputation as a novel thinker to Key's work.[22]

In some ways Key was an acolyte of McLuhan. He had attended McLuhan's famous seminars at the University of Toronto where the prophet expounded on the significance of communications as well as the future of society. He repeated some of McLuhan's axioms about the media in his own work. His style of presentation was reminiscent of McLuhan's grand proclamations, except that Key lacked McLuhan's skill with words – much of *Subliminal Seduction* was pedestrian. But the most telling sign of McLuhan's influence was Key's extension of the propositions about a conspiracy of elites evident in *The Mechanical Bride*. Where McLuhan had been so excited by the way Madison Avenue and Hollywood constructed paradoxical symbols that were apparent to the eye, Key focused on the words and images hidden in ads – that is, subliminals that could not be consciously perceived. Beginning roughly thirty years before, according to Key, 'every major advertising agency in North America' plus 'the FBI and the CIA' had sponsored research studies on the phenomenon of subliminal perception (180). All sorts of authorities, including the political parties, had come to use sexual 'embeds' to condition the public mind. This had happened apparently unnoticed by social scientists, something Key clearly regarded as suspicious, evidence of a conspiracy of silence. Likewise, newspapers and broadcasters had failed to blow the whistle, further proof of how the gospel of profit, of selling, dominated the practices of journalism. The main villain was, nonetheless, the advertising industry. 'Every major advertising agency has at least one embedding technician in its art department,' he declared. 'The technique is taught in most commercial art schools' (109). Nowhere did he supply an affidavit, a testimonial from some renegade admaker that might demonstrate the accuracy of such a bold claim, not even an incriminating document or an overheard comment to prove that embedding was even an occasional practice, never mind a common practice.

What Key did supply, and in large doses, were examples of this assault upon the psyches of Americans. One of the best of these appeared early in his account, a close reading of an ad for Gilbey's London Dry Gin (reprinted in the book), initially published on the inside back cover of *Time* (apparently on 5 July 1971). The ad looked fairly innocuous: a photograph of a sparkling bottle, open, its cap lying on a shiny surface, next to a tall glass filled with ice, tonic, and gin. Key directed his readers to see the faint outline of the word 'SEX' spelled out

in the ice cubes. (And, yes, if you look closely you can 'see' the word.)
That was just the beginning. He also found some faces, voyeurs apparently, in these same ice cubes, as well as some reflections that could well
be 'a man's legs and partially erect genitals.' The melting ice on the bottle suggested seminal fluid. Yet another reflection 'could be interpreted
as lips – vaginal lips, of course.' There was even more imagery, if you
looked hard. But Key had made his point: the 'subliminal promise to
anyone buying Gilbey's gin is simply a good old-fashioned sexual
orgy' (7). Elsewhere in the book he discovered a promise of adultery in
a Seagram's ad for whisky, a *Playboy* cover that replayed the Oedipal
drama (the nursing mom and the castrating dad), phallic symbols and
death symbols – a skull, scorpions, three wolf faces – in an ad for Cal-
vert's whisky, how the *Vogue* woman was actually a 'symbolic hermaphrodite,' a polar bear (or perhaps a dog) embracing a nude woman
for Sprite, a woman (briefly!) sucking the surrogate of a male penis in a
television commercial, images of masturbation in two cigarette ads.
Plus, always, hidden words that spoke of sex: in a later work he even
claimed that Nabisco embedded the word 'SEX' on Ritz crackers – 'SEX
Can Also Be Crunchy.'[23] Key certainly had an active imagination. In
fact he had adopted the voyeur's gaze, and with a vengeance: everywhere he looked in the ad world he saw something that signalled
graphic, often illicit, sex. His ability to eroticize the commonplace was
not new. Salvador Dalí had been able to look at ordinary things, as he
recalled in his autobiography, and see the most bizarre and often
emphatically erotic figures and scenes. But Dalí created art. Key produced dogma.

Time and again Key repeated that people never noticed these subliminals unless guided by a knowledgeable observer. So, for example,
he explained how he had tested the responses of more than a thousand
men and women to the Gilbey's ad. Many – 62 per cent, in fact – had
admitted feelings of arousal or excitement. But none had been aware of
the subliminals. In various places he outlined how the reader must
relax, adopt a trance-like state, and search these ads until the mind did
perceive what was so well hidden. The fact that virtually no one could
spy the subliminals was actually proof of their potency. Like McLuhan,
Key was ready to ascribe awesome power to the mass media. The subliminals were a major reason why people bought products, apparently.
'Ice cubes likely sell more alcohol for the distilling industry than attractive models in cheesecake poses,' he declared. 'The inconspicuous ice
cubes often hide the invisible sell – invisible, that is, to the conscious

mind' (96). The presence of all these subliminals, he feared, might be making people mad and encouraging 'perversion.' They certainly encouraged the over-indulgence of Americans, itself a sin in a world of scarcity and starvation – Key, briefly, took on the pose of a moral critic. But, above all, subliminal advertising represented an invasion, a brand of pollution, a rape of the inner mind that had to be exposed to enable Americans to defend themselves against further manipulation.

Such alarms raised a question. How could something invisible have any effect upon the behaviour of Americans? Here Key was beholden to his second mentor, Sigmund Freud. You could find traces of Freud and Jung in a variety of places in *Subliminal Seduction*. Both theorists had made much of the role of symbols in the psyches and culture of humanity: there was, for instance, a discussion of 'archetypal symbolism' (à la Jung?) in a dissection of the meaning of an orange in a Seagram's ad for gin (61). But the most important borrowing was Freud's idea of the dynamic unconscious. Key treated the unconscious as a separate entity – another person in our heads, as it were, who had an extraordinary capacity to capture information that the conscious self either avoided or repressed. He deemed repression the single most important defence mechanism because it blinded the conscious eye to what was shameful or fearful, an argument that reflected Freud's own emphasis on the importance of repression in the construction of the psyche.[24] But Key went a step farther to assert the ability of the unconscious to perceive all. One glance was sufficient to imprint a subliminal on the unconscious, even if the image or the word were upside down or blurred. And this unconscious was always lecherous, always alert to some 'dirty' sign the media might send its way. Indeed not only did the unconscious find the phallic symbol or the embedded 'SEX,' it stored these fragments, if not forever then certainly for a long time, in some gigantic database that linked together desire, provocation, and the brand, where they might trigger action at a much later date. Key clearly worked with the model of hypnosis in mind, and he asserted that the embed acted like 'a posthypnotic suggestion' (93). The really scary claim, however, was that the contaminated unconscious ruled the roost, that it could command what the self thought and did. 'Theories of the unconscious suggest that it actually dominates human behaviour,' Key wrote, 'controlling motivations, value systems, interpersonal relationships, personal identities, and, in effect, all major and minor aspects of life which differentiate humans from animals' (48). Control the unconscious, then, and you controlled the individual. That was how the admakers had turned the consumer into a slave: they had colonized the psyches of the nation.

There were three major problems with Key's argument. First, no evidence has ever emerged to demonstrate that admakers actually employed subliminals to convince consumers to buy products. The industry always rejected what professionals regarded as a canard. An extensive survey of practitioners in 1994, for example, learned that 90 per cent of the 256 respondents denied 'any use of or knowledge of use of "words, pictures, or shapes that are purposely inserted in advertising materials so that the viewers of the material cannot process the imagery at a conscious level, but rather at a subconscious level."' Of the 10 per cent who answered yes, apparently only one respondent could accurately describe subliminal advertising, and he claimed 'its use in one ad was "an inside joke."'[25] According to another source, two ad agencies did use masked images in admitted parodies of Key's subliminals for liquor ads. 'In an ad for Seagram's Extra Dry Gin, for instance, a tiny golfer is tucked away in a splash of gin. The ad reads: "Look for a wedge and a splash, and find the hidden pleasure in refreshing Seagram's Gin."'[26] The reason for such neglect of subliminal persuasion was straightforward. 'Advertising wants to impact on people's consciousness,' claimed Bob Garfield, a columnist for *Advertising Age*, 'not on their unconsciousness.'[27] Now this claim went too far, and masked the import and importance of innuendo, suggestion, and symbolism. But, this caveat aside, the common-sense assertion did explain why the denials of the advertising industry were credible.

Second, there was scarcely any evidence to back up Key's conclusions about the impact of subliminals. This lack was not the result of neglect. The topic attracted some researchers before and after Key's 'exposé.' Their work demonstrated that subliminal perception did exist: people could be influenced by signals of which they were unaware. But time and again these experiments demonstrated that this kind of influence was both limited and weak, unable to program the mind in the fashion Key had outlined.[28] A series of studies of subliminal self-help tapes, a rage in the early 1990s, found that they had no discernible effect, even when users thought they did.[29] Not that this bothered Key very much. During a trial where he appeared as an expert witness in 1990, he made clear his disdain for the assertions of the scientific community: 'Science is pretty much what you can get away [with] at any particular point in history and you can get away with a great deal.'[30]

Beyond these two problems, the fundamental difficulty with Key's horror story was its reliance on Freud's topography of the mind, and this Key shared with other critics such as McLuhan and Baudrillard, and, for that matter, with the great promoter Ernest Dichter. 'There is no evidence the brain works the way Key says,' argued Don Schultz, a professor of advertising at the Medill School of Northwestern University. 'I mean, if you can't find the phallus after staring at it, how's the brain going to process the information?'[31] Recall that Freud had first posited a troubled consciousness, always imperilled by the demands of a potent unconscious, and later a hapless ego caught between the conflicting pressures of the id and the superego. The dynamic unconscious, and later the id (although these terms were not equivalent), was a chaotic domain of the psyche, dominated by the instincts, especially the sex drive, where the pleasure principle held sway.[32] It had a symbolic dimension, but of a most peculiar kind, bereft of logic, untroubled by contradiction, as Freud wrote, where for instance the meanings of 'faeces (money, gift), baby and penis are ill-distinguished from one another and are easily interchangeable.'[33]

Even Key recognized that many a psychologist doubted the existence of such an entity, this just after the heyday of Freud's influence, and the doubts have grown since the early 1970s.[34] A dictionary of cognitive psychology, the dominant brand of psychology in the anglophone world at the end of the twentieth century, actually had no listing for the term 'unconscious,' evidence that it now lacked scientific credibility.[35] But such a conclusion could not readily deny the importance of a variety of what were sometimes termed 'nonconscious' or 'subconscious' phenomena – the processing of data, for example, that generates flashes of intuition – which occur in the mind beneath the threshold of awareness. The experiments done on subliminal perception or hypnosis did illustrate that portions of the psyche operated outside the normal range of cognitive faculties. Some of the findings of neuroscience suggested that much routine human behaviour was certainly conditioned, and even determined, by control mechanisms of which individuals were usually unaware.[36] None of these findings, of course, confirmed the existence of Key's understanding of the mind.

The unconscious encompasses a variety of drives, which we can deem innate or biological, plus a repertoire of desires and fears, born of personal experience and social pressures, that persist sometimes in opposition to our moral beings or, if you like, our superego. There is a sense in which the unconscious, in some people, at some times, may also harbour something like Freud's id, a collection of antisocial urges. The actual strength and importance of any particular desire (or fear) will vary from one personality to another, however. Both Dichter and Baudrillard, for example, admitted that the need for security was widespread throughout the populace. Even McLuhan allowed that there were other sorts of appeals to other needs than sex that might captivate the American public. Put another way, the desire for sexual pleasure may well be the model of all other pleasures, as Freud suggested, but its impact on the behaviour of any person was not constant: many other factors, social and personal, conditioned its import.

Besides which, this unconscious is not a separated part of the self, a homunculus that resides hidden away somewhere in the brain. Indeed, desires and fears often do become conscious. We are aware of our wishes and our anxieties, of painful or lascivious memories, even if we endeavour to suppress these on a day-to-day basis. One problem of life is that these demons are never fully exorcised, that the Freudian notion of repression really does not work, at least not always, especially if external stimuli endeavour to awaken desire. In any event, the unconscious does not routinely control the behaviour of the mind. The self, conscious and aware, does.

No wonder the advertising industry could easily dismiss what one of its apologists called 'this troubled man's paranoid nightmares.'[37] In 1986, in fact, the American Association of Advertising Agencies actually mailed out a poster of a glass containing liquor and ice to newspapers, magazines, and universities designed to debunk Key. According to the copy, 'People have been trying to find the breasts in these ice cubes since 1957,' the date of the first scare over subliminal advertising. 'Well, if you really searched, you probably could see breasts,' the ad stated. 'For that matter, you could also see Millard Fillmore, a stuffed pork chop and a 1946 Dodge.'[38] Ironically, Key had the last word, though. In a later book, he admitted that none of those objects existed in the ad. Instead he found 'a collection of grotesque faces, animals, a shark and other bizarre imagery ... and an erect penis'![39]

Which prompts the question, why was he so successful? Why did the American public first believe, and then continue to believe, in what experts and the industry said was a myth? The answer lay in the public's unshakable view that Madison Avenue and its like constituted, at one level, a sort of a conspiracy against the moral health of the nation. Witness this observation from an assessment published in 1994: 'On the whole, consumers thought advertising created many undesirable effects ranging from increased cost of goods to spreading materialism, promoting sex and other unwholesome values and taking undue advantage of children.' In particular, nearly three-quarters of the respondents believed that 'there was too much sex in TV advertising.'[40] Such findings were not at all uncommon – indeed it was news when some study came along suggesting a more favourable attitude towards advertising.[41] Key had tapped into this conviction that advertisers and admakers were waging a species of psychological warfare against Americans. The public could, after all, detect the signs of the erotic sell all over their lives. Even if Key's claims seemed outlandish, they connected with the everyday experience of Americans, providing a useful explanation of the available 'facts' about consumption, materialism, and excess. Perhaps one further source of the appeal of Key's books was that they let the consumer off the hook, blaming someone else for the sin of over-indulgence. Subliminal seduction has remained a legend of modern times.

4 Killing Us Softly (1979)

Some of the loudest of the naysayers in the anti-advertising camp were feminist voices. That was hardly surprising given the links between the capitalist version of eroticism and the world of pornography. Betty Friedan coined the phrase 'the sexual sell' in her famous book The Feminine Mystique (1963). Indeed, she devoted a whole chapter to the phenomenon.[42] But what she meant was not the eroticization of the material world. The sexual sell was, for her, a part of a general wave of propaganda that had served to discipline the minds and habits of American women during the late 1940s and the dismal 1950s.

Friedan explored the blighted lives of educated, middle-class wives like herself, who now had no identity except as spouse and mother and consumer, no approved occupation beyond being a housewife. They found themselves trapped in the padded prisons of suburbia, enslaved to kids and husband, endlessly cleaning house, washing clothes, and cooking meals. These women suffered 'the problem that has no name' – a sense of malaise, a loss of self – and so they had succumbed to all manner of physical and emotional ailments. They had no way out, other than an obsessive search for erotic pleasure, with a husband or with another man, which rarely brought joy because the problem was rooted not in sex but in a kind of oppression: whatever their supposed rights, women could not be like men; they could not have a meaningful career in the world of work where their creative urges might be satisfied and their talents recognized.

The source of this oppression was the hegemony of 'the feminine mystique,' both an ideology and a set of practices that restricted women's lives' to the sphere of the home (allowing, perhaps, some activity in the wider community on behalf of children and the like). Since the Second World War women had been indoctrinated to believe that biology was destiny and that femininity could flourish only in the confines of the family. The agents of the mystique were the fiction and features of women's magazines, the ideas and effects of Freudian psychology, the curricula of schools and universities, but above all the whole apparatus of American business, the manufacturers and retailers, the advertising agencies, and especially motivational researchers who advised the lot. 'The manipulators and their clients in American business can hardly be accused of creating the feminine mystique,' she argued. 'But they are the most powerful of its perpetuators; it is their millions which blanket the land with persuasive images, flattering the American housewife, diverting her guilt and disguising her growing sense of emptiness' (228). Her strictures were based on a scrutiny of the files of none other than Ernest Dichter, who, generously – and Friedan admitted his kindness, however ironic that seemed – had allowed her access to the mass of interviews and reports his institute had assembled over the years, so that she could understand how and why the sexual sell worked.

What advertising did was provide women with an identity as consumers, channelling their creative energies into the purchase of goods. Friedan quoted copiously from Dichter's studies to show how to fool a woman into believing that housework was fun, how to boost her self-esteem by suggesting she was an expert, no less than a home engineer, and why she might accept the gospel of 'happiness through things' (219). A sense of guilt – about the kids, say – a certain envy – over what neighbours had, perhaps – all this and much more were exploited by the adroit manipulators. Sex was part of the mix. 'How skillfully they divert her need for achievements into sexual phantasies which promise her eternal youth, dulling her sense of passing time' (228–9). You could not buy love – 'smoking a Marlboro will not get her an invitation to bed' (229) – but you could make her believe that buying something would ensure her 'status as a desirable sexual object' (271). So in the search for ever greater profits American advertising had stoked the sexual hunger of its victims.

Friedan's critique was part of her overall suspicion of the erotic as a tool neither of liberation nor of play but of mastery, a way in which men had used sex to blind women to their real need: freedom. This attitude expressed more than just a hostility to the regime of stimulation that had emerged – although she noted wryly how one report 'advised sellers to "put the libido back into advertising"' to rejuvenate the passions of married life (225). Friedan extended her critique to all of the agents of the feminine mystique, not only ads, because they had worked to reduce 'several generations of able American women' to 'sex-creatures' (261). In a chapter entitled 'The Sex-Seekers' she displayed considerable disdain for contemporary representations of sex, which she characterized as 'joyless,' 'diseased,' or even 'perverted' (261–3). There were moments, in short, when Friedan appeared to be something of a prude who found the appetite for sexual fantasy demeaning and the obsession with erotic pleasure dangerous. This suspicion of eroticism would persist in the rhetoric of feminism.

Soon after Friedan published her book, of course, the situation grew a lot worse, at least from a feminist perspective. That resulted from a convergence of the sexual revolution in the wider society and the so-called creative revolution in advertising, both during the late 1960s, which together fuelled yet another boom in publicity as erotica.[43] One person who took issue with the rush of erotic imagery was Jean Kilbourne, then a young activist. In 1968 she had begun collecting magazine ads that, in one way or another, demeaned women, eventually turning these into slides to illustrate lectures she delivered inside and outside schools on the evils of advertising.[44] She had considerable success, especially on college campuses. In 1979 she turned this show-and-tell exercise into a half-hour documentary entitled *Killing Us Softly: Advertising's Image of Women*. By all accounts that proved one of the most popular educational films of the times, shown, so she claimed, 'throughout the world,' and certainly commonplace in university classrooms. The documentary eventually went through two reincarnations, in 1987 and again in 2000, where she updated her collection of ads.[45]

Killing Us Softly was both an exploration and a polemic that sought to make advertising 'speak its own truth.' Kilbourne proved a very effective lecturer: she had a good presence, a fine voice, and an easy manner. The camera occasionally took a shot of the audience just to certify the impact of her delivery. Kilbourne made her arguments clearly, avoiding jargon, offering a few statistics, and occasionally spicing her polemic with witty comments at the expense of the slides she was showing. These slides were the key to the whole effort: she had selected a series of ads – many touting cosmetics, food, liquor, or tobacco – that served as examples of why, as she put it, people ought to take advertising very seriously. Sometimes it was difficult to make out just what was being promoted, though that mattered little because Kilbourne was not really concerned with the market power of an individual brand. Nor did Kilbourne offer much of a context: rarely did she give a date or a source for an ad, which meant it was impossible to tell how significant the example was – whether it was typical or singular.[46] Instead she emphasized the properties of the images and, sometimes, the copy: how the figures looked, their body language, their dress or undress, their relative positions, the shape of the product, innuendo, subliminals, and the like.

Everyone, men as well as women, should be concerned, Kilbourne argued, because advertising was an extraordinarily sophisticated tool of persuasion – nothing happened by chance in these ads – a tool for shaping the values, attitudes, and habits of the public. It was ubiquitous and inescapable and, perhaps most troubling, it was uncontested. In passing she referred to advertising as a form of 'pollution,' designed to make people buy what they did not need. But that was not her primary objection. The advertising she targeted was both an agent and a reflection of a sexist culture, steeped in gender stereotypes. What she was talking about, consequently, was 'ideology' and 'hegemony'; what she was doing was a brand of 'ideology critique'; and what she wanted to achieve was to 'demystify,' to awaken people from their dangerous slumber. (She did not use any of these terms, of course. That would have made her performance far too heavy for the occasion.) She focused attention on the way admakers (her preferred term was 'advertisers') promoted particular images of women, notably as sex objects or moronic housewives, on how they excluded or denigrated other kinds of views, thereby obscuring the social reality, and on how they naturalized and universalized the image of the body beautiful. If this species of propaganda harmed women most of all, it also perverted masculinity, making advertising a double threat to the social and moral health of the country. Kilbourne explicitly invited men to join in the crusade. She looked towards a utopia of gender equality where men and women shared agency and independence and where everyone might practise the so-called masculine and feminine virtues as part of a common humanity.

Kilbourne's first slide was a close-up of the face of Farrah Fawcett, then a reigning celebrity, noted for her blonde hair and her sex appeal. Here was the basic criticism: that advertising propagated an impossible image of women, expressing a masculine ideal of erotic desire.[47] The pictures Kilbourne presented highlighted very attractive young women, all fitting the mode of the classical figure, slim, tall, well-endowed, elegant, glamorous, flawless. Hardly any real woman could or would look like this, no matter what she bought or how hard she dieted. That, of course, was only the beginning of the harm. Women's bodies were dismembered, their faces or hair, legs or breasts treated as objects of lust that required constant work to ensure that they appealed to men. Even the smell of women needed improvement, and Kilbourne waxed indignant over the promotion of feminine hygiene products, not just because the ads were insulting but also because the products were dangerous to health. Fat became the grand sin since it rendered a woman unattractive to most men: a diet ad, complete with before and after pictures, that declared 'I'd probably never be married now if I hadn't lost 49 pounds,' Kilbourne noted, had led one woman to state, this 'was the best advertisement for fat she'd ever seen.' Youth was overvalued: an elderly woman lost her sexual appeal, and had to compensate by desperately offering food. Work was undervalued: even the new stereotype of the liberated woman (she cited the famous Virginia Slims campaign) presented such a person as yet another type of body beautiful.[48]

How men and women were represented, especially in tableaux where both appeared, expressed the imbalance in the relations of power between the two genders. Men were typically given the right of command. Their bodies were rarely so obviously eroticized. Indeed they were clothed in macho dress, as it were, making them dominant and sometimes aggressive – she lamented the 'violent, brutal image of masculinity.' Women were tamed so that their sexual power did not pose a threat. They were divided – Kilbourne showed a Hanes ad where a man, if not married then certainly attached, gazed longingly at another woman. Women were engaged in a constant struggle to capture and hold a man, always threatened by the wiles of a younger and sexier rival. They were infantilized, represented as simpletons, unable to think logically, or shown clowning about in some giddy mood of foolishness, or portrayed as passive or submissive, always dependent on a man's gaze. They were even represented as children, objects of innocence and lust: an ad for Baby Soft (a baby powder) showed a woman, with a lollipop and a cleavage, dressed in a girl's outfit, her skirt slightly lifted, next to four samples of the product, each in a phallic-shaped container. (She also noted the reverse process, where girls were sexualized.) They were threatened, by violence or abuse – a mock rape, a dog that grasped a woman's limb, a sinister shadow that intimidated, the display of an exposed throat. Advertising's purpose, from this standpoint, was oppressive, to keep women down, where they belonged. (Kilbourne quoted from one ad whose copy read 'keep her where she belongs.' The image she displayed showed a woman, lying down on the floor, smiling at a man's new shoe.) It worked to perpetuate all the sins of a sexist society, to degrade women, to mock feminine virtues, to doubt women's intelligence, to encourage abuse, and to separate the sexes. This line of argument was very familiar because it repeated the assaults on patriarchy that had become so much a part of feminist rhetoric during the 1970s.

The stereotype of woman as sex, her body always an object of desire, allowed admakers to deploy women to sell nearly any product to men. Some winsome beauties in skimpy outfits graced an ad for outboard motors. The spread of the shapely legs of a woman (yet another dismembered soul) was juxtaposed with the stance of a tripod for a camera. The back view of a naked and voluptuous female was supposed to attract the male gaze to the products of an unnamed maker of construction materials. The copy?: 'She's built like all our products ... Heavy where she has to take the strain.' Apparently influenced by Key, Kilbourne found all manner of sexual images in ads – subliminals of a sort, though overt rather than embeds: a tough-looking Winston woman who declared, 'Winston wasn't my first cigarette'; a close-up of lipstick touching full, red lips, a reference to oral sex; a smiling woman, lightly clad, sitting on top of a spread of skis.[49] Even more striking, however, was an ad for Tabasco sauce entitled 'The Exciter.' The bottle rushed down from above to project a drop of sauce on the exposed white flesh of a baked potato. 'Add your own dash at the table.' Here, thought Kilbourne, was a direct allusion to sexual intercourse – the intent, she claimed, was to register this message on the unconscious. 'That's hard core,' she declared. 'The advertisers are America's real pornographers.'

Such was Kilbourne's most sensational charge against advertising, and she repeated the charge twenty years later in the remake of 2000.[50] But stigmatizing advertising this way was misleading. Pornography was a good deal more explicit and graphic than a bottle spraying a potato with some spicy sauce, however lusty the aura. More to the

point, an admaker could never have employed, not in the 1970s anyway, an image of a man ejaculating on a woman, which surely would
have been deemed pornographic according to the prevailing standards
of obscenity. Kilbourne had masked the significance of this otherwise
modest ad. The makers certainly did borrow a common porn image,
the so-called money shot, in which a penis ejaculates onto some part of
a woman's body. But they had also translated and cleansed that image,
removing the 'dirtiness,' making it humorous. The purpose was to
evoke 'the money shot,' to get the conscious (not the unconscious) to
process this striking image so that it engaged the male consumer, per-
suading him to give the brand a try. Admakers might be pornographers if judged by the standards of some kinds of feminist morality.
However, they were also something much more effective, the techni-
cians of sensuality, masters of a form of publicity that was also erotica.

Kilbourne's error grew out of a deeper misunderstanding of the
nature of advertising, indeed of publicity in general. The appeal of
advertising lay in the realm of fantasy, itself a type of play where
adults might indulge their 'illicit' or 'forbidden' wishes, to borrow an
argument from Freud. The fact that advertising obscured the reality of
women's lives was a function of this brand of discourse: advertising
obscured men's lives as well. Judging publicity by the standards of
news, expecting advertising to tell us who we were, rather than who
we might like to be – that approach was always flawed. Like McLuhan
before her, Kilbourne recognized the humorous side of advertising. But
she never welcomed the ironic tone or the mockery present in many of
her ads, signs of the playfulness of advertising, because of what she
deemed their baneful effects, one reason why her analysis seemed at
times a bit humourless and prudish.[51] Implicit in *Killing Us Softly*, as a
kind of subtext, was a deep suspicion of any display of sex, perhaps
because the ads Kilbourne noticed always expressed the inequalities of
power between women and men. There was little appreciation, in
short, of either the power of erotics or the erotics of power: both the
male gaze and the female spectacle were ruled out of bounds.

The related problem with *Killing Us Softly* (and in all its versions, not
just the 1979 edition) was Kilbourne's neglect of fashion, even though
many of her ads, for cosmetics as well as dress, certainly referenced
that system. At first glance the presence and power of the fashion
industry might seem to buttress her charge of the harm advertising did
to women, a theme picked up in the work of other feminists such as
Ms. magazine or Susan Faludi's *Backlash*.[52] After all, the fashion houses

of Dior and St Laurent, Ralph Lauren and Calvin Klein, Giorgio Armani, and the like, sponsored waves of publicity full of beautiful bodies to get women to buy all manner of clothes, perfumes, and accessories. One of the cardinal features of fashion was, as Fred Davis put it, the constant operation of 'the dialectic of the erotic and the chaste,' which worked to hide, to reveal, and to accentuate the allure of the flesh.[53] This was never just a tyranny of appearances, however. Women could and did resist, witness in particular the decade-long popularity of the 'dress-for-success' code, from the late 1970s into the 1980s, which eschewed the visible signs of femininity and erotic allure in the business world. That, too, passed, especially as it became increasingly boring and, to some degree, unnecessary. What fashion publicity conjured up was the stuff of fantasy, another version of that erotic utopia in which women could and did play by choosing the items that suited their own personal inclinations. 'The potent imagery of fashion art,' wrote Anne Hollander, 'provides the glow and generates the true art of dress, feeding the imagination and pushing the visual possibilities of clothing into new emotional territory.'[54] By the 1990s a later generation of feminists, notably those associated with *Bust* magazine, had come to accept how fashion publicity could serve the desires of women as voyeurs, dreamers, and consumers.[55]

Jean Kilbourne attained much personal success as a result of her long crusade against advertising. Her website supplied a list of these achievements.[56] Since 1984 she had been attached to Wellesley College as a visiting scholar. She worked with local and federal governments in the wars against smoking and alcoholism. She made a number of other documentaries about the way advertising promoted an obsession with thinness and addictions to alcohol and tobacco, and eventually published a book against advertising. Above all, she continued her brand of public education: she lectured, eventually, 'at over one-third of all the colleges and universities in the United States and all the major universities in Canada, as well as scores of private and public schools,' an extraordinary achievement. Obviously her crusade against the industry won the attention of all sorts of people, most especially young women. Like Key, Kilbourne had exploited fears of a conspiracy against the moral and public health of America. But unlike Key, her pillory of sexist advertising rested upon the demonstrated practices of the industry. Women had no difficulty finding examples of the erotic sell that might distress or insult, whether in 1979 or in 2000.

5 The Erotics of Power

'But Madonna, I contend, never does anything just for publicity.' That comment came from Camille Paglia, a Madonna fan, a cultural critic, and a celebrity in her own right, certainly someone who had proved adept at the task of generating attention. 'Rather, publicity is the language naturally used by the great stars to communicate with their vast modern audience. Through publicity, we live in the star's flowing consciousness.'[1] The comment I take to mean that the icons of entertainment deploy publicity to fashion and then refashion their own personae, an explanation that seems to fit Paglia's intent, since she goes on to talk about how Madonna constantly evolved, changing her body, her voice, her style. In effect, publicity constructed these icons as 'simulacra,' to borrow a concept from the vocabulary of Jean Baudrillard, although this decidedly was not Paglia's argument, since at the time she was a noted hater of any form of French theory. Simulacra are free-floating signifiers, images without authenticity, images that make their own reality, created and circulated in an environment dominated by the mass media to suit the pleasure of the masses and the profit of the elite. Advertising, more generally all forms of promotion and propaganda, constituted the key mode of designing and delivering simulacra.[2] Whatever the general merit of Baudrillard's proclamations, they do seem well suited to two of the most successful examples of the prevalence of the erotic at the end of the twentieth century, the stories of James Bond and Madonna. Publicity was the means, to revert to Paglia's prose, whereby fans could live in the erotic fantasies of their icons.

There is, however, yet another reason to dwell on the stories of Bond and Madonna: the different ways their exploits reflected the fascination (and the repulsion) of sado-masochism. Recall that Freud regarded this deviance as a kind of model because it resulted so clearly from 'a mixture of the two classes of instinct, of Eros and aggressiveness.'[3] In retrospect it seemed to be the signature 'perversion' of so violent and sexy a time as the twentieth century.[4] Likewise, Foucault, though for very different reasons, thought S/M central to the understanding and the future of sexuality. Partly that was because its practitioners were 'inventing new possibilities of pleasure with strange parts of their body – through the eroticization of the body.' But more significant was the way S/M eroticized power, or as he preferred 'strategic relations,' meaning the game of master and slave in which the roles could be reversed. It was interesting that he also recognized, and this was in 1982, that the new pleasures S/M generated would soon be appropriated by advertising, or in other words by the regime of stimulation.[5] Well, in some measure, that was exactly what happened in the case of Bond and Madonna, both of whom indulged in erotic games of power as a way to sell their wares. And both generated billions of dollars in revenues for the corporations that financed these properties.

I will focus on what proved the most interesting and effective agents of publicity, the trailers for the Bond movies and the music videos of Madonna. The trailers distilled not just the stories of the movies but the special qualities of the Bond character. The music videos were an enormously successful form of entertainment that served to popularize and promote Madonna in her various guises. In each case they conveyed that special linkage between the display of vigour and the allure of sensuality, so making clear how eroticism sexualized power.

1 The Bond Saga

Early in 2002, *People* magazine designated Pierce Brosnan 'the sexiest man alive,' though just for 2001, adding him to a list of hunks that already included Brad Pitt (2000), Tom Cruise (1990), and Mel Gibson (1985). 'This breathtaking Irishman,' so 'suave and sophisticated,' was chosen not just for his own considerable physical charms, however. What really worked in his favour was the famous role Brosnan had played in three recent hit movies: the fictional hero called James Bond, also known as '007' because of his 'licence to kill' in the course of his missions, that most famous of secret agents. 'Brosnan "has all the sensibilities of his character," says Bond coproducer Barbara Broccoli. "He also has the rugged good looks and the charm. He's manly."'[6] It was no accident that an earlier Bond, indeed the 'original' Bond, the actor Sean

Connery, who had starred in the first of the extraordinary series of movies launched in 1962, had also been honoured with the accolade back in 1989. Even if he was a wholly invented character, played by six different actors, Bond was always the sexiest man alive, to borrow the hype.

The fame of 007 reflected in part the extraordinary cult of the action hero that swept through the world of entertainment in the West during the late twentieth century. Here indeed was the modern self triumphant: a person, normally a man, who knew what he wanted and how to get it. He was a moral being, indeed a social good, for he sought to restore order by destroying the evil that menaced the community. Most important, he was effective: he proved able to overcome all obstacles, even the stupidities of his own side, to kill his enemies, usually in an orgy of violence, all to achieve his aims. Therein lay the excitement of a narrative of retribution that so captivated audiences. So popular was this figure that he turned up in novels and comics, toys and games, television shows and above all movies as a spy (television's Napoleon Solo of *The Man from U.N.C.L.E.* in the sixties), a detective or a cop (the 'Dirty Harry' series of movies, beginning in the seventies), a soldier (G.I. Joe) or superhero (Marvel Comics), and innumerable warriors (notably the roles played by Arnold Schwarzenegger in movies after 1980).[7] In the movies the hero himself might be sexy, but usually the narrative was not. Eros was seconded to Thanatos in such Freudian dramas. Sex was repressed, present only in the play of muscles on the hero's body or the way he might put on his gear or the big guns and other such weapons he employed – here was the armed phallus. Sex was sublimated, the libido channelled into war on the streets of America or the jungles and deserts and cities of the world. That was where 007 was so different, so unusual: the Bond movies were also erotic thrillers.[8]

Bond must count as one of the most successful franchises in the annals of pop culture. He first appeared in Ian Fleming's *Casino Royale*, published in Britain in 1953, whose success, albeit modest in the beginning, led to further novels, fourteen in all, the last released just after Fleming's death in 1964.[9] The Bond adventures belonged to an already established tradition of spy thrillers, although Fleming modernized the characters and the scenarios to suit a world where the British Empire was in decline and the global arena was dominated by the Cold War. Although Fleming did not have any direct field experience as a government agent – indeed, he was really a journalist who had become a newspaper manager – he had served as a personal assistant to the

Director of Naval Intelligence during the Second World War. But what most characterized, say, *Doctor No* or, even more, *Goldfinger* – neither of which could make any plausible claim to realism – was not so much a knowledge of secret operations as a marvellous imagination that produced entertaining fantasies of a life and a man both exciting and impossible. In 1958 Paul Johnson, an acerbic critic, claimed that the appeal of *Doctor No* was rooted in 'sex, snobbery and sadism.'[10] Fleming once admitted that he wrote for 'warm-blooded heterosexuals' in need of diversion, that his target 'lay somewhere between the solar plexus and, well, the upper thigh,' that he attempted 'the total stimulation of the reader all the way through, even to his taste buds.'[11] He certainly succeeded. Sales of his books took off at home in the late 1950s, effectively bringing the paperback revolution to Britain.[12] His fame soon spread to the United States, especially after President John F. Kennedy revealed in 1961 that Fleming was one of his favourite authors.[13] And sales continued upward even after his death: by 1977 close to 28 million Bond paperbacks had been sold in Britain, an unmatched achievement at the time.[14] Indeed his appeal proved to be global: in 2002, when Penguin chose to reissue the books (in hardcover, paperback, and now audio) the publisher claimed that the 007 novels had sold approximately 60 million copies.[15]

A lot of these sales were actually driven by the popularity of the 007 movies, which eventually proved the main vehicle of the whole Bond phenomenon (see figure 5.1). By the end of the century, it was estimated that nineteen 007 films had produced about U.S.$3 billion in box office around the globe, plus other lucrative revenues from television, video, and DVD sales. According to one guess, between one-quarter and one-half of the world's population had seen at least one Bond film.[16] The series was the brainchild of two experienced, independent producers active in Britain, Harry Saltzman (a Canadian by birth) and Cubby Broccoli (an American), working together as Eon Productions, who were able to secure financing (slightly less than $1 million) from United Artists to produce *Dr. No* (the spelling of the movie title differed from that of the book) in 1962. The success of that initiative led to *From Russia with Love* (1963), then *Goldfinger* (1964), and *Thunderball* (1965), the last two smash hits sufficient to set off a kind of 'Bondmania.' Eon and United Artists introduced what would become a common practice in the marketing of blockbusters: they distributed a large number of copies of a film (1,100 in the case of *Goldfinger*), a strategy that not only ensured the maximum benefit from all the pre-release

Figure 5.1: The Bond Movies
The first twenty-one movies, listed by date of release, title, the actor playing Bond, the main Bond 'girl' (or girls), and the chief villain(s).

Year	Title	Actor	Bond 'girl' (or girls); villain(s)
1962	Dr. No	Connery	Honey Rider; Dr No
1963	From Russia with Love	Connery	Tatiana Romanova; 'Red' Grant and Rosa Klebb.
1964	Goldfinger	Connery	Jill Masterson and Pussy Galore; Auric Goldfinger
1965	Thunderball	Connery	Domino Derval; Emilio Largo
1967	You Only Live Twice	Connery	Kissy Suzuki and Aki; Blofeld
1969	On Her Majesty's Secret Service	Lazenby	Tracy Di Vicenzo; Blofeld
1971	Diamonds Are Forever	Connery	Tiffany Case; Blofeld
1973	Live and Let Die	Moore	Solitaire; Dr Kananga/Mr Big
1974	The Man with the Golden Gun	Moore	Andrea and Mary Goodnight; Scaramanga
1977	The Spy Who Loved Me	Moore	Major Anya Amasova; Jaws and Carl Stromberg
1979	Moonraker	Moore	Dr Holly Goodhead; Jaws and Hugo Drax
1981	For Your Eyes Only	Moore	Melina Havelock; Aristotle Kristatos
1983	Octopussy	Moore	Octopussy; Kamal Kahn
1985	A View to a Kill	Moore	May Day and Stacey Sutton; Max Zorin
1987	The Living Daylights	Dalton	Kara Milovy; General Georgi Koskov
1989	Licence to Kill	Dalton	Pam Bouvier and Lupe Lamora; Franz Sanchez
1995	GoldenEye	Brosnan	Natalya Simonova; Xenia Onatopp and Alec Trevelyan
1997	Tomorrow Never Dies	Brosnan	Paris Carver and Colonel Wai-Lin; Elliot Carver
1999	The World Is Not Enough	Brosnan	Dr Christmas Jones; Elektra King and Reynard
2002	Die Another Day	Brosnan	Jinx; Miranda Frost and Gustav Graves
2006	Casino Royale	Craig	Vesper Lynd; Le Chiffre

publicity but also meant the movie would reach a large audience quickly, making its success an event that could only increase the frenzy.[17] Bond might remain most popular in Britain, but he won lots of fans in France, Italy, Japan, and, most important, in the United States, which took to *Goldfinger* eagerly. The even more popular *Thunderball* generated around $140 million at the box office on four continents, half of this in Britain alone, an extraordinary sum in the 1960s.[18] The upshot was a boom in sales of 007–themed merchandise, the popularity of spy books of all sorts, and a host of imitations and spoofs at the movies, notably Derek Flint and Matt Helm in the United States.[19] Thereafter the Bond movies followed regularly, usually every two years, even though the initial wave of Bondmania receded before the close of the decade.

Bond and his adventures changed in the process of translation from novel to screen. Sean Connery's Bond was more self-assured, more witty, and decidedly more erotic than the original model, not the least because of the sexual magnetism of Connery himself. The stories were altered not only to suit the visual imperative of film but also to connect with trends in movie making and even the political fashions of the times.[20] During the 1970s and 1980s the films starring the more debonair if less sexy Roger Moore, the actor who replaced Connery in *Live and Let Die* (1973), took on the guise of parody, and more and more of the chases and confrontations were played for laughs.[21] *Live and Let Die* borrowed some of the style of black exploitation movies; *The Man with the Golden Gun* (1974) had a kung-fu scene; the climax of *Moonraker* (1979) occurred in space, making this a sci-fi film; and the villain in *A View to a Kill* (1985) sought to overturn the world by flooding Silicon Valley. Of these *Moonraker* proved a major success, earning back more than six and a half times its cost of around $34 million at the worldwide box office.[22] The practice and the troubles of détente, that uneasy accommodation of the Soviet Union and the United States, proved a continuing motif in the series. The replacement of an aged Moore by the more youthful and aggressive Timothy Dalton in *The Living Daylights* (1987) and *Licence to Kill* (1989) produced a much more serious Bond, reminiscent of the kind of heroes of law and order common in some American versions of action cinema. But, as *Newsweek* later put it (22 November 1999), Bond had 'a near-death experience' when *Licence to Kill* only generated about $32 million in the United States, though it did considerably better elsewhere.[23] The break with the now well-established conventions of the Bond adventures, in particular the rougher, less elegant Bond played by Dalton, obviously did not impress audiences.

What happened later was an astonishing revival of the franchise in the 1990s, according to the press mostly because of the efforts of executives at MGM, which had taken over the financing and marketing of Bond when the company acquired United Artists.[24] MGM and Eon set out to update 007. One crucial aim was to connect with youth, to update the Bond persona and his adventures to suit the tastes of the teenagers and young adults whose favour now made a movie into a blockbuster. Production budgets were doubled. The action scenes were exciting and imaginative. The special effects were outstanding. Bond's official superior, M, became a woman. The villains were more youthful and more aggressive. A rock band, Garbage, performed one of the signature songs, as did Madonna a few years later.[25] Denise Richards, a hot property with young audiences, was hired to play one of Bond's 'girls,' as a nuclear physicist in *The World Is Not Enough* (1999). Even better, the major new star Halle Berry, the winner of an Oscar, was signed for Bond number 20, *Die Another Day* (2002). But, above all, the choice of Pierce Brosnan as the fifth Bond was inspired: his elegance, his ruthlessness, his sexiness recalled the brilliant performances of Connery that had first made the franchise a global triumph. '"Bond resonates with the culture," says Sharon Lee of Look-Look, a market-research company specializing in the 15-to-30 crowd. "Today, brawn has to be sleek. Heroes aren't pumped up. While Arnold [Schwarzenegger] hasn't updated his image, Bond has. These kids list Muhammad Ali, Kurt Cobain, John Lennon and Andy Kaufman as their heroes. For them, Bond works."'[26]

The rebirth came with *GoldenEye* (1995), ironically named after Fleming's home in Jamaica, although the story was new: costing about $50 million to produce, it generated $106 million in the United States and $340 million worldwide in three months.[27] Two years later *Tomorrow Never Dies* (costing $80 million) also took in well over $300 million, as did *The World Is Not Enough* (costing $100 million), and *Die Another Day* (costing $140 million) earned $430 million worldwide.[28] This was all the more remarkable because of the fierce competition: Hollywood was now churning out a series of action movies with proven stars like Arnold Schwarzenegger, Bruce Willis, Wesley Snipes, Mel Gibson, Sylvester Stallone, and Vin Diesel.[29] MGM had also sold TV rights to various past films first to TBS (1991) and later to ABC (2001) in the United States. It had even launched a successful video game series, first on the Nintendo 64 platform and later on the Sony Playstation. Then there were the ongoing DVD sales: in its first day of release in the United States, *Die Another Day* reportedly sold 1 million copies at roughly $14 a unit.[30] It was not surprising that the rejuvenated Bond franchise alone was sufficient, sometimes, to push MGM's finances into the black.[31]

There was yet another way in which MGM profited from 007: the films of the 1990s became a selling vehicle in their own right. In fact, from the beginning, James Bond had constituted an advertising resource. The first wave of Bondmania in the 1960s had Sean Connery, more often Bond lookalikes, and the name James Bond selling elegant shirts and suits, shoes, lipstick and lingerie, and assorted liquors. In Australia Pelaco advertised 'the Shirt with a Licence to Thrill,' complete with the picture of a handsome man pointing what looked like a gun at the viewer and, naturally, backed by an excited and exciting blonde woman. During the 1970s and 1980s, the Bond persona advertised, for instance, Rolex watches, a bevy of kids' toys, Mountain Dew, and Peugeot (in France, in the 1980s). Two award-winning Peugeot commercials had a Bond type, menaced by helicopters and planes, doing some spectacular stunts in his Peugeot to win the fancy of beautiful women – these parodies of the typical Bond adventure were a bit strange, though, given that the Peugeot appeared to be a very ordinary car, not at all like the elegant and aggressive vehicles 007 usually employed.[32]

Legend had it that *Dr. No* was among the pioneers of product tie-ins when it featured the Aston Martin as Bond's car and Smirnoff vodka as his favourite alcohol. Marlboro cigarettes appeared twice in *Moonraker* (1979). Ten years later Philip Morris paid an estimated $350,000 to have a package of Lark cigarettes featured in a particularly intense scene of the movie *Licence to Kill*.[33] The costs of such placements mounted rapidly. According to one source, Ford supposedly paid an estimated $35 million to have three of its cars, an Aston Martin, a Thunderbird, and a Range Rover, driven by Bond and his eventual ally (Halle Berry as Jinx) in *Die Another Day*.[34]

MGM carried this kind of association a step farther, emulating what had first occurred in the realm of children's hit movies. Bond became, in the words of one scholar, 'a kept man.'[35] The company arranged cross-marketing agreements and promotional partnerships with a variety of manufacturers and retailers in order to promote their brands as well as the forthcoming movies through advertisements and commercials and displays, using Pierce Brosnan or his image to drive home the message that these brands were Bond's choices. Such arrangements enabled MGM to mount a marketing blitz for *Tomorrow Never Dies*, for example, estimated at $100 million, most of this paid for by what were now Bond's sponsors. Under these agreements Bond had, at different times, his own car (BMW), his vodka (Smirnoff) and champagne (Bollinger), his cell phone (Erickson), his computer (IBM), his credit card (Visa), and his watch (Omega). Early in 2002, Best Buy Stores, which owned a series of chains in North America that marketed electronic goods, signed on to launch Bond-themed packages, to design special in-store displays, and to market *Die Another Day* to its 50 million customers. Soon after, Philips became the official supplier of shaving goods for the forthcoming film, and it planned to launch a series of Bond-branded products to coincide with the film's international premiere. "'We have looked for an icon who personifies the merits of design and technology innovation of Philips," said a spokesman for the company. "James Bond was the natural choice for that role."'[36]

Why was he 'the natural choice'? The appeal of 007 had always extended broadly across the normal divides of age, class, locale, race, and even gender. The movies had a global reach. Kids relished the Bond adventures. Television ratings in Britain and the United States, presumably from the late 1970s or 1980s, showed that Bond found a lot of favour with women.[37] Of course, Bond was most fancied by men. That fact was signified by the early interest of *Playboy* magazine in the whole 007 phenomenon. Bond shared many of the qualities of the male ideal propagated by Hugh Hefner, not just a roving eye and an extraordinary sexual prowess but a taste for excellent clothes, prestige cars, expensive liquors, the best champagne, exotic places, and much more – Bond enjoyed consuming the finest things in life. The magazine had carried an interview with Ian Fleming in December 1964, just after he died, where it mused Bond 'may well be not so much the child of this century as the next,' presumably because he was a new kind of man. It later ran photo essays on the 'Bond girls,' including a semi-nude and nude feature on Barbara Bach around the release of *The Spy Who Loved Me* (1977), in which she starred with Roger Moore.[38] Most telling, however, was the result of the Christmas rebroadcast of Bond films by TBS during the 1990s in the United States: this attracted not only more men than women, an unusual situation around holiday time, but a lot of upscale males as well.[39] Men with money to spend were an irresistible attraction to advertisers, particularly to companies who sold luxury cars, expensive toys, all sorts of gadgets, fine liquor and wine, and quality men's products. Indeed Bond had a proven track record as a salesman: according to the *The Times* of London (13 December 1997), BMW had managed to generate 10,000 advance orders for its new sports car, worth about $300 million, as a result of its association with *GoldenEye*.

All of which points to the particular charisma of the Bond franchise and the subversive pleasures it promised fans.[40] In the world of 007, life was organized by the rule of the phallus, meaning that masculine principle of challenge, command, and conquest in which sex and violence were inextricably linked.[41] The rule was only one variety of the overall regime of stimulation already in place. But it was an especially powerful expression of that regime. Consider its effect on one sensitive child, then living in Vancouver. 'I was only eight years old at the time and I was not allowed to go to the cinema to see *Dr. No*,' the novelist Jay McInerney recalled. 'On hearsay, my parents judged it to be far too racy for me. There were kids at school whose parents were not so strict, and these lucky few told the rest of us exactly what we wanted to hear, and what our parents feared – that the movie was full of hot babes and cool weaponry. Not to mention Bond, James Bond, himself, who was reportedly everything we wanted to be.' When he and a friend finally did sneak into a cinema to see the later *Thunderball*, where they found the underwater love scene between Claudine Auger and Sean Connery the most intriguing, he concluded that 'the message of Bond ... was about sex.'[42] One charge against Fleming's novels was that they constituted a pioneering form of the kind of soft-core pornography that became so popular in the consumer society, and he himself admitted his work was 'the author's pillow fancy' full of 'bang, bang, kiss, kiss – that sort of stuff.'[43] Although Harry Saltzman, one of the producers, denied that the movies were pornographic – the sex, after all, was consistently 'lightweight' and never graphic – he did admit that 'Bond is sadism for the family.'[44] He could have added that this sadism was spiced with large doses of erotomania, voyeurism, and exhibitionism.

That was apparent in one of the signatures of the Bond series (though absent from *Casino Royale*), the title sequence near the beginning of most films where women, sometimes in silhouette, were shown cavorting with or around guns – McInerney's 'hot babes and cool weaponry' – while the theme song played. These sequences acted as an ad embedded within the movie itself. They teased and tantalized, they promised excitements, they suggested what was on offer. That was how the pre-release publicity worked to attract clients to the box office:

the promotions, the posters, the teasers, and the trailers established, to borrow the words of John Ellis, the 'narrative image' of the movie, always an enigma that the film promised to resolve, though in the case of 007 the particular images of each adventure had to fit the conventions of the brand.[45] The publicity also amounted to a statement of the core messages of the Bond franchise, not just a commercial instrument but a cultural tool, a way of understanding the appeal of the character and his world.[46]

The posters could do no more than indicate the motifs and the style of a film, which meant that they became imaginative commentaries or collages. 'With the Bond pictures, we set out to sell – in a stylish, classy way – the girls, the action, and, to whatever extent we could, the gadgetry particular to the film,' recalled Donald Smolen, a marketing executive with United Artists who handled eight 007 campaigns after 1965. 'The central "idea" was always this: Bond is cool in the midst of the beautiful girls, the villains out to get him, and the chaos bombarding him.'[47] Many of these were fine examples of the art of movie promotion. Indeed some of the vintage posters commanded a high price among collectors: a United Artists' poster for *Goldfinger* went for £8,225 at one auction in 2002.[48] Usually Bond was armed with his pistol and linked to beautiful women, in tight or revealing clothes, who, sometimes, were also armed. There was, of course, a surfeit of phallic imagery: a huge cannon blasted out its payload from a position close to Bond's crotch (*Live and Let Die*); an enormous golden gun pointed menacingly at the Bond figure (*The Man with the Golden Gun*); a tough Timothy Dalton, legs apart, posed to shoot, the two women he seduced placed in a boxed insert beneath his crotch (*Licence to Kill*). The controversial poster for *For Your Eyes Only*, an object of feminist disdain on some university campuses in the United States, forefronted the back view of a young woman standing with her legs apart – we see her silver high heels, tanned shapely legs, the cheeks of her bottom partly enclosed in tight blue panties, and a hand holding a black crossbow – with a smallish Roger Moore, gun at the ready, facing the viewer but positioned in the triangle created by the woman's pose. That single image was more erotic than any in the movie itself. A spare, stylish poster for *The World Is Not Enough* showed the silhouettes of two figures, Bond in black, his weapon raised up, and a woman in yellow and orange, apparently on fire, her gun held low. It evoked the contrast between yin and yang, a fitting theme since this adventure featured, for the first time, a woman as a master villain, whom Bond would bed and, eventually, would kill. Colourful, menacing, sexy, elegant: the Bond posters captured what was the central effect of the series, the eroticization of violence.

The trailers revealed much more, especially the theatrical versions that ran over two minutes and longer in the case of the early Bond movies.[49] Aside from some additional graphics, especially common in the 1990s, these ads were composed of scenes from the actual movies, though often with a voice-over explaining who was who, hinting at the nature of Bond's quest, and promising all sorts of thrills. The trailer for *Dr. No* amounted to a synopsis of the movie, narrated largely by Connery himself, perhaps because this was the first adventure. One of the trailers for *The Living Daylights* focused solely on a single action sequence, set in and around Gibraltar, when Bond parachutes from a plane and, after various scuffles, ends up on the yacht of a woman searching for 'a real man.' Both were uncommon. The plot usually disappeared in the translation from movie to trailer. Most commercials were a sequence of jolts – a sexy image, some peril, a scrap of conversation, a fight or a death, perhaps a quip, an explosion, an elegant moment – that conveyed the impression of all sorts of stimulation. The pace of this sequence became especially frenetic when MGM set out to reach young people: one *GoldenEye* trailer, 170 seconds long, contained roughly 135 separate cuts (and even more separate images), though some of these were linked around a particular motif, be that sex, chases, explosions, or confrontations.

The stories these trailers told accord well with that general pattern in the universe of the European imagination discerned by Mikhail Bakhtin: the dichotomy of two worlds, distinct but linked, peopled by very different beings. (A point of clarification: in the following discussion the title of a movie refers to its trailer[s], not to the actual movie.) The first world – of authority, affluence, and elegance – received relatively little attention, much less than in the films. The circle of authority, centred largely in the offices of the secret service, which in some of the movies constituted a kind of church, full of ritual and ceremony, was almost completely absent. But not so all its residents – two powerful souls, known only by an initial, dwelt here: 'M,' the person in charge, was the patriarch and later the matriarch who launched 007 on his mission; and 'Q,' the master of the laboratories, was the wizard who equipped Bond with the tools that enhanced his prowess. (No such wizard appeared in the movie *Casino Royale*.) Neither sex nor violence happened in this well-ordered environment, and that explained its neglect by publicity.[50] The neglect was akin to the absence of the factory in most forms of consumer advertising: the place of origin counted much less than the goods on offer.

By contrast, the circle of affluence was more common, represented by places like Bond's stylish apartment, the casino, luxury hotels, a fancy party, an exotic beach, an Indian palace, plush bedrooms. In such sites Bond made contact with all sorts of beautiful women, sometimes enemies, often victims, occasionally friends – what were called 'Bond girls.' 'The girls are willing,' promised the announcer in *The Man with the Golden Gun*. The exact meaning of 'making contact,' of course, might range from merely saying hello (to 'Plenty O'Toole,' say, in *Diamonds Are Forever*), to hurting or threatening a recalcitrant beauty (the mistress of 'Scaramanga' in *The Man with the Golden Gun*), to the moment of seduction (the elegant 'Octopussy' in the movie of the same name). And these were places of tease, where viewers might be treated to a glimpse of the charms of a Bond girl – the famous shot of Ursula Andress on the beach in her stunning bikini (*Dr. No*), replayed by Halle Berry (*Die Another Day*) when the upper portion of her body rose out of the water; a quick focus on the semi-exposed breasts of Diana Rigg (*On Her Majesty's Secret Service*) at the casino; a glimpse, from the back, of the doomed 'Paris Carver' taking off her gown (*Tomorrow Never Dies*) in the bedroom, replayed by the treacherous Miss Frost doing the same (*Die Another Day*). Occasionally Bond himself might display his own body, at least when he was played by a relatively young actor. Pierce Brosnan showed off his hairy chest while relaxing in a swimming pool (in *GoldenEye*, his first try at 007); Daniel Craig revealed his well-muscled torso in a swimsuit shot (referring back to the famous Andress/Berry scenes) in the trailers for *Casino Royale*. Here then was the promise of erotic titillation.

Considerably more attention was lavished on that other world, however, the world of carnival, where all the thrills and mayhem were concentrated. Like its rival, carnival was also composed of two areas, the midway and the citadels of evil. The midway could be just about anywhere, since it was the region of action. It was full of games of skill and peril, car chases, battles in the air and under the water, a flight and fight on skis, an extraordinary bungee jump (in *GoldenEye*), fist fights and gun fights galore. Especially in the 1970s the action might be played for laughs: so Roger Moore ran his speedboat through a wedding, much to the horror of the bride (*Live and Let Die*). But the humour was often much darker. The *Thunderball* trailer, for instance, opened with three commands to the audience: 'Look Up,' 'Look Down,' and 'Look Out.'

The first sequence caught Bond as he flew into the sky on a personal rocket, away from the gunshots of his pursuers. The second saw Bond descend into the depths of the ocean, filled with the menace of underwater personnel carriers and frogmen, armed with spearguns. The third command led to a scene on the beach where 007 fired his own speargun into an unwary villain, nailing him to a tree: 'I think he got the point,' quipped Sean Connery. There were many such moments marked by a touch of sadism. Perhaps that explained the penchant for shark attacks and the like, where nightmares became actual. An incompetent gunman was thrown into a shark-infested swimming pool on the orders of his disgusted superior (*Thunderball*). Another failed servant, this time a woman, was dropped into a pond full of piranha – she screamed her pain as she was consumed (*You Only Live Twice*). Roger Moore and Carol Bouquet, tied together, were dragged through coral, their blood attracting sharks – yes, sharks in the Mediterranean (*For Your Eyes Only*). The trailer for *Licence to Kill* actually opened with a twenty-five-second clip showing Bond's friend and ally, the CIA operative Felix Leiter, about to be fed to the sharks by the drug king Sanchez. There was, inevitably, the threat of castration. A laser cut its way toward the crotch of Sean Connery, trapped, lying spread-eagled (*Goldfinger*): that scene found its way into both the American and the German trailers. Roger Moore fired a rifle between the legs of a weapons-maker who would not talk (*The Man with the Golden Gun*). Some years later he blasted an ornament out of the way as he slid down the handrail of a staircase (*Octopussy*).

The Bond trailers, in short, promised a dose of what the culture critic Tom Wolfe once called 'pornoviolence,' a staple of action cinema, except the theme was sex as well as violence.[51] 'When danger becomes a temptation,' exclaimed a hushed voice in the teaser for *Die Another Day*, 'when every move brings you closer to the edge, when you live each day like it's your last, there's a surprise around every curve.' Thereafter the screen burst into action, a racing car, explosions, Brosnan firing, Brosnan running, Brosnan fighting, and Brosnan kissing – an orgy of brief, violent jolts, interspersed with moments of sex and some shots of the attractive Halle Berry. There were weapons everywhere. Even Berry had a big gun. It was hard to miss the symbolism: here, full of colour and sound and excitement, was the rule of the phallus made manifest.

The midway was populated with odd characters, some bearing the mark of the grotesque, reminiscent of the 'freak shows' of many a carnival. There were a couple of anti-Bonds, consummate killers like 'Red

Grant' (*From Russia with Love*) or the renegade '006' (*GoldenEye*), who matched Bond in skill though not in elegance or sexiness. 'Pussy Galore,' 'Kissy Suzuki,' 'Dr Holly Goodhead,' and 'Xenia Onatopp' were all women whose erotic potential (and in one case whose sexual preference) was emphasized or spelled out by their very names. 'Odd-job' was a squat, powerful Korean who killed with a bowler hat. 'Sheriff J.W. Pepper' was a course, loud-mouthed American sheriff who made appearances in two movies (the trailer for *The Man with the Golden Gun* emphasized his return). So did 'Jaws,' a hulk of a man sporting metallic teeth who gave the kiss of death when he sank these teeth into the neck of a victim, a bizarre mix of Dracula and the infamous shark of the movie *Jaws*. 'May Day,' played by Grace Jones, was a tall, androgynous woman, tough as nails, an object of desire and fear, with whom Bond fought, loved, and eventually allied (but in the movie *A View to a Kill*, not in its trailer). She was just one of a whole bevy of female warriors, both attractive and dangerous, a mixture of the feminine and the masculine, like 'Bambi' and 'Thumper,' two female guards Bond had to overcome (*Diamonds Are Forever*); 'Octopussy's' platoon of fighters, clad (naturally) in revealing outfits; or the Russian 'Anya Amasova' (*The Spy Who Loved Me*) and later the Chinese 'Wei Lin' (*Tomorrow Never Dies*), both Communist counterparts of 007, who worked with Bond.

The most perverse characters were the lords of misrule, the men of power who wished to reverse the order of things. The Bond franchise had an extraordinary gallery of these ultimate villains, all of whom bore some sign of their wickedness, rendered visible by the trailers: 'Dr No,' the man with artificial hands; 'Blofeld,' head of SPECTRE, whose familiar was a cat; the encased 'Hugo Drax,' dressed in grey, seemingly closed to human contact; 'Zorin,' a youthful looking psychotic, marked by his white hair and wild eyes; 'Elliott Carver,' the media mogul, the man with a sick laugh; and 'Reynard,' the anarchist whose brain harboured the bullet that would kill him. These megalomaniacs often resided in weird citadels of evil, such as the enormous underwater laboratory of Carl Stromberg (*The Spy Who Loved Me*), built like a huge spider, where they dreamed up strange ways of killing Bond and of endangering the Free World. Time and again, the citadels became the site of a grand battle, which ended in a set of giant explosions in the movies. The trailer for *Dr. No* closed (though that was not true of the publicity for later movies) with a series of fights and blasts in the mad scientist's base. Trailers for later movies often incorporated multiple scenes of devastation and destruction. These blasts, so loud, so gorgeous, the billowing clouds of yellows and reds filling the screen, were akin to the notorious 'money shot' of porn films: they signified completion, the final victory of the phallic hero.

James Bond bridged the divide between the two worlds: he was both High and Low, a hybrid of sorts. As 007 he was an agent of authority, as Bond he was at home in the circle of affluence, but his profession demanded he act in the world of carnival. Always he played out the roles of the gentleman, the warrior, and the satyr, all of which were well-established figures of masculinity in the fiction and fantasy of the West. The various Bonds all bore the body of the classical hero: well-proportioned, flawless, slim, vigorous, hard, experienced. They were clad in the garb of elegance, Bond's version of the streamlined body – at times it seemed the evening suit was Bond's second skin, making 007 very different from most of the heroes of American action cinema (witness 'Dirty Harry,' 'Rambo,' or 'John McClane' of *Die Hard* fame). And these Bonds were intelligent, men of the head rather than the heart, their sentiments calculated, their actions ruthless. It was 'M' who suggested that Bond resurrect his affair with 'Paris Carver' to extract information regarding the ambitions of her powerful husband, and 007 did so (*Tomorrow Never Dies*). But Bond was also a creature of his appetites, indeed the acolyte of a rampant and rampaging heterosexuality. Sean Connery set aside his mission to Jamaica, briefly, to dally with an attractive young woman who had found her way to his apartment (*Dr. No*). Roger Moore postponed an escape to give a willing 'Solitaire' 'lesson number three' in the ways of life (*Live and Let Die*). Timothy Dalton was ready to delay reporting back to headquarters to indulge his taste for a new lady (*The Living Daylights*). Bond's passion for sex was only matched by his addiction to jeopardy and violence. Sometimes they came together: a determined Pierce Brosnan, naked to the waste, his arm outstretched, his hand holding a big gun, all to menace an unseen woman in some darkened bedroom somewhere. His comment?: 'No more foreplay' (*GoldenEye*). And he cocks the pistol.

That pistol highlighted another way in which the Bond character was double-natured: he was a cyborg, both man and machine, whose extraordinary powers as a warrior derived from his command of technology. Thus a small monitoring device was inserted into the wrist of Daniel Craig to ensure his continuing contact with headquarters. Many of the teasers or trailers, at least after the movie *From Russia with Love*, highlighted some of the marvellous tools 'Q' provided for Bond, whether the streamlined and weaponized cars, special planes, all manner of spy devices, secret weapons, and on and on. So in the German trailer for *Licence to Kill*, 'Q' brings Bond a souped-up camera that dispenses a deadly laser beam. He was, in his warrior mode, an assemblage, a network of flesh and machine, of passion and skill, always with the purpose of dealing in death.[52]

Bond's 'licence to kill' marked him as a privileged being – the early trailers made much of this special status (for example, *Dr. No*: 'licenced to kill whom he pleases, where he pleases, when he pleases') – but this was unnecessary as the series progressed and people became familiar with the mythology of 007. One aspect of this privilege, however, was constantly reaffirmed, namely Bond's licence to look everywhere, anytime, and at anyone.[53] Consider the recurring fascination with seeing and sight in the trailers. Especially in the early movies Bond took on the guise of the tourist, consuming exotic sights far from home: so a trailer for *You Only Live Twice* featured shots of Japan, including the signature Sumo wrestlers, as well, of course, as its beautiful women and its fierce fighters. Near the opening of *For Your Eyes Only*, the camera disclosed the large, staring eyes of a young woman, captivated by the prospect of adventure. Right at the end of *GoldenEye*, a wary Bond slowly opened a door to reveal ... what is never made clear. In *A View to a Kill* Bond and 'May Day' engaged in a small duel of wits. 'May Day': 'Someone will take care of you.' Bond: 'Oh, you'll, uhrr, see to that personally, will you?' She turns, and he stares at her knowingly over the top of his champagne glass. An announcer told prospective viewers that 'wherever Bond stops to visit, he leaves his mark ... on everything': the first sight was an explosion, the second a willing woman, lying ready in bed (*Live and Let Die*). One visual cliché appeared in some form or other in virtually every trailer, even into the 1990s when the style and pace changed dramatically.[54] An eye filled the screen, focused on the small figure of 007; suddenly, he turned and fired directly into the eye; occasionally, a curtain of red came down from the top of the screen, sometimes the eye itself was red, presumably to suggest blood. No other character could wield so effectively the power of the gaze, not even the lords of misrule. Only Bond could survey all, and his was a gaze both sexual and violent, penetrating and dangerous, so much so that it verged on the pornographic.

The Bond films were not usually perceived as porn, however, either by regulators or by audiences.[55] The reason lay in the control his makers had over the sign. The movie Bond was hardly a disembodied signifier: there was always a referent of sorts, first Fleming's fictional hero and then over time the collection of past performances. But the origina-tors of the Bond franchise had taken great pains to cleanse their prod-uct: no nudity, no intercourse, nothing gruesome. The corporate makeover of the 1990s preserved the integrity of the franchise and the Bond persona. Two slogans used in that decade exploited the familiar-ity of this persona: 'Nobody does it better' and 'You can still depend on one man,' references to Bond's reputation as the always competent figure of heterosexual and violent power. (It is intriguing that in 1997 William Rees-Mogg echoed Paul Johnson's slur on Bond forty years before: 'He is a high technology killer, a sadistic womanizer, and a pseudo sophisticate.')[56] The erotic appeal worked through suggestion and innuendo. The publicity showed how consumers, how the whole family, to paraphrase Harry Saltzman, could enjoy the thrills of a bit of sadism. Special effects supplied the excitement of violence without its horrors. The camera might focus on fights and gunplay, and there was sometimes blood, but never did the trailers or the movies display the gory details (excepting in *Casino Royale*). Occasional shots of flesh, some revealing costumes, a knowing glance, body language, repartee, innuendo, foreplay, all worked to arouse the libido and to confirm the sovereignty of the phallus, but not – at least not often – to offend. The mix of jolts was held together with a dose of levity and a sense of fun. The Bond saga was a fine example of the ways business could stimu-late, via stealth, the prurient tastes of consumers.

The one serious vulnerability occurred whenever there was a transi-tion to a new Bond actor (witness the failure of Lazenby or Dalton), who might be unable to make the role of 007 credible. No wonder that when the time came to replace Brosnan, the search for the sixth Bond consumed many months and much energy, and set off an orgy of press speculation about who might be chosen, before the blessing fell on the blonde head of Daniel Craig late in 2005.[57] His Bond proved a less fin-ished and much rougher reincarnation of the classic hero, a good deal more brutal than his predecessors, emphasized by scenes of a vicious fight early in the trailers. No doubt that was fitting, given the fact that *Casino Royale* was presented as 'Bond begins' – about a newly minted 007. But he was still a sexy brute, still an action figure able to live very well, elegantly clad in his tuxedo, accompanied by a beautiful woman. And Craig's version of Bond did intrigue the public: in its opening weekend at the end of November 2006, the movie (according to the Internet Movie Database) took in $41 million in the United States and £13 million in the United Kingdom at the box office.

2 Madonna's Rise

Hugh Hefner built an empire by delivering an unending series of erotic spectacles. James Bond won fame because he was the grand master of the voyeur's gaze. Madonna Ciccone did both: she not only wielded the gaze, she made the display of 'perversions' into a compelling spectacle of desire. 'Sex makes the world go round,' she once told a television audience.[58] It certainly energized her career, at least during the 1980s and the early 1990s when she became so extraordinarily famous – and notorious. She flourished as one of America's great sex symbols, then certainly its most controversial, an icon of her time sometimes compared to Marilyn Monroe of the 1950s, a woman whose look Madonna emulated. Except that Monroe had found her own stature troubling: 'A sex symbol becomes a thing. I hate being a thing.'[59] Not so Madonna.[60] For ten years she fashioned herself as an erotic commodity, creating (not alone, but with the help of many people and the backing of Time-Warner) a Madonna brand, an original style of performance, often outrageous, always sexy, that was manifest in videos, records, concerts, a book, and movies consumed by millions at home and abroad. In the process she became America's queen of vulgarity.[61] The wild ride lasted until 1995 when she retreated, a victim of her own notoriety.

Despite all the hype, Madonna was not really an original. She played out a role as an entertainer that was already well-established in the annals of female performance in American mass culture. Women had often achieved fame by daring to transgress, by using sex to cause a sensation and captivate audiences.[62] Madonna was actually more akin to Mae West than Marilyn Monroe. In the early decades of the twentieth century, West had fashioned a style and a persona that drew on burlesque, on black dance, and eventually on gay performances to excite her work on the stage in New York.[63] She was denounced as vulgar and subjected to censorship and even prosecution, much of which served to publicize her fame. In her case she was able to translate that fame, and her New York sensibility, into success in Hollywood, something that would elude Madonna. But the point is that Madonna, despite her innovations, was following in the footsteps of other women who managed to succeed as sinners in a world of entertainment dominated by men.

Madonna's rise was both a consequence and a cause of the exploding popularity of music television, a novel form that emerged in America during the 1980s. This mix of sight and sound offered viewers a never-ending series of short rock and pop videos. The irony was that what music television played as entertainment amounted to commercials meant to sell the star and the record. Music videos were initially a form of publicity provided free of charge by record companies to promote their wares. That explained why these videos usually adopted the techniques of advertising rather than the conventions of film, using collections of fragmented and startling images, fast cutting, extreme camera angles, and the like, to capture and hold the attention of youthful audiences. These were performances, sometimes dances, sometimes dramas, where the flow of images might prevail over the music itself. It was not long before music videos were condemned because they dealt too much in sex and violence. Nor was it long before they were also celebrated as a new art form, and an especially postmodern form of television. 'Music video is arguably the contemporary carnival on television,' declared an admiring John Fiske, a champion of the then emerging school of cultural studies.[64]

The main force in music television was MTV, a twenty-four-hour commercial channel on cable, launched in August 1981 by Warner Amex Satellite Entertainment and acquired by another large corporate entity called Viacom in 1987. MTV was mostly about marketing – selling stars; their records, styles, and looks; advertisers' goods; and always itself, according to one of its early chroniclers.[65] Three years after it had started, MTV already commanded an audience of around 22 million viewers, mostly young people (aged between twelve and thirty-four), and earned more than $1 million a week in ad revenues.[66] In 1985 it started VH-1, a second channel aimed at baby boomers, in other words an older audience whose taste in music was less adventurous. By 1992 the MTV services were reaching approximately 56 million homes in the United States, making the channels not only a major success story in the cable industry but a significant force in the music industry as well.[67] MTV scheduled the music videos in a fashion like that of rock radio (complete with 'vjs,' or video disk jockeys), in light, medium, or heavy rotation, meaning that they were repeated throughout the day and the week. It was this constant replay that could boom the popularity of a singer or group and their records. The favour of MTV was crucial to the success of newcomers like Michael Jackson, Prince, the British group Duran Duran, and, of course, Madonna.[68]

Did Madonna set out to scandalize America? Probably, although her biographers have placed more emphasis upon her fierce ambition, her desire to win fame fast. Madonna trained first as a dancer and then took up singing: she remained, always, a visual performer whose extraordinary stage presence carried over well onto the small screen. She belonged to an avant-garde of artists and performers in New York city, tied both to the club scene and to the sexual underground, whose spirit of excess and of difference she carried into her performances. In 1982 she signed with Sire Records, a branch of Warner Brothers, later Time-Warner, a major entertainment conglomerate. She emerged on the video scene in 1984, causing a big sensation when she simulated sexual frenzy while performing her song *Like a Virgin* live on stage at the MTV music awards.[69] Two years later, after multiple video hits, she received a special 'Video Vanguard Award' from MTV. Indeed her music videos earned over forty nominations and won ten awards in the annual MTV contests between 1984 and 1994. She co-starred in the popular movie *Desperately Seeking Susan* (1985), which apparently brought her to the attention of adults. Her tours were very successful, initially winning notice because they were so popular with young girls, known as 'wannabes,' who dressed up in the peculiar garb – 'a cross between a bordello queen and a bag lady' – that Madonna sported in the mid-1980s.[70] 'I thought she was really cool, I wanted to be like her,' recalled one fan later. 'You know, like in [the] *Desperately Seeking Susan*-era, and who didn't want to be like her?'[71] She even had her own fashion look of belt buckles, clunky jewellery, cut-off gloves, pop tops, and skirts rolled down to expose the belly, celebrated in look-a-like contests in suburban malls and exploited by some retail outlets.[72] She made notorious the wearing of a crucifix as an ornament rather than a religious symbol, a gesture that seemed especially sacrilegious given her sexy ways. But it was her record sales that really impressed observers: except for 1988, when she did not release a record, she always placed a single in the Top 40 of the Billboard chart, and many of these sold well over a million copies.[73] Furthermore her music was enormously popular outside the United States as well. The *True Blue* album (1986) sold 7 million copies in the United States and 13 million worldwide.[74] In 1987 her albums were going for U.S.$75 on the black market in Moscow.[75]

By 1990 Madonna was listed as the world's top female entertainer, earning close to $40 million that year.[76] She had already generated half a billion dollars in sales for her parent company, Time-Warner. *Forbes* considered her America's top businesswoman. With good reason. She appeared in the much-hyped movie *Dick Tracy* (1990), next to her lover-of-the-moment, Warren Beatty – although she would never realize the degree of fame in Hollywood that she wanted. She masterminded a controversial but acclaimed documentary of her sell-out Blonde Ambition tour under the title *Truth or Dare* (1991), where she revealed her passion for control, for sensation, and always for sex. Indeed it was here that she celebrated her status as a hedonist, a constant seeker of pleasure and of power, whatever the consequences, a person who had full control of her environment. Purportedly it was also the highest grossing documentary up to that point in history.[77] A year later she launched Maverick Entertainment, a multimedia enterprise, backed in part by Time-Warner, to enable her to pursue opportunities in music, video, film, and the like. Then there was the commercial success of yet another new venture, entitled *Sex* (1992), a book of her erotic fantasies and photographs, the subject of an extraordinary publicity campaign and the attendant media excitement. One sample was the launch party, which, according to *People* magazine (2 November 1992), occurred in a setting designed like 'a dungeon worthy of the Marquis de Sade, featuring models in leather and mesh, acting out fantasies with whips, handcuffs and heavy-duty chains.' Madonna herself came as a mix of wanton and innocent, 'a voluptuous Heidi, clutching a toy lamb.'[78] Although published only at the end of the year and selling at a hefty cost of nearly $50, *Sex* was an instant bestseller, ranked number ten that year and earning Madonna an estimated $20 million: the hype had made all sorts of people, not just fans, desperate to get hold of a copy.[79] Madonna, it seemed, was having lots of fun making lots of money.

Madonna's popularity soon attracted the attention of the academy, where the analysis of mass and popular culture had become a matter of consuming interest during the 1980s.[80] Feminist scholars found the success of Madonna both fascinating and problematic because she seemed to mock as well as to embrace the prevailing codes of sexuality, which in turn reflected the machinations of their bête noire, patriarchy. Was she friend or foe? Queer scholars were intrigued, and sometimes also troubled, by the ways in which Madonna expropriated the styles and the images of lesbian and gay sex. Did her borrowings advance the cause of sexual diversity? Much of this work occurred under the rubric of cultural studies, a relatively new academic enterprise, British in origin but then making rapid progress in the United States, which focused on the generation and circulation of meanings in contemporary societies. The result was a series of articles and books, in the United States and elsewhere, that analysed her 'texts,' her audiences, and her significance.[81]

The process transformed Madonna into a tool used to explore, say, postmodern times, gay culture or gender troubles, and always the power of commercialism. She became, in short, an object and a site, often a contested site, of theory. Cultural studies was high on the virtues of theorizing, whatever its topic of analysis, nearly always a source of derision among journalists, who, then at least, were ignorant of theory, unable to understand its insights, and therefore ever ready to condemn the Madonna scholars for writing jargon-ridden explanations that provided little that was new or worthwhile.[82] Freud, Jung, and Lacan, especially Jacques Lacan, whose work had caught the fancy of literary analysts, received much play, though the ideology of psychoanalysis no longer commanded the respect it had enjoyed among an earlier generation of academics. Well represented, of course, were feminist theorists, notably Judith Butler – and that advocate of postfeminism Camille Paglia, who found in Madonna 'the future of feminism.'[83] All kinds of French writers were quoted, men such as Roland Barthes (of semiotics fame), Guy Debord (the theorist of spectacle), Michel De Certeau (the sociologist of everyday life), Gilles Deleuze (a philosopher of difference), and Georges Bataille (though, ironically, not because of his work on eroticism), all this a sign of the infatuation of the American academy with French theory in the late 1980s and early 1990s. Also present were Horkheimer and Adorno, leaders of the Frankfurt School of critical theory, who back in the 1940s and 1950s had treated mass culture as 'mass deception.'[84] This view was no longer favoured by the champions of cultural studies, who denied that ordinary people, the consumers or rather makers of popular culture ('makers' because they negotiated their own meanings out of songs and sitcoms and ads), were dopes or dupes of Hollywood or Madison Avenue or Nashville: some of the scholars actually studied how fans and haters derived different meanings from watching Madonna on screen or stage.[85]

Three additional names stand out in this extensive menagerie of theorists, Jean Baudrillard, Michel Foucault, and Mikhail Bakhtin, because in my view their arguments seem so well suited to understanding the Madonna phenomenon. Baudrillard directed attention to his fabulous domain of hyperreality where images were sovereign and where images, or rather 'simulacra,' were disembodied signifiers, cut free from their referents and their meanings. Madonna flourished in an environment dominated by the mass media; and that, of course, was one reason she seemed the postmodern icon nonpareil. Time and again the scholars quoted a conversation from *Truth or Dare* where Warren Beatty commented wryly on Madonna's addiction to the public stage. A doctor was examining Madonna's suffering throat, injured by the strain of so many performances during the Blonde Ambition tour:

> DOCTOR: Do you want to talk at all off-camera? You have nothing to say?
> MADONNA shakes her head no. Beatty laughs.
> BEATTY: She doesn't want to live off-camera, much less talk.
> DOCTOR: That's it, yes that's what I think it is.
> BEATTY: There's nothing to say off camera. Why would you say something if it's off-camera? What point is there of existing?

As one of the paparazzi put it, she was 'a publicity whore.'[86]

Everything Madonna did seemed orchestrated for effect: she was the master publicist who fashioned her own self as myth, one reason why people wondered whether there was anything authentic about Madonna and why biographers later had such difficulty separating the fact and the fiction in her life.[87] 'My sister is her own masterpiece,' commented her brother, Christopher Ciccone.[88] She was an expert in making claims that excited the media. Andrew Morton, one of her biographers, pointed out how her first interviews amounted to propaganda for her own self-vision: 'the ghetto childhood; the schoolgirl rebel; the flirty young Lolita who became a sexual athlete; the mistreated Cinderella, complete with Wicked Stepmother; the misunderstood artist.'[89] She was the ever-changing chameleon, playing a tomboy or a vamp, Mae West and Marlene Dietrich, a virgin or a dominatrix, albeit over the span of a decade. 'Madonna says we are nothing but masks,' wrote an admiring Camille Paglia.[90] Madonna constantly worked to market shock in her performances on television and on stage. When *Penthouse* and then *Playboy* announced in 1985 that they intended to run nude photographs of a pre-stardom Madonna, just at the time she was betrothed to the actor Sean Penn, that set off an orgy of speculation about what this revelation might do to her career, and her prospective marriage. The frenzy did her no public harm, given her reputation as something of a sex radical. Indeed, at least one magazine concluded that she had engineered the whole affair.[91] There were times when her face seemed to be everywhere. She worked with Time-Warner during the five months prior to the publication of *Sex* in 1992 to keep the story of its arrival in the public eye. Initially, far fewer books were printed than were required to meet the demand generated, in order to create scarcity and feed the buying frenzy, making the release a marketing event in its own right.[92] 'Madonna has no equal in getting attention,' concluded Carrie Fisher.[93]

Her command of artifice showed best in her music videos (see figure 5.2). The lyrics and the music of her songs, however appealing, were ancillary to her visual performance. Madonna put considerable time and money into crafting what were often very elaborate productions: reportedly she invested a million dollars in the making of *Express Yourself*, which was based on Fritz Lang's 1929 science-fiction classic, *Metropolis*.[94] She and her associates really did appear to practise Baudrillard, meaning they appropriated and juxtaposed all manner of different images.[95] But, contra Baudrillard, these images were not completely disembodied; they carried with them the traces of their earlier meanings, even if they had been ripped free from their original contexts. The cinematography was superb, at least after the initial cheaply produced videos. She used panoramic shots and close-ups, pans, quick cutting, alternating black-and-white and colour inserts, fades, fuzzy and sharp images, changing angles, superimposed images, and on-screen text. Sometimes the videos had a surreal quality, as in the case of *Express Yourself* or *Fever*. Often they told some kind of story, even acting out a drama – note, in particular, *Papa Don't Preach*. She staged the productions in exotic places, both high and low: the canals of Venice (*Like a Virgin*), the settings of Hollywood (*Material Girl* or *Vogue*), a Parisian hotel full of sin (*Justify My Love*), a Third World street (*La Isla Bonita*). She drew upon the signifiers of her own Italian-American and Catholic background, on gay and black culture, on the past stars of Hollywood. Often her performances were organized around stark contrasts: the classic virgin/whore distinction (notably represented by her wedding dress in *Like a Virgin*), the dichotomy between sleaze and innocence (the peep show versus the happy street in *Open Your Heart*), or the erotic play of top or bottom (the changing positions of the sexual athletes in *Justify My Love*). She assembled her identity of the moment out of costumes (which she might change in the course of a video), her hair colour and hair-do, gestures and poses, other performers, words and music, to make herself, for example, Marilyn Monroe or Marie Antoinette. Always she played with symbols: the lion and the lion-headed man as her lover in *Like a Virgin*; or the bodies trapped in a tight-fitting box in *Human Nature*. Nearly all of the videos featured dance, either Madonna alone or Madonna and a troupe of mostly male performers,

Figure 5.2: Madonna's Music Videos
Listed below are the videos cited in the text because, in one way or another, they manifest Madonna's version of eroticism. I have identified the overall style of the video and, briefly, described its topic or character. Madonna did release other kinds of music videos in this period, of course.

Borderline   1984   Director: Mary Lambert
Drama: Madonna plays with love (a Latino youth) and fame (a fashion photographer), resisting the demands of both men to have her own way.

Lucky Star   1984   Director: Arthur Pierson
Display: Madonna appears as a sex kitten, enticing the voyeur with her poses and dancing energetically.

Like a Virgin   1984   Director: Mary Lambert.
Vignettes: Madonna expresses the joys of being in love, 'kissed ... for the very first time.' This was considered the first of her great videos.

Material Girl   1985   Director: Mary Lambert.
Drama: Madonna playing Marilyn Monroe in the movie *Gentlemen Prefer Blondes* affirms and denies materialism.

Papa Don't Preach   1986   Director: James Foley.
Drama: Madonna confronts her father over 'keeping her baby.'

Open Your Heart   1986   Director: Jean-Baptiste Mondino.
Drama: Madonna performs for voyeurs but runs away with a young boy.

La Isla Bonita   1987   Director: Mary Lambert.
Vignettes: Madonna yearns for the carefree and erotic life of 'San Pedro.'

Like a Prayer   1989   Director: Mary Lambert.
Drama: Madonna, among much else, saves a black man falsely accused of raping and murdering a white woman.

Express Yourself   1989   Director: David Fincher.
Vignettes: Madonna leads a sex revolt among the toiling male masses in a remake of Fritz Lang's *Metropolis*.

Vogue   1990   Director: David Fincher.
Display: Madonna and her dancers draw on gay imagery and the camp style to worship the memory of celebrity.

Justify My Love   1990   Director: Jean-Baptiste Mondino.
Vignettes: Madonna enjoys the pleasures of lust with her lover and others in a hotel dedicated to sin.

Erotica   1992   Director: Fabien Baron.
Vignettes: Madonna as dominatrix orchestrates and participates in a series of adventures.

Bad Girl   1993   Director: David Fincher.
Drama: Madonna as a woman of low morals and much unhappiness is being stalked, though perhaps by her guardian angel.

Fever   1993   Director: Stephanie Sednaopi.
Display: An extended dance number featuring glossy, throbbing, and boldly coloured images of Madonna and a semi-naked man.

Human Nature   1995   Director: Jean-Baptiste Mondino.
Display: A defiant Madonna and her dancers respond to those who have trashed her crusade for sexual liberation.

where her amazing ability to enact emotions and strike poses was always on display. The moods changed: *Like a Prayer* mixed fear and joy; *Justify My Love* was full of lust; and *Erotica*, the 'dirtiest' of her videos, was both ironic and sinister. Things usually turned out well in the end; indeed some of her endings were joyful, though in one strange video (*Bad Girl*) Madonna watched as the police carried her dead body out of her apartment.

The music videos were Madonna's key mode of publicity. But they were also more than that: they were the artistic renditions of her fantasies, her desires, the narcissism of her many selves. The dreams she told the public much of the time were about sex and power, and in particular about evading or resisting the reign of orthodoxy. She became an advocate in some of her videos, actually delivering commands to her fans such as 'open your heart,' 'express yourself,' and 'strike a pose.' *Erotica* was an extended ode to the forbidden pleasures awaiting whoever opened themselves up to the demands of desire. 'Power is a great aphrodisiac,' she once claimed, 'and I'm a very powerful person.'[96] That was why Foucault's teachings seemed so appropriate. Madonna, to borrow his terminology, was the product of relations of power, meaning that she was constructed as a sexual object in a world where men, more properly heterosexual men, enjoyed the larger share of social and economic authority. She did not try to deny the tyranny of the stereotype, to enact the oppositions of a classic feminism. Rather she relished – in fact, celebrated – her status as a sex goddess who commanded the attention of men and women. Where she resisted was by putting herself, that is by putting women, at the centre of this economy of power and pleasure. She articulated and performed a gospel of 'libidinal autonomy.'[97] During the course of *Like a Virgin*, she pointed and boldly declared to her man, to all men, 'You're mine.' She opened *Express Yourself*, sitting atop an eagle with a man's face, by singing 'Come on girls ... don't go for second best ... put your love to the test,' exhorting women to make men declare their love in a way so emphatic that they knew it was 'real.' Some of the video displayed not the female body but the muscular torsos of young males toiling away in the bowels of the 'city': they were the objects of the voyeur's gaze. Yet other scenes depicted Madonna being sexy, dressed in the garb of black negligee, garters, and nylons; chained to a bed, an iron band around her neck; or crawling, better yet slinking, across a glossy floor on her hands and knees.

It was this combined persona of sexuality and independence that so appealed to women, especially young women. 'I like the way she handles herself, sort of take it or leave it; she's sexy but she doesn't need men ... she's kind of there all by herself,' stated one teenager. 'She gives us ideas. It's really women's lib, not being afraid of what guys think,' said another.[98] 'She's tarty and seductive,' noted an Australian girl, fourteen years old, 'but it looks all right when she does it ... with her it's OK, it's acceptable ...'[99] An English fan, aged fifteen, recalled how 'It's like after you've watched her on telly or something, you walk, no you flaunt out of the room, thinking, well if she can, why can't I?'[100] That same persona clearly disturbed some men, though: one poll in 1990 revealed that 60 per cent of the boys interviewed did not want to sleep with Madonna, perhaps because, as another teen had put it, 'she'd give any guy a hard time.'[101]

The effort to liberate sex and centre women took two forms. Initially, roughly speaking in the years 1984 to 1986, she enacted the cause of teen rebellion in videos where she posed as a sexy creature, especially in *Lucky Star* and *Like a Virgin*, who refused to submit to rules imposed by a boyfriend (*Borderline*), money (*Material Girl*), or a father (*Papa Don't Preach*). Then she shed her teen look and toned her body, becoming wiry, even muscular and androgynous, adopting the pose, in Paglia's words, of 'hard glamour.'[102] This marked the translation of her resistance into a wider challenge to the sexual codes of America, where she embraced deviance, drawing on the sexual culture of outsiders, notably Latino and black, gay and lesbian, and the aficionados of S/M.[103] It was during these years, roughly 1986 through 1993, that she fashioned her most outstanding and controversial videos, *Express Yourself*, *Like a Prayer*, *Justify My Love*, and *Erotica*. *Like a Prayer* derived some of its force from suggestions of sex between a white woman and a black man, always a touchy subject in America. The last video in the series was all about the extraordinary pleasures of pain, about the joys of surrender and domination, some of the themes elaborated in *Sex*: indeed the song 'Erotica' was actually a part of the package that people bought when they got the book.

One place where this rebellion was constantly played out, particularly during the second phase of her project, was in Foucault's domain of the eye. Foucault had argued the eclipse of spectacle and the significance of surveillance in the technologies of modern power.[104] He focused attention on the person who wielded the gaze, be that a doctor, a teacher, a prison guard, a manager, anyone who looked upon the body and the soul of another. Madonna worked to disturb this sovereignty of the gaze through the adroit manipulation of camera angles. The voyeurs in the peep show of *Open Your Heart* were themselves objects of a mocking gaze: two plasticized homosexuals, a cool lesbian, a naive country boy, one slob and one creep, a dirty old man, even an academic complete with pencil and paper, all were shown looking at her perform an erotic dance. The master of the city in *Express Yourself* held the monocle, 'a symbol of male voyeuristic power but also a signifier of lesbianism in the 1920s,' according to one commentator.[105] Yet at the end of the video it was the outline of Madonna's face, and especially her huge eyes, which look out on the city. Sometimes Tony Ward, then Madonna's actual lover, was the voyeur, sometimes he was the spectacle, in *Justify My Love*. Christopher Walken played the stalker in *Bad Girl*, but at the end, both he and Madonna, seated in directors' chairs above the action, watched as the body of the 'bad girl' was removed from her apartment. The gaze, in short, shifted here and there, back and forth, offering no solid purchase on who held the power, except eventually Madonna herself.

Madonna's videos demonstrated not the eclipse but the significance of spectacle, thus contradicting Foucault. Right from the beginning she took great pleasure in playing the exhibitionist: that was the overriding message of *Lucky Star* where she offered shots of her belly button, where she appeared as a sexy little girl, where she gave the 'come-on' sign to viewers. She set out to seduce both her suitors and the audience when she re-performed Marilyn Monroe's number in *Material Girl*.[106] In the much more elaborate *Vogue*, based on the styles of fashion photography and classic Hollywood, Madonna and her troupe took up enigmatic but stylish poses. The force of *Justify My Love* grew out of the display of 'perverted' sex play. During the course of *Erotica* the words 'I'll ... teach ... you ... how ... to' flashed on the screen. Teach what? The *Sex* book supplied the answer – how to 'fuck.' That illustrated a common purpose: Madonna had constantly employed spectacle to construct the viewer as a sexual player ready to enjoy all sorts of erotic fantasies.

Here is where Bakhtin's concept of the carnival becomes a useful tool of explanation. Recall that carnival was that other world of laughter and sin and excess where people could escape the authority and the rules of the mundane world of hierarchy and privilege. In Madonna's videos the arrival of carnival was always represented through the beginning of dance that signified the release of the body. At the end of *Open Your Heart* Madonna and the young boy, holding hands, danced happily away from the sordid abode of the voyeurs. In *Like a Prayer* the joyous dancing and singing of a choir in a black church signified the escape from the racism and violence of white America. The lyrics of *Vogue* actually referred to life as a heartache. There was, fortunately, 'a place you can get away. It's called a dance floor ...' The song went on to command, 'let your body groove to the music,' 'let your body go with the flow.' The body triumphed over the head, the physical over the moral, expression over repression. No wonder that command was repeated time and again in *Human Nature*, Madonna's answer to her critics: 'Express yourself, don't repress yourself.'

During *Express Yourself* Madonna suddenly appeared in drag, wearing a dark, loose-fitting man's suit, on a raised stage where her dance parodied the macho style of male performers, grabbing her crotch and pulling open her jacket to reveal her bra. In *Sex* Madonna admitted, though not in these words, that she was the realization of that Freudian nightmare the phallic woman – 'I think I have a dick in my brain.'[107] This too signified her entry into a carnivalesque world, a place inhabited by all sorts of vulgar types: clowns and freaks and gluttons, fake priests and false kings, conjurers and profaners, whores and thieves. Such people can be loosely gathered within the social category of the grotesque, whose appetites and actions threatened the order of the mundane world. The grotesque remained a source of repugnance and fascination because he or she represented that which had been suppressed by the mainstream, a reformulation of the Freudian notion that whatever was repressed must eventually return as an object of desire.[108] Madonna performed as the erotic version of the grotesque – and a very dangerous one, too – a sort of Pied Piper who set out to entice the public, notably youth, especially teenage women, down the forbidden paths of sin and pleasure. There was more than a whiff of polymorphous perversity, that characteristic of childhood identified by Freud, in her version of eroticism.

Consider *Justify My Love*, where Madonna deployed a range of means designed to scandalize. Masquerade: Madonna appeared once again in the guise of Marilyn Monroe. Parody: looking a bit stunned or drugged, she roamed through the halls of a hotel in Paris that amounted to a twisted version of the honeymoon resort. Erotomania: suddenly she dropped her suitcase. Then she stroked her body, slid to the floor, opened her coat, revealed her upper legs, and touched her crotch, all the while imagining herself and her man. That man slowly approached Madonna and they began to kiss. The lyrics, sung in a husky voice, emphasized how she was overcome by lust, how she wanted her lover to pleasure her completely. 'Wanting, needing, waiting, for you to justify my love.' Exoticism: the camera then revealed how the hotel was frequented by lesbians, bisexuals, transvestites, and androgynes, all happily on display. Occasionally it focused on the slim body of what was probably a man, wearing a kind of jump suit, his hands ending in long nails, who swayed and danced to the music. Degradation: she and the other players appropriated the signs of pornography, including swelling breasts, the garter belt, black panties and bras, leather and chains, the corset, the high heel (all of which separately or in other contexts could have different meanings). But there was not, aside from a brief shot of one woman's breasts, much nudity, no naked Madonna, no male erection, which would offend the rules of television broadcasting. This fantasy had to be tailored to the law. Blasphemy: the symbols of Catholicism, a crucifix worn this time by her lover and a wall plaque showing a crucified Christ, became part of the ongoing erotic play. As always, her very name, 'Madonna,' seemed sacrilegious in so sinful an environment. Excess: there was a constant game of tease, of hiding, revealing, and suggesting all kinds of 'dirty' behaviours, including a lesbian kiss, simulated intercourse (both 'missionary' and 'queen'), the exchange of partners, bondage and rough sex, foot fetish, orgy and masturbation, even total sex where the whole body was treated – admired, stroked, or licked – as an erotic object. Humour: how funny it was – well, she did laugh – when one lesbian drew a moustache on the face of another. Irony: after all the play, she ran through the halls of the hotel smiling and laughing, perhaps because she had been so pleasured, perhaps over the bizarre sights, anyway privy to some hidden joke. The finale was an on-screen declaration: 'Poor is the man whose pleasures depend on the permission of another.' The sense of fun had lasted right to the end.

Such performances infuriated many a viewer. As John Fiske noted, Madonna excited the passions, she was 'much loved or much hated.'[109] A trio of scholars looked closely at the pattern of responses of the Madonna haters. What they found was a deep sense of revulsion, in effect a recognition that she had played out the role of the grotesque. Time and again she was referred to as a tramp or a whore, the lowest form of a woman. 'Madonna is a sleez [sic], she's a tramp, she's a slut,' wrote a thirty-one-year-old mother. 'She's a disgrace to the woman's race.' 'Any slut can strip and sing professionally,' claimed another woman. 'She's a repulsive ho.' A male asserted that Madonna was 'a child molester' because she had kissed the lips of the young boy in *Open Your Heart*. Another male viewer of the same video thought Madonna 'a sex-crazed nymph.' One imaginative, and religious, soul decided that the Antichrist would declare his love for Madonna, because 'she is obedient to my will and does a good job in luring the impure, unchaste, and unstraight to my cause; like pride, greed, drugs, crime, sodomy, she tempts the weak and rebellious, adding to my army.'[110]

Inevitably Madonna was attacked by moral authorities. *Material Girl* sparked media complaints about her celebration of materialism, though she actually rejected the lure of money in the minidrama. Planned Parenthood charged that *Papa Don't Preach* encouraged premature sex and teenage pregnancy. The Reverend Donald Wildmon of the American Family Association took issue with the blasphemy of *Like a Prayer*, where Madonna and a black saint had sex in a church. The controversy over *Like a Prayer* early in 1989 led Pepsi-Cola, because of fears of a boycott, to drop a commercial linked to the video, a species of cross-marketing, though the company still paid Madonna her $5 million fee. The next year even MTV balked over *Justify My Love*: the channel refused to air the video. Her Blonde Ambition tour of 1990 ran into difficulties, briefly, in what she called 'the fascist city of Toronto,' more seriously in Italy because of the Vatican's displeasure.[111]

Madonna fought back. The MTV ban on *Justify My Love* brought a celebrated appearance on ABC's *Nightline* (3 November 1990), a late-night public affairs program.[112] Madonna adopted the pose of the wronged artist – she was beautifully made up in an elegant but severe black jacket, with most of her neck covered – who had fallen victim 'to the wave of censorship over the nation.' She had acted responsibly: her video was about sexual honesty, 'about the celebration of sex.' The trouble was, 'sexuality is something that Americans would really rather sweep under the rug.' She denied, in short, the carnivalesque purpose of her own performance. Forrest Sawyer, her inquisitor, was unconvinced, because she always seemed ready to push the limits of acceptance. And she did warn, 'I'm gonna keep pushing buttons.' Besides, he suspected that this was all a publicity stunt to market still more of the Madonna brand, notably the video single, something never done before. Wasn't she known in the industry as 'one of the best self-marketers in the business'? All the excitement over the ban was just a win-win situation for Madonna. And in fact she did sell around 800,000 copies of the video. It was an interesting reflection of the moral temper of the times that Madonna's ability to profit from her art, indeed from the sale of her publicity, was still counted against her claims that she was the victim of censorship.

In other circumstances, though, Madonna imagined herself playing a more aggressive role in the ongoing culture wars. 'I think I am a sexual threat,' she told Vanity Fair (April 1990). 'I think it is easier for people to embrace people who don't poke at their insides and make them think about their own sexuality.'[113] In Truth or Dare she admitted, 'I'm interested in pushing people's buttons, and being provocative, and being political.' Indeed, she told Newsweek (2 November 1992), 'I do in a way see myself as a revolutionary at this point'; and she told BBC Radio One (30 December 1992), 'I only have to be rebellious because others are so reactionary.'[114] So she positioned herself as something of a catalyst for sexual change in America. That too was part of the publicity machine for her Sex book, of course. It was also a trifle specious because, in fact, she had restrained her sexual fantasies to meet the conventions of mainstream publishing: Sex did not display erections, penetration, or bestiality (although one photograph did suggest having sex with a dog).[115] There was a definite limit to how provocative – to be blunt, how grotesque – Madonna would or could become, as long as she wished to work within the confines of the existing corporate system of entertainment in America.

In fact Madonna had already gone beyond the bounds of the permissible, at least according to the reigning moral authorities. Sex looked too much like pornography: not even the skills of the fashion photographer Steven Meisel, who shot her fantasies, could dispel the sleaze. Christian advocates, feminists, gays, even one-time friends were, in different ways, critical and sometimes appalled, although this opinion was not universal and certainly did not slow sales of the book.[116] The full weight of media outrage came down on her head, however: Sex, no matter how popular, was deemed pornographic or boring or oversold – once more she was denounced because she had exploited, or promoted, 'perversion' for profit, a veiled reference to the notion that Madonna really was a whore. She also received 'sackloads of hate mail' (up to 200 a day) from irate individuals and groups.[117] This time Madonna retreated in the face of such a display of righteous anger. She did, admittedly, complete her Girlie Show tour in 1993, which had its randy moments. But her publicity antics and music videos were toned down. And, in a September 1994 interview with The Face, a magazine in London, she claimed it was time for 'a tamer image.' 'I'm being punished for being a single female, for having power and being rich and saying the things I say,' she said. 'I'm being punished for having a sex life, for saying that I enjoy it. So I've decided to leave it alone.'[118] Madonna, for the moment, had again taken on the pose of the victim.

Her most public response to the controversy came the next year when she released *Human Nature*. It was an extraordinary performance, the mood out of keeping with what she had done before. Madonna, dressed in a shiny black one-piece suit that, once more, suggested fetish garb, and her troupe of men and women, also in black, expressed in song and dance a disdain for all of the critics who had slammed her erotic crusade. At times she snarled at the camera. She and the others kept repeating, 'And I'm not sorry.' She struck out at obstacles that restrained her. 'I'm not your bitch, don't hang your ... on me.' She boxed an imaginary opponent. 'You're the one with the problem.' She and her dancers rolled around as if in combat. 'Did I say something wrong? Oops, I didn't know I couldn't talk about sex.' There were scenes of stroking and rubbing and licking, especially of Madonna's body, some bondage, ropes and chains, and Madonna playing with a whip. At the end she even took a feminist line, the lyrics conveying the sad 'truth' that her plight was the result of being a woman, not a man. There was little of the old spirit of fun here, but a lot of defiance. Not to much purpose, however, except the satisfaction of striking back: this bitter outburst marked the end of the wild ride.

There are ways in which the career of Madonna parallels that of Dalí. Both were independent-minded and energetic. Both were masters of their respective art forms who earned a reputation for brilliant work that expressed their own erotic fantasies. Both sought wealth and fame by playing out the social role of the grotesque, challenging the sexual morality of their times. Dalí translated the surrealist vision into a marketable signature. Madonna appropriated the deviance and the styles of the sexual underground to fashion a spectacularly successful brand. They each suffered criticism because they achieved success in the marketplace: Dalí was labelled 'Avida Dollars' and rejected by his erstwhile compatriots; Madonna was deemed a pervert and a whore and condemned by the media.

Neither, in the end, could continue to perform as the grotesque. Still famous, still wealthy, Madonna sought respectability after 1994: she starred in the movie *Evita* (albeit as another woman of dubious morals), soon became a mother, found spiritual renewal, and eventually remarried. Count here the import of aging and the moderating effects of success. Beyond that, the role of the grotesque was inherently unstable, since it required that its actor always exploit some new sin to excite the passions of the public. This demand must eventually clash with the limits of tolerance. Consider the following example of a desire never voiced or imaged. Throughout, Madonna had made reference to her troubled relationship with her father – indeed, her sense of rejection, her wish to be loved, became a part of the mythology of the persona that she kept presenting to the world. In *Truth or Dare* she made a passing, and clearly humorous, comment about spending time in his bed. But would Madonna have held her fans had she obviously transgressed the taboo of incest in one of her performances? The answer is surely no. That taboo was just too strong, especially given the rise of a moral panic over child abuse in the 1980s and its persistence in the 1990s.

Where Madonna differed from Dalí was that she came at the end of the Eros project – the regime of stimulation was already in place. Madonna's success was underwritten by corporations who dominated the entertainment business. She could never have secured the degree of fame and notoriety and power she had won by 1990 without the exposure she received on MTV. Her success as a singer was closely linked to the resources and reach of Warner Brothers, later Time-Warner, who marketed her songs. By the same token Time-Warner had earned extraordinary profits because she was so popular, generating an estimated $1.2 billion worth of record sales by 1996, according to *Vanity Fair*.[119] Time-Warner had discovered a brand that captured the appeal of deviant sex, that offered consumers the possibility of enjoying guilty or forbidden pleasures in privacy and safety. They could use Madonna's wares either to sample her erotic fantasies or to enliven their own. Time-Warner had made money not just out of satisfying desire but out of exploiting 'perversion,' out of sinning; or, to cast this in more theoretical terms, the company had effectively sponsored the rebellion of the carnivalesque and been handsomely rewarded for its endeavour.

6 A Theatre of the Libido

Watching television one night in Germany in 1994, I found an exuberant celebration of appetite on a local television channel.[1] The vehicle was a commercial for Langnese's Viennetta, a frozen dessert made up of layers of vanilla ice cream and chocolate and powdered with cocoa. The ad had begun innocently enough with some shots of a loving couple, apparently at ease, perhaps on a bed, making eyes at each other. But suddenly the camera switched from the dreamy face of the woman to a close-up of the product; now the camera showed how the sensual folds of creamy delight simulated intercourse, one shiny shaft entering what looked very much like a smoothed vagina. That launched a series of vignettes: some of bodies engaged in sex play, hugging and nibbling and sucking each other; others of people – well, mostly mouths – eagerly consuming a Viennetta, eating with the same kind of passion as if making love; plus assorted pictures of the 'making' of the product, one creamy layer of ice cream or chocolate falling so perfectly on top of another. The commercial positioned the dessert as a substitute for sex; better yet, it extended the definition of sensual passion to include the consumption of food.[2] The pleasures of food and sex, the common delight of sensuality, the satisfaction of desires, all were presented in the space of thirty seconds. Here was an example of what has sometimes been called 'food porn.'

The Viennetta commercial appeared in a cluster of ads where more than half of the nine messages had an erotic tinge, particularly featuring shots of beautiful women. That number was on the high side. Most clusters during the evening were not so sexy. Still, my survey of the ads shown in London, Madrid, Cologne and the Rhineland, Paris, and Stockholm revealed how common it was to find erotic commercials on television, especially in the evening hours.[3] There was hardly a cluster that did not sport a bit of flesh, some erotic yearning, perhaps a love scene.[4]

And not just in western Europe. According to some estimates, 'as much as one fifth of advertising' in America employed sex in one way or another at the end of the 1990s.[5] Magazines on both continents carried a whole series of sensual and erotic messages: indeed they have remained the boldest among the advertising media, the home of the most risqué imagery. The French magazine *Photo* (November 2000) offered its readers a gallery of the most sexy and shocking ads, these as a form of art, replete with images suggesting bestiality, violence, prostitution, fetish, and on and on. Movie trailers were infamous for teasing cinema goers with glimpses of sex and violence. Radio commercials commonly used sexual innuendo to attract the notice of listeners. Posters and window displays staged a public version of this libidinal dreaming: the Saatchi agency (London) won a Grand Prix at the Cannes advertising festival in 2002 for a series of outdoor ads for Club 18–30, a travel group, featuring 'scenes of vacationing 20–somethings that, on closer inspection, include an array of erotic situations.'[6]

By the 1990s advertising had built theatres of the libido where sex was used to sell a broad range of goods to people in the affluent zone of countries. These theatres were located in the minds of people watching, reading, and listening, at home, on the road, and in movie houses, bars, restaurants, and the like. They were sites where people consumed, contested, enjoyed, resisted, and accepted the assortment of commercial messages. They were crucial to the functioning of the libidinal economy since publicity as erotica produced the assemblages that linked self, object, and sex in the material world of Eros. This enterprise fitted the temper of the times. More people at home were enthusiastically enjoying what historian Edward Shorter has called the pleasures of 'total body sex,' oral, anal, role-playing, and so on, including much that would once have been deemed improper, if not illegal.[7] The cinemas and television were full of examples of 'porno-chic,' a term that Brian McNair, a media scholar, coined to refer to the spread of pornographic imagery and styles into the mainstream.[8] Indeed much advertising could be fitted into that category, except that its imagery and styles were usually cleansed to produce something other than porn.

1 Erotic Trajectories

It was erotic commercials on television and, sometimes, at the cinema that offered the most complete and compelling examples of publicity as erotica. There were many reasons why the audiovisual commercial would prove the most effective way to render the world of goods sexy.[9] Cinema had conquered much of the globe by mid-century, meaning it reached huge numbers of people over the course of a month, and in western Europe (later in North America) it served as a vehicle of advertising. Television was nearly everywhere in the affluent zone of countries by the end of the 1960s. It penetrated markets more slowly elsewhere – but it was potent throughout the developing world and the successor states of the Soviet empire in the 1990s. Increasingly, especially after 1980 when public television in western Europe went into decline, the most successful services around the globe were commercial, their programming geared to please the widest audiences and their purpose to sell the attention of viewers, their eyes and ears, to advertisers of all sorts. By the early 1980s, the TV set in homes of all classes was turned on for large chunks of time, around eight hours a day in North America and Japan. No wonder national and global marketers spent huge sums trying to reach this enormous constituency of consumers, amounting to about $60 billion alone in the U.S. market of 2000.[10] Hence the common refrain, usually a complaint, that people were exposed to hundreds of TV ads a week, thousands in the course of a year, millions even before they left school.

TV and cinema ads well suited the triumph of what Jean Baudrillard, now a postmodern guru, once called the 'era of simulation,' when reality had been murdered by a profusion of mass-produced illusions or simulacra.[11] The very design of the commercial enabled it to fashion, far better than print ads, those libidinal assemblages of bodies and body parts, of personas, commodities and services, objects, places, and situations that were the mainstay of the erotic sell. Images could startle and excite; moving images could involve and engage; coloured images could sensualize a brand; music might promote a particular mood; words spoken or written could activate the erotic imagination. The commercial excelled at association: it could link together disparate elements, the signs of the desirable body and the name of the product, whether Levi jeans or Absolut vodka, in displays and stories that fostered a narrative of desire, sometimes one that attached an erotic charge to a brand. Perhaps best of all, the commercial easily moved beyond both truth and falsity – so it could never be unmasked – by positioning its sexual scenarios as fantasies played out in some realm of dreams far away from the mundane world of ordinary life.[12]

The date of the first erotic commercial is likely lost forever.[13] It happened before the arrival of television, though. In the early 1930s in France, Scandale Girdle sponsored at least three slightly risqué ad films featuring young, attractive women in their underwear.[14] During the 1950s, the first full decade of television in the United States, American admakers were much more shy in their use of sex appeal, as it was then called. Only a few ads in the first Clios, an industry selection of esteemed classics, employed sexual innuendo, displayed a well-shaped ankle, or emphasized a striking face.[15] Even a famous commercial of 1957 for Miss Clairol was just an oh-so-tame chronicle of the life and looks of a young mother, despite its slogan: 'Does she ... or doesn't she?'[16]

The moral restrictions placed on advertising did loosen during the next decade because of the onset of both the sexual revolution in the broader society and the 'creative revolution' in Madison Avenue. Agencies now emphasized such novel selling strategies as a youth focus (since even older folk responded well to images of young bodies and appeals to a youthful state of mind), the related ploy of rebel talk (where the brand became a mark of distinction and opposition), the use of humour and irony (even to the point of mocking the brand itself, as in the case of the Volkswagen 'Beetle' campaigns), as well as the practice of 'making sexy.'[17] Indeed the erotic sell became both more common and more overt in magazines: thus the advertisers in *Chatelaine*, the most important women's magazine in Canada during the 1960s, made sex appeal a major theme in their messages to homemakers.[18] But television was a different story, at least in America: the Pepsi Generation campaign, for example, was more suggestive than revealing when it highlighted the firm bodies of young men and women at play. The sexy sell was much milder and less familiar on television, presumably because admakers and advertisers, not to mention network censors, thought eroticism would not go over well when shown in the living room, especially where and when children might be watching.

That situation changed slowly between the early 1970s and the mid-1990s. The 'creative revolution' had redefined television advertising as a form of popular culture, a type of entertainment that was supposed to offer viewers a small dose of pleasure in its own right. One result was efforts to capitalize on the tease: a survey of the award-winning commercials in the yearly Cannes (and sometimes Venice) international advertising festivals demonstrated how the practice of mobilizing the libido became a standard ploy of admakers. The focus and the progress of the erotic sell were always uneven, however. Everywhere, the female body was much more likely to be sexualized than the male: you could find plenty of cleavage, lots of shapely legs and pouty mouths, increasingly a man's bare chest, occasionally naked female breasts, but rarely the vulva, and never an erection (though one Austrian cigarette ad did show a man's penis covered by a yellow sheath – it looked very much like a banana). [19] That said, admakers in Britain and France, joined a bit later by their compatriots in Italy, West Germany, Brazil, and post-Franco Spain, were more adventurous than their counterparts in North America. At first the British went in for innuendo (there were restrictions on what parts of the body could be shown) while the French were more prone to visual display. As the 1980s advanced the (usually) brief exposure of a young woman's breasts became increasingly commonplace on the continent – ads in Germany, in fact, came to specialize in a peek-a-boo effect, a sudden and unexpected display of a bare female chest. One Danish film, for the tabloid *Ekstrabladet*, offered a few seconds of full frontal nudity, revealing the lush bodies of some beautiful young women enjoying a rest in a sauna – though the ad hid the resulting erection of the male voyeur beneath the newspaper. [20] During the 1980s, agencies in Brazil fashioned award-winning TV spots that embodied the famed sensuality of their country's culture: one such ad would never have run in North America because its sexualizing of a girl's body appeared so indecent. [21]

In English Canada, by comparison, a brand of prudery seemed to reign over television advertising until the late 1980s, at least if the commercials awarded prizes in the Bessies competition were indicative. [22] A similar kind of reticence prevailed in capitalist Asia, though with a twist: even when a Japanese agency made an erotic ad the woman featured usually appeared to be European or American (as if to preserve the 'purity' of the Japanese woman?). An analysis of prime-time commercials running in the United States as late as April 1993 found that less than a tenth of the actors present practised what the author considered sexy behaviour. [23] Contrast that with the findings of a survey of the characters appearing in American magazine ads in the same year: 18 per cent of men and 40 per cent of women were dressed provocatively, a significant advance over the situation a decade previously. [24] 'I think in European commercials, shocking ideas are more preponderant than the product itself,' mused the French model Magali, who had appeared in some slightly sexy commercials made for Schick in 1995.

'In American commercials, it's more important to sell the product and to be politically correct.'[25] It was not until the end of the 1990s, perhaps because of a burst of prosperity, probably as well because of the widening acceptance of pornography, that the erotic sell became much more widespread on North American television.

Which raises the question, who led the advance onto television? The other way to chart this progress is to look at what brands, what kinds of products, took up the erotic sell first. There were, of course, a wide range of individual spots that might display a bit of flesh to catch the viewer's eye.[26] But the global pioneer was Levi Strauss, a San Francisco-based manufacturer of jeans, because it had a mass product meant for young people (in age or in spirit) everywhere. No other company was so early and so consistent in its use of commercials to attach an erotic charge to its brands. It set out to make what was already a smash hit among the youth of America equally popular in western Europe and eventually across the world.

An ad designed for European markets entitled *Walking Behinds*, one of Levi's early efforts, won the Grand Prix Cinema at the Venice awards ceremony in 1972, meaning it was judged the best commercial aired anywhere in the year before.[27] The ad was little more than a fast-paced collage of beguiling images of young bums, tight and firm, male and female, but clad in Levi's, in a variety of different settings, set to the energetic music of 'Tutti Frutti.' But it embodied the three features that would reoccur time and again in Levi's commercials: the use of popular music, normally American, especially the hits of rock 'n' roll (here Little Richard's tune); an American flavour (among other references a brief shot of a 'U.S. Army' label); and some sort of erotic sign, particularly behaviour (as in the unclothing of a statue's bum).

During the 1980s and well into the 1990s, Levi's would remain a leader in Europe, and especially in Britain, with its style of sexy commercials, particularly for its 501 brand. One of the signatures of this campaign was the way the ads eroticized the male body, featuring handsome and well-muscled young men who exuded sex appeal and Americanness. That quality of being American was inflected with a sense of class: Levi's heroes were rugged, populist figures, akin to the action heroes of many a Hollywood movie. So an especially heated ad called *Climate* (Britain 1988) featured a hunk who turned male and female eyes in a diner situated somewhere in the American west: the camera focused on his massive thighs and his crotch, notably as he put on his ice-cold 501s (they had been stored in a refrigerator overnight).

All the while there played the raucous sounds of a rendition of the powerful Muddy Waters blues song 'Mannish Boy,' a paean to high-spirited masculinity.[28] An earlier ad in the campaign, *Laundrette* (1985/6) made its actor, Nick Kamen (who stripped down in a laundromat to the surprise and pleasure of assorted watchers), a star and re-released the Marvin Gaye song 'I Heard It through the Grapevine' onto the hit parade.[29] This and a partner ad helped to spur the British sales of 501s from 80,000 a year to nearly 650,000.[30] Indeed these campaigns were as much an aesthetic triumph as a marketing success: in the three decades after 1970, Levi's won awards for ads made in the United States and Canada, across western Europe, and in Argentina, Japan, and Australia. It was only after the mid-1990s that the Levi's star began to wane.

Long before then, Levi's had acquired many competitors in the marketplace of erotic signs. Some of these were also manufacturers of jeans, especially the so-called designer jeans aimed at upscale consumers: companies like Brutus in Britain or Jordache and Calvin Klein in the United States who took to television in the late 1970s. Brutus won a Cannes award in 1981 for a spot in which a collection of security cameras, acting as male surrogates, got so agitated by the sight of a woman trying on her jeans in a clothing store that they finally exploded, the equivalent of an orgasm. In the United States Calvin Klein caused the most public excitement when the famous Brooke Shields commercials aired in 1980, in which the camera slowly and lovingly explored the young woman's lithe and sensual body, sufficient to elicit cries of child porn: in one of the spots, the fifteen-year-old Shields uttered that memorable statement, 'Know what comes between me and my Calvins? Nothing.'[31] Apparently sales boomed nearly 300 per cent after the initial wave of commercials.[32]

But now these manufacturers were joined by a host of other companies whose brands promised to enhance the allure of the body. Chanel No. 5 won fame in the United States with *Share the Dream* (1983), a study in elegance full of phallic imagery, notably a huge, pointy skyscraper with a blinking star on top. That same year Berlei, a lingerie maker, was the first company to air a spot in the United States featuring a naked woman (the model Debra Diehl), although she was only shown from behind – at least until she was clothed.[33] In France Dim, eventually a leader in intimate wear, had started advertising on television in 1969 and soon fashioned a sexy style that it extended to all kinds of nylons, bras, and men's and women's underwear. This so-called Parisian spirit of play actually involved the lavish display of the legs, the breasts (clothed and sometimes unclothed), and the bums (male as well as female) of active, joyful models. Although Dim expanded into North America in the early 1980s (and its first made-for-America commercial aired in 1985), its sexiest commercials were confined to France where the spectacle of flesh caused much less offence than in anglophone countries.[34] It was the maker of a shower gel, Neutralia, that aired the first spot in Britain, early in 1994, featuring a woman's nipple, an action that produced nearly 200 complaints to the regulator of commercial television.[35]

Not far behind were the purveyors of food and drink. The improved technology of colour photography meant admakers could better show the sensual properties of a product – say, an extreme close-up of an orange burst open so that it released a stream of delight. In one suggestive French spot (Boursicot 1976?) a woman's elegant hand stroked a bottle of Perrier, which slowly enlarged, began to fizz, and finally unscrewed its cap to spray out the eager contents in a fountain of refreshment. But there were many other ways to link appetite and sex. So Tip Top Bakeries in Australia ran a marvellous spoof (Cannes 1981) in which an Old World farmer, though enticed by all sorts of well-endowed peasant women, persisted in making his bread, only to consume the delicious treat fast and then rush to satisfy his other urge. 'Man does not live on bread alone,' admitted the voice-over, in a rather coy fashion, 'but with Bornhoffen he comes close.' Suntory in Japan (IBA 1982) used a dancing Cheryl Ladd, one of the sexy stars of the TV hit *Charlie's Angels*, clad in a tight and revealing black evening dress – with lots of blonde hair, cleavage, and leg on display – to hype its American Brandy. Langnese in West Germany ran a long spot (Cannes and IBA 1982) of life one hot summer afternoon, where it mixed brief shots of jiggling breasts (and one exposed breast), some bums, and lots of phallic symbols (a lollipop going in and out of a woman's mouth, for example) with more mundane images of kids, teenagers, dogs, fishing and boating and talking, and just people having fun, usually consuming some Langnese product and mostly outdoors. All of these ads were about realizing desire, about satisfying the urges of the flesh.

Consider just one example of what this change might signify about the meaning of a product. Even in English Canada the character of beer ads, a staple on Canadian telecasts of sporting events, sometimes taken as a national sign of friendliness, indicative of the spirit of the country, began to falter under the pressure of competition among brewers to capture the lucrative youth market. Previously, commercials had featured the guys getting together for a friendly brew, maybe a bunch of happy adults, sometimes women as well as men, enjoying the good times outdoors in some sport like skiing or windsurfing or even ballooning.[36] But in the mid-1980s Molson Breweries boosted its 'Canadian' brand by launching some MTV-style spots that mixed rock, dancing, playing around, and flesh to win the attention of young male drinkers. A few years later Carling Breweries sponsored a particularly bold campaign, for Canada anyway, to export the appeal of an old brand, 'Black Label,' which had apparently caught the fancy of the avant-garde in Toronto's youth district. The ads positioned the brand as sexy, though in different ways: allusions to oral sex; a camera focus on breasts, bums, or the crotch; shots of fetish garb; scenes of posing and voguing. The initial campaign was sufficiently startling to capture the fancy of the judges of the industry's awards, the Bessies, in both 1989 and 1990. More to the point these ads worked to make beer not just the instrument of good times but of hot times, of sexual excitement, even of forbidden pleasures.

By this time, of course, the erotic sell had swarmed out from its place of origin, namely the advertising of body goods, to infect the whole field of television promotion, excepting political advertising where sex was still kept at bay. Clothes, umbrellas, pictures, watches, shoes, towels, a couple, all made love in a French ad (Cannes 1986) for Dunlopillo, a maker of beds and mattresses: the commercial ended when the television turned on to show a train entering a tunnel. Yamaha sold its motorcycle in West Germany (Cannes 1987) with a spot that 'drove' the camera over the naked body of a woman, concluding when she had an orgasm and uttered the name of the brand. Rikk-Bank in Russia (Boursicot 1995) featured a bored woman who tried to entice her male colleagues with coy gestures and a lot of leg, all to no avail because here people worked hard to make money. Sony Europe (2002) pushed the virtues of the built-in camera of its Vaio notebook in a little sex drama where a stunning wife, dressed for lust, jumped on her stay-at-home husband (working with the computer), not realizing that the men in the boardroom could see all the action. After the first wave of the AIDS panic, condom ads all over the world sought to attach their product to the pleasures of sex rather than the terrors of disease. Even advocacy ads joined the frenzy: so the Vegetarian Society of Great Britain (Boursicot 1998) filled one spot with images of vegetables or fruits stroked, a pea dangling in a pod as a clitoris, a dripping asparagus as a penis, and so on. A washing machine in Britain, opticians in Spain, the postal service in Holland, a tabloid in Norway, and the *Washington Post* in the United States, a mobile phone company in Portugal, booksellers in Argentina – by the 1990s, each of these sponsored commercials that deployed the signs of sex to win attention.

The most spectacular of these signs were the supermodels: Cindy Crawford, Naomi Campbell, Linda Evangelista, Claudia Schiffer, Christy Turlington, and Elle Macpherson, to name but the most prominent of this species, who rose to fame in the late 1980s and persisted as celebrities throughout the 1990s. 'They're everywhere,' exclaimed *Time* (16 September 1991) in a cover story announcing the newest craze in publicity. '*Vogue, Elle*, feature pages, ad pages, gossip pages. Selling couture and catalogs, soap and sportswear.' These international icons embodied beauty, glamour, and fashion, so much so that they were able to generate enormous incomes, a feat that fascinated the media because it signalled success.[37]

The supermodels resulted not just from genetics – the good looks granted by birth – or even hard work, diet, exercise, and denial. Beauty, as Turlington put it, was a 'gift,' a 'curse,' a 'talent,' 'a very complicated little thing.'[38] What counted was the whole body of these women. Yes, much attention was paid to their beautiful faces. But they were also honoured for their shape and look, the luxurious hair, their slimness, their breasts ('Especially breasts, which are a sine qua non of stardom in the '90s'),[39] their long, shapely legs, the clothes they wore. They were chameleons, able to express any sort of mood – wanton, elegant, innocent, available, or distant, but always erotic. Every inch of their bodies seemed worked over and perfected to render their look into a kind of art piece. 'We don't exist in reality,' said Lauren Hutton, a model famous in the past. 'We've been created.'[40] The creators of these streamlined bodies were the make-up artists, the fashion designers, and, in particular, the photographers.

Turning this manufactured beauty into a promotional text was the result of a further process of inscription.[41] The public significance of the supermodels was produced by a network grounded in the fashion complex. They were discovered by photographers and trained by model agencies, hired by designers to promote their clothes on the runway, their images plastered on the cover pages of beauty and fashion magazines, and their fame and fortune chronicled and enhanced by the news media. It was this fame that made them such superlative instruments of publicity who could be added like a magic ingredient to messages of all sorts to enhance their impact. Admakers assumed, better yet celebrated, the 'fetishism' that underlay the fashion industry, as one writer put it, the belief that 'we can acquire the power of glamor, its omnipotence and invulnerability, by donning the sacred articles of the mannequin's clothing and mimicking her hieratic gestures.'[42]

The 'natural' home of these marvels was the pages of women's magazines. The supermodels were so potent, however, that they soon spread into television advertising. Indeed, Cindy Crawford appeared in one of the most famous American ads of the era, *Kids* (IBA 1992), that was used to introduce the new look of the Pepsi-Cola can. Two boys ogled Cindy Crawford, very much the wanton, as she sashayed over to a vending machine to purchase and consume a Pepsi on a very hot day somewhere in the west. The boys were most impressed by the can, but viewers, notably male viewers, were particularly taken with the soft-focus shots of her slim body, her face, and her wild hair.[43] Throughout the 1990s, Crawford and her kindred, Naomi Campbell, Claudia Schiffer, and Christy Turlington, appeared in ads for Pepsi-Cola (U.S.), Spumanti Martini in (Italy), Guess perfume (U.S.), L'Oreal skin care (France), Camay and Maybelline (U.S.), the railway Deutch Bahn (Germany), Olympus cameras (U.K.), and Moulinex (France), to name but a few of the many sponsors who found that their presence enhanced the allure of the brand. Turlington even made some public-service announcements for the American Cancer Society and the Newspaper Association of America. 'The more you read,' claimed that last ad, 'the better you'll look,' an ironic comment on the potency of the supermodel.

That potency began to wane towards the end of the decade, a victim of over-exposure and the costliness of the models and, increasingly, the effects of age.[44] Younger, cheaper, less famous models, who would not overshadow the clothes, were hired by designers to show their fashions.[45] Movie actresses began to take the place of supermodels on magazine covers and in ads. In 2000 Revlon dropped their famous 'face' Cindy Crawford, then thirty-four, apparently because of her age (and her large annual salary).[46] The 'fall' of the supermodels was one indication of a lessening of the erotic frenzy, partly due to the fact that the display of sex and sin was no longer so novel.[47]

In truth, the conquest of television, if that is the correct phrase, had never been complete because of the different levels of sensitivity about the public display of sex in various parts of the world. What was acceptable in a secular society like Sweden was not imaginable in Saudi Arabia or other Moslem countries.[48] The boldest instances of publicity as erotica were made for markets in western Europe rather than in North America, where being too explicit invited censure. In the Canadian province of Ontario, for example, an ad for Carlsberg beer (AdCritic 2000) that featured women discussing how one boyfriend was a specialist in cunnilingus (that was never shown, of course) provoked expressions of distaste from a local politician. And admakers in Asia were usually much more restrained than their North American brethren, if only because political or legal authorities might act against the ad and the sponsor. In 2002 Fox television online carried a portion of a commercial for Swenson's Light in which a lusty scoop revealed the outline of a naked woman, emphasizing her breasts, in a sea of ice cream. The ad was banned in Thailand.[49]

Still, the advance of the erotic commercial suggests the existence of global phenomena that underwrote and so encouraged the erotic sell everywhere in the affluent world. The craft of advertising was marked by both emulation and imitation. What worked in one place or for one brand was soon copied by rivals and others at home and elsewhere – explaining why settings, images, tunes, and the like reoccurred. More important, the advance was a response to both heightened competition and advertising clutter in the marketplace of goods and signs: the use of sexy imagery was a way of meeting the problem of promotional noise. Finally, the erotic commercial was itself both a result and an agent of the way in which sexual liberation had come to characterize the popular culture of the West.

2 Displays of Sin

A sexy young woman strides onto the screen. She wears a tight white bra and a matching small skirt, dark nylons and a soft, perhaps silk, blue gown, opened to reveal her assets. She prances as if on a fashion runway. The accompanying music is full of drums. Briefly the camera cuts to a different woman, a blonde this time, lying down, dressed in a black bra that also shows off her cleavage. Then the question, or rather each of the elements of this question, flash on screen: 'WHAT ... IS ... SEXY ... ?' The answer comes quickly, a succession of images of half-clad women, always voluptuous, posing for effect, some with adoring men, and at the end the brand name, 'Victoria's Secret' (AdCritic 2001).

Veteran viewers of American television likely did not need to be told who had sponsored such an ad. Since the late 1990s Victoria's Secret had fashioned a special brand of lingerie promotion that shouted glamour, pizzazz, and sex. [50] In 1999 the company organized a 'Victoria's Secret Fashion Show' only on the Web, running a superbowl ad to announce the event, that proved sufficient to tie up Web traffic for hours as fans searched for the sight of beautiful women. Two years later this event, what really amounted to an hour-long infomercial, moved to prime time on NBC where it captured more than 12 million adult viewers. The publicity for Victoria's Secret drew on the imagery of both porn and fashion – one ad was termed '30 seconds of lace-trimmed jiggle' – in a successful effort to appeal to men as well as women. By 2003 Victoria's Secret was the leader in the field of intimate apparel in the United States.

But compare *What Is Sexy?* to an award-winning spot, indeed the Grand Prix winner at the Cannes festival in 1992, a Spanish ad for Talons Rubber Cement called *Nuns*. This little drama was set in a peaceful convent, the mood of worship emphasized by the sounds of a church choir. While walking quietly together, two young nuns discover a problem – something has fallen off the statue of a baby Jesus: his tiny, slightly curled penis. They delicately wrap the object in a lace handkerchief and carry the discovery to a stern, and much older, Mother Superior. Although a bit surprised (she does raise her eyebrows), out comes the Talons and off she marches to the statue, with the two nuns following behind her. After inspecting the problem, she puts a little glue on the penis and carefully reattaches it to the statue. Except she puts the penis on upside down. When she leaves the scene, one of the young nuns, the prettier of the twosome, quickly turns the penis the right way up. That gives the male voice-over the excuse to explain how flexible Talons is. The last scene is the young nun about to pray to God for her bold act.

The spot was part of a small genre of humorous commercials evident across the affluent zone of countries in which people used glue to attach all sorts of odd things, like fixing a man to a ceiling or binding together cans of Coke and Pepsi (thus ending the Cola Wars?). But the Talons spot did carry viewers into the world of sex, a human space made by convention and symbol and action where Eros reigned supreme. More to the point, *Nuns*, like *What Is Sexy?*, evoked the idea of transgression. The Victoria's Secret ad was bold, emphatic, in your face, a display of sexy women cavorting for the pleasure of any voyeur. *Nuns* was much more subtle and yet more transgressive because it put sex into the chaste context of a convent. The tiny penis, even so innocuous an object as the stone member of a baby Jesus, had symbolic power. The two young nuns knew that, as did the Mother Superior. But the older woman did not remember how a penis ought to look. The young nun did, presumably because she had seen the real thing recently. That was a form of forbidden knowledge in the place she now lived and worked, at least according to stereotype. So, at the end, she had to make an act of contrition to atone for her small sin.

Television and cinema commercials constantly reworked this theme of transgression, drawing here on the age-old depiction of sex as subversive, especially the public display of sex, a belief embodied in the discourse and imagery of pornography. Sometimes the ad might be little more than a dirty joke; sometimes it was chock full of sexy stuff – images, words and allusions, symbols, sounds, and innuendo. Generally it was about some sort of activity that challenged prevailing standards of moral conduct. The focus on transgressions, however minor, gave the ads their bite, their ability to capture the fancy of viewers. One analysis of the collages people created to represent desire demonstrated just how often these involved images of immorality or danger – rebels and criminals, wild animals, threatening masks – signalling an escape from social control and the ethics of restraint.[51] What was once taboo was now exciting.

The American maestro of shock was Calvin Klein, one of New York's celebrity designers. Rumour had it that his penchant for racy advertising reflected his own wild lifestyle through the 1970s and into the 1980s: he was one of the great players at the city's infamous Studio 54, a site of decadence noted for sex and drugs.[52] His advertising was designed in house, though he hired top fashion photographers such as Richard Avedon and Bruce Webber to give the ads a special aesthetic quality. The Brooke Shields campaign of 1980 was only the beginning. Next came some startlingly homoerotic portraits of beautiful men, nude except for Calvin Klein underwear, some of which appeared on gigantic billboards, a sight never before seen in the American cityscape.[53] The most stunning picture was of the bare, bronze, and hard body of Olympic pole vaulter Tom Hintaus, apparently at rest catching some sun, his legs open and his penis just barely evident underneath the marvellously white cotton briefs.[54] 'The Calvin Klein Underwear Man is the dominant sexual icon in modern-day America,' declared the *Washington Post*, evidence of how the campaign had garnered media attention.[55] The late 1980s campaigns for Obsession, a new fragrance, featured images of nudity, lots of coupling, and even some group sex. In 1991 Klein sponsored an extraordinary 116–page insert in

Vanity Fair, photographed by Bruce Webber, full of flesh and titillation, mostly to highlight the designer jeans. Along the way his advertising made famous the model Kate Moss and her 'waif' look: Moss was so slim she struck people as a poster girl for anorexia – critics actually pasted 'Feed Me' signs on some of her posters.[56] The whole point was to excite consumers with images of sin, perhaps to generate some free publicity from an outraged media, in order to give the brand a distinctive image as bold, avant-garde, and on the edge.

The practice of outrage finally got Klein into a lot of trouble. In August 1995 his company launched a television and print campaign to promote CK jeans, chiefly seeking to win the attention of the teenage market. The commercials took the form of an audition, situated in a cheap, wood-panelled playroom in a basement, where an off-camera male asked intimate questions of nervous or coy 'girls' and 'boys' dressed scantily in Klein's underwear and denim. The print images captured these same characters in various provocative poses, often showing their underwear: indeed, it was the image of a male teen his legs open, his crotch on display, that caused so much upset because of its novelty. This was too much for moralists inside and outside the media. The conservative-minded American Family Association, headed by Donald Wildmon, denounced the campaign as kiddie porn. Many news outlets echoed the charge, angrily attacking Klein's blatant use of 'dirty' sex to sell his clothes.[57] The FBI investigated whether the ads did amount to child pornography, though in the end the investigation turned up nothing substantial. Although Klein denied the porn label, he had to retreat: he apologized for causing offence, and the television ads were withdrawn. Even so, the campaign and the furore generated an extraordinary amount of free publicity. *Newsweek* (11 September 1995) observed that teenagers in 'the shopping malls of America' wondered what all the fuss was about and seemed impressed with the style of the campaign. 'Even when he seems to lose,' claimed one journalist of Calvin Klein, 'he wins.'[58]

Normally admakers strove to avoid the sleaze, and so the offence, attached to sexual allusions and images. The reason Calvin Klein was widely abused was because his ads evoked all too effectively the aesthetic of child porn: the high-fashion gloss that characterized the Shields ads was missing from the CK jeans commercials. By contrast, what cleansed the Victoria's Secret ad was the use of an aesthetic drawn from fashion, and what cleansed *Nuns* was the gentle humour. Admakers, at least the television variety, were not (usually) pornographers. They strove to ameliorate the transgression in some way or other.

Table 6.1 outlines 100 numbered examples of erotic commercials – some of these particularly extreme examples – chosen to illustrate the wide range of 'sins' displayed, the brands advertised, the countries of origin, and the techniques employed to achieve, and to moderate, the sexual stimulus. It does not represent an attempt to produce a sample based on any quantitative methodology, although the examples are drawn from a survey of thousands of award-winning and notable ads from around the world.[59] The emphasis is upon difference rather than upon repetition, upon what is striking more than what is typical.[60] I have collected the assorted transgressions into three grand categories, variously named erotomania, the old 'perversions,' and violation. Erotomania, once thought of as Bill Clinton's disease, amounts to an unseemly or an overwhelming fascination with sex. It encompasses everything from an obsession with the erotic to scenes of actual intercourse, even suggestions of an orgy. The old 'perversions' refers to sexual acts that diverge from the 'normal' or accepted brand of heterosexual intercourse, acts that were once considered criminal offences in some jurisdictions, certainly as evidence of some moral or mental disorder. Most of these acts have since won acceptance as alternative forms of sexual behaviour in law; still they, or at least their public display, retained the flavour of the taboo, the forbidden, at least into the 1990s. Missing from the list are such still dishonoured practices as necrophiliac or coprophagic sex, neither of which turned up in my survey of erotic commercials, presumably because no one had figured out how to 'cleanse' this kind of behaviour. (I did, however, find one oblique reference to bestiality, this a Danish ad [Boursicot 1994] for Carlsberg: the action occurred on a sheep farm where a well-endowed woman served beer to the animals, and notably a commanding dog whose bottle she opened between her ample breasts.) The final category, violations, does include a series of acts, most of which remain crimes, in which one person exercises power over another to secure some sexual pleasure or personal advantage. That could mean no more than the invasion of a person's privacy, though in one case the person involved was a child (no. 73), a production that evoked, at least to my North American eyes, the horror of paedophilia. [61] But ads did allude to the murder of a philandering lover (no. 90), the castration of a male (no. 96), and the rape of a female (no. 98), three of the most violent acts in the world of sex. In any case these 100 examples differed widely in terms of the erotic charge

Table 6.1
Transgressions

No.	Activity * = 'Hot'	Product	Country and date	Source	Music	Fashion √ = nude/semi-nude scenes	Humour
A. Erotomania							
Obsession							
1	Frenzy	Chanel Egoiste	France 1990	Boursicot	Classical	Elite	Excess
2	Frenzy	Creem Jeans	Sweden 1992	Boursicot	Rock	Carnal	
3	Wanting	Stimorol Chewing Gum	Europe 1992	Boursicot	Rock song	Commonplace	
4	Talking Sex	Jean-Paul Gaultier	France 1994	Boursicot	Jazz	Avant-garde	Wit
5	Wanting	Turelli Pasta	Sweden 1994	Boursicot	Rock song	Commonplace	Excess
6	Overwhelmed Man	L'Air du Temps	France 1995	Clios	Choir (sacred)	Bizarre	
7	Wanting	Hanes Clothing	Spain 1996	Boursicot	Pop	Commonplace	Incongruity
8	Wanting	Old Spice After Shave	USA 1996	Boursicot	Jazz	Commonplace	Unexpected
9	Wanting	Pepsi Manzanita	Mexico 1997	Boursicot	Pop/Jazz	Commonplace	Unexpected
10	Wanting	Brut Anti-perspirant	USA 1999	AdCritic	Pop	Commonplace	Parody
11	Conquest	Lynx Body Spray (men)	UK 2000	Showcase	Rock	Diverse	Excess
Pornography							
12	Phone Sex	Bulevard Rosa	Spain 1995	Cannes		Commonplace	Unexpected
13	*Consuming	Fredgaard Televisions	Denmark 1996	Boursicot	Jazz	√Carnal	Unexpected
14	Consuming	Apple Tango (soft drink)	UK 1997	AdFilms		Bizarre	Incongruity
15	Home Videos	Volkswagen	USA 1999	AdCritic		Commonplace	Accident
16	Producing	Diesel Jeans	Sweden 1999	Diesel	Pop	Commonplace	Reversals
Philandering							
17	Illicit Sex	Topp Kopie (photocopy)	West Germany 1989	Cannes		Commonplace	Discovery
18	Stealing the Woman	Martini & Rossi	USA and France? 1996	Clios and Boursicot	Jazz	Upscale	

Table 6.1 (continued)

No.	Activity * = 'Hot'	Product	Country and date	Source	Music	Fashion √ = nude/semi-nude scenes	Humour
19	Promiscuity	Bonds Clothing	Australia 1997	Showcase	Pop/Jazz	√Commonplace	Unexpected
20	Unsafe Sex	Volkswagen Golf	Italy 1997	Boursicot	Rock	Carnal	Stereotype
21	Illicit Sex	Milk	Australia 1999	Showcase	Big Band	Commonplace	Unexpected
22	Illicit Sex	Castelmaine XXXX	UK 2000	Showcase	Pop song	Commonplace	Unexpected
Love-making							
23	*Languid	Relax (male cologne)	Germany 1992	Boursicot	Pop song	√Carnal	
24	*Frenzied	Man & Woman (fragrance)	Argentina 1992	Boursicot	Rock	√Carnal	
25	*Thwarted	Foster's Draught Beer (and Häagen-Dazs ice cream)	UK 1993	Cannes	Rock song	√Carnal	Unexpected
26	*Paused	Moritz Ice Cream	New Zealand 1994	Boursicot	Pop (soft)	√Carnal	Unexpected
27	Frenzied	Expressen (magazine)	Sweden 1994	Boursicot	Circus	√Commonplace	Excess
28	*Out of doors	Gapa (condom)	Brazil 1995	Boursicot	Rock	√Carnal	
29	*Frenzied	Calvin Klein Escape	International 1995	Boursicot	Pop	√Carnal	
30	*Lasting Intercourse	Durex Condoms	Belgium 1996	Boursicot	Pop	√Carnal	Parody
31	Impossible	Solo (soft drink)	Norway 1997	Showcase	Rock	√Carnal	Unexpected
32	*Interrupted	Aprilla Rally 50 (scooter)	Italy 1997	Showcase	Rock song	√Carnal	
33	*Post-Coital	Ronson Cigarettes	Austria 1998	Boursicot	Jazz Rock	√Carnal	
34	*Imagined	Gini (soft drink)	France 1999	Boursicot	Rock	√Carnal	
Orgy							
35	Party	Kaiser Beer	Brazil 1995	Boursicot	Pop Rock	Carnal	Excess
36	Party	Spumanti Martini	Italy 1995	Boursicot	Pop song	Elite	Incongruity
37	Group Sex	Gancia	Argentina 1996	Boursicot	Latin Rock	Upscale	
38	Party	Dockers Khakis	USA 1999	AdCritic	Dance	Carnal	Excess

Table 6.1 (continued)

B. The Old 'Perversions'

No.	Activity * = 'Hot'	Product	Country and date	Source	Music	Fashion √ = nude/semi-nude scenes	Humour
Mixing							
39	Race	Ella Baché	Australia 1997	Boursicot	Jazz song	Upscale	
40	Age	Nestlé Cappuccino	France 1996	Boursicot	Classical	Upscale	
41	Class	Saila Mints	Italy 1996	Showcase	Classical	Elite	Degradation
Oral/Anal Sex							
42	*Cunnilingus	Jade Man	Germany 1992	Boursicot	Classical (soft)	√Carnal	
43	Fellatio	Calvin Klein Underwear	USA 1992	Boursicot		√Carnal	Jokes
44	Fellatio	Mega Superstores	Norway 1998	Showcase	Rock song	√Bizarre	Unexpected
45	Anal	Soesman	Germany 2000?	AdCritic	Rock song	Commonplace	Incongruity
Exhibitionism							
46	Admiring the Man	H.I.S. Jeans	Germany 1995	Boursicot	Rock song	Commonplace	
47	*Vamping and Looking	Bugle Boy Denims	USA 1992	Boursicot	Rock song	Carnal	Contrasts
48	Showing Off	Tirlement Sugar	Belgium 1995	Boursicot	Rock	Carnal	Joke
49	*The Unveiling	Victoria's Secret	USA 1999	AdCritic	Drums	Carnal	
50	Showing Off	Levi's 501s	USA 1996	Cannes	Rock	Carnal	Incongruity
51	Vamping	Pepsi One	USA 2000	Advertisementave.com	Rock song	Carnal	Incongruity
Masturbation							
52	Playing with Another	Jane More Fashions	Japan 1982	Cannes	Pop song	Upscale	Incongruity
53	Multiple Jobs	Hit 100.6	France 1985	Cannes	Rock	Commonplace	Excess
54	Indulgence	Yves St Laurent Opium	France 1988	Boursicot	Classical (soft)	Elite	
55	Hand Job	Kama Sutra Condoms	India 1991	Boursicot	Semi-classical	√Carnal	
56	*Frenzy	Voda Zap Pager	UK 1997	Showcase	Rock	Carnal	Unexpected

Table 6.1 (continued)

No.	Activity * = 'Hot'	Product	Country and date	Source	Music	Fashion √ = nude/semi-nude scenes	Humour
Fetishism							
57	*Leather Fetish	Collective du Cuir	France 1991	Boursicot	Rock song	√Avant-garde	
58	*Beer as Fetish?	Export 33	Lebanon 1995	Boursicot	Pop	√Carnal	
59	*Foot Fetish	Christian Louboutin Shoes	UK 2000	Showcase	Jazz (soft)	Carnal	Unexpected
Homosexuality							
60	Gay Kiss	Solo (soft drink)	Norway 1995	Boursicot	Classical (soft)	Upscale	Unexpected
61	*Lesbian Kiss	Boisvert Lingerie	UK 1996	Boursicot	Drums	Carnal	Unexpected
62	*Lesbian Desire	Clothestime	USA 1997	Showcase	Rock	Carnal	Discovery
63	Gay Play	Ewe XL Kitchens	Austria 1998	Boursicot	Jazz	Commonplace	
S&M							
64	Bondage	J&B Scotch	International 1995	Boursicot	Semi-classical	Avant-garde	Incongruity
65	Bondage	Hot Bods Bra and Panties	Australia 1997	Boursicot	Pop	Bizarre	Incongruity
66	*Dominatrix	Schiesser Underwear	Belgium 1999	Boursicot		Carnal	
67	Whipping	Color Line	Sweden 1997	Boursicot	European Folk	Commonplace	Accident
Ambiguities							
68	Revealed Natures	Smirnoff Vodka	Europe 1995	Lowe Howard Spink	Discordant	Bizarre	Parody
69	Transvestite	Cooler Club	Thailand 1996	Boursicot	Disco	Carnal	Unexpected
70	Transvestite	Bourgyes Telecom	France 1997	Boursicot	Rock song	Upscale	Incongruity
71	*Transgendered	Holiday Inn	USA 2000	AdCritic	Pop	Carnal	Incongruity

Table 6.1 (continued)

No, Activity * = 'Hot'	Product	Country and date	Source	Music	Fashion √ = nude/semi-nude scenes	Humour
C. Violations						
Exposure						
72 *Peeping Tom	Ekstrabladet	Denmark 1987	Cannes	Pop (soft)	√Carnal	Incongruity
73 Paedophilia	Phebo Body Lotion	Brazil 1988	Cannes	Pop song	√Carnal	
74 Exposing Female Breasts	Anti-Cancer	Spain 1994	Cannes	Classical	√Commonplace	Incongruity
75 Peeping Tom	Pepsi-Cola	USA 1997	Showcase	Rock song	Carnal	Unexpected
76 Peeping Jane	Underdaks (male underwear)	Australia 1996	Showcase	Pop song	Commonplace	Incongruity
Entrapment						
77 Woman as Bait	Diesel Jeans	International 1993	Diesel	Heavy Metal	Carnal	Unexpected
78 Bound Male	Ypno (perfume)	Germany 1994	Boursicot	Classical	√Carnal	
79 Overwhelmed Male	Victorio & Lucchino's Carmen (perfume)	Spain 1994	Boursicot	Classical (the opera)	Bizarre	
80 *Bound Male	Soviet Jeans	S. Africa 1994	Boursicot	Classical	√Carnal	Unexpected
81 Cheating Male	Guess Clothing	USA 1995	Clios	Pop	Carnal	Unexpected
82 Female Assault	Chiemsee Underwear	Germany 1996	Boursicot	Classical/Rock/Classical	Commonplace	Unexpected
83 Touching	Vaseline Lotion	Canada 2000	Bessies	Pop (soft)	Commonplace	Accident
Stalking						
84 *Hunted Man	Panasonic Audio	UK 1991	Boursicot	Rock song	Carnal	Excess
85 Hunted Woman	Diesel Jeans	International 1994	Diesel	Heavy Metal	Carnal	Unexpected

Table 6.1 (concluded)

No.	Activity * = 'Hot'	Product	Country and date	Source	Music	Fashion √ = nude/semi- nude scenes	Humour
86	Hunted Man	Deutch Bahn	Germany 1996	Boursicot	Jazz	Commonplace and Carnal	Incongruity
87	Hunted Child-Woman	Chanel No. 5	USA 2000	AdCritic	Classical (+ choir)	Bizarre	Unexpected
88	Hunted Woman	EB Beer	Poland 1995	Boursicot	Pop	Commonplace	Unexpected
Battery/Murder							
89	Aged Don Juan	Mazda	Holland 1992	Cannes	Rock song	Upscale	Stereotype
90	*Avenging Female	Campari	Italy 1994	Boursicot	Pop	Avant-garde	Unexpected
91	Avenging Female	Vivazz Nylons	Chile 1995	Boursicot	Jazz	Upscale	Unexpected
92	Murderous Female	Don't Tell It	UK 1996	Showcase	Jazz/Pop	Sloppy and Carnal	Reversal
93	Voodoo	Denim Cologne	Italy 1997	Boursicot	Discordant	Carnal	Incongruity
94	Voodoo	World Championship Wrestling	USA 1999	AdCritic	Various and Discordant	Bizarre	
Castration							
95	Avenging Female	Clairol Glints	UK 1984	Cannes	Pop (fast)	Avant-garde	Unexpected
96	Femme Fatale	Edgars Denim	S. Africa 1996	Boursicot	Rock song		Unexpected
97	*Avenging Female	Levi's 501s	USA 1998	Showcase	Rock	Carnal	Unexpected
Rape							
98	*Male Predator	Best Montana Jeans	International 1995	Boursicot	Country and Western	√Carnal	
99	Man as Victim	SAS Youth Ticket	Sweden 1997	Clios	Rock song	Bizarre	Accident
100	*Female Predator	Camel	Switzerland 1998	Boursicot	Hard Rock	√Carnal	Incongruity

they carried. Some featured naked or semi-naked bodies, even graphic or explicit images of sexual joy. A few examples, not always the same ads, were full of sexual hunger and sexual tension, at least in my judgment, and these I have designated 'hot.'[62]

There were many ways in which the admaker might signal the entry into the world of sex. The spot could employ verbal cues, say a reference to impotence in a Kia ad (AdCritic 1999) called *Performance Issues* or to the accidental return of a private recording of sex play (no. 15) in *THAT Video*. An ad meant to demonstrate why learning English (no. 45) was necessary showed a very staid German family, two parents and two children, who listened intently and happily to a song on the car radio with only one set of lyrics: 'I want to fuck you in the ass.' One of the actors in a spot for Relax (no. 23) actually told his audience they were about to see his recollection of a hot day spent outdoors in a Louisiana plantation. A bit more subtle was the use of sounds or music. A French ad for Darty (Cannes 1983), intended to sell the sound quality of its stereo systems, began when a tape played the cries of a woman enjoying an orgasm loudly and clearly throughout the store. Much later Herbal Essences sponsored an ad in which a woman mimicked an orgasm in the aisles of an American supermarket (AdCritic 1999). *Body by Victoria* (AdCritic 1999) incorporated sounds of heavy breathing to emphasize the effects of the lingerie on a spectator. *Wild Thing*, an ad for leather (no. 57), opened with the lusty song of the same name by the Los Angeles rapper Tone-Lōc.

These words and sounds, however, were always backed up by images of one kind or another, the most common method of signalling the erotic. That could mean leavening the mix with phallic symbols and the like.[63] A French spot (no. 53) for Hit 100.6, a rock radio station, opened on a collection of men, a bit sweaty, certainly expectant, seated in their cars. A woman arrived carrying a metal tuner, shaped like a penis, which she proceeded to stroke and turn. Up went the antennas of the cars. The men showed all the signs of sexual agitation. Then the music blasted out. The husky female voice-over exclaimed, 'She goes all the way ... She tunes you on.' In an Indian ad for Kama Sutra condoms (no. 55) the phallic object was a shower head a woman stroked, that image juxtaposed with pictures of her rough-looking man returning home from work at sea. In two fragrance ads, an Italian ad for Spazio Krizia (Boursicot 1994) for men and a French ad for Givenchy's Oblique (Boursicot 2000) for women, the object was the bottle itself, a not uncommon attribute of the perfume business. The Italian spot for

Spumanti Martini (no. 36) tracked a champagne cork, released by a handsome man in Rome, that crossed the Atlantic where it wedged in the naval of Naomi Campbell. But an American commercial called *Little Red Riding Hood* for Chanel (no. 87) was the most clever of all. For the young woman walked through a padded tunnel (in short, a vaginal symbol) to find the magic bottle of Chanel No. 5. She applied the perfume, then opened a huge door to reveal ... yes, the Eiffel Tower! Along the way, with just a finger and a 'shhhh,' she also stilled a wolf who hunted her, before going onward towards the tower. The wolf could only howl. The whole ad was suffused with an aura of sophistication and sensuality.

A second way to signal the erotic was via the use of an attractive celebrity – normally female, though a few male stars were available to signify sexiness (Brad Pitt was one outstanding example). Thus Cindy Crawford was the dream date of the nerdy man so happily asleep on the smooth-riding Deutch Bahn (no. 86) that he did not want to awake. Rivalling the appeal of the supermodels were the stars or near-stars of movies and sometimes television: Demi Moore for Diet Coke (U.S. 1987), Kim Basinger for Golden Lady nylons (Italy 1992) and Freixenet wine (Spain 1993), Halle Berry for M&M's Crispy (Superbowl 1999), Catherine Zeta-Jones in a very heated number for Alfa Romeo (Italy 2000), or Kim Cattrall in a campaign for Pepsi One (2000/1). Cattrall, for example, played out the persona of Samantha Jones that she had made famous in the TV series *Sex and the City.* Just as Samantha led a life of promiscuity in the HBO series, selecting and discarding men as she pleased, so Cattrall as a sexy Lil' Red Ridin' Hood (no. 51) judged various diet colas, and always turned men's heads, until she found the Pepsi One that served her needs. Which was the point: all these female celebrities enacted the role of sex symbols whose past performances now worked to establish the erotic credentials of the ad.

Much more common, however, was the display of the Body Beautiful and the Body Handsome, especially in the United States where admakers came to specialize in such spectacles (never so graphic, though, as in western Europe). Here lesser mortals were sufficient, men as well as women, as long as they boasted the right physique. Most people were white, although even where a black man or woman was featured the treatment of the body was much the same. Even in ads with a homoerotic flavour, the standards of beauty common in the straight community ruled: the style of the so-called 'lesbian chic' (no. 61 and no. 62), for example, featured women who were slim, soft, well-endowed, long-legged, and perfectly made-up.[64] Male bodies were powerful, muscular, and rugged, hypermasculine in short.[65] The rapper Marky Mark showed off his muscles, and in one ad an erection (covered by his underwear), in a campaign for Calvin Klein shorts (no. 43) that also featured the semi-naked supermodel Kate Moss. Lucky Vanous, a male model, took off his t-shirt so that he could appear as an object of lust for female office workers in a famous commercial for Diet Coke (U.S.) in 1994. The camera alternately revealed an elegant and beautiful woman slowly putting on her intimates and sashaying through a crowded restaurant, complete with men ogling her, in a British ad for Boisvert Lingerie (no. 61). The camera flashed one shot after another of the uncovered breasts of startled, indeed horrified, women, albeit to underline a message about cancer, in a Spanish public-service message (no. 74). Often the camera acted as the instrument of the voyeur's gaze, lingering on a woman's luscious hair, pouty mouth, cleavage or breasts, well-rounded bottom, and long, shapely legs. A Bugle Boy spot (no. 47) was little more than an extended series of such shots in which the women posed for the pleasure of the male viewer. Running text beneath these salacious pictures told viewers to buy the coloured denims if they wanted to see more of this kind of peep show, or else the sponsor would insist on boring shots of male models.

What the erotic commercial excelled at was the tease. One clever French commercial for Scandale (Cannes 1989) actually showed a sophisticated and attractive woman who explained what she was wearing underneath her clothes – a silky bra, panties embroidered with lace, and a matching garter belt – only to add, 'I have no intention whatsoever of showing them to you.' The response of the male voice-over?: 'That's a scandal!' The message could stand as a motto for the whole genre, the purpose of which was to impress, to excite, to titillate, but never to actually satisfy any desire the ad might awaken, since that desire could only be realized by purchasing the advertised brand.

This ensured that even the most graphic commercials usually spent little time showing the sexual activity, whatever it might be – just a sufficient amount to evoke the sense of transgression. The camera in the Swedish magazine ad (no. 27) focused most of its attention not on the couple caught up in the frenzy of love making but on the devastation they wreaked on the room where they sought pleasure. Viewers never saw the retired milkman (no. 21) sleep with his past clients; they only saw the pleased, and in one case slightly dishevelled, women – plus the sprightly ease with which this Don Juan skipped from house to house, proof of the virility milk conveyed on a man. The shots of the Jade Man (no. 42) as he slowly moved to pleasure his companion were interspersed with screens of text telling viewers to enjoy themselves. One exception to this restraint was a condom ad (no. 30) full of images of the twosome coupling, in different positions and in different parts of the home, all this to prove how long the sex play could last with Durex.

The ads were even more coy when they dealt with actions that might strike some viewers as shocking or offensive. Yves St Laurent (no. 54) only suggested that the elegant, upscale woman had retreated to her bedroom to pleasure herself. Neither the male nor the female 'prisoner' in the two Hot Bods ads (no. 65) was actually tortured, even though the camera showed the pleasure dungeon, the tools of sexual pain, the austere masters, and their expectant slaves: what was broken was an egg that fried on the hot skin of the slaves. We saw the avenging female (no. 90) raise her enormous knife, but what she struck was not her philandering lover but an orange, which she proceeded to open: some of the peel went into his Campari, and the orange she squeezed in his hand so that it splattered his face. Similarly, although the femme fatale in one retail ad (no. 96) carried a huge pair of scissors, briefly highlighted by the camera, what she cut off the man asleep in the train was not his member but the top button of his jeans to add to the collection on her backpack. Best Montana (no. 98) hinted at a forthcoming rape by mixing scenes of a woman at rest with pictures of two men capturing a wild stallion. The Swiss ad for Camel cigarettes (no. 100) might show a beautiful woman who quietly entered an apartment (she did have the key) and attacked the hunk sleeping there; but very quickly he joined in the wild lovemaking. The frenzy ended when she clamped her hand on, of all things, a large, smiling, fake Camel, meaning the tobacco. The erotic commercial never delivered on the sexual promise, unlike pornography: the effort was meant to attach, in some way or another, the erotic charge to the particular good or service.

Just as important, the admakers employed a number of techniques to filter out the dirt that attached to the pornographic display. Music and song could both mellow and enhance the effect of the imagery, perhaps point the viewer towards some preferred reading of the pictures. A classical piece gave an air of distinction to a message, particularly when the pictures shouted sex (no. 42 and no. 80) or degradation (no. 41). A popular song might add to the poignancy of the minidrama: 'Your Cheatin' Heart' played through one depiction of infidelity (no. 22). Likewise the Animals' hit of the sixties 'Don't Let Me Be Misunderstood' underlined a man's plea (no. 89) in a portrayal of unwanted affection that led to one senior battering another. Jazz conveyed a sense of mystery, even mischief, in studies of foot fetish (no. 59), some intended gay play (no. 63), and race mixing (no. 39). A bit of old-fashioned folk music marked the homey character of a travel ad that featured an accidental whipping (no. 67). A circus tune emphasized that the crazed love making of one couple (no. 27) was played for laughs. Rock, especially hard rock or heavy metal, was a way to signal frenzy and excess, whether in love making (no. 100), dance (no. 56), or stalking (no. 85).

The second mode of cleansing relied on the aesthetics of fashion, meaning the nature of both the dress and the photography, to give a particular look to the commercial. Some ads, it is true, avoided any special look, seeking instead to portray what was commonplace: a particularly sweet commercial for Vaseline (no. 83), for example, showed scenes of a blind man on a subway who accidentally touched the arm of a fellow passenger, only to discover 'How beautiful feels.'[66] But that was not true of the majority of commercials. Not surprisingly what prevailed was the carnal style, whether that involved nudity or semi-nudity. As in art, so in advertising, nudity was a kind of costume a character put on to impress the observer.[67] The characters, clothed or unclothed, boasted the so-called high body, meaning well-defined, almost polished, closed, symmetrical, finished, toned, and muscled. The low or ugly body was not usually present, except as a contrast, and then the individual was usually fat (no. 8, no. 75, no. 77).

Sometimes the action was fast paced. The spot for Fredgaard Televisions (no. 13), done in black and white, which heightened its artistic quality, cut between scenes of a male model undressing on television and a female voyeur stroking herself in response: the man's eyes indicated that he well knew the effects of his spectacle on her libido. The camera gave us glimpses of his shoulder, her hand stroking her breast, his six-pack, her hand pushing on her crotch, lips opened in sexual excitement, even the first signs of his pubic hairs as he began to pull down his undershorts. The lighting was carefully focused to highlight the showing of each of the body parts. Call this the passionate eye.

But in other cases the action was much slower. The Relax spot (no. 23), also in black and white, featured scenes of the naked couple, the man and the woman, posed to show off their perfect flesh as if on a fashion shoot: their bums, her breasts and his chest, her hair and his muscles, their slim bodies, and so on. Instead of just lust, the ad was imbued with an aura of romance. The Phebo ad (no. 73), in colour, gently surveyed, almost stroked, the surfaces and the curves of the young mother and her daughter as they softly pampered their skin with the body lotion. In *Ladies Room* (no. 62) one woman carefully (indeed the action is obviously slowed) inspected the simple, short and sleeveless, but clinging, orange dress of another. Call this the amorous eye. No matter: the result of both approaches produced something more akin to art than pornography, or at least the standard fare of porn movies.

The combination of elite, avant-garde, and upscale styles constituted another fashion cluster, this marked more obviously by class, where the dress of the characters established an air of distinction. Women in evening gowns (no. 1), an old man in a sports jacket and tie (no. 89) or a handsome black man in fine casuals (no. 39), some jaded creatures in exotic garb (no. 4) or two women in PVC ware (no. 95), all of these signs worked to ameliorate whatever was the transgression, putting the action in the context of a special community of privileged players. The sophisticated and stylish clothes of the older woman in a Nestlé ad (no. 40), showing that she was indeed desirable, excused the sudden expression of young lust when her friend's son could not resist grasping her hand. That kind of licence was also present where the dress was obviously bizarre. The strange rubber costume doffed by a pudgy man (no. 14) telegraphed that this ad was a spoof of pornography. In *Wedding* (no. 68), part of the ongoing 'Reflections' campaign, a seedy journalist looked through a bottle of Smirnoff vodka to see the true, often sexual, nature of the wedding party: the bride who was really a vampire; a sailor who became a gigantic, aroused rooster at the approach of a shapely woman; and a distinguished gentlemen actually wearing women's underwear. We had entered the realm of the carnivalesque.

Even more effective as a cleansing agent, of course, was a bit of humour. Laughter softens, excuses, justifies. Some ads were clearly parodies right from the beginning, such as Ken's vain attempt to make love to Barbie (no. 31) or the over-hyped, hard-sell style of a Brut commercial (no. 10). Others so exaggerated a scene that it became funny. An aristocratic woman cleaned a filthy sports car with her own body, slithering over roof and hood, all to get a candy (no. 41) from her chauffeur. A host of sophisticated women yelled out their sexual frustration and their anger in a Chanel Egoiste spot (no. 1), which ended on an especially bizarre note: they compulsively, hysterically opened and closed the windows of their rooms in a very posh hotel, all the while shouting the name of the brand. Even wit could go to excess: the upscale women in a surreal ad were so clever, and so jaded, that they became objects of humour – and, so it seemed, prime candidates for Jean-Paul Gaultier's perfume (no. 4).

The right amount of comedy could serve to draw the sting of a transgression, particularly near the end of the commercial. That was why so many of the jokes revolved around what was unexpected or incongruous. The portrayal of phone sex (no. 12) seemed very funny when the woman hung up on her client because she learned how dowdy his clothes were. A lover would sleep with his best friend's wife, but he would never drink the last can of his favourite beer (no. 22). The shoeshine boy paid the elegant and sexy woman after he shined – well, actually stroked – each of her fancy, high-heeled, black leather shoes (no. 59). One of the most elaborate efforts, for Levi's 501s, drew on the culture of voodoo (no. 97), only to end when the jilted woman failed to drive a spike into her lover's crotch because of the metal button on his jeans. The way the camera at a class reunion (no. 71) focused on the walk, the lips, the legs, and the chest of a mystery woman, and the shots of men looking her over, all seemed fair when it was revealed that the erstwhile 'Bob Johnston' had completed a total, and expensive, makeover: this to emphasize the result of the extensive renovations at Holiday Inn.

Just as common were misperceptions: we were led to think that a woman was being hunted (no. 85 and no. 88) until we realized at the end it was all make-believe. The guy with the chain saw (no. 85) in the Diesel ad was not a fearsome stalker but actually going home for what turned out to be a surprise birthday party, and he used the saw to cut the cake, not his girlfriend. Indeed Diesel seemed to pride itself on producing ads in the 1990s that suggested 'perversion' or violation only to end on some ironic note, presumably to heighten its profile as a youth favourite in the highly competitive market for jeans. One of the best (no. 16) tracked a man who was making pornographic films, then showed him leaving his place of business to become the devoted husband and father, the champion of family values. Yet right at the end his children, seated in the back seat, began to make the same kinds of sex noises – the exaggerated groaning – that he had encouraged his actors to voice. The ad said absolutely nothing about the character or the quality of the jeans but it certainly did identify the brand as distinctive.

The Diesel campaign often verged on the grotesque, offering images that were excessive, absurd, gross, or vulgar, sometimes bodies that were misshapen or ugly, always to provoke laughter.[68] Nor was it alone. A Japanese spot (no. 52) depicted a European woman playing in a fountain and using her foot to stimulate the penis of a stone statue, a little boy 'peeing' out water, so much so that the stream suddenly exploded in her face – one take on the infamous 'money shot' of pornography. All this to hype a brand of fashion. A Norwegian ad (no. 44) showed a doctor who greeted one of his female compatriots at home wearing nothing but a flashing sign that covered his penis, the sign reading 'eat me.' This to get consumers to go to a store for better 'dinner' ideas. An American commercial (no. 94) featured an over-muscled, long-haired doll, representing a wrestler, who worked voodoo magic – using needles and such – on another doll to force an actual woman – pained, twisted, puzzled, eventually loved – to watch the wrestling championships on television.

Even where the images were not grotesque, even where there was no humour, still the realm of sex portrayed by this species of erotica seemed like a gigantic carnival. It was the stage for endless sin and endless play with lots of flesh always on display, for festivals and abundance, for some romance and more amusement – occasionally a bit sinister, often sensual, and always lustful. It was a place of rebellion, of a kind of ersatz subversion, where people flouted convention and found pleasure. It was also, of course, a marketplace, since the self-evident goal was to sell the consumer a good or service. There are a myriad ways in which this theatre of the libido realized, in however perverted a fashion, that utopia of carnival outlined so long ago by Mikhail Bakhtin.

3 Fables of Lust

One of the most startling commercials of the 1990s was a British ad (no. 92) entitled *Reservoir Bitch*, presumably after the movie *Reservoir Dogs*, renowned for its scenes of violence. There were only two characters, an adult male and an adult female, fine examples of the Body Handsome and the Body Beautiful. The 'hunk' was more than a bit shabby, dressed in an opened work shirt, white t-shirt, jeans, and boots; the 'beauty,' by contrast, wore a sexy black dress that revealed her black bra and her cleavage plus her long, shapely legs. The camera cut back and forth between the two bodies, paying particular attention to her breasts, her rear end, her stunning face, her red, red lips, and her bouncy hair. Meanwhile the man acted as the herald: 'There's a new fashion magazine ... for women ... and men. A magazine that only wants to know you ... if you know what you want. It's engaging, provocative, and totally modern ... with so much va-voom and it's called ...' He never finished speaking. The woman had become increasingly upset with his announcement. Suddenly she pulled a gun out of her purse and began shooting, and kept shooting. He fell to the floor, the wounds obvious, his prone body jerking at each shot, his work shirt stained with blood; indeed, eventually the screen itself was splattered. One of her shots was aimed between his legs, a clear sign of her contempt for his sex. At the end she walked away, while on screen, above the man's ruined body, written in red, appeared the name of the sponsor, 'Don't Tell It.' All this served to demonstrate that the magazine was both different and shocking.[69]

What made the spot so unusual was that admakers rarely deployed the images of violence so common elsewhere in mass culture. The spot was, indeed, an especially graphic example of the way advertising could employ the sin of murder to promote a product. But not just that: for *Reservoir Bitch* was also an example, albeit an extreme example, of a particular set of erotic commercials I call the fables of lust, because they acted as morality plays – 'immorality' plays might often seem a more appropriate label – that sought to explain the place of objects and persons in a world made sexy. These were always dramas, not just displays: so *What Is Sexy?* and nearly all of the Victoria's Secret ads were not fables of lust because they did not tell much of a story, although they certainly were about lust. Nor was *Nuns* a fable, because it did not directly address the issue of lust, even if it was a little play that spoke of sex and sin. By contrast, *Reservoir Bitch*, like many erotic commercials, did tell a story about lust, in this case about the uncontrollable passions of hate.

The fables of lust were symbolic enactments of libidinal assemblages. They connected problems, people, objects, the prevailing discourses and scenarios of conduct, and nearly always particular times and particular spaces.[70] These fantasies of life were narratives, albeit compacted and often rudimentary, but boasting a chronology and causality, some sort of plot that explained cause and effect, thus serving as a mode of instruction.[71] That was crucial because it exploited the significance of story telling as a mode of self-fashioning. Narrative was one important way in which most people made sense of the world, organized experiences, and constituted their identities. The narratives of ads, even if they were more fragments than whole stories, worked to engage the passions, the bodies, and the selves of consumers in the workings of the libidinal economy. Above all, these narratives offered up at least the illusion of agency, so that a person might transform himself or her situation for the better. It was here that erotica as publicity came to take on some of the attributes of utopian literature. Table 6.2 utilizes thirty fables, selected from the previous collection of 100 commercials, to highlight aspects of the organization of these assemblages.[72] Such a summary, abstracted from the actual commercials, cannot encompass the full variety or richness of any one of these semiotic networks. But the summary does enable an analysis of how these assemblages worked.

Morality plays of this sort had definite motifs that gave the fantasies coherence and meaning. Only five of the most prominent and common motifs are listed in table 6.2.

(i) *spying and teasing*: The discourse of pornography was always full of people watching others, particularly of women, consciously or not, showing off their bodies to please lusty men. So too the tradition of the nude in the art of western Europe. Nearly all of the erotic commercials contain some sort of display of bodies or body parts. But this group of fables actually played around with the nature and the consequences of voyeurism and exhibitionism. A woman used the very nylons (no. b91) that enhanced her legs and excited the voyeur to fashion a catapult that hurled a vase, destroying his telescope and injuring him – we heard the scream. Another woman, white, equally beautiful, stood in front of a young black man (no. c50) whom she thought was blind (he wasn't) and slowly, just to taunt him, buttoned up her fly in a seedy washroom – later, the man shook his head in wonder. And a third woman, this one plain, a security official at an airport (no. d76), had fixed the metal detector so that it always rang when a handsome male went through – that way she could enjoy watching him strip down to his underwear. The last example invoked one instance of the regime of surveillance that became more and more pronounced in the 1990s. It was not alone: surveillance units, video cameras, and cameras of all sorts were commonplace in the fables of lust. But this ad, like the others, undid the threat of Big Brother, turning the regime of surveillance into a regime of stimulation.

(ii) *seductions*: Seduction was another theme familiar to fans of

Table 6.2
Libidinal Assemblages

Ad	Problem	Bodies [m] = male [f] = female	Personas	Brand	Spaces	Moments	Behaviours	Intensities
A. Spying and teasing								
a 85 Diesel Jeans International 1994	Fear	[f] beauty [m] armed [m] ugly	[f] Victim [m] Predator	Symbol: difference	Street Home	Night	Stalking Partying	Relief
b 91 Vivazz Nylons Chile 1995	Revenge	[f] beauty: long legs [m] plain and short	[f] Temptress [m] Voyeur	Agent	Homes	Play	Male gaze Female retaliation	[f] Triumph
c 50 Levi's 501s USA 1996	Flight	[f] white beauty	[f] Temptress	Symbol: individuality	Gas station washroom	Night	Undressing/ dressing Male gaze	Boldness
d 76 Underdaks Underwear Australia 1996	Yearning	[m] young black [f] plain [m] hunk	[m] Voyeur [f]Voyeur [m] Object	Symbol: sexiness	Airport	Work as play	Undressing Female Gaze	Obsession
e 82 Chiemsee Underwear Germany 1996	Revenge	[f] young beauty [m] middle-aged	[f] Femme Fatale [m] Victim	Symbol: supremacy	University library	Day Work	Sexual assault	[f] Triumph vs [m] Frustration
f 75 Pepsi-Cola USA 1997	Yearning	[m] plain teenager [f] Claudia Schiffer [f] fat and ugly	[m] Voyeur [f] Object [f] Spoiler	Symbol: freedom	Shower	Dream	Male gaze Washing	[m] Desire and horror
B. Seductions								
g 79 Carmen perfume Spain 1994	Boredom	[f] beauty [m] hunk	[f] Temptress [m] Victim	Agent	Stage	Work/Play	Posing	Attraction
h 81 Guess Clothing USA 1995	Exposé	[m] old [m] hunk [f] two beauties	[m] Joker [f] Temptress [m] Victim	Instrument	Office and bar	Day and night Work/Play	Entrapment	Curiosity Love Greed Obsession
i 6 L'Air du Temps France 1995	Yearning	[m] hunk [f] beauty, bizarre creatures	[m] Victim [f] Temptress	Instrument	Paradise/Hell	Dream	Posing Dreaming Entrapment	
j 58 Export 33 Lebanon 1995	Yearning	[m] handsome [f] beauty	[m] Voyeur [f] Object	Agent		Dream	Revealing	Attraction

Table 6.2 (continued)

Ad	Problem	Bodies [m] = male [f] = female	Personas	Brand	Spaces	Moments	Behaviours	Intensities
k 18 Martini & Rossi USA and France 1996	Fidelity	[m] cool hunk [f] beauty [m] ugly and old	[m] Tempter [f] Object [m] Authority	Instrument	Riviera	Play	Smooching Drinking Walking	Attraction
l II Lynx Body Spray UK 2000	Revenge	[m] cool hunk [f] many beauties [m] fat and old	[m] Tempter [f] Victims [m] Authority	Instrument	Town	Day Work as play	The Pied Piper Acts of submission	Attraction
C. True lust								
m 25 Foster's Draught Beer and Häagen-Dazs UK 1993	Joy	[f] beauty [m] hunk	[f] Lover [m] Lover/Fan	Agent	Home	Play	Love making Eating and drinking	[f] Frustration [m] Satisfaction
n 80 Soviet Jeans South Africa 1994	Yearning	[f] beauty [m] hunk	Lovers	Target	Home	Play	Love making	[f] Happiness [m] Anger
o 7 Hanes Clothing Spain 1996	Admiration	[m] hunk [m] middle-aged [f] young beauty	[m] Object [m] Seeker [f] Object	Target	On the road	Night and day	Hitch-hiking Driving Trading	Acquisition
p 32 Rally 50 Scooter Italy 1997	Yearning	[f] beauty [m] hunk	Lovers	Target	Home	Play	Love making Driving	[m] Frustration [f] Happiness
q 19 Bonds Clothing Australia 1997	Loss	[f] old [f] two beauties [m] hunk	[f] Seeker [f] Seeker Objects	Target	Homes	Night Play	Love making (straight and lesbian) Driving	Acquisition
r 9 Pepsi Manzanita Mexico 1997	Yearning	[m] hunk [f] beauty	[m] Object [f] Seeker	Target	Bar	Play	Drinking Licking	Embarrassment
D. Escape								
s 3 Stimorol Chewing Gum Europe 1992	Boredom	[m] hunk [f] beauty	Lovers	Agent	Brokerage On the road Homestead	Work Transition Play	Day dreaming Driving Welcoming	Happiness

Table 2. (concluded)

	Ad	Problem	Bodies [m] = male [f] = female	Personas	Brand	Spaces	Moments	Behaviours	Intensities
t 46	H.I.S. Jeans Germany 1995	Loss	[f] beauty [m] ugly [m] hunk	[f] Lover [m] Chauvinist [m] Lover	Instrument	On the road	Day	Arguing Assembling: a new man	Happiness
u 86	Deutch Bahn Germany 1996	Peace	[m] plain [f] stunning: Cindy Crawford	[m] Object [f] Temptress	Instrument	On the railway	Dream	Sleep/Wake	Happiness
v 64	J&B Scotch International 1995	Tradition	[f] classy beauty [m] macho hunk	Lovers	Symbol: novelty	Church	Day	Wedding Partying	Modernity
w 29	Calvin Klein Escape International 1995	Yearning	[f] beauty [m] hunk	Lovers	Agent	Maze	Dream	Running Love making	Obsession Pleasure
x 8	Old Spice After Shave USA 1996	Entrapment	[m] hunk [f] beauty [m] fat, old, and ugly	[m] Tempter [f] Tempted [m] Authority	Symbol: freedom	Diner	Day Work	Dressing [m] Female gaze Driving	Happiness

E. Vulgar pleasures

	Ad	Problem	Bodies [m] = male [f] = female	Personas	Brand	Spaces	Moments	Behaviours	Intensities
y 26	Moritz Ice Cream NZ 1994 [Boursicot]	Yearning	[f] beauty [m] hunk	Lovers	Agent	Home	Play	Love making Eating	Indulgence
z 5	Turelli Pasta Sweden 1994 [Boursicot]	Boredom	young old	Lovers Spouses	Agent	Restaurant	Day Dinner	Eating as loving	Passion
φ 30	Durex Condoms Belgium 1996	Persistence	[f] beauty [m] hunk	Lovers	Instrument	Home	Night	Love making	Indulgence
χ 20	Volkswagen Golf Italy 1998	Risk	[m] hunk [f] beauty	Seekers (actually a couple)	Answer	Dance club	Night Play	Dancing Flirting	Thrill
ψ 33	Ronson Cigarettes Austria 1998	Yearning	[f] beauty [m] hunk	[f] Temptress [m] Object	Instrument	Home	Night	Post-coital play	Indulgence
ω 38	Dockers Khakis USA 1997	Durability	[m] young black [f] many beauties	[m] Tempter [f] Voyeurs	Instrument	Dance club	Play	Dirty dancing Flirting	Energy

pornography. Like spying and teasing, seduction was about relations of power, how people managed to impose their will upon others to realize the imperatives of lust. A woman overwhelmed a stranger with her scent (no. i6), transporting him into a bizarre land where he must search for her presence, whatever demons hindered his progress. A mayor tried to cheat the Pied Piper of his just reward (no. l11), so the young man used his body spray to entice all the women to leave the village in his wake. A private detective employed beautiful women (no. h81) to test the fidelity of a boyfriend of a client. 'Sure it's entrapment. My girls look great. They know how to dress and they know how to talk to a man.' And in this case 'Julie,' his star temptress, did her job well, revealing that the all-American guy was indeed a cheat. Sex always trumped other desires in this group of fables. So a beautiful woman (no. k18) left the rich old man to run away with a cool, handsome fellow who promised much greater excitement. The morality celebrated here was the pre-eminence of the libido. The person who won this game of sex was the one with a body that commanded attention.

(iii) *true lust*: This cluster of fables, however, broke away from the norms of pornography because now the protagonists chose not sex but the brand. A couple (no. m25) were eagerly making love (and eating ice cream, the love food) when the man suddenly found a bottle of beer in the fridge, opened it, and turned on the soccer match. A woman (no. q19) made love with another woman simply to retrieve the t-shirt she had lost in an earlier encounter with a man. Indeed one man (no. o7), albeit older and so in need of some assistance, gave up his money, his car, and his girl just to get the right t-shirt. It was also about power and about appetite, but the lust was for the product. A woman (no. r9) gazed longingly at a man quaffing a soft drink; when he wiped the last drop on his arm, she grabbed the arm and began licking it as if caught up in a sexual frenzy. Then she, and he, looked very embarrassed. But she had demonstrated the law of true lust: what counted in the end was consumption.

(iv) *escape*: The logic of escape, by contrast, dictated that people had to liberate themselves from a situation that somehow thwarted their lusts. It might be no more than a need to escape the ordinary. A man suffering the boredom of work (no. s3) fled the brokerage to find happiness in the company of his old girlfriend.[73] A woman threw over her job in a dingy diner (no. x8) to run away with a

handsome man. Or it could mean shedding the past. A couple discarded tradition (no. v64) to stage an avant-garde wedding – and
that included a gift of handcuffs to the bride for some future bondage drama. Then there were those poor souls who felt a terrible
lack. A woman, jilted and deserted by her cad of a boyfriend, actually witnessed the assembling of a new hunk (no. t46) who granted
her the love she so desperately wanted.[74] Desperation and want
lay behind the two besotted souls in a Calvin Klein drama (no.
w29) who made passionate love in a private world of their own.
Power mattered not at all to these lovers, only pleasure. The escape
was into the realm of sex where their flaming desire could be realized.

(v) *vulgar pleasures*: These fables celebrated appetite, indulgence, and
excess – the body freed from its restraints – a logic that could easily
slip over into the carnivalesque. A young couple expressed their
love (no. z5) while eating pasta, sucking each strand so passion-
ately they excited a gnarled wife to try the same with her ancient
husband, except that she demanded plate after plate of pasta. The
sexy dancer, a young African-American man, found that his cool
look and smooth moves (no. ω38) were admired not just on the
dance floor but outside in the world at large – everyone, or rather
every woman, wanted a piece of him. Making love was not
enough: one woman indulged in a sinful, chocolate-covered, ice-
cream bar (no. y26) and another lit up two cigarettes (no. ψ33), one
for her and the other for the naked man she had just slept with. A
man and a woman, supposed strangers, performed the risky game
of flirtation at a dance club, enjoying the promise of dangerous sex
(no. χ20), each action underlined by warnings about playing it safe
that were flashed on the screen. What a disappointment when it
was revealed at the end this was all a game: the twosome were
really a couple, owners of a Volkswagen, just trying to rekindle the
old thrills of night life.

   Whatever the motif, however, the key player in these fables of lust
was more often than not the brand. The brand became a fetish, doubly
so, in the sense of both Marx and Freud. The term 'fetish' had its origins in anthropology, where it referred to the belief, supposedly common among adherents of 'primitive' religions, that some objects had a
built-in magic, that they were actually inhabited by spirits, if not the
gods. For Marx the commodity, once produced, transcended its origins

to become a fetish, a thing endowed with life, indeed with mystical properties that enabled it to act in the world almost as though it were a person.[75] For Freud the fetish was any object, animate or inanimate, that people believed had some enormous sexual significance, rather like the phallus.[76]

The brand in the fable of lust was such an object, a non-human actor, made powerful and sexy by the operations of the libidinal assemblage. The images in a Lebanese ad (no. j58) jumped back and forth between shots of the beer and shots of a woman's bosom and her behind: eventually the man undid her bra to reveal one nipple and the screen overlaid a picture of the foaming bottle of beer. The bottle had become her body; opening its cap promised the man the pleasures of sex, a promise emphasized by the silhouette of the two faces about to kiss. The brand might be the actual agent that drove or transformed what happened in the minidrama: thus one fragrance called Carmen appeared in the ad (no. g79) as the notorious Carmen of opera fame who proved she could seduce any man. The brand might be an instrument used by the protagonist to achieve an erotic purpose: the Guess clothes worn by the temptress (no. h81) were necessary to trap the cheater. Or it could be a target motivating the various participants, an object of such attraction that they were compelled to acquire it, whatever the consequences. In every case, then, the brand was presented as one crucial cause of events in the fable.

Even when the brand acted only as a symbol, what it stood for, the particular spirit, imbued the commercial. Consider a bizarre ad for Chiemsee underwear (no. e82). The beautiful young student teased the older professor, actually tearing off his trousers and putting her hand into his underpants. He tried to rip open her sports bra, marked with the logo of Chiemsee, to reach her ample bosom – but to no avail. She played with him, she demonstrated her supremacy, leaving him in a state of disarray and frustration. At the end she exited the university library smiling, and we heard his howl of anguish. The brand symbolized her indomitable will, her defiance of convention and authority.[77]

Marx also perceived in the drama of production a process of reification, the conversion of people into things.[78] Certainly some of the participants in the fables were reduced to objects, passive not active, present because they or some part of their bodies was deemed beautiful or handsome. But the protagonists were never just objects; rather, they were calculating subjects, able to use things and make choices – in short, a version of the modern self. But only a version, because these people were led not so much by reason as by emotion, or, to put this in Freudian terms, by desires lodged in the id. The one outstanding exception, at least in the collection I have assembled here, was the businessman in the Guess ad (no. h81), a joker who had organized the phoney seduction to earn his living. Most other protagonists played out such personae as the temptress and the tempter, lovers and seekers, the occasional femme fatale, people moved by impulse and whim. In one of the Pepsi-Cola fables (no. f75), a young lad, not especially good looking, got asked what he wanted. 'Hey, Tony, now that you've changed to Pepsi, what else would you change?' He sidled up to the camera and exclaimed, 'I'd like to be soap on a rope in Claudia Schiffer's shower.' What better place, so he calculated, to see the supermodel in all her naked splendour, thus evoking that age-old scenario in art and pornography where the man looked at the woman washing her body? The calculation was only partly correct, unfortunately. Yes, he did see the supermodel in action, preparing for her shower. But then, suddenly, another person, an older fat woman, rushed into the show to take her place – worse yet she used the soap on a rope to wash herself and to wash him down the drain. What he got to see was only the grotesque body.

Much more often the protagonists did achieve their will. In the appropriately named *X-Rated* (no. n80), a man and a woman made passionate love in a secluded room while outside the rain poured down. They stripped each other, kissed and coupled, and fell upon the bed. She tied his hands to the bed post and turned around to secure his feet, all the time pleasuring him with her legs and her body. Suddenly she reached down to the floor and pulled up his discarded pair of Soviet jeans. Desire struck. She brought them to her mouth. She couldn't resist the impulse. She put on the jeans and her coat, giving her bound lover, now raging to get free, a look of contempt. She opened the door to escape into the rain with her prize. She had calculated her chances well. But she too had been moved by desire. Time and again the protagonists acted on impulse – to show off (no. c50), to exact revenge (no. b91 and no. 111), to break away (no. s3 and no. x8), to satisfy a yearning (no. p32). These characters were reminiscent of the desiring (and fearing) machines celebrated by Gilles Deleuze and Félix Guattari: that is, subjects always wanting and needing, who connected to others and to objects to satisfy the commands of the id. In the world of sex, at least as the admakers imagined that world, the unconscious really was 'a factory, a workshop' producing a never-ending flow of desire. The admakers did what Deleuze and Guattari claimed capitalism always did; their fables of lust engineered that desire, transformed it into wants and lacks, mobilized the libido, all in the interest of the marketplace.[79]

The fables linked the brand and the self to particular places and particular moments. Space mattered because it grounded the drama in the matrix of ordinary life. True, while it was important that the disruption of the professor in the Chiemsee ad (no. e82) occur in a workplace, a space that spoke of authority, that could have been his office rather than the library. But consider the importance of stereotype in other fantasies. A washroom, albeit a men's washroom in the case of the Levi's ad (no. c50), was one public space where by accident a man might witness a strange woman changing clothes. The fact that the scenario took place in a church, albeit a very homely one, was crucial to J&B's message (no. v64) about the need to break with tradition. Nor was it surprising that the extended display of love making in the Durex commercial (no. φ30) was situated in the various rooms of the home. Perhaps Carmen (no. g79) could have worked the magic of her scent in the street, a restaurant, or at home; even so, the stage setting was essential to emphasize the link with the opera and so with the myth of the temptress. Likewise the Riviera locale in the Martini & Rossi fable (no. k18) set the scene for images of the wealthy and their hangers-on living a life of leisure and luxury. These settings establish a context full of expected or familiar details – the grunginess of a man's washroom, the furnishings of a home, the aura of a dance club or bar – to inform, sometimes to counter, the fantasy, making it possible to suspend disbelief.

Time mattered even more than space, however, because the moment justified the fantasy. Admakers displayed a preference for times of licence, dreams, playtime, and most especially the night. Work time, like the workplace, was something people escaped, by either leaving (no. s3) or undoing, turning work into play (no. 111 and no. d76). Because he was dreaming, the nerd really could think he was desired by such a person as Cindy Crawford (no. u86). Play meant the denial of all the pressures of normal life, work and social obligation, a loss of restraint, the time to indulge. Night was still occasionally, as of old, a sinister time where dangers lurked: thus the stalking drama (no. a85) sponsored by Diesel Jeans. But now, even more, night, a night well lit by electricity and full of people and activity, was when the imperative of lust could reign supreme. Consider one briefly famous American commercial for Michelob beer (Cannes 1987) called *Night Moves*. Throughout, Phil Collins's haunting song 'In the Air Tonight' carried the message of sexual excitement, the yearning for adventure and novelty. The action occurred in a big city in the evening, full of cars and street lights and tall buildings – but no sounds other than the music. There were assorted shots of a disc jockey, a man playing a guitar, a band. The most compelling images were hazy, slowed, sometimes even fuzzy shots of attractive young men and women together and apart, looking around, searching for something or someone, on the street and in clubs. This nighttime was given over to the pursuit of pleasure. And Michelob was a part of that scene: the images of the young people were occasionally interspersed with shots of the brand label and the beer itself. 'The night belongs to Michelob' was the moral on screen at the end of the commercial.

The night didn't belong to Michelob, anymore than it belonged to Guess or Levi's or Volkswagen. But admakers could hope. The libidinal assemblages organized by the admakers were meant to entice and excite: Diesel was playing the game of irony when it referred to its bizarre ads as guides 'to successful living.' These fables were far more sophisticated and much less didactic than, say, the Barbie advertising of the 1960s, except that they too could perform like Freud's dreams. For embedded in these fables were narratives of self and soul: in the mid-1990s Levi Strauss actually set up a website for *Washroom* (no. 50) where it filled out the story, explaining how the woman in disguise was trying to escape with a load of found money (the results of gambling), fearful of discovery by her boyfriend or the police. The point was not only to connect the brand to the culture, chiefly the pop culture and the lifestyles of youth, but to mobilize the libido, as Baudrillard had argued many years before, to channel that hunger in ways best suited to the imperatives of consumption. The fables worked to assemble the social out of material, cultural, and even moral elements.

4 Audiences and Impacts

'Does sex sell?' The answer might seem obvious. It did to one columnist in *Advertising Age* (28 January 1991), who could not resist mocking the prose of academic researchers who had tried to find out the effectiveness of sex in advertising.[80] That was part of a massive enterprise launched by professors of marketing in the United States to discover

'What did ads do to people?' Since the early 1970s, an increasing number of these professors had explored what arousal meant, what kinds of images or words worked or did not work, why some people were offended, whether sex induced thought, how it affected attitudes towards the brand, what media were best, and whether sex strengthened the intention to purchase. The chosen method was a kind of survey research where the scholars constructed experiments that tested the responses of audiences, normally made up of university students, to ads that were sometimes fabricated or modified to suit the needs of the investigation. Although that tradition persisted into the new century, by 1990 it was being challenged by a new body of academics, influenced by cultural theory and cultural studies, who asked, 'What did people do with ads?,' including, naturally, ads that featured the erotic.[81] That produced analyses of ethnographic texts, sometimes informed by insights from Freud and Foucault and other luminaries – the texts derived from interviews with actual consumers, many of whom again were undergraduates – in a search for how ads entertained, what meanings people derived from ads and whether these might serve to build identities or enhance life projects.[82] Together, the result was an extensive body of literature scattered across a series of scholarly journals and the occasional book of essays.

The findings could strike outsiders and practitioners – and a critic like the *Advertising Age* columnist – as ambiguous, trivial, even contradictory, and too often embedded in opaque texts that were full of jargon. Nonetheless, the research literature did show that the answer to whether sex sells, in print and on television, was much more complicated than common sense might assume. Certainly it dispelled the old idea of a submissive or brainwashed audience, a notion that was popularized by Vance Packard's bestselling exposé, *The Hidden Persuaders* (1957), and that lingered on in the minds of some critics of advertising.

The first problem was to understand how the public responded to advertising in general. The fact is that response was conditioned by a deep sense of ambivalence.[83] People were not passive vessels but 'active readers of texts,' meaning words and images, who sought to interpret and change what they saw or heard.[84] Advertising was never a discourse of truth, at least not to veteran consumers, who approached ads with an intriguing mix of belief and disbelief – sometimes bored, occasionally fascinated, and both irritated and pleased – so that they were usually ready to discount any claims the ad might make.[85] After conducting some tests, one group of researchers observed, a bit ruefully, that 'consumers were much easier to turn off than to turn on. It almost seemed as though they were subconsciously looking for some reason not to become involved in the commercial – a reason for screening it out.'[86] Very often, of course, such consumers tried to avoid ads altogether, leaving the room when a commercial break came on television or tuning in other channels to see what was on before returning to their programs.[87]

But consumers, sometimes the same consumers, did treat ads, or rather certain ads, as a form of entertainment, watched because they produced a sense of pleasure, whether intellectual or aesthetic or emotional, particularly when the style or execution was novel.[88] People did incorporate the sayings of widely known campaigns into their daily lives.[89] One group of English teens would continually re-enact and retell content from TV ads, transforming the claims and styles of these commercials to suit the occasion, usually in some humorous fashion, all as part of an ongoing effort to maintain a sense of fellowship.[90] People, in short, used ads *as* play and *to* play.

That was especially true of erotic ads. The sex often trumped the brand, meaning that watchers could become so fascinated (or horrified) by what they saw that they focused on the ad rather than the product.[91] Yet people did not always respond the same way in the theatre of the libido. Perhaps, as one set of researchers wrote, 'all pleasure is secretly sexual,' briefly indulging in a Freudian moment. However, like the master himself, they recognized that the pursuit of this pleasure was constrained by moral convictions.[92] Overall, sex in advertising had a paradoxical effect on audiences: the displays of sin and the fables of lust certainly attracted more attention, but they also caused more upset, especially when the treatment was extreme.[93]

Those moral convictions reflected the import of demographics and psychographics. Unfortunately the influence of class was masked by the character of the research literature, which did not look closely at the effects of income or different levels of education. By contrast, the research thoroughly explored the role of gender. Women were much more likely to take offence at sex than men, because of the impact of feminism plus the fact that women's bodies were so often the target of the voyeur's gaze.[94] A little bit of romance in the ad did sometimes help to soothe a ruffled female soul.[95] Even then, women were especially sensitive to the product advertised – what was fine for perfumes and clothes was not justified for other kinds of goods. Men were more liberal in their attitudes towards sex, more tolerant of an admaker's images (excepting signals of homosexuality), and indeed more likely to see the signs of sex in advertisements.[96] So 'a student talked about how his flatmates would applaud when they saw a television ad featuring an attractive woman.'[97] There was evidence, though not uncontested, that age sometimes had a bigger impact on response than gender: young adults were more inclined than older people, at least in some studies, to accept nudity and the like.[98] Youth of both sexes were prepared to agree that 'romantic sexuality can add symbolic value to consumption,' while the focus groups of middle-aged respondents were not.[99] Then there was nationality. Two cross-country studies, one in Europe and the other in Asia, did demonstrate different kinds of responses, likes and dislikes, to the same stimuli.[100] Americans were certainly inclined to think that television commercials too often promoted sex.[101] In one extensive report the British seemed more willing to accept nudity and the erotic, though only late at night when the children and seniors were presumably in bed.[102] That report also detected a range of personalities, labelling some respondents 'puritans' (the embarrassed) and 'moralists' (who would ban sex) and others 'crusaders' (who hoped the imagery would undo prudishness) and even 'libertines' (who wanted more nudity). At which point the picture of the audience becomes too confused and contradictory to yield much useful information.

Another way to explore the impact of sexy ads is to move out of the laboratory and the classroom to study examples of what might be called success stories in the 'real' world. We will see, however, that the three cases confirm the findings of sex researchers who have explored the mechanics of sexuality. Their efforts have highlighted the crucial importance of fantasy in the work of arousal; indeed, sex counsellors commonly tell patients to generate fantasies or view pornography in order to master their inhibitions.[103] Here admakers provided the fantasies, or at least the catalyst for whatever dreams and fears individuals might elaborate. The researchers have also demonstrated that the fantasies of men and women do differ. Men often dream of adventure, meaning lots of sex, multiple partners, their own agency, and sometimes the domination of others. Women often fantasize about romance, meaning a loving partner, moments of tenderness and togetherness, pleasant and aesthetic surroundings, commitment, and receptivity.[104] Likely, that also was not news to these admakers, who clearly understood how to curry favour with particular audiences, although their success with one gender did not necessarily translate into success with the other.

(i) The Swedish Bikini Team (SBT), 1991

The SBT saga was more a case of a cultural triumph than a marketing coup. The Stroh Brewery wished to revitalize the advertising for its Old Milwaukee brand of beer. It told its ad agency, Hal Riney and Part-ners/San Francisco, to fashion a new campaign, aimed at young males, that would preserve the existing 'equities' of past endeavours: blue collar appeal, outdoor settings, high energy, an emphasis on fun, and, of course, the slogan, 'It doesn't get any better than this ...'[105] The agency came up with the idea of a mock rescue that would parody the style of sexy beer ads prevailing in the United States at the time. The resulting three commercials featured a group of guys outdoors some-where – the mountains, a beach, in the water – who would toast how 'it doesn't get any better than this ...' Except it could: the ad showed just how much better. Suddenly, out of nowhere, five beautiful and smiling women, in blonde wigs and swimsuits and showing lots of flesh, espe-cially lots of breast and bottom, arrived with beer to make the party (there was rock music of course) much more interesting. This was the Swedish Bikini Team, no more than an ad creation, and actually com-posed of five American actresses.

The SBT was a clever expression of a long-standing male, heterosex-ual fantasy: sexy and willing women arrive to save lusty men from a life of boredom – or in this case from thirst as well. It had obvious por-nographic overtones. It embodied the widespread stereotype of the gorgeous Scandinavian blonde, a woman made for sex. And it was funny, or at least meant to be taken as humorous. No wonder the cam-paign received a lot of free publicity from the media. The late-night TV comedians Jay Leno and David Letterman featured the team in their monologues. Indeed the SBT became a commodity in its own right, the women appearing in two episodes of the hit situation comedy *Married with Children*. They also graced the cover of *Playboy* magazine in Janu-ary 1992.

Before then, the campaign had already run into a lot of trouble in the media. The parody had not worked to cleanse the sex. This was a time of considerable upset in the United States over issues of sexism and sex-ual harassment, when the public sphere was much agitated by the Wil-liam Kennedy Smith rape case and the Anita Hill controversy (part of the Senate hearings over the nomination of Clarence Thomas to the Supreme Court). In this climate the SBT campaign looked more and more like a tasteless attack on women. It was condemned by various public associations, including women's groups, for being irresponsible and sexist. *Time* magazine decided it was one of the worst ad campaigns of the year. Most serious, a number of female employees at Stroh's St Paul brewery launched sexual harassment suits against the company, citing the ads as one cause of the hostile climate of opinion at the plant.[106] 'The Swedish bikini ads portray women as giggling, jiggling idiots who have large breasts and small minds,' asserted Lori Peterson, the attorney for the aggrieved workers. 'Stroh's is promoting an attitude about women, and the employees are imitating it in the workplace.'[107] Brand sales actually declined, or so it was claimed afterwards.[108] The upshot was the cancellation of the campaign and the official end of the Swedish Bikini Team. The sexual harassment suits were settled out of court two years later.[109] Beer advertisers even worked to find alternatives to the 'babes' and 'bimbos' who had cavorted in their commercials.

Still the story would not die. The SBT fiasco remained fresh in the minds of anti-feminists, who saw Stroh's retreat as a victory for political correctness. Men recalled the team fondly as a marvellous fantasy: so in 1999 one writer admitted, 'I've dreamt for years – probably inspired by the beer commercials featuring a bunch of guys partying with the Swedish Bikini Team – of beautiful, adoring Swedish girls kidnapping me.'[110] A bit later one entrepreneur revived the name, producing a new team for a spy spoof called *Never Say ... Never Mind* (2001). Bikini teams were made available for hire to people who wanted to liven up a party. Meanwhile the industry had returned to its old ways. In 2003, for example, Miller Lite generated some controversy with *Catfight*, a commercial in which, as one critic put it, 'the busty, comely dames dive into a reflecting pool, tearing each other's clothes off, with the camera providing enough underwear and bra shots to launch 1,000 lingerie fetish sites.' That scene was later revealed as a dream of two guys, another fantasy of sex made visible.[111] Pabst, which had acquired the Stroh company, resurrected the memory of the campaign on its website for Old Milwaukee: they provided a poster of three beautiful blonde women, in bikinis, posed next to an enlarged bottle of the beer.

The poster was reminiscent of the style of the pop art painter Mel Ramos. Recall how he had linked bodies and brands, sex and consumption. The poster pointed to the lasting significance of the campaign. The SBT saga was representative of a particular kind of libidinal assemblage sponsored over and over again by the beer industry, because at least sometimes (though apparently not this time) it worked. And not only in

North America: in Brazil, for instance, Kaiser beer (no. 35) ran a commercial where handsome men and sexy women, skimpily clad, drank and played on a beach. That ad, like many others, suggested an orgy. Young males as subjects, beautiful, sometimes semi-nude women as objects, and always good times, much music and much fun – these were all connected in a fable of lust where the key ingredient was the brand of beer that made possible the pleasures of the 'real' guy.

(ii) Jessica's Tale, 1993–4?

This was a story of a more private, indeed intimate, kind of fantasy. A young woman called 'Jessica' by the British academics who interviewed her told about the ways in which she and her group of university friends played sex games with Häagen-Dazs ice cream.[112] The women, aged between nineteen and twenty-two, had lived close to each other in two rented houses for two years. At the time Häagen-Dazs was sponsoring a campaign that eroticized the brand through words and images emphasizing sensuality and love making, all in an effort to enhance the appeal of their product to the adult market. The campaign involved television as well as magazines, though it was not clear how much attention Jessica and her friends paid to television. They certainly were taken by the ad images in the magazines, however.
    'I think we basically liked the connotations of the ads ...,' recalled Jessica, 'and we believed the idea that Häagen-Dazs was sexy because the ads told us it was sexy, so when we had the ice-cream in front of us we felt that the pot was very sexy, a sexy pot.' They would seek out the ads and talk about their meanings. Some of the women filled their rooms with empty tubs of the ice cream and put up ads from the campaign on the walls as signifiers of the erotic. The friends would get together to eat the ice cream, play music, and talk dirty, treating men as objects of visual pleasure. The brand and the advertising gave the women licence to act in what now seemed to Jessica a vulgar fashion, even though sometimes they realized, given the prevailing morality in feminist circles, how ironic it was for women to adopt the voyeur's gaze: 'I mean we did stop and think "Oh my God this is really horrible," but we'd just laugh it off.' They might even involve Häagen-Dazs in their erotic liaisons with the men they brought back to their rooms. 'The connection between Häagen-Dazs and sex ... well it would be a part of sex, be used with sex. It would be added. It would be something, an added extra to sex.' On reflection Jessica admitted it might all

seem a bit silly now that the group had split up (and apparently the academics had some difficulty getting her to talk). But she had no regrets: 'their advertising's worked on me and everything, but if I enjoy the product I'd still let the advertising work on me.'

Of course we only have Jessica's word for the truth of this tale of ad seduction. But it was plausible. One of the academics and his team of researchers did interview some other people, both eighteen- to twenty-three-year-olds and forty- to fifty-five-year-olds, about the Häagen-Dazs campaign, as well as other advertisements. The informants were shown magazine ads – 'Melt Together' and 'Feel Me' – that linked consumption, indulgence, and sex play. The older group was not at all impressed; indeed they found the claims and suggestions crude, if not disgusting. By contrast the younger group were, like Jessica, attracted by the aura of romance as well as the sexual suggestion. 'Until that I wouldn't have thought of ice-cream as sexy,' claimed one woman. 'I would like to put it on someone's body and lick it off,' said another. Still a third claimed, in the spirit of the discussion, 'I would use it as a substitute for a guy.' [113] Clearly the Häagen-Dazs campaign had engaged the sexual fancies of some people.

Here, then, was another successful assemblage, but this time appealing more to young women than men. The fantasies of indulgence connected the brand to sexy bodies, moods of romance and sensuality, and acts of love making – which was exactly what Foster's beer (no. m25) satirized in its story of love making thwarted: a man chose beer and soccer over Häagen-Dazs and sex.

(iii) The Viagra Case, 1998–2002

Finally, consider the so-called techno-body fashioned by the use of Viagra, which has the additional advantage of demonstrating Donna Haraway's notion of the import of both technology and information, especially since the drug produced what has been called a 'cyborg phallus.'[114] At one end of the assemblage was Pfizer Incorporated, the makers of Viagra; at the other end was the perfect erection, the result of consuming Viagra. In between ran connections among, first, the drug, the bloodstream, and of course the penis; second, lots of publicity, the eyes and ears that absorbed it, and the imagination it excited; and, again, the man's eyes, presumably focused on the object of his desire, then the man's libido, and finally his penis.[115] Arousal was the result of both fantasy and consumption.

What conditioned the user's psyche, what prepared him for the magic of the drug, were two different waves of publicity. The unofficial publicity of news, gossip, and jokes spread throughout the media treated Viagra as an effective aphrodisiac that could help all men, including the young, to secure and retain 'a hard.' The official publicity, generated by Pfizer, variously depicted Viagra as a medical cure for erectile dysfunction in older and middle-aged males. A series of American television commercials running in 2002 emphasized how Viagra could restore a man's self-esteem because it reaffirmed his masculinity. The ads were entitled *What's Different?*, *Baseball*, *Free Sample*, and *That's My Number*, the last two using a racing-car motif to convey speed and vigour. In *What's Different?* a middle-aged African-American man, looking pleased and confident, arrived at the office where his co-workers, both male and female, knew that something good had happened to him: was it a new haircut, new shoes, exercise, a promotion? None of these of course – the viewer was led to believe that the happy man had started taking Viagra.[116]

The 'Viagra Success Stories,' located at viagra.com, allowed seniors and their wives to explain how using the drug had revitalized their lives, their marriages, indeed their romance. Witness this comment from one of the men: 'When you are not performing, you wonder if you are doing your job, you know. And maybe they [the wife?] won't say something, you know, but you are always thinking that they will, sooner or later.' And from one of the women: 'It was like a honeymoon. After twenty-two-and-a-half years of not being able to have physical relations, it was just like a honeymoon.' All of this publicity promised men something once deemed impossible, namely the ability to control the penis, a notoriously uncooperative organ boasting, as one historian put it, 'a mind of its own.'[117]

The campaign had even created its own poster boy, the one-time Republican presidential candidate Bob Dole, who had acted as the first spokesman for Viagra on television and had since become a slightly comic symbol of the always erotic and ever-ready male.[118] No wonder Viagra had swiftly attracted a clientele around the world among men of all ages, including the youthful *Maxim* crowd (named after a male magazine of the day), who supposedly devoted themselves to wild parties of sex, booze, and drugs.

In 2001 a group of researchers in New Zealand probed the views of Viagra users and their partners, most of whom were in their old age.[119] Pfizer had launched a campaign in that country similar to their advertising in the United States. The team found a much more diverse response to the drug than was represented in the campaign, including outright dissent, especially from the few men who had found the drug of limited or no use, as well as from some of the women who now felt pressured to have sex. But what was striking was the level of agreement among the men with the motif of renewal, the return of adventure, in the rhetoric of Pfizer. Viagra was 'a godsend,' 'a gift from heaven': as Derek put it, 'it's given you your manhood back again so to speak.' 'Oh, it's the greatest sex I've ever had in my life ... I'm sort of 18 again,' claimed Nicholas. 'Your erection's just super hard, super big and you can just go on and do different things and there's just no worries, it's just great.' One man could have intercourse three or four times a night, presumably as in the days of his youth. Another embarked on a life of sexual experimentation with other partners, unknown to his wife. In short Viagra was a way to realize the sexual fantasies of many of these men who had felt lessened by the problem of what was once called impotence.

There were few other products or brands where a libidinal assemblage was so obvious (although one earlier instance might be that female body fashioned by the use of the vibrator to ensure the once tabooed pleasures of masturbation).[120] But the Viagra case represented the ideal result of the sexy sell, where capitalism as eroticism had constructed a type of body and self organized around techniques of stimulation. Consumption became one of Foucault's 'technologies of the self,' a technique for the self-fashioning of the modern woman and man, making her and him better, happier people.[121] This was the function of an enormous barrage of advertising, beginning in the 1960s and cresting in the 1990s, for clothing, food, cosmetics, even cars and electronics, that had swarmed through the affluent zone of the world. The ads sought to eroticize brand and user: enhance the skin or the face, accentuate the bottom or the breasts, please the stomach or freshen the mouth – to list only some of the many promises. In all, this advertising had worked to realize a kind of body, of appetites and orifices and extensions, imagined by Bakhtin, celebrated by Bataille, but now connected to the world of commerce.

5 Sexy Posters

A refugee from the Soviet Union in the late 1970s was asked what she had first found different about North America. '"The pornography," she said immediately. "It's everywhere, even on billboards." '[122] What had once seemed so striking a feature of the visual landscape of cities in North America has now spread to much of the rest of the world.

At the turn of the millennium, one of Beijing's most famous shopping areas was Wangfujing Street, located downtown just east of the Forbidden City, within easy walking distance of a number of luxury hotels. Wangfujing seemed a particularly exotic intrusion, full of glamour and glitz, in a central Beijing characterized by many narrow streets and dilapidated storefronts, a few enormous avenues and the giant Tiananmen Square, huge government buildings, plus assorted museums and tourist sights.[123] The four blocks of shops, a department store, even a mall entrance, were closed to traffic, which meant that shoppers and lookers could amble about largely unhindered. And so they did: throngs of people filled the street on a Saturday night, both Chinese and visitors, and the numbers were still noticeable on the Sunday morning.

What was most striking, however, were all the erotic ads, displayed on an ever-changing video wall, in window and street-level displays, and on billboards mounted on the buildings.[124] This was despite the fact that the local authorities were still leery of allowing the public spectacle of too much flesh.[125] Here was the face of the supermodel Cindy Crawford fronting for Omega watches. A young, passionate Western couple, courtesy of Esprit, kissed above the entrance of a department store. Another young Western body, looking Scandinavian, and very much the wanton, smiled slightly as she eagerly displayed her shapely torso in a billboard for O-N-L-Y, a brand of clothes made by Bestseller. A Nine West woman and the Armani man were both in window displays. Some of the smoothed faces and streamlined bodies were Chinese, however: a young woman, presumably naked, reading in a bathtub (Roca); a slim, half-naked woman carefully covering her breasts (Qume); the beautifully made-up face of a woman, her full lips rouged, her skin flawless, her eyebrows enhanced, looking directly at passers-by (Tony Studio). Call this the poster art of the regime of stimulation.

All of which made Wangfujing into an outpost of a utopia of Eros that had spread throughout the affluent zones of North America and western Europe. You could find similar posters, some even more alluring and revealing, in such upscale shopping sites as Yorkville in Toronto or the Via Veneto in Rome or Avenida de la Libertad in Lisbon. In October 2000 the upper reaches of Times Square in New York were dominated by huge billboards of a headless woman showing lots of skin (an ad for a TV series on the women of Wall Street), a bit of necrophilia (Perry Ellis), a coy but inviting Christina Aguilera (pushing a new album), and a man showing off his fine physique (Hilfiger underwear). This poster art, however, had swarmed into many other areas of Western cities. A residential street in Nice in France (May 2001) had ad kiosks suggesting both lesbian sex and a female masturbating. Near one of the most famous of the old-style sex districts, the Reeperbahn in Hamburg, were cigarette billboards (September 1999) showing off the bare torso of a male hunk and the shiny body of a voluptuous woman in a skimpy bathing suit. A series of buses in Barcelona (June 2000) were festooned with assorted eroticized images touting a new man's perfume from Carolina Herrera of New York.

Consider just one of these posters. The ad was for Collistar, the Italian manufacturer of a variety of products that claimed to energize the skin and banish the effects of aging. It appeared (September 1999) in the window of a pharmacy in the coastal Italian town of Amalfi, as a backdrop to an actual display of various Collistar products. The background of the ad was spare, divided between a light brown swatch that suggested the beach and a light blue and white section that signified the sea. Along one side ran the company name. In the middle was a streamlined nude: a very attractive young woman, wet and tanned, her body caught in a strange but revealing pose. She rested on the beach, her head back, her neck strained, her arms behind (though one was not visible) thrusting her torso upward to display full, perfect breasts. Her nipples were erect. Her bare midriff was extraordinarily slim. She had lifted one smooth leg, for balance, but also to hide her vulva. Not surprisingly her skin was flawless, with no marks or wrinkles, and certainly no cellulite. Her wet hair rested on one shoulder and hung down from her head. It was impossible to see her expression clearly, though her eyes seemed closed and her mouth opened. She was oblivious to all but the rays of the sun, caught up in a mood of ecstasy that had an obvious sexual connotation.

How are we to understand such an image? The posters might be counted as yet another example of Jean Baudrillard's simulacra, images without an original, or perhaps images that masked 'the absence of a profound reality,' since they referred to a world of dreams.[126] Except that the posters did draw upon a reality, namely the sexual underground as well as the practices of beauty. Or they might be labelled 'semiophores,' in the terminology of Krzysztof Pomian, making the posters the visible representatives of an imaginary utopia of sex.[127] Except Pomian believed that 'semiophores' had no practical value, a belief which hardly suited ads whose purpose was to stimulate.

The posters were more akin to what Roland Barthes termed bourgeois myth many years ago in *Mythologies*, a classic work on semiotics.[128] Barthes considered myth a special type of speech, one that was frozen in time, thoroughly depoliticized, and dressed up as fact. He posited the example of a picture on the cover of *Paris-Match* of an African soldier saluting the tricolour. He did not doubt that the picture had a specific meaning about the actions of one uniformed man paying his respects to the flag. But he was much more interested in how the sign operated at another (or as he claimed second) level, as a signifier that conveyed a concept of 'French imperiality' of much wider significance to the status quo.[129] He drew on Freud's notion of the manifest (as remembered) and the latent (as interpreted) content of dreams. Barthes argued that there could be many different signifiers used to connote a single concept, although he emphasized how myth preferred simple or closed images.[130] Each of these signifiers of myth had 'an imperative, buttonholing character' that served to hail the viewer or reader as a believer.[131] The concept, or signified, was itself rooted in the wider ideology of the ruling elite so that the picture of the saluting African soldier became a reference meant to establish the validity of the French empire. The shift into myth produced a sign that had removed the image from history, from actual experience, transforming the meaning so that it spoke of what was both natural and eternal, a statement of an essence.[132]

The sexy posters were not altogether the equivalent of Barthes's guardians of bourgeois society and morality. To a degree the posters actually challenged an older set of moral norms that still exercised some influence on behaviour. Yet, in a similar fashion, the Collistar ad as myth did evoke the modern Eros of streamlined bodies and stylized faces that made such expressions of perfection into ideals of sensuality. So, too, did most of the Beijing ads, where what was on display was a beauty both purified and enticing. Some of the Western posters, notably the two in Nice, evoked instead the carnival of sex, albeit in a more restricted fashion than the fables of lust, where transgression had been cleansed through aesthetics and the like. All these posters constituted, à la Barthes, a host of different signifiers, different performances, though there were only two signifieds. All were linked to a broader ideology, in this case of eroticism, that served the purposes of a host of international corporations. Nearly all the images were carefully arranged and organized, a type of closed text, to ensure that they effectively conveyed the meaning preferred by the sponsors of the ad. And, excepting the special case of the Omega ad, because of the well-known face of Cindy Crawford, all of the images were removed from history, rendered as eternal statements of stimulation, desire, and lust.

The significance of these posters lay in what their presence said about life. They were evidence of how the regime of stimulation had colonized the visual surround in the affluent West and beyond. How admirably they fitted the definition of the 'modern' outlined by Bruno Latour, who has pointed to the contradictory but complementary practices of 'purification' and 'translation' that have shaped the life and times of the past two centuries.[133] The posters spoke of purified and ideal forms, of a world of sex that had been cleansed and streamlined and perfected. But they also fostered networks among people and objects, sometimes places as well, to actually gain access to that world. The Collistar ad sought to build an assemblage of consumers, branded products, and an erotic ideal that would supposedly profit user and maker alike. The Beijing posters worked to link disparate souls to the wider realm of international brands in order to speed sales at a range of local retail outlets. The manifest purpose of these posters was to stimulate sales. The latent purpose, however, was to signify the triumph of the Eros project.

Conclusion

I began the book by repeating some passing comments made by Michel Foucault. Now I will show how the story of the Eros project fits, and where it extends, his great unfinished drama of the history of sexuality in the modern West.[1]

Foucault's drama was outlined in the first volume of his *History of Sexuality* (1976), as well as in a series of papers, lectures, and interviews that he gave up until his death in 1984. Foucault denied the accuracy of the liberation theory of Reich and Marcuse: indeed, Foucault preferred to call this 'the repressive hypothesis.'[2] Whatever the facts of sexual repression (which usually he did not deny), the crucial feature of the nineteenth century was instead the explosion of talk about sex, in all its myriad forms, about desire, actions, 'perversions,' and identities.[3] According to Foucault, this proliferation of discourse was one sign and one aspect of the deployment of a technology of sexuality throughout Europe and America, itself part of a wider phenomenon he called the rise of 'biopower,' where authority sought to administer life.[4] Emerging in the eighteenth century, biopolitical institutions, whether run by the state or private organizations, employed mechanisms of truth such as statistics and demography to generate data able to divide the people into governable categories and to comprehend these categories as populations – of a city, region, or country; of a class, gender, or race; and of a type: delinquents, fathers, or the masturbating child. The results were efforts to improve health and sanitation, to foster hygiene and longevity, and to regulate sexuality. Whatever the instinctual roots of desire (and he did, at times, give biology its due), the many devices of sexuality actually produced and excited desire, making Foucault's drama an extreme example of social construction.[5] The purpose of this human technology, he asserted, was not to serve the interests of capitalism, at least not directly, nor to discipline the masses, for labourers at first evaded its effects, but rather to advance the cultivation of the bourgeois self, a crucial objective in the task of governing the national populations of Europe.[6] The result was to define the person as a sexual being and a 'desiring subject' whose identity and whose truth were determined by the effects of sexuality.[7] No wonder Foucault doubted the promise and the reality of sexual liberation: the decline of restrictions in the twentieth century, he asserted, merely registered a change in the operations of sexuality.[8] The existing regime of knowledge and power remained in place.[9]

This was not the end of the drama. In the years after the publication of his first book on the subject, Foucault became more and more interested in relations of power and the construction of the self, a focus that effectively swallowed up his history of sexuality.[10] Foucault argued that no system of domination, at least not in modern times, was ever perfect: relations of power invariably necessitated areas of freedom, provoked cycles of resistance, and fostered games of strategy.[11] He was particularly intrigued by the way liberalism promoted a style of governance that allowed the individual a degree of autonomy.[12] Similarly he wrote of 'technologies of the self' whereby individuals could engage in forms of self-improvement and self-fashioning.[13] He spoke in interviews about the excitements of the games of power played out in the world of sado-masochism, where the total body became an erotic object.[14] He recognized at least some advance of freedoms (though he remained leery of the word 'liberation') in the rise and partial acceptance of gay rights.[15] In short Foucault's drama of sex presumed a mixture of emancipation and domination in the practices of daily life as the twentieth century advanced.[16]

But Foucault never paid close attention to how the deployment of sexuality changed after 1900: his historical research drew him back to the story of desire in ancient Greece and Rome and early Christianity. The trajectory and nature of the Eros project demonstrate that Foucault's rejection of liberation theory was too extreme.[17] The reason Foucault once railed against 'Reichianisms' and 'Marcuseries' was because they enjoyed such currency in the debate over sexual liberation.[18] The radical Freud rooted humanity's unhappiness in the repression of the sexual instincts; the popular dream of a sexual revolution planned the happiness of this humanity via the freeing of pre-existing desires. Whatever intellectual substance there was to the Eros project came from liberation theory. Consider the assumed prehistory of the project: the belief in a sad past when the prude and the censor reigned over sex was fundamental. Those two eager promoters of the project Dr Ernest Dichter and Hugh Hefner clearly did subscribe to versions of the repressive hypothesis. One justification for *Playboy*, for instance, rested on the claim that the magazine was waging the good fight to free the instincts of Americans. And publicity as erotica worked off the presumption of a benighted past and a legacy of prudery that hampered the pursuit of erotic pleasure. That was how, in part, admakers hoped to evoke the thrill of transgression. So those twin ideas – that is, the assumed existence of repression and the virtue of liberation – were crucial ingredients in the intellectual stew.

The origins of the project lay in the interplay of disparate mechanisms of desire, much in the same fashion that, as Foucault had argued, the apparatus of sexuality took shape centuries earlier. The effort to eroticize the world, to make places, bodies, and above all objects sexy, did not emerge full blown out of the head or behaviour of any single group or institution. Indeed one of the small ironies of history was that the Left first imagined the eroticizing of life and the world that capitalism would eventually carry out, although in a way very different from the initial design. The project drew upon existing practices, some reaching well back into the past. The most obvious was pornography, as much a discourse as a practice, which furnished the repertoire of images that would later be cleansed to sell products. Walking through one of the sex museums, especially those in western Europe, is like visiting a veritable laboratory of the Eros project. You could find amid the clutter of historical collections the kinds of displays of flesh – admittedly raw, blatant, often uncouth – that would reappear in a milder form much later in movies, magazines, and television during the last half of the twentieth century. Here too you could see ordinary objects like playing cards, pipes, or household ornaments full of images or sculptings that transformed them into erotic commodities: a primitive version of the way in which brands would later be stamped with the erotic. There were even attempts at humour: say, a Chinese wall hanging that mocked men's phallic obsession or a nineteenth-century cartoon of a politician undone by his excessive wants. Such examples showed how the raw display of desire might be dressed in ways that rendered it more palatable. The evolution of pornography seems an especially apt example of what Foucault termed 'a mechanism of increasing incitement' that had dominated the discourse of sex.[19] But the very existence of this pornography, however restricted its reach prior to the late nineteenth century, does also suggest the importance of a counter-tradition, that of the 'Other Victorians,' to the supposed prevalence of 'modern puritanism.'[20] In any case it was this counter-tradition, admittedly much refined, that came into its own after 1900.

There were other predecessors to the project. Just as old as pornography in Europe was erotic art, or rather the genre of the nude, which linked together the activation of desire and the sensual portrayal of female flesh. A more recent innovation, represented by the work of Dalí, showed how the signs and symbols of 'perversion' could be turned to the task of promotion. From the mid-nineteenth century in America, and tied to what has been called the carnivalesque tradition of advertising, admakers occasionally employed sex appeal to sell drinks or soap, eventually corsets or cigarettes, and similar products for the body, to the buying public. Popular entertainment, certainly from the last decades of the nineteenth century, often promised sexual display to attract a clientele. After 1900 many female stars, notably Mae West in New York during the 1920s and 1930s, played the vamp, deploying an exaggerated sexiness to hype their performances on stage or in movies: the style was replayed by Marilyn Monroe in the 1950s and Madonna in the 1980s. After 1920 some male performers, notably the sensual Rudolph Valentino but also the swashbuckling Douglas Fairbanks, became signifiers of virility and objects of desire, a ploy that continued to work in the promotion of Hollywood movies thereafter.

These trends and experiences began to converge in the making of a new mechanism of desire, especially after 1945 and in the United States. This did not mark any decline in the vigour of the discourse or technology of sexuality. Rather the opposite: the swelling volume of sexual information, imagery, and discussion seemed, at times, about to overwhelm the whole of Western society. But the 'great sexual sermon' was now joined by a novel kind of erotic preaching.[21] Still, the why and how of that convergence is better explained by the insights of Reich, Marcuse, and Baudrillard (at least the early Baudrillard) than Foucault. For the single most important cause was rooted in the evolution of the marketplace. The onset of mass production in America during the early decades of the century resulted in an economy characterized by escalating abundance rather than continuing scarcity. The priority shifted from production to consumption.[22] How could business foster the passion to acquire, ensuring that it was always heated and never satisfied, a manoeuvre necessary to the health and progress of the industrial machine? One way was to make the new brands sexy. As Marcuse suggested, capitalism came to sponsor a kind of eroticism that offered instant gratification and sensual pleasure. And, as Baudrillard explained, the admakers created elaborate constructs of illusion and desire to mobilize the libido and harness the energy to inspire purchase. It was this spirit and this situation that pop art managed to capture in its assorted works about affluence and America.

At its core, then, the Eros project was very much a selling scheme. But in time, beginning in the 1960s, it became much more than just that. It amounted to a conglomeration of the sort Foucault outlined: a network of production, meanings, and domination, although centred around communications and signification.[23] Count the project another instance of biopower, wherein authorities (albeit largely non-state in this case) set out to shape and manage a significant aspect of life. It drew upon the teachings of marketing, itself a rapidly developing discourse of truth, that employed sales surveys, questionnaires, statistics, and eventually focus groups to arrange people into different populations – men and women, well-off and ordinary, rural and urban – who could then be educated as consumers and organized as markets. It borrowed freely from the presumptions and practices of the psychological sciences, notably psychoanalysis, yet another instance of biopower, to understand the why of consumption and to shape the behaviour of consumers. The project could boast an aesthetic and a rhetoric, an ideology and a set of values, plus an apparatus of manipulation. Out of such materials the actions of an ensemble of companies, agencies, and individuals assembled a particular regime of stimulation to serve the needs of a libidinal economy. In his actions and his writings Dr Ernest Dichter was at once the most articulate, aggressive, and far-fetched of the promoters of the new regime. In interesting ways Dichter upended the radical Freud to argue that virtually any product was a fetish that evoked sex, if not 'perversion,' in the psyche of consumers. He urged these Americans to shed their (supposed) puritanism and embrace hedonism, to revel in the pleasures of an abundance both material and erotic. If anyone might be called the master of what Marcuse termed 'repressive desublimation,' then it was Dr Dichter, although his books positioned him as a liberator.

The crucial instrument of the Eros project was the media. Foucault never paid much attention to the organs of mass communication in any of his works. Marcuse did, in *One-Dimensional Man*, where he analysed the ability of the media to build a prison house of language in which the mind of the citizen might be trapped.[24] But the key was not so much words as the profusion of images. The regime of stimulation certainly required the techniques of surveillance that had once so exercised Foucault.[25] Marketing experts like Dichter were forever assessing the attitudes, wishes, and habits of the consumers. Much attention was paid to the tastes and expectations of target markets, as in the case of Maidenform bras, *Playboy*, and Barbie. Even so, the regime rested more on spectacle, the constant production of visual stories that could act as stimuli.[26] Dalí showed the way when he developed a signature style to eroticize faces, bodies, and objects. Popular magazines proved an excellent vehicle because, as McLuhan suggested and later Kilbourne demonstrated, they could offer colourful tableaux to captivate the eye. But the import of magazines was soon superseded by forms of spectacle that mixed colour, sound, and movement: movies, television ads, or music videos. These forms were able to realize the potential of storytelling as the great mode of persuasion.

The libidinal economy was itself an assemblage of signs, practices, and products so intertwined that the brand was always an amalgam of the material and the symbolic. The Maidenform bra, for instance, only acquired its particular appeal as an erotic instrument because of continuous advertising. The first showcase of this economy was designed by Hugh Hefner: the pages of *Playboy* linked together images of flesh and desire, displays of products, reviews of consumption, and brand advertisements in ways that argued how fitting such goods were as accoutrements and instruments of the knowing male consumer. Much later, in the 1990s, the masters of the Bond saga would achieve something similar with the Brosnan movies, where the hero extended his aura of sexiness to a variety of goods, whose makers were willing to pay well for the honour of appearing in the melodrama.

The advance of the libidinal economy was fuelled by prosperity so that in times of recession, such as the mid-1970s, the early 1980s, or the early 1990s, that advance slowed. But the wave of eroticism always returned when the good times came back, spurred on especially by the imagery of television. By the 1990s television, though most especially in western Europe, had fashioned an ongoing theatre of the libido that reached across the affluent world. At first the objects eroticized were mostly associated with the body, clothes and fashion, drinks, and foods. By the end of the century virtually any product might take on an erotic guise. The presence of those sexy posters in Beijing indicated that the economy now had a global reach sufficient to leave its mark in the capital city of an ostensibly communist country.

The cumulative purpose of the publicity was to construct the individual as a desiring, and sometimes fearing, creature. What the regime offered its subjects was one of those 'technologies of the self' that Foucault came to believe were crucial to the identity and management of populations – or, in this case, markets. What was cultivated by this renovated apparatus of sexuality, however, was not the bourgeois self, certainly not in any form once recognized as ideal, but the erotic self, irrespective of class, age, gender, or race. The discourse of sexuality had always sought to make of the person as producer and citizen a sexual being; it now sought to transform the person as consumer into a passionate being as well. The whole body was subject to exhortation and manipulation; nearly every part, from the hair and the eyes down to the ankles and feet, was to be rendered sexy. To repeat the jocular comment of Foucault: 'Get undressed - but be slim, good-looking, tanned!'[27] Publicity harvested figures, scenarios, and motifs from mass culture to fashion dreams of happy consumption (and occasionally nightmares of lack). Subjects were expected to build their erotic identities, to improve their social behaviour, according to the dictates of this publicity.[28]

No wonder the regime of stimulation fostered a very different taxonomy of sexual figures and erotic acts than did Foucault's discourse of sexuality. He noted the rising prominence during the course of the nineteenth century of 'the hysterical woman, the masturbating child, the Malthusian couple and the perverse adult' who became the 'privileged objects of knowledge.'[29] He found the emergence of a huge body of concern over the problematic actions of a collection of aberrant types.[30] But the displays of sin and the fables of lust so common on television by the 1990s were full of images of the Body Beautiful and the Body Handsome who appeared as ideals of perfection and sensuality. Occasionally the allure of these 'babes' and 'hunks' was highlighted by the presence of the grotesque, people rendered ugly by too much fat, by age, or by neglect (of health, hair, scent, etc.). The heroes of these minidramas engaged most often in spying and teasing, in seduction scenarios, in acts of true lust (for the brand rather than the body), in an escape from the ordinary, and in an assortment of vulgar pleasures. The watcher of these images was, of course, positioned as a voyeur, an act that was commonly celebrated in all this publicity. In short, sex was coded in ways that accentuated the positive, not the negative, that offered visual pleasures now and personal satisfaction or social success later.

Viewers were also given licence to explore, however vicariously, the pleasures of aberration and 'perversion.' Of the set of 'perversions' Foucault claimed sexuality had implanted in the mind of the nineteenth century, a small sample were now regularly dressed up as exciting or humorous kinds of transgression designed to titillate and excite. The radical Freud and Left Freudians thought of sadism, or more broadly the erotics of power, as one of the ills of the age. Foucault found that the deployment of sexuality had actually fostered 'a sensualization of power and a gain of pleasure.'[31] Consider then how the motif of dominator/dominatrix was referenced in the Bond trailers, which offered doses of sex and sadism and, even more, in Madonna's music videos, where for a time she played out the role of sexual provocateur. Though television commercials were usually more cautious in what they might show, they too offered scenes that spoke of crossdressing, homoeroticism, orgies, or S/M.

More generally, publicity as erotica displayed one of the characteristics of the discourse of sexuality identified by Foucault, namely that fetishism was 'the model perversion' in the discourse of sexuality in the late Victorian era and beyond. Of course Foucault went on to specify that fetishism 'served as the guiding thread for analyzing all the other deviations.'[32] In short, it remained an aberration. But not in the ideology of eroticism, where fetish, at least by one definition, played a central role. The task of all the images and rhetoric was to make the brand into a signifier of sexual desire and, often, an instrument of sexual pleasure. It was here that the project constituted such a threat to an older morality of right behaviour.

All of which might suggest that Marcuse was correct when he charged that capitalism had reinvented dystopia through a process of repressive or institutionalized desublimation. He presumed that process was part of a totalizing endeavour mounted by elites to construct a 'one-dimensional' society and to establish a 'new totalitarianism' in which revolt, or even negation, was impossible.[33] Certainly the regime of stimulation offered the kind of gratifications and satisfactions, even liberties, that might make people more willing to accept their lot in life. Desire was conditioned by ideology: 'Pleasure, thus adjusted, generates submission.'[34] (Here the views of Marcuse and Foucault were similar, although the former continued to believe in a pre-existing or instinctual form of desire.)[35] The trouble was, Marcuse also argued that such a process de-eroticized the environment, when in fact the Eros project actually fostered a world made sexy. Second, he saw 'a localization and contraction of libido, the reduction of erotic to sexual experience and satisfaction,' when in fact the project expanded enormously the sphere of the erotic and the reach of desire.[36] Third, Marcuse's lament assumed that repressive desublimation had triumphed, that its victory over the human spirit was well-nigh total. That certainly was not true of the regime of stimulation. Indeed the Eros project was never as directed or as effective as Marcuse's despairing account of 'one-dimensionality' would lead a person to believe.

The moral authority of publicity as erotica did not go unchallenged. Advertising was never regarded as a discourse of truth by the public at large – often, indeed, it was treated as a discourse of deceit. Sex was not totally governed by the calculations of business.[37] The emergence of the regime of stimulation soon provoked the very kind of resistance Foucault's hypotheses about power predicted.[38] Marshall McLuhan sounded the first alarm. He was succeeded by a bevy of other intellectuals, including Marcuse and Baudrillard, as well as more popular figures such as Key and Kilbourne. Their warnings reflected a more general mood of suspicion, if not opposition, among the public. Key, in particular, benefited because his outlandish charges of a conspiracy had tapped into popular fears of manipulation. The stigma of sleaze always stayed with *Playboy*, even as its mix of sex and style was superseded by the more blatant imagery of more raunchy rivals. At another level the attack on erotic and sexist publicity became a staple in the arsenal of American feminism in much of the 1970s and 1980s. It was echoed by similar complaints from the New Right, whose spokespeople and constituents occasionally inveighed against the amounts of salacious and indecent advertising on television and in the other media.

Indeed, in America during the 1990s there were sporadic rebellions against the operations of the regime of stimulation, notably the attacks on Madonna (her *Sex* book) and Calvin Klein (his 'kiddie porn' campaign), both of whom had wandered across the boundaries of the permissible. The objection might be to the aesthetics or rhetoric of a campaign, to the effort to sexualize a particular brand – say, by objectifying a woman's body – or to the excessive materialism of the whole enterprise, which harnessed sex to commerce. Witness the controversy provoked by the Swedish Bikini Team campaign in the United States in the early 1990s. But in all cases the resistance was rooted in the ethics of right conduct. That was one reason admakers went to such efforts to cleanse their publicity, especially to lighten the sex with a bit of humour. The point was that publicity as erotica was always restrained by notions of public decency, some of which were enshrined in law and thus subject to the action of the courts.

There was another way in which people might resist, or more properly evade, the full effects of the regime of stimulation. Foucault talked broadly of the import of games, or 'relations of power and relations of strategy,' in modern systems of domination in the liberal West.[39] Individuals could and did employ the missives and the objects designed by business to seek out their own pleasures. It was, after all, girls who created the fetish Barbie denied by Mattel's advertising. The case of 'Jessica' and her housemates was another example of such play, although that worked to the advantage of Häagen-Dazs as well. Straight men made the Swedish Bikini Team into their own fantasy of a desire satisfied. More common, so it would seem, viewers converted the fables of lust on television into entertainments, thereby subverting the intent of their makers.

What was much more difficult to evade was the impact of eroticism on the perception of the material world of places, bodies, and objects. There might be terrible public moments such as 9/11, tragic circumstances like the ongoing AIDS crisis, moral and intellectual convictions such as feminism, or personal troubles relating to age, health, and especially a lack of money, any of which could check the effects of mass eroticism on the public and on individuals. But its presence was felt nearly everywhere in western Europe and North America in the last decades of the century. How people experienced shopping malls or vacations in the lands of the sun was always coloured by the stimuli of sex. So in the 1990s one cruise company launched a famous campaign that capitalized on the dream of getting away to a place of sensuality and joy in the Caribbean.[40] The way people looked at the shape and the dress of themselves and others was through lenses constructed, in part, by the ideology. That same campaign depicted the cruise couple as streamlined bodies, him as hard and muscled, her as soft and enticing – this even though upscale cruises were largely filled with older people who had the necessary money but not the perfected physiques. Why people were attracted to one commodity or one person was affected by notions of what was, or was not, 'sexy.' Indeed the term itself acquired status as a commanding metaphor, a word as commonplace as 'hot' or 'cool' to designate what was so appealing.

The ubiquity of such perceptions might just as easily be taken as a sign of liberation as control. Instead of the 'surplus repression' (imagined by Marcuse) of the preceding century, think of a 'surplus eroticism,' something generated by the regime of stimulation but beyond its immediate needs – much more incitement than was necessary to promote a brand. That captivated the publics of countries in all parts of the globe. Whether you assume that desire was mostly natural and eternal (as did the radical Freud) or mostly constructed and provoked (as did Foucault), the Eros project seemed to free desire from the apparent restraints of an earlier morality. Was this no more than an instance of 'the pseudo-liberation of modern culture,' as Marcuse had presumed?[41] That depended in large part on one's political and moral outlook. The animosity of Marcuse was a sophisticated expression of views that were not uncommon, then or later. But these views were hardly mainstream.[42] Consuming Chanel No. 5, Dim nylons, or Absolut vodka was a method by which people did connect with the erotic. Enjoying the look of a supermodel or dreaming about being Madonna, these were in their times common, if small, sources of pleasure. For a sizeable group of young people the ideology of eroticism even served as a design for living. Clearly the vast majority of consumers in the affluent zone relished spending some time, and some money, in this utopia of Eros. If this was evidence of 'false consciousness,' then it was part and parcel of a state of desire that a lot of citizens, especially the young in fact and in spirit, enjoyed (or wished to enjoy) across the globe.

By the end of the century the Eros project had emerged as a leading nexus of power, profit, and pleasure. Its character can be described as a particular arrangement of what Foucault sometimes called technologies of power and understanding.[43] None of these technologies ought to be treated as separate: their operations overlapped, and their activities were to some extent coordinated, working together as parts of a singular enterprise.

(i) *production, the realm of things*: the rise of a libidinal economy, the motive force of the enterprise, that fashioned and distributed an expanding variety of sexy brands in search of national and eventually global markets. Such an economy was both an agent and a result of an ongoing process of liberation that was freeing the expression of erotic desire from the trammels of moral restriction.

(ii) *rule, or systems of control*: the emergence of a regime of stimulation, linked closely to the marketing industry and financed by business, that deployed the techniques of surveillance and even more the apparatus of spectacle to determine the conduct of consumers. The regime adopted one of the standard practices of biopolitics, namely an effort to normalize, in this case setting standards of beauty or fashioning typical wants, as well as to pathologize, thus dishonouring ugliness or indifference, and especially the imperfect body.[44]

(iii) *communication, the domain of signs*: the escalating growth of public-ity as erotica, the most important technology, delivered by maga-zines, television commercials, movie trailers, ad posters, music videos, and the like, to huge audiences that soon extended well beyond the affluent zone of countries. None of this material actu-ally created desire, which was a part of the *bios* of humanity. The immediate purpose was to direct the existing flows of desire by fashioning erotic fantasies, manufacturing wants, and offering solutions to satisfy the appetite for sex. The broader social effect was to contribute to the spread of an eroticism cut free from the biological imperative to reproduce. The workings of these signs constituted the biopolitical core of the Eros project: they designed – or rather sought to design – populations of consumers that were governable.

(iv) *the self, the realm of belief and action*: the spread of an eroticism that enticed individuals to devote themselves to the pursuit of plea-sure, to seek happiness and perfection through the consumption of sights, places, and commodities. 'Enticed' did not mean com-manded – consumers might and did use the signs of the erotic to construct their own meanings or to inform their own play. This technology of the self was the reason the project also counted as a form of emancipation (as well as domination): the erotic being was a 'knowing subject,' not just a creature of appetite or a victim of programming, but an active rather than a passive individual, engaged in 'a practice of self-formation.'[45]

The eroticism is also why the Eros project was one of the most suc-cessful of modern enterprises, or remodernizing agencies, where authorities used systems of persuasion to mould and guide the actions of the populace. That kind of endeavour was common to the exercise of biopower in the twentieth century: the success of efforts to educate peo-ple (itself an example of nineteenth-century biopolitics) and the rise of mass media enabled authority to use communications to work not just

on the bodies but on the minds or consciousness of the citizenry. Corporations, the state, and moral associations deployed the 'powers of freedom,' to borrow the words of Nikolas Rose, by cajoling populations in
the causes of happiness, health, and prosperity.[46] The Eros project was
similar to the various regimes of propaganda in which public and private agencies employed advertising first to encourage war patriotism,
then to defeat assorted vices (drinking and driving, drug use, smoking), and eventually to encourage right attitudes (about women or
minorities or even nature).[47] But the Eros project proved much more
effective than any public communication campaign because its guid-
ance offered ways to realize desire and enhance pleasure. More effectively than most forms of advertising, the project harnessed the long-
standing tradition of the carnivalesque, employing the elements of sex,
laughter, and appetite to craft an unending fantasy of play. It worked
with mass culture – indeed, becoming a part of a popular entertainment
suffused with sensual imagery. It worked with the freeing of sexual
activity, the enthusiasm for erotic experimentation, the growing acceptance of what were once deemed 'perversions,' the novel idea of 'total
body sex,' all those attributes of a sexual revolution that transformed so
much of intimate life in the lands of affluence during the late twentieth
century. The project might not make people any happier (and how
accurately could anyone judge such a condition or identify its cause?),
but it did multiply the avenues of enjoyment for many, many people. In
short the project really had delivered the goods.[48]

Notes

1 Foucault, *History of Sexuality*, vol. 1: *An Introduction* (first published in French in 1976). In that book Foucault had argued that 'the repressive hypothesis' was inadequate. He saw the nineteenth century as a time when power increasingly organized sexuality and constructed an ever-expanding body of knowledge about desire in order to govern individuals and populations.

2 Foucault, 'Body/Power,' 57–8.

3 The description is derived from an explanation of how power operates that Foucault provided in a 'conversation,' really more of a round-table inquisition, that he carried on with a variety of luminaries in 1977. It was reprinted as 'The Confession of the Flesh,' in *Power/Knowledge*, and the quotations appear in his initial commentary, pages 194–5, though he explores this issue throughout the discussion. Foucault was not referring to any particular regime, however.

4 Hollander, *Feeding the Eye*, 150.

5 So the account amounts to a study of governmentality, or rather one aspect of that burgeoning enterprise. The founding text of such studies is a book edited by Burchall, Gordon, and Miller, *The Foucault Effect*. One of the essays in that book is Foucault's 'Governmentality,' which was first given as a lecture at the Collège de France in 1978. The quoted phrase appears on page 93.

6 Consider James Peterson's *The Century of Sex* and Tom Hickman's *The Sexual Century*, both appearing in 1999. The first, an American work subtitled *Playboy's History of the Sexual Revolution*, was written by an employee of the magazine at the suggestion of its founder, Hugh Hefner, who also introduced the book. The second, a British entry that purported to demonstrate *How Private Passion Became a Public Obsession*, was twinned with a six-part

video documentary made by Carlton Communications. Both delivered a by then standard story of repression and struggle and liberation. There are, of course, more nuanced histories, notably David Allyn, *Make Love, Not War*; Steven Seidman, *Romantic Longings*; and John D'Emilio and Estelle B. Freedman, *Intimate Matters*.

7 See Shorter, *Written in the Flesh*, for a strong statement of the import of biology in the study of sex.

8 For an excellent example of the way desire is translated and transformed by culture, see Laqueur, *Solitary Sex*.

9 *Giorgio Armani*, organized by Germano Celant and Harold Koda, with Susan Cross and Karole Vail.

10 I say 'misappropriate' because Lyotard was really concerned with the libido as an economy, and not the reverse. Lyotard, *Libidinal Economy*.

11 For an extensive exploration of how one brand of 'perversion' has found expression in the fashion industry, see the classic work by Valerie Steele, *Fetish: Fashion, Sex and Power*.

12 The phrase was the subtitle of Marshall McLuhan's most famous work, *Understanding Media*.

13 The language used is derived from Hal Foster, 'Hey, That's Me,' 13, 14.

14 'In fact, it is possible to argue that much that is shown on the runways is viewed as the pure art of fashion – meant to stimulate, excite and disquiet more than to be worn.' McDowell, *Fashion Today*, 386.

15 Hollander, *Feeding the Eye*, 147.

16 The term 'ideology' is subject to a host of different definitions. I see ideology in the way Terry Eagleton outlines its meanings in his *Ideology*, where he puts a special emphasis on the link between systems of belief and structures of power.

17 Zygmunt Bauman has called eroticism a 'cultural processing' of sex that works with the excess of sexual energy supplied by 'nature.' Indeed he claims that, 'Postmodern eroticism is free-floating; it can enter chemical reaction with virtually any other substance, feed and draw juices from any other human emotion or activity.' See Bauman, 'On Postmodern Uses of Sex,' 26. This was part of a theme volume on eroticism and love.

18 See, for instance, Joel Whitebook, *Perversion and Utopia*. I say a reluctant Freud because, as we shall see later, he doubted the possibility of liberation.

19 Bataille, *Erotism*. The book was originally published in 1957.

20 The idea that the self is narrated, created, and confirmed through stories generated by and outside the individual became fashionable in a number of disciplines during the 1990s. See Somers, 'The Narrative Construction of Identity,' and Ochs and Capps, 'Narrating the Self.'

21 On the process of inventing the self, and the modern self as a type, see Rose, *Inventing Our Selves*. On the history of the self, see Seigel, 'Problematizing the Self.'

22 This understanding of body types is derived, in part, from the discussion of high and low bodies in Stallybrass and White, *The Politics and Poetics of Transgression*, 21–2, and elsewhere.

23 See Deleuze and Guattari, *Anti-Oedipus*, and Deleuze and Guattari, *A Thousand Plateaus*, where the two men presented a radical re-imagining of the body and self. The term 'desiring machine' was coined in the first book and 'libidinal assemblage' in the second.

24 See also the views of Donna Haraway, who imagined a woman's body as 'a hybrid of machine and organism' that was penetrated and shaped by 'communications technologies and biotechnologies.' Haraway, 'A Cyborg Manifesto: Science, Technology, and Socialist-Feminism in the Late Twentieth Century,' in *Simians, Cyborgs and Women*, 140, 163.

25 'Assemblages' are similar to the networks of Actor-Network Theory, employed in the field of science studies. There is an extensive literature on ANT: see, for example, the articles in Law and Hassard, eds, *Actor Network Theory and After*. The most prominent figure in science studies is Bruno Latour: there are some fine examples of the use of networks as a tool of explanation in his *Pandora's Hope*.

26 The terminology is from Harvey, 'The Body as an Accumulation Strategy,' 402. Harvey was referring to the body in general, not specifically the erotic version.

27 The notion of the 'extended self' entered marketing theory with an article by Belk, 'Possessions and the Extended Self.'

28 For a slightly tongue-in-cheek discussion of marketing and utopia, see Brown, Maclaren, and Stevens, 'Marcadia Postponed.'

29 Ricoeur, *Lectures on Ideology and Utopia*, 310. Ricoeur, however, saw utopia as opposed to ideology.

30 The reference is to Bakhtin's classic work, *Rabelais and His World*. The book was originally published in the Soviet Union in 1965, on the basis of a work largely written in the 1930s.

31 The brief explanation of the 'double task' of modernity comes from Latour, *We Have Never Been Modern*, 10.

32 The term 'second modernity' seems preferable to alternatives, such as 'late modernity,' since it registers a change in the nature of modernization, once identified by the concept of 'postmodernity,' which, however, has proven a permanent condition. *Theory, Culture and Society* 2003 devoted an issue (vol. 20 no. 2) to the notion of remodernization and second modernity: see, in

particular, Bech, Bonss, and Lau, 'The Theory of Reflexive Modernization,' and Latour, 'Is *Re*-Modernization Occurring – and if So, How to Prove It?' But in a different vein see Habermas, 'Modernity: An Unfinished Project.'

33 The Eros project, then, was one answer (though hardly the preferred answer) to the indictment of modernity contained in that classic anti-utopian work by Horkheimer and Adorno, *Dialectic of Enlightenment*, first published in 1944.

1 Exhibiting Eros

1 The description called to mind Jean-François Lyotard's startling vision in one of his books: a human body opened up to the aggressive gaze of lust, the organs exposed, the skin stretched out, twisted into a Möbius strip, along which and through which constantly pulsated sexual energies that invested every corner of the now bizarre and grotesque object. Lyotard, *Libidinal Economy*, 1–5.

2 Hamilton, 'In a New Museum, a Blue Period.'

3 Ibid.

4 Daniel Gluck, cited in *The New York Times*, 18 January 2000.

5 See Dubin, 'How "Sensation" Became a Scandal.' In an earlier book, *Arresting Images*, Dubin explored the fury of moral conservatives and some political officials over the display of new art in America. The public display of the erotic in galleries and museums in Canada, especially in publicly funded venues, has often produced controversy and attempts to censor such an offence to morality, especially when the displays involved scenes of gay or lesbian sex: see Gilbert, ed., *Arousing Sensation*. Clearly, North America in the late twentieth century had a lower tolerance for exhibiting Eros, by comparison with Europe.

6 On that site was the mission statement, a list of the Board of Advisors, pictures of the model building, and a series of articles from the press. The media represented in this collection were, respectively, *Architecture, ARTNews Magazine*, CNN, *Crains, Elle, ID Magazine, L'Espresso, Lingua Franca,* London *Daily Telegraph*, London *Sunday Times*, London *Times, Newsday, New York Daily News, New York Times, New York Times Magazine, New Yorker, Philadelphia Inquirer, Playboy*, and *Time*. I have used this material, as well as a story in the *New York Post*, 10 April 1998, to reconstruct the career of the publicity campaign.

7 Hunt, 'Introduction: Obscenity and the Origins of Modernity, 1500–1800,' in Hunt, ed., *The Invention of Pornography*, 13.

8 See Hedger, 'Kinsey Collections Reveal the Value of Variety.'

9 Allison Xantha Miller, 'Sex in the City.'
10 Here is a list of the dates when I visited the sex museums: Copenhagen (August 1999), Barcelona (September 1999 and June 2000), Hamburg (September 1999 and September 2001), Paris (February 2000 and May 2003), Berlin (June 2000), Amsterdam (September 2001), Madrid (September 2001), Shanghai (May 2002), New York (December 2002 and April 2004).
11 The National Museum of Erotica in Canberra opened in 2001 but closed in 2002. Apparently it was a small affair and lacked sufficient material to win much local favour. See Adams and Francis, 'Lifting the Veil.'
12 See, for example, McDonald, 'Chinese Sexual Museum Has High-Minded Goals'; Schauble, 'Life's Basics Are Food and Sex'; Lakshmanan, 'China Gets Officially Hot and Bothered'; Hewitt, 'China Sex Museum Goes Public'; and Johnson, 'Great Wall of Sex Silence.'
13 Ni, 'This Museum Won't Give Up.'
14 Eventually, in 2003, Liu Dalin had to move from the second site in Shanghai as well, apparently because he could not attract sufficient custom to meet expenses – nor could he secure official approval as a tourist site. The collection was moved outside the city to Tongli, which was a tourist area. See 'Q&A: Liu Dalin and His Sex Museum,' and '6,000 Years of Sex at Chinese Museums.'
15 Her story was featured in one of the special display areas in the museum. What follows is drawn from a number of English-language reports, especially in *Time*, 13 April 1981, and the *Independent on Sunday*, 6 November 1994.
16 Beck and Hafferkamp, 'Sex Please, We're Tourists.' The story was initially produced for the *Toronto Sun* and first featured only in January 1999. There was no mention of who did the surveys or how, but it was cited elsewhere by a spokesperson for the city's tourist service (see the second reference). Other museums also made claims of lots of visitors: 125,000 a year in Copenhagen, a quarter of a million in Barcelona, half a million to the Sex Museum in Amsterdam, 80,000 in Hamburg, or 8,000 a month in Paris. These figures appeared in an article at the online site of *Libido, The Journal of Sex and Sensibility*, available in January 2002: Beck and Hafferkamp, 'The Era of Sex Museums.'
17 Beck and Hafferkamp, 'The Era of Sex Museums.'
18 The book, however, did not replicate the exhibition, providing different kinds of material, though all to the same purpose of explaining the history of the sexual underground. There was, in addition, an excellent introduction by the executive curator, Grady T. Turner, entitled 'Sodom on the Hudson.'

19 A mere 10 DM in Berlin, 5.5fl in Amsterdam, 15 DM in Hamburg, 995 pesetas in Barcelona, 850 pesetas in Madrid, 40FF in Paris – likewise U.S. $4 in Shanghai, though $12 in New York.

20 The 'Different Spaces' lecture was given in 1967 and was first published in 1984. The term 'heterotopia' also appears briefly in Foucault's *The Order of Things: An Archaeology of the Human Sciences*, xvii-xviii, where their existence and operation contests the very foundations of language.

21 The sex museums, even more than the erotic exhibitions, are clearly a type that differs in character from the kind of public museums much criticized by scholars of a Foucauldian persuasion. Witness this comment: 'Museums deputize the muses of knowledge to instruct the masses who, in turn, visit them to learn about deeper realities, even as those realities are being written and wrought by elites around them in museums.' Luke, *Museum Politics*, xix.

22 So they play out the general role of museums identified by Krzysztof Pomian, practising 'a unique type of behaviour, consisting in the formation of collections, in an attempt to create a link between the visible and the invisible.' *Collectors and Curiosities*, 5.

23 For a brief discussion of types of museums, different systems of objects, and distinct types of viewing subjects, see Hetherington, 'From Blindness to Blindness.'

24 See Bennett, *The Birth of the Museum*.

25 Many of these were available on the museum's website as of May 2000.

26 Which, of course, is one way of portraying all sorts of museums. On the import of the museum, and of museum studies, to the historian, see Starn, 'A Historian's Brief Guide to New Museum Studies.'

27 Quotations from Museu de l'Eròtica, Barcelona; followed by a paraphrase of a statement from the Musée de l'erotisme, Paris: 'Contrairement à l'Occident, où le plaisir a toujours été considéré coupable, en Orient, le sexe y était considéré comme source de félicité et de santé.'

28 *Sex among the Lotus: 2,500 Years of Chinese Erotic Obsession*, which was one of a number of exhibitions shown in 2004.

29 Supposedly dated 1971. Present on the website of the museum.

30 From Beck and Hafferkamp, 'The Era of Sex Museums.' The same article also claimed that 'the Eros Foundation' had launched the National Museum of Erotica in Canberra in 2001 to counter a National Museum of Australia that neglected sexuality.

31 'Foreword,' in Mundy, ed., *Surrealism*, 7.

32 Combalía and Lebel, eds, 'Introduction' to *Jardín de Eros*, 381.

33 Guy Cogeval (Musée des Beaux-Arts, Montreal), Jean Clair (Musée national

Picasso, Paris), Maria Teresa Ocaña (Museu Picasso, Barcelona) in the 'Preface' to *Picasso Érotique*, np.

34 Described in Alison Smith, ed., *Exposed*, 180–3.

35 See, for example, an interesting study of the attitudes of thirty-two Canadian women who, collectively, feared porn, especially when it mixed sex and violence, though they accepted sexy imagery. M. Shaw, 'Men's Leisure and Women's Lives: The Impact of Pornography on Women.'

36 Jerrold Levinson, 'On Erotic Art,' in *Routledge Encyclopedia of Philosophy*, Online, Version 1.0 (London: Routledge), in August 2002. He has elaborated this position in his 'Erotic Art and Pornographic Pictures.' That view was in accord with the arguments of anti-pornography feminists. See, for instance, the essays in Dines, Jensen, and Russo, *Pornography: The Production and Consumption of Inequality.*

37 Rowan Pelling, ed., *The Erotic Review*, an English publication, quoted in the Toronto *National Post*, 8 April 2000, Arts 2. She added: 'Erotica is about not telling or showing you everything; it's about suspense, detail and buildup; it's about being teased, and kept on the burn for a while.'

38 See, for example, Amy Allen, 'Pornography and Power,' 512–31, which surveys the debate over the relationship between porn and authority.

39 Arcand, *The Jaguar and the Anteater: Pornography and the Modern World*, 60.

40 *Hieronymus Bosch*, Museum Boijmans Van Beuningen, Rotterdam, 1 September – 11 November 2001.

41 See Dean, 'History, Pornography and the Social Body,' 227. See also her book *The Frail Social Body: Pornography, Homosexuality, and Other Fantasies in Interwar France*, where she explores in detail the narrative of 'the inviolable body' (2). Recently there has been considerable work done on pornography from different perspectives, and this has complicated and broadened the scope of understanding. A useful survey of this work is contained in Attwood, 'Reading Porn.'

42 One of the scholars who first took up the modern study of pornography as a genre put this argument another way, talking about 'the confession of previously invisible "truths" of bodies and pleasures in an unprecedented "frenzy of the visible"' in a study of pornographic films. Linda Williams, *Hard Core*, 7. Williams was among a small group of feminists in the 1990s who worked to present porn as 'an unruly force' in opposition to the anti-porn rhetoric of Catherine McKinnon and Andrea Dworkin. The phrase appeared in a story about this group by M.G. Lord, 'Pornutopia: How Feminist Scholars Learned to Love Dirty Pictures.' See also Pamela Church Gibson and Roma Gibson, eds, *Dirty Looks*, for a series of feminist essays that broke with the anti-pornography position of one brand of radical feminism.

43 Bataille, *Erotism*, 192. The pleasures of watching and causing suffering had a long history before Bataille, of course. See Halttunen, 'Humanitarianism and the Pornography of Pain in Anglo-American Culture.'

44 Here Bataille shared much with the surrealists, a group he worked with and criticized. See Carolyn J. Dean, *The Self and Its Pleasures*, especially her discussion of 'Sade's Selflessness,' 123–99. For a sympathetic exploration of the views of Bataille and, more generally, of surrealism on the nature of eroticism, see Richardson, 'Seductions of the Impossible.'

45 Cited in Arcand, *The Jaguar and the Anteater*, 171.

46 Paglia, *Sexual Personae*, 3. She added: 'A perfectly humane eroticism may be impossible. Somewhere in every family romance is hostility and aggression, the homicidal wishes of the unconscious' (4).

47 Grosz painted girls, often looking very young, engaged in sex play; Bellmer's female doll was photographed wearing clothes that suggested her youth and in settings that suggested abuse; some watercolours in Berlin showed a youthful but voluptuous teenage female stripped and whipped by her mother.

48 Bakhtin, *Rabelais and His World*.

49 This last claim is an addition to Bakhtin's theory elaborated by Stallybrass and White in *The Politics and Poetics of Transgression*.

50 Robert Stam has also discussed the juxtaposition of Bakhtin and pornography, which at the most he would see as a form of 'degraded carnival.' One of Stam's chief concerns was to ensure that Bakhtin's theories are not harnessed to the defence of pornography. Stam, *Subversive Pleasures*, 166–71.

51 This despite the fact that Martin Myrone has pointed out how the British response to nudity and to prudery was much more complicated than once was thought. See his 'Prudery, Pornography and the Victorian Nude (Or, What Do We Think the Butler Saw?).'

52 See Kendrick, *The Secret Museum*, and Hunt, ed., *The Invention of Pornography*.

53 There are authors who argue, however, that the carnivalesque has spread throughout the pop culture of the present. Larsen, 'South Park's Solar Anus, or, Rabelais Returns.'

54 In this it conformed to the general character of carnival in the modern world. See the discussion of carnival and renewal in Denis-Constant Martin, 'Politics behind the Mask.'

55 The illustrations were by Martin Van Maelle. There was no specific date but a range listed, 1895–1918.

56 The reference here is, of course, to Michel Foucault's first volume of *The History of Sexuality*.

57 Paglia, *Sexual Personae*, 32.
58 Infante, *La Habana Para un Infante Difento* (first published 1979), 226.
59 Freedberg, *The Power of Images*, 28. The book is a superb discussion of the way images have worked in the West in the centuries up to roughly the age of the photograph. Freedberg deals here with instances of pornography before the term itself was invented.
60 Obscene material of various kinds, both words and images, has existed for many years and in many different places. What we take to be pornography, though, was born in western Europe: supposedly the first master of this form was the Italian Pietro Aretino, active in the early sixteenth century. Hunt, 'Introduction,' in Hunt, ed., *The Invention of Pornography*, 9–45.
61 This paragraph is based largely on the material in Lisa Z. Sigel, 'Filth in the Wrong People's Hands.'
62 It was counted a 'perversion' by Freudians when looking became the preferred form of sexual activity. Rycroft, *A Critical Dictionary of Psychoanalysis*, 194–5.
63 It is not clear to what extent women have become regular consumers of pornography, especially in recent years when access to porn videos has become so easy. But it is clear that many women, often with their men, do use pornographic and erotic material. Arcand noted, for example, statistics that indicated between 60 and 40 per cent of the audience for pornographic films was female: Arcand, *The Jaguar and the Anteater*, 90. Jane Juffer has gone to great lengths to demonstrate the increasing place that pornographic material has in the lives of women in the United States: Juffer, *At Home with Pornography*.
64 From the translated version of Clos's foreword to the catalogue of *jardín de eros*, edited by Combalía and Lebel, 380.
65 On the ways in which sexualized images 'look' back at the viewer, see Elkins, *The Object Stares Back*, especially 106–7 and 118–20.
66 Lane had visited Copenhagen's Erotica Museum.
67 This conflicted response, the capacity of porn and erotica to both attract and repel, has afflicted scholars of sex as well. 'Like many people, I engage with the materials of sexual representation on a deeply personal level, experiencing at one moment desire and another revulsion; at one moment arousal and another guilt.' McNair, *Mediated Sex*, 4.
68 Elias's *The History of Manners* was initially published in 1939. The version I have used forms a part of his *The Civilizing Process*.
69 Ibid., 160.
70 'This transformation of what manifested itself originally as an active, often aggressive expression of pleasure, into the passive, more ordered pleasure

of spectating (i.e., a mere pleasure of the eye) is already initiated in education, in the conditioning precepts of young people.' Ibid., 170.

71 'And for what is lacking in everyday life a substitute is created in dreams,
in books and pictures. So, on their way to becoming courtiers, the nobility
read novels of chivalry; the bourgeois contemplate violence and erotic
passion in films.' Ibid., 375.

72 Stallybrass and White, *The Politics and Poetics of Transgression*, 191.

73 As in, for example, Freud's essay 'Repression.'

74 Cited in Roegiers, 'The Bobkin, the Vulva and the Eye-Popping Gaze of the
Painter,' 72.

75 Berger, *Ways of Seeing*, 47.

76 On the gaze, Michel Foucault supplied one of the most elaborate discussions of its power in *The Birth of the Clinic*. Foucault's study focused on the
emergence of the medical gaze in the late eighteenth and early nineteenth
centuries, though in his conclusion he noted similarities between the texts
of medicine and the texts of the Marquis de Sade (195).

77 On spectacle, see the madcap work of Guy Debord, *The Society of the Spectacle*, initially published in French in 1967. In a discussion of both Foucault
and Debord, Martin Jay has called surveillance and spectacle 'complementary apparatuses' that are 'so central to the maintenance of disciplinary or
repressive power in the modern world.' Jay, *Downcast Eyes: The Denigration
of Vision in Twentieth-Century French Thought*, 383.

2 Liberation Theory

1 Discussed in Roudinesco, *Jacques Lacan*, 265.

2 The term appears as part of the title of a 1915 translation of part of an essay
Freud wrote initially in 1908, eventually recalled in its complete form as
'"Civilized" Sexual Morality and Modern Nervousness.' John Forrester
notes two instances in the 1910s when Freud privately expressed his opposition. See Forrester, *Dispatches from the Freud Wars*, 45.

3 Both examples cited in Petersen, *The Century of Sex*, 40, 75.

4 Friedan, *The Feminine Mystique*, 104. The book was first published in 1963.

5 Franz Alexander, 1953, cited in Shorter, *A History of Psychiatry*, 186.

6 Martin Wain, for example, has argued that psychoanalysis established a
new foundation for governance in the twentieth century. Here Freud takes
on a sinister cast. Wain, *Freud's Answers*.

7 Young, 'Darwin, Marx, Freud.'

8 Manuel and Manuel, *Utopian Thought in the Western World*, 788–800.

9 This comment is not meant to cast any aspersions upon the 'critical theory'

of the Frankfurt School. The attempt to combine Freud and Marx was a feature of the work of the school, of which Marcuse was a member (Reich was not). Critical theory was and remains a major tool of analysis of all manner of social and cultural phenomena. See Jay, *The Dialectical Imagination*.

10 Reich, 'Dialectical Materialism and Psychoanalysis.' Reich wrote the essay in 1927–8, published it first in 1929, and republished it in 1934 with additions (an extra chapter and some footnotes). So the essay was initially prepared before *Civilization and Its Discontents* appeared. Fromm, 'The Method and Function of an Analytic Social Psychology: Notes on Psychoanalysis and Historical Materialism.' Fromm also added footnotes to explain where his opinions now diverged from the original formulation in the essay, first published in 1932.

11 Freud himself would never have accepted such an amalgam – in fact *Civilization and Its Discontents* can easily be depicted as a refutation of communist dreams. Reich in 'Dialectical Materialism' admitted as much in his 1934 preface: 'The connections between Marxism and psychoanalysis were fundamentally rejected by Freud, who said that the two disciplines were opposed to each other.' The Manuels called Freud 'the dark prince of the modern anti-utopians.' Manuel and Manuel, *Utopian Thought in the Western World*, 790.

12 Gay, *Freud*, 547.

13 The actual size depends on the edition used. The essay in the *Penguin Freud Library* runs to ninety pages (this in volume 12, *Civilization, Society and Religion*). I have employed the Dover Thrift Edition, published in 1994, which 'is an unabridged republication of the translation by Joan Riviere originally published by the Hogarth Press, London, 1930.' That is seventy pages long. The citations in the text of this section are to the Dover Edition.

14 Gay, *Freud*, 552.

15 See Fromm, 'Analytic Social Psychology,' 110, and Reich, 'Dialectical Materialism,' 6.

16 'The instinct is a "borderline concept between the psychic and the somatic."' Here Reich, 'Dialectical Materialism,' 15, was quoting from Freud's early work on sexuality.

17 According to Fromm, 'Analytic Social Psychology,' 111, the right kind of analytic social psychology 'seeks to understand the drive structure through the understanding of life history.'

18 'The id, again, is not something supernatural but is an expression of the biological sector of the personality. A part of it is the unconscious in the sense just described, that is to say it belongs to what has actually been repressed.' Reich, 'Dialectical Materialism,' 22.

19 'Psychoanalysis has shown that man's conscious psychic activity is only a relatively small sector of his psychic life, that many decisive impulses behind psychic behavior are unconscious.' Fromm, 'Analytic Social Psychology,' 110

20 'We cannot disregard the conclusion that man's sense of guilt has its origin in the Oedipus complex and was acquired when the father was killed by the association of the brothers.' Freud, *Civilization*, 57. This line of argument depended upon another controversial theory, outlined in a 1913 essay (1918 in English), 'Totem and Taboo,' where he posited a initial act of patricide in the primal horde, in which the sons killed their father to secure the women and so launched civilization.

21 'Our present point of view can be roughly expressed in the statement that libido participates in every instinctual manifestation,' he mused, 'but that not everything in that manifestation is libido.' Freud, *Civilization*, 48, n2.

22 Most famously in his 'Three Essays on the Theory of Sexuality' (1905).

23 'Thus the extraordinarily wide dissemination of the perversions forces us to suppose that the disposition to perversions is itself of no great rarity but must form a part of what passes as the normal constitution.' Ibid., 86.

24 Ibid., 72.

25 'Sadism is the great instinctual reservoir, to which one appeals when one has no other – and usually more costly – satisfactions to offer the masses; at the same time, it is useful in annihilating the "enemy."' Fromm, 'Analytic Social Psychology,' 113, n1.

26 'It is said, however, that each one of us behaves in some respect like the paranoic, substituting a wish-fulfilment for some aspect of the world which is unbearable to him, and carrying this delusion through into reality.' Freud, *Civilization*, 15.

27 Freud, 'Creative Writers and Day-Dreaming,' 146.

28 Ibid., 149.

29 Ibid., 153.

30 'Psychoanalysis can show that man's ideologies are the products of certain wishes, instinctual drives, interests, and needs, which themselves, in large measure, unconsciously find expression as rationalizations – i.e., as ideologies.' Fromm, 'Analytic Social Psychology,' 127.

31 Fromm's variant is developed in a different article, also published in 1932, called 'Psychoanalytic Characterology and Its Relevance for Social Psychology.' Here Fromm outlines the hypothesis that the spirit of capitalism is anal, the restriction of genital sexuality having produced a character type that reflects 'an intensification of the anal libido' (155). Naturally Fromm repeats 'the equation of feces and money' found in Freud's works such as

'Character and Anal Erotism' (1908) and 'On Transformations of Instinct as Exemplified in Anal Erotism' (1917).

32 Reich, 'Dialectical Materialism,' 26, and Fromm, 'Analytic Social Psychology,' 117.

33 'Sexual oppression serves class rule; ideologically and structurally reproduced in the ruled, sexual oppression represents the most powerful and as yet unrecognized force of oppression in general.' Reich, 'Dialectical Materialism,' 51, n54. This claim was added by Reich to his 1934 version of the essay.

34 Deleuze and Guattari, *Anti-Oedipus*, 265.

35 See, for instance, the comment on Reich in Patricia Anderson, *Passion Lost*, 77.

36 Visited in August 1999.

37 A historian of sex reform in Germany, however, has argued that Reich, while prominent, was never pre-eminent on the Berlin stage, and that a number of other individuals were much better known and respected in the ranks of the movement. See Atina Grossman, *Reforming Sex*, especially 124–7.

38 On the Frankfurt Institute and the import of Freudianism, as well as Fromm's efforts, see Jay, *The Dialectical Imagination*, especially the chapter 'The Integration of Psychoanalysis,' 86–112.

39 Reich, 'Dialectical Materialism,' 8.

40 See 'Preface to the Second Edition (1936),' in Reich, *The Sexual Revolution*, xxvi.

41 Cited in Wilhelm Reich, 'What Is Class Consciousness?,' 350.

42 Reich purportedly used this terminology, though in another context. Boadella, *Wilhelm Reich*, 85.

43 Rycroft, *Wilhelm Reich*, 7.

44 Grossman, *Reforming Sex*, 124–5.

45 Rieff, *The Triumph of the Therapeutic*, 144.

46 The citations in the text of this section are to the 1974 edition.

47 'Qualitatively and quantitatively, the unconscious is itself conditioned by culture.' Reich, *The Sexual Revolution*, 19.

48 'The moralistic regulation of instinctual life creates precisely what it alleges to keep in check: the antisocial drives.' Ibid., 20.

49 Marcuse, *Eros and Civilization*, 239

50 Cited in Robinson, *The Freudian Left*, 72.

51 'The experiences gleaned from the restructuring of individuals will serve merely to establish general principles for a new form of education of infants and adolescents in which nature and culture, individual and society, sexu-

ality and sociality, would no longer contradict each other.' Reich, *The Sexual Revolution*, 9.

52 Huxley, *Brave New World*, 41.

53 Ibid., 13–14.

54 That file was made available under the Freedom of Information Act and published on the web at http://foia.fbi.gov/reich.htm, and accessed in June 2001.

55 Cited in Katz, *Herbert Marcuse and the Art of Liberation*, 186.

56 Robinson, *The Freudian Left*, 185. Robinson's chapter on Marcuse is both an excellent discussion of Marcuse's intellectual development and a closely reasoned analysis of *Eros and Civilization*.

57 Kellner, *Herbert Marcuse and the Crisis of Marxism*, 155–7. Horkheimer and Adorno had published a very dismal analysis of 'the work of the administered life' in 1947: see the preface to the new edition (1969), *Dialectic of Enlightenment*, ix.

58 The citations in the text of this section are to Marcuse, *Eros and Civilization*.

59 Kellner (188) thought the result was 'more Freudian than Marxian.' By contrast Robinson (*The Freudian Left*, 201) decided that Marx 'was clearly the unacknowledged hero of *Eros and Civilization*.'

60 Whitebook has suggested that the 'perversions,' along with fantasy life, constituted for Marcuse 'the good Other of the repressive ego': *Perversion and Utopia*, 32.

61 'The perversions suggest the ultimate identity of Eros and death instinct, or the submission of Eros to the death instinct.' Marcuse, *Eros and Civilization*, 51.

62 This stance was the reason why Whitebook has argued that Marcuse 'was, if not eschatological, at least radically utopian. Because the forces of production had developed immeasurably further under capitalism than Marx had ever imagined, the long transitional phase of socialist accumulation he had envisioned would not be necessary. It was possible, Marcuse argued, to move directly to a "communist" society, where the amount of time and energy necessary to negotiate the basic reality principle would be reduced to a minimum. This would, in turn, make it possible to eliminate surplus repression and emancipate the polymorphous perverse dimension of human sexuality that had remained loyal to the pleasure principle.' Whitebook, 'Michel Foucault: A Structuralist in Marcusean Clothing,' 64.

63 'However, progressive alienation itself increases the potential of freedom: the more external to the individual the necessary labour becomes, the less does it involve him in the realm of necessity.' Marcuse, *Eros and Civilization*, 223. He then went on to write of an 'expanding realm of freedom' that reshapes aspects of the world.

64 'But, within the system of unified and intensified controls, decisive changes are taking place. They affect the structure of the superego and the content and manifestation of guilt feeling. Moreover, they tend toward a state in which the completely alienated world, expending its full power, seems to prepare the stuff and material for a new reality principle.' Ibid., 95. See also passages on 129, 150–1, 153–4, and 215.

65 One chapter of *Eros and Civilization* was devoted to a discussion of those other archetypes of the ancient Greeks, whom Marcuse opposed to Prometheus, 'the archetype-hero of the performance principle' (161).

66 He regained some of his earlier optimism, at the height of the student protests, when he published *An Essay on Liberation*.

67 Marcuse, *One-Dimensional Man*. The detailed discussion of repressive desublimation occurs in chapter 3. I deal again with this issue in the conclusion.

68 Witness this comment from *Eros and Civilization*: 'The argument that makes liberation conditional upon an ever higher standard of living all too easily serves to justify the perpetuation of repression. The definition of the standard of living in terms of automobiles, television sets, airplanes, and tractors is that of the performance principle itself. Beyond the rule of this principle, the level of living would be measured by other criteria: the universal gratification of the basic human needs, and the freedom from guilt and fear – internalized as well as external, instinctual as well as "rational"' (153).

69 For a more detailed discussion of the operations of repressive desublimation, see Reiche, *Sexuality and Class Struggle*. Reiche also wrote in the tradition of Freudo-Marxism. The fact that eroticism was sweeping through the affluent West was only cause for despair. How could the Left compete, how could it free sex or use sex to bring about the desired social revolution? Reiche had no answers. He ended his 1970 'Postscript' with the revealing and hopeless declaration, '*Long live victory in the class struggle!*'

70 Cited in Parkin, 'The Sex of Food and Ernest Dichter.'

71 Noted in Easton, 'Consuming Interests.' In fact there were other inputs that shaped the campaign, both from the Elmo Roper researchers and the Leo Burnett advertising agency. I have discussed at length the Marlboro campaign, which was masterminded by the Leo Burnett advertising agency, in Paul Rutherford, *The New Icons? The Art of Television Advertising*, 38–44.

72 Cited in Packard, *The Hidden Persuaders*, 28.

73 See Pratkanis, 'The Cargo-Cult Science of Subliminal Persuasion.'

74 Martineau, *Motivation in Advertising: Motives That Make People Buy.*

75 Easton, 'Consuming Interests.' This article concentrates on the story of SRI.

76 Goodman, 'Freud and the Hucksters,' 144.
77 Packard, *The Hidden Persuaders*, 22.
78 The comments on Gardner and Weiss and Geller are from Goodman, 'Freud and the Hucksters,' 143, 144.
79 Cited in, respectively, Fox, *The Mirror Makers*, 184, and Goodman, 'Freud and the Hucksters,' 144.
80 Packard, *The Hidden Persuaders*, 1. The book was initially published by David McKay in 1957.
81 The book's popularity is discussed in Horowitz, *Vance Packard and American Social Criticism*, 1994), 133. Horowitz notes that it had sold about 3 million copies by 1975.
82 The discussion of Dichter's life is drawn from a number of different sources: Horowitz, 'The Emigré as Celebrant of American Consumer Culture: George Katona and Ernest Dichter'; Mayer, *Madison Avenue, USA*, particularly 235–43; 'Ernest Dichter,' *Current Biography*, 1961, available online from the H.W. Wilson Company; 'Ernest Dichter: Motive Interpreter,' *Journal of Advertising Research* (February/March 1986): 15–20, a reprint of a 1977 interview; and Barbara B. Stern, 'The Importance of Being Ernest.'
83 Friedan, *The Feminine Mystique*, 206–32. Friedan did not 'name' Dichter in the text of the book, only in the footnotes, perhaps because he had been so willing to assist her. She actually referred to him as 'this most helpful of hidden persuaders' (208).
84 Hopkins was one of the most famous champions of the more traditional, 'reason-why' school of advertising. The quotation is from Mayer, *Madison Avenue*, 239.
85 Witness the slightly disparaging comments on Dichter in a contemporary work by another researcher, this person attached to McCann-Erickson: Harry Henry, *Motivation Research*, 216–217.
86 Meyer, *Madison Avenue*, 235.
87 Cited in Horowitz, 'The Emigré and American Consumer Culture,' 160. Horowitz makes much of Dichter's view of consumption as therapy. The second quotation comes from the book itself. The book was reprinted in 1952, apparently as *Successful Living*.
88 He had, however, used focus groups much earlier to generate discussions about particular brands and products.
89 Cited in Fox, *The Mirror Makers*, 186.
90 Cited in Mayer, *Madison Avenue*, 239–40.
91 Dichter, *The Strategy of Desire* and *Handbook of Consumer Motivations*. Hereafter the page references in this section are to one of these books, abbreviated as SD and HCM respectively.

92 Parkin, 'The Sex of Food and Ernest Dichter,' is an extended discussion of how he gendered all manner of foods: so steak, asparagus, wieners, or coffee were masculine; tea, rice, and cake feminine; and roast chicken and oranges bisexual.

93 These references are all to the *Handbook*, respectively pages 332, 10, 108, 71, 177, 134, 148, 31–2, and 56–7. Along similar lines, Dichter had apparently told the Fitzgerald advertising agency in a 1955 report that, 'The wedding cake [is] ... the symbol of the feminine organ. The act of cutting the first slice by the bride and bridegroom together clearly stands as a symbol of defloration.' Cited in Parkin, 'The Sex of Food and Ernest Dichter.'

94 *Handbook*, 346 and 347, 46 and 339, 46, 184, 249–52.

95 There is some debate over the reasons why the Edsel failed, though not over the fact that the failure was spectacular. 'No other product was so widely anticipated before being so emphatically rejected as the Edsel. When Ford unveiled the new model on September 5, 1957, nearly three million people stopped for a look. Few liked what they saw. Although the Edsel opened to mixed reviews, within weeks it had become the car people liked to hate. Ford had projected sales of over 200,000 during its first year. Actual sales did not reach a third of that number, and when Ford discontinued the line in November 1959, shortly after the start of its third model year, total sales were just over 100,000.' Dicke, 'Review of *Disaster in Dearborn: The Story of the Edsel* by Thomas E. Bonsall.'

96 One scholar has subjected the *Handbook* to a close analysis and concludes 'that the text relies on dream-logic found in modern literature and advertising more than on the rigorous flow of ideas readers have come to expect in scientific prose.' Barbara Stern, 'Literary Criticism and the History of Marketing Thought,' 334.

97 Although Dichter suffered a coronary in 1970, Horowitz claims he remained very active as 'a lecturer, consultant, and author' right into the 1980s. Horowitz, 'The Emigré and American Consumer Culture,' 163–4. Barbara Stern notes that he has been largely forgotten in the academic literature on marketing: 'As of 2000, Dichter had disappeared from the academic establishment, for out of 15 consumer behavior texts, only 3 mention him in connection with MR.' Stern, 'The Importance of Being Ernest,' 165.

98 Schiffman and Kanuk, *Consumer Behavior*, 79.

99 Shalit, 'The Return of the Hidden Persuaders.'

3 The Erotic Sell

1 A copy of the ad is included in Sivulka, *Soap, Sex, and Cigarettes*, 112.

2 The slogan was part of the Woodbury Deb campaign, about women who won their mates because they used the right soap. The ad appeared in *Ladies' Home Journal*. Samples of the campaign were available online through the Ad*Access database of Duke University in November 2001.

3 The general story of the erotic sell in the United States has been told in Reichert, *The Erotic History of Advertising*. See his chapter 2, 'Smoke and Leers 1850–1900,' 45–66, for a discussion of early examples of the use of sex in advertising.

4 See figure 7 in Sobieszek, *The Art of Persuasion*, 31. Sobieszek does not identify either the brand or the country of origin.

5 Loeb, *Consuming Angels: Advertising and Victorian Women*, 60–71.

6 Lears, *Fables of Abundance*.

7 Two images from the campaign were on display at the website of the John W. Hartman Center for Sales, Advertising and Marketing History of Duke University in October 2001. These were drawn from *The Second Annual of Illustrations for Advertisements in the United States*, 1923, produced by 'The Art Directors Club.'

8 This important shift in the thinking of admakers in the United States has been analysed by Merle Curti and Roland Marchand. See Curti, 'The Changing Concept of "Human Nature" in the Literature of American Advertising,' and Marchand, *Advertising the American Dream*, 52–87.

9 See Buckley, *Mechanical Man: John Broadus Watson and the Beginnings of Behaviorism*.

10 Poffenberger, *Psychology in Advertising*, 57. Poffenberger was, however, unwilling to accept the Freudian insistence on the pre-eminence of the sex drive. See also Lucas, *Psychology for Advertisers*, 64; Braddock, *Psychology and Advertising*, 84–5; and Burtt, *Psychology of Advertising*, 79–80.

11 Sivulka, *Soap, Sex, and Cigarettes*, 214. There was at least one earlier use of a photograph of a nude woman, outside the United States, in 1922 in Japan for Akadama Port Wine (later Suntory). See Sobieszek, *The Art of Persuasion*, 38–9.

12 On Freud in America, see Hale, Jr, *The Rise and Crisis of Psychoanalysis in the United States: Freud and the Americans, 1917–1985*, especially chapter 16, 'The "Golden Age" of Popularization,' 1945–1965,' 276–99.

13 On the changing culture of the United States, see D'Emilio and Freedman, *Intimate Matters*, especially 239–300. On the rapidly expanding market for pornography in Britain, see H.G. Cocks, 'Saucy Stories,' especially 477–82.

14 And, increasingly, women as well. By 1970 it was estimated that around 80 per cent of boys and 70 per cent of girls in the United States 'had seen visual depictions or read textual descriptions of sexual intercourse by the age of eighteen.' Allyn, *Make Love, Not War*, 186.

15 This information thanks to Ms Elizabeth Leiss-McKellar. She received the story during an interview with Bud Turner, the retired president of McLaren Advertising, an interview she conducted on 18 July 2000.

16 All quotations in this and the next paragraph are from George Orwell, 'Benefit of Clergy: Some Notes on Salvador Dali,' in *Dickens, Dali and Others*. Orwell tells the story of the suppression of the essay in the 'Notes' to his own book.

17 Ian Gibson constantly refers to the autobiography, which he calls a 'biographical minefield,' in his excellent and comprehensive biography, *The Shameful Life of Salvador Dalí*. An earlier biographer, Meryle Secrest, claimed that the autobiography made one wonder, 'How much was sheer braggadocio, how much clear fabrication, and what truths might be concealed?' Secrest, *Salvador Dalí*, 8. Robert Radforth decided the *Secret Life* was Dalí's 'preferred orchestration of his own myth: the story of the creation of a "genius."' Radforth, *Dalí*, 8. David Vilaseca used the autobiography as the main source for his psychoanalytical inquiry into the mind of Dalí: in his *The Apocryphal Subject*. Haim Finkelstein thought that the autobiography marked an end and a beginning in the evolution of Dalí's aesthetic vision, standing between his surrealist period of the 1930s and his postwar work: *Salvador Dalí's Art and Writing, 1927–1942*. Finkelstein also perceived the commercial intent of the *Secret Life*, which he calls 'a construction created for the purpose of selling a particular image of Dalí to his new American public' (256).

18 My account is based on the Dover edition of the original 1942 book: the text is unabridged, but the colour plates have been repositioned to the inside covers. The one important item missing from the Dover paperback is Dalí's famous painting of the 'soft watches,' *The Persistence of Memory*, which had appeared in colour on the front of the jacket. Dalí, *The Secret Life of Salvador Dalí*. Unless otherwise indicated, the page references to quoted material in the text of the rest of this section are to the Dover edition.

19 Gibson, *The Shameful Life*, 407–9, has a superb summary and critique of the autobiography.

20 Ibid., 417–19. Gibson gives a summary of the critics' responses.

21 Freud had explored the theme of repression, more properly 'the return of the repressed,' in *Delusions and Dreams in Jensen's Gradiva* (1907). The case had been a particular favourite of the surrealists in general. The importance of the Gradiva myth, and its link to Gala, is dealt with at length in Finkelstein, *Salvador Dalí's Art and Writing*, 257–9.

22 Gibson, *The Shameful Life*, 73. This diary he kept only briefly. Gibson notes that in a later confessional work Dalí admitted to reading a pornographic

work which confirmed his view that he was physically inadequate, unable to perform the acts of sexual prowess of the hero.

23 Cited in Dawn Ades, *Dalí*, 68. Bataille was a surrealist at odds with André Breton, the leader of the movement.

24 This admission came in an interview in 1979 when he talked about his problems with premature ejaculation. Gibson, *The Shameful Life*, 74.

25 The article was published in an avant-garde magazine. Cited in Jordana Mendelson, 'Of Politics, Postcards and Pornography,' 165.

26 Cited in Gibson, *The Shameful Life*, 175.

27 Combalía and Lebel, eds, *Jardín de Eros* catalogue, 79.

28 Orwell, 'Benefit of Clergy,' 175–6.

29 'The grotesque body is not separate from the rest of the world. It is not a closed, completed unit: it is unfinished, outgrows itself, transgresses its own limits. The stress is laid on those parts of the body that are open to the outside world, that is, the parts through which the world enters the body or emerges from it, or through which the body itself goes out to meet the world. This means that the emphasis is on the apertures or the convexities, or on various ramifications and offshoots: the open mouth, the genital organs, the breasts, the phallus, the potbelly, the nose. The body discloses its essence as a principle of growth which exceeds its own limits only in copulation, pregnancy, childbirth, the throes of death, eating, drinking, or defecation.' Bakhtin, *Rabelais and His World*, 26.

30 Bataille's comments are cited in Descharnes and Néret, *Salvador Dalí 1904– 1989*, 143.

31 'I, however, affected the opposite position, and often said, "I love getting publicity, and if I am lucky enough to have the reporters know who I am, I will given them some of my own bread to eat, just as Saint Francis did with his birds."' Dalí, *The Secret Life*, 330.

32 Cited in Gibson, *The Shameful Life*, 391.

33 Cited in Descharnes and Néret, *Salvador Dalí*, 322–3.

34 Cited in Gibson, *The Shameful Life*, 415.

35 Radforth, *Dalí*, 222.

36 See Descharnes and Néret, *Salvador Dalí*, for a sample of such pictures: Lady Louis Mountbatten, 1940 (330), Helena Rubinstein, 1942–3 (351), Mrs Luther Greene, 1942 (356), Mrs Harrison Williams, 1943 (360), or Mrs Mary Sigall, 1948 (417).

37 Gibson, *The Shameful Life*, 431.

38 See Richard Martin, *Fashion and Surrealism*, 203.

39 See Descharnes and Néret, *Salvador Dalí*, 376. Not all of the ads were so bizarre: for a later, more subdued ad see R. Martin, *Fashion and Surrealism*, 130.

40 Secrest, *Salvador Dalí*, 189.

41 Cited in 'Foreword' to Mundy, ed., *Surrealism*, 11.

42 'The surrealist object is one that is absolutely useless from the practical and rational point of view, created wholly for the purpose of materializing in a fetishistic way, with the maximum of tangible reality, ideas and fantasies having a delirious character.' Dalí, *The Secret Life*, 312. A replica of Dalí's *Scatological Object Functioning Symbolically,* a 1930 reflection on shoe fetishism, was on display in the *Surrealism: Desire Unbound* exhibition.

43 'Bra Battle Centers on New Ads, New Angles, New Users,' 14.

44 Including Sweden, Holland, France, Hong Kong, Singapore, and South Africa. Hughes, 'Maidenform Dreams Big,' 39.

45 A portion of one television commercial, in 1959, appeared in a CNN story in 1995. See also the comment in Howard, '"At the Curve Exchange": Postwar Beauty Culture and Working Women at Maidenform,' 600.

46 Howard, '"At the Curve Exchange,"' discusses how Maidenform organized its own 'Pin-Up Girl of the Month' in its own company, chosen from among its employees and featured in its newsletter.

47 See 'Maidenform's Mrs. R.,' 76.

48 The ad, under the title 'Gaine Scandale,' in the Film Library established by Jean-Marie Boursicot at www.adeater.com. American firms had also employed sexualized imagery at an earlier date: so Warner showed off its wares in a 1937 ad where the women were preparing to go skiing. This last ad was in Néret, *Dessous*, 94.

49 See Coleman, 'Maidenform(ed)' for an extended discussion of the supposed meanings, including the phallic overtones, of this bra style.

50 The description of the Chansonette is taken from the company pamphlet: Maidenform, Inc., 'A Company Built by a Brand.' The nickname is from Marilyn Yalom, *A History of the Breast*, 177.

51 See also Coleman, 'Maidenform(ed),' 11, regarding the bra as a badge of modernity.

52 Hughes, 'Maidenform Dreams Big,' 118.

53 Adding credibility to this claim is a copy of a draft ad in which a woman dressed in slip and heels picks up objects, and the tagline reads, 'I dreamed I went shopping in my Seamprufe slip!' The first Maidenform ad dealt with shopping as well. Sacco, 'Dreams for Sale.'

54 *Harper's Bazaar*, October 1955, 102.

55 Hughes, 'Maidenform Dreams Big,' 120.

56 Norman had been senior vice-president of Weintraub H. Weintraub and Company, in charge of the Maidenform account. In 1955 he and some associates bought out Weintraub, and the company became Norman, Craig

and Kummel. For a discussion of Norman, see Meyer, *Madison Avenue, USA*, 59–62.

57 Freud, *The Interpretation of Dreams*, 344. Freud devoted a small section to these fantasies, under the chapter heading 'Typical Dreams.' He was primarily interested in the dreams of men, though in a footnote added to a later edition of the original text he made reference to similar dreams of women recorded by his follower Sándor Ferenczi.

58 Calt, 'Advertising's Debt to Dr. Freud,' 98. Calt was associated with the agency Young and Rubicam.

59 Packard, *The Hidden Persuaders*, 72–3. Unfortunately Packard did not list any sources for the comments he placed in quotation marks. *Advertising Age*, much later, again without any references, claimed the company had conducted research 'that indicated deep down, every woman is really a born exhibitionist.' Baltera, 'Maidenform Goes on Stage for Dream Theme Revival.'

60 Cited in Mayer, *Madison Avenue, USA*, 36.

61 Cited in Montgomery, 'Norman, Craig and Kummel, Inc.,' 1154.

62 Cited in Hughes, 'Maidenform Dreams Big,' 38, 39.

63 *Harper's Bazaar*, September 1951.

64 The undated ad was available online at Bedroom Boudoir, members.aol.com/aster314/, in October 2001.

65 The ad was from 1962. It was available online at www.rareads.com/rareads/webmiscell.html in October 2001.

66 Coleman, 'Maidenform(ed),' 15–16.

67 *Ladies' Home Journal*, May 1958.

68 *Harper's Bazaar*, October 1951.

69 This is an ad where the Maidenform woman dreamed she was on an election campaign. *Woman's Day*, October 1956.

70 *Harper's Bazaar*, May 1954.

71 Maidenform, Inc., 'A Company Built by a Brand.'

72 The ads are from *Vogue*, December 1955; online at www.tias.com; *Woman's Day*, 1 August 1957; *Harper's Bazaar*, June 1961; *Harper's Bazaar*, September 1965.

73 Hughes, 'Maidenform Dreams Big,' 118.

74 This observation draws on Howard, '"At the Curve Exchange,"' 601.

75 Cited in Reichert, *The Erotic History of Advertising*, 151.

76 Nelson, 'Dream Lovers.'

77 Moog, *'Are They Selling Her Lips?': Advertising and Identity*, 23.

78 The figures are from Hughes, 'Maidenform Dreams Big,' 35; 'Maidenform's Mrs. R.,' 75; and 'Ida Rosenthal,' 92.

79 Baltera, 'Maidenform Goes on Stage,' 39.

80 See, for example, a series of ads in *Harper's Bazaar* for Formfit Rogers (March 1963, 39), Vanity Fair (March 1963, 47), Warner's (February 1964, back cover), Jantzen (April 1965, 50 and 51), Poirette (April 1965, 84), and Warner's again (February 1966, back page). Even Sears, Middle America's favourite store, had 'gone wild!,' as one of its bra ads declared in the *Ladies' Home Journal*, March 1969, 63.

81 According to Gay Talese, 'the magazines that were saturated with sex – the cheaper pulp magazines and *Enquirer*-style tabloids – presented it as an abomination to be endlessly explored with such headlines as: 'How Wild Are Small-town Girls?' or "The Lowdown on the Abortion Business or "The Multimillion-dollar Smut Racket."' Talese, *Thy Neighbor's Wife*, 75.

82 *Newsweek*, 23 May 1960, 72.

83 This example is discussed in Dines, 'Dirty Business: *Playboy* Magazine and the Mainstreaming of Pornography,' 50.

84 The quoted description comes from one of the more famous articles in feminist journalism, first written in 1963, by Gloria Steinem, a piece reprinted as 'I Was a Playboy Bunny' in her *Outrageous Acts and Everyday Rebellions*, 29–69.

85 *The Observer* (London), 18 May 1999.

86 This was not a compliment. According to Reynolds, 'the only kick I got out of the whole thing,' meaning the Cosmo appearance, 'was that I was sending up *Playboy*, which I hate desperately.' Cited in Allyn, *Make Love Not War*, 232.

87 Talese, *Thy Neighbor's Wife*, 16–17.

88 Cited in Ingham and Feldman, 'Hefner, Hugh Marston,' 217.

89 Cited in Kallan and Brooks, 'The Playmate of the Month,' 329. The authors claim that roughly one-third had husbands.

90 Allyn, *Make Love, Not War*, 88.

91 *Playboy*, November 1956.

92 Talese, *Thy Neighbor's Wife*, 87.

93 Russell Miller, *Bunny: The Real Story of Playboy*, 55.

94 The formula is discussed in Kallan and Brooks, 'The Playmate of the Month.'

95 Witness this judgment of the commentary on *Playboy*'s sex: 'Critics repeatedly attack the magazine's "obsession" with the "quality" of the nude photographs, and accuse the playmates of being "idealized", "sanitized" and "plastic", terms that define them as artificial and lacking in authenticity.' Jancovich, 'Placing Sex.'

96 *The Times* (London), 9 December 1996.

97 This comment draws on the work of John Berger in his analysis of the European nude: 'To be on display is to have the surface of one's own skin, the hairs of one's own body, turned into a disguise which, in that situation, can never be discarded. The nude is condemned to never being naked. Nudity is a form of dress.' Berger, *Ways of Seeing*, 54.

98 The phrase is borrowed from Benjamin De Mott's well-considered denunciation of *Playboy*, where he charged that, 'the editors offer a vision of the whole man reduced to his private parts.' De Mott, 'The Anatomy of "Playboy,"' 113. In fact the editors did not do that, nor would Hefner have succeeded so well if that was all *Playboy* did.

99 Russell Miller, *Bunny*, 65.

100 Ibid., 66.

101 That saying irked at least one feminist. See Dines, '"I Buy It for the Articles."'

102 'The Playboy Philosophy,' *Playboy*, December 1964.

103 See chapter 4 of Ehrenreich, *The Hearts of Men*.

104 Wylie was most especially noted for his 1942 piece *Generation of Vipers*.

105 This came about in a discussion with three clerics, discussed below. One of the clerics, Rabbi Marc Tanenbaum, summarized the charges of Philip Wylie about Momism and suggested that *Playboy* had sought to 'restore the balance' and to help man 'to reassert his masculinity.' 'You've just touched upon the very heart of the matter, I think,' replied Hefner. 'This is the real key to an understanding of *Playboy*, and its success, in contemporary society.'

106 However, in a passage shortly afterwards, he explicitly denied the Freudian notion that sex could be effectively sublimated through cultural activity or artistic creativity.

107 *Newsweek*, 6 January 1964, 48.

108 This description draws from a page devoted to selling the magazine's ad services, with the title 'What Sort of Man Reads Playboy?'

109 Talese, *Thy Neighbor's Wife*, 126.

110 These descriptions are borrowed from two contemporary analyses, respectively Gerson and Lund, '*Playboy* Magazine,' 221, and De Mott, 'The Anatomy of "Playboy,"' 111.

111 See Hollows, 'The Bachelor Dinner: Masculinity, Class, and Cooking in *Playboy*, 1953–1961,' for an extended discussion of how *Playboy* sought to masculinize cooking.

112 For example, the April 1958 edition carried a feature on making sauces that emphasized the sensory adventure awaiting the man daring enough to take on the challenge of preparing all manner of delicious sauces the proper way.

113 'Gift Gallery Preview,' *Playboy,* November 1956, 18.

114 Which was why Robert Guccione would challenge in 1969 with *Penthouse,* promising 'pictures without the lectures' and 'pinups without the hangups.' See Jancovich, 'Placing Sex.'

115 Ingham and Feldman, 'Hefner,' 224.

116 Reprinted in Lord, *Forever Barbie,* 15.

117 My thanks to Heidi Bohaker, a colleague in history at the University of Toronto, who provided me with this reference and the pictures.

118 In fact the story comes in different shapes. I have drawn this bare-bones version from Susan Stern, *Barbie Nation,* and Lord, *Forever Barbie.*

119 Lord reprints a series of promotional images for Lilli in *Forever Barbie,* 27–31. She also explains that Lilli was 'a symbol of illicit sex.'

120 The comment appears in Schneider, *Children's Television,* 25. Schneider wrote the first Barbie commercials.

121 The first statistic is cited in Owen, 'Where Toys Come From' (the article was part of Infotrac, a web service, hence unpaginated); the second statistic and quotation are from Quindlen, 'Barbie at 35,' 119.

122 One collection of academics figured out much later that the chances of an actual Barbie turning up in a population were less than one in 100,000. Norton, Olds, Olive, and Dank, 'Ken and Barbie at Life Size.'

123 Ken was apparently introduced because a survey of girls indicated they thought Barbie should have a boyfriend.

124 According to Lord, *Forever Barbie,* 49–50, the initial accessories for Ken tried to compensate for his lack: a long stick, a hunting rifle, a baseball bat, 'a pendulous stethoscope.'

125 This account is based on the material in Lord, *Forever Barbie,* 36–42.

126 Cited in ibid., 39.

127 Ibid., 42–3.

128 Cited in Rand, *Barbie's Queer Accessories,* 98. The story was purportedly about a thwarted shopping trip in 1963. Of course, the reliability of this story of what a woman recalls from when she was three years old is not high. Likely the memory could only persist if it was rehearsed much later, becoming a part of family lore. Even so, the story neatly expresses the problem mothers had with Barbie.

129 Wolitzer, 'Barbie as Boy Toy,' 208.

130 Mattel had used television earlier to sell its wares to children, buying a quarter hour on the popular Mickey Mouse Club in 1955 for $500,000. 'It's Not the Doll, It's the Clothes,' 52.

131 Ted Rakstis, 'Debate in the Doll House,' 30.

132 Recognize, however, that this figure includes all Mattel products, although

of course Barbie was the hot item in those days. Philip Seitz, 'The Mattel Story: Success,' 72.

133 G. Wayne Miller, *Toy Wars*, 69.

134 O'Sickey, 'Barbie Magazine and the Aesthetic Commodification of Girls' Bodies,' 23.

135 'This commercial received more response than any previous commercial in the first 25 years of television.' Schneider, *Children's Television*, 31.

136 Ibid., 31.

137 Westenhouser, *The Story of Barbie*, 15.

138 Lord, *Forever Barbie*, 138.

139 Seitz, 'The Mattel Story: Success,' 70.

140 She did have a last name for a time – Roberts (named after the advertising agency Carson/Roberts); she came from a small town called Willows in Wisconsin; and her parents' names were George and Margaret. See Rand, *Barbie's Queer Accessories*, 47–52. According to Florence Theriault, Barbie had no definite age, though Mattel believed girls thought her roughly six years older than they were. Theriault also listed her weight as 110 lbs, her height as five feet, eight inches. Theriault, *Theriault Presents Barbie*, 6.

141 And that is exactly what happened, according to Bob Garfield, an ad columnist, speaking perhaps as a parent: 'Anyone who has seen young girls "play Barbies" understands that the dolls do indeed unleash imaginations. The clothes and the accessories and those damned little high-heel landmines inevitably are cast aside while the Barbies themselves take center stage in elaborate, stream-of-consciousness role playing.' Garfield, 'Barbie Becomes More Than Just a Pretty Face,' 45.

142 Cross, 'Toy.' Perhaps tongue in cheek, Cross suggested she was also 'a harbinger of modern feminism.'

143 So this comment by Ruth Handler: 'parents like to thank us for the educational values in the world of Barbie. They say that they could never get their daughters well-groomed before – get them out of slacks or blue jeans and into a dress, get them to scrub their necks and wash their hair. Well, that's where Barbie comes in. The doll has clean hair and a clean face, and she dresses fashionably, and she wears gloves and shoes that match.' Cited in Zinsser, 'Barbie Is a Million-Dollar Doll,' 73.

144 Hook, 'Material Girl,' 173.

145 *Ken & Barbie* was available on the Kodak Showcase videotape of 1997 commercials.

146 One commentator asserted that 'Barbie's dream world' effectively sexualized the lives of girls 'as young as five or six' because it compelled them

'to confront the problems of teenagers.' Cox, 'Barbie and Her Playmates,' 306.

147 'According to Mattel, a little girl gets her first Barbie™ at age three and is given six more until age 12.' This from the website of the Provincial Museum of Alberta in 2001, which held an exhibition on Barbie in 1999.

148 Brandt, 'Barbie Buys a Bra,' 53.

149 Stephens, 'Barbie Doesn't Live Here Anymore,' 193.

150 Rand, *Barbie's Queer Accessories*, 102–3.

151 Maynard, 'Looking Back at Barbie,' 19.

152 Lisa Jones, cited in Ducille, 'Dyes and Dolls' (online copy, Infotrac, August 1999). Late in 2005, a group of British researchers reported their finding that some girls gleefully tortured and mutilated their Barbies. ' "The girls we spoke to see Barbie torture as a legitimate play activity, and see the torture as a 'cool' activity in contrast to other forms of play with the doll," said Agnes Nairn, one of the University of Bath researchers. "The types of mutilation are varied and creative, and range from removing the hair to decapitation, burning, breaking and even microwaving." ' *Toronto Star*, 20 December 2005, A18.

153 The reference is to Freud's classic work *The Interpretation of Dreams*.

154 For instance, see Susan Stern, *Barbie Nation*.

155 Bess, 'The Menace of Barbie Dolls,' 26.

156 Chamberlain, 'Idolatry: Barbie Dolls and Feminism' (online copy: Infotrac, August 1999).

157 Witness this quotation from an article in the feminist periodical *Ms.*: 'Most people I've met think that Barbie teaches young girls to be sex objects and consumers, that they have to have all the new costumes and a new outfit for every occasion.' This from Sibyl DeWein, a collector and author of a book on collecting Barbies. It was cited with approval by Jane Leavy in 'Is There a Barbie Doll in Your Past?,' 102.

158 Wolfe, *Promiscuities*, 14.

159 Ducille, 'Dyes and Dolls.' This despite the fact that Mattel did produce a black doll, Christie, in 1968, and multicultural Barbies in the 1980s.

160 'She helped reduce play to collecting and led kids into a fantasy world alien to the child's world.' Cross, 'Toy.' Cross is a historian and author of a book on toys and childhood.

161 For a broader definition of the brand as fetish, see pages 226–7 of this book.

162 The reference here is to Sigmund Freud's brief, controversial essay entitled 'Fetishism.' There, Freud focused on fetishism as a male 'perversion.' He also argued that the fetish was a substitute for the mythical mother's

penis (!) and bespoke the male fear of castration. The formula of expectation, absence, and fear is abstracted from this line of argument.

163 Baumgardner and Richards, *Manifesta*, 136.

164 Wolfe, *Promiscuities*, 16.

165 See Dubin, 'Who's That Girl? The World of Barbie Deconstructed,' 32–3.
Or consider this recollection: 'Someone came over – a guy – and he made
Barbie and Ken do things that I was so embarrassed about, like taking off
Barbie's clothes.' Cited in Rand, *Barbie's Queer Accessories*, 121.

166 The comment was actually about another branch of the line, 'Palm Beach
Midge.' It was available at Epinions.com in July 2002.

167 The collage, for example, appeared in Twitchell's *Adcult USA*, 210, as part
of a discussion of pop art and advertising; it was one of the featured pictures in the catalogue *High and Low: Modern Art and Popular Culture*, by
Varnedoe and Gopnik, in the chapter entitled 'Advertising,' 320; and it
served as the cover art for Sinclair, *Images Incorporated*.

168 Hamilton, *Collected Words 1953–1982*, 24.

169 Though not obvious to any casual viewer, the carpet was 'a detail of a
high-contrast black-and-white photograph of hundreds of people on a
beach,' presumably a reference to the importance of the masses in the contemporary society and marketplace. Livingstone, *Pop Art*, 36.

170 The description comes from a biography on the web (http://
www.cmgww.com/sports/atlas/ biograph.html), available in December
2001, sponsored by CMG Worldwide, which described itself as 'the home
of properties and personalities considered to be among the most presti-
gious in the licensing industry.' Atlas had won the accolade in a contest at
Madison Square Garden in 1922.

171 Livingstone, *Pop Art*, 36.

172 Cited in Ratcliff, *Andy Warhol*, 82.

173 For a brief description of the 'machine aesthetic,' see Ewen, *All Consuming
Images*, 89–90 where he talks about commercial photography. Ewen does
use the term 'streamlining' elsewhere (145–9), but he does not apply that
to bodies so much as objects.

174 There is a possibility of some confusion here. There was, at the same time,
a related movement, known as the art of assemblage, which involved collages of largely pre-existing material: see Lucie-Smith, *Movements in Art
since 1945*, 119–22, and McCarthy, *Pop Art*, 22–3. But I am using the term
'assemblage' in the broader sense outlined in the introduction.

175 See Varnedoe and Gopnik, *High and Low*, 365.

176 Mamiya, *Pop Art and Consumer Culture*, 99.

177 The Erotisch Museum in Amsterdam actually did display Barbie as Mari-

lyn, her white dress permanently raised by wind, and in ironic juxtaposition to a series of male dolls with their long, flaccid penises hanging
out.

178 Kuspit, 'The Uses of Irony: Popularity and Beauty in Mel Ramos's Painting.'

179 Witness this comment by Lichtenstein about his art: 'It's not saying that
commercial art is terrible, or 'look what we've come to' – that may be a
sociological fact, but it is not what this art is about.' Again, elsewhere, he
said, 'In parody, the implication is the perversion [of the original source],
and I feel that in my own work I don't mean it to be that. Because I don't
dislike the work that I'm parodying ... The things that I have apparently
parodied I actually admire.' Cited in Decker, 'Pop Goes the Easel.' Or this
reflection by Hamilton: 'Pop Art is a profession of approbation of mass
culture, therefore also antiartistic. It is positive Dada, creative where Dada
was destructive. Perhaps it is Mama – a cross-fertilization of Futurism and
Dada which upholds a respect for the culture of the masses and a conviction that the artist in 20th century urban life is inevitably a consumer of
mass culture and potentially a contributor to it.' Cited on a website maintained by St Mary's College of Maryland, December 2001.

4 Signs of Angst

1 Tarpley, 'History: 1970s,' 791.
2 This draws upon discussions of advertising and television in my book *The
New Icons? The Art of Television Advertising*. Census data are taken from the
website of the Census Bureau of the United States.
3 Fox, *The Mirror Makers*, 199–207.
4 McLuhan, *The Mechanical Bride*, v. Hereafter the page references in this section are to that book.
5 *The Mechanical Bride* was initially published by Vanguard Press and later
reprinted by others, though it did eventually go out of print. A new, fiftieth-
anniversary edition was issued by Gingko Press in 2002.
6 The review was available on the Web at various sites: I acquired the copy at
http:///www.english.upenn.edu/~afilreis/50s/mcluhan-bride.html, in
December 2001.
7 'When I wrote The Mechanical Bride some years ago I did not realize that I
was attempting a defense of book culture against the new media. I can now
see that I was trying to bring some of the critical awareness fostered by literary training to bear on the new media of sight and sound. My strategy
was wrong, because my obsession with literary values blinded me to much

that was actually happening for good and ill.' McLuhan, 'Sight, Sound, and the Fury' (reprinted from the *Commonweal*, 1954).

8 Although a Winnipeg boy, now teaching in a Canadian university, McLuhan was never much interested in Canada. His focus was on the United States and, more generally, on the mass culture and eventually the media born in the United States. The border was a political fact but hardly a cultural obstacle.

9 Philip Marchand, *Marshall McLuhan*, 107.

10 Ever the literary zealot, McLuhan cited as his model Edgar Allan Poe's 'A Descent Into the Maelstrom,' where the sailor saved himself by understanding the action of the whirlpool in which he was trapped.

11 See Jonathan Miller, *McLuhan*, 76.

12 One of the first and most famous of these studies of capitalism and culture, published initially in 1967, was Guy Debord's *The Society of the Spectacle*, which argued that capitalism had taken command of the visual surround. A year later, in West Germany, Reimut Reiche published *Sexuality and Class Struggle*. Reiche investigated in some detail the process of repressive desublimation, which he feared was manufacturing people who suffered from feeble egos, unable to resist authority or initiate revolution. Shortly thereafter, from East Germany, came W.F. Haug's *Critique of Commodity Aesthetics*, which explored the mechanics of the commercial appropriation of sex and how that worked, especially on young people. Then there was John Berger's very successful *Ways of Seeing*, also a BBC documentary series, which contained what became a classic chapter on art and advertising from a Marxist (but not a Freudo-Marxist) standpoint. In addition there were two works by French theorists on the synthesis of Marx and Freud, although they did not treat advertising specifically. The philosopher Gilles Deleuze and the psychoanalyst Félix Guattari used Marxism and Freudianism to eviscerate Freud, psychoanalysis, and capitalism in their theoretical blockbuster *L'Anti-Oedipe* (1972): this was later published as *Anti-Oedipus*. Then came an even 'crazier' book, Jean-François Lyotard's *Economie Libidinale* (1974), which downed Marx by reworking Freud, among others, positing the expansion of a hungry sexuality across the whole expanse of life: this was published as *Libidinal Economy*.

13 Baudrillard, *The System of Objects*. Hereafter the page references in the text of this section are to the Verso edition.

14 Baudrillard, *The System of Objects*, 185. The quotation was actually drawn from one of the pieces in Dichter's newsletter, *Motivations*, of 1956, and the quotation has since become modestly famous as a statement of the intent of the advertising industry or American business (which, of course, it was

not) in the 1950s. The quotation opened with this sentence: 'The problem confronting us now is how to allow the average American to feel moral even when he is flirting, even when he is spending money, even when he is buying a second or third car.' It is not clear where Baudrillard found the quotation. He gave *The Strategy of Desire* as the source, which was incorrect, though the thoughts embodied in the quotation were certainly apparent in that book.

15 Levine, 'Search and Find: Subliminal Advertising Theoretician Wilson Bryan Key Survives Ridicule,' 134.

16 Respectively, *Subliminal Seduction: Ad Media's Manipulation of a Not-So-Innocent America* (1973); *Media Sexploitation* (1976); *Clam-Plate Orgy* (1980), later updated as *Subliminal Adventures in Erotic Art* (1992); and *The Age of Manipulation: The Con in Confidence, the Sin in Sincere* (1991).

17 In fact the appropriate word might better be 'remade,' because there had been an earlier scare over subliminal advertising in the late 1950s when James Vicary, a marketing expert, reported how he had used hidden commands to encourage movie goers to eat popcorn and drink Coca-Cola. The claim was never substantiated, and later Vicary admitted it was something of a hoax. See Pratkanis, 'The Cargo-Cult Science of Subliminal Persuasion.'

18 Cited in an Associated Press report, 13 September 2000, entitled 'Advertising Industry Sees Hidden-Message Ads as Fiction.' The report was available online from CNN in January 2002.

19 The 1983 report is discussed in Pratkanis, 'The Cargo-Cult Science of Subliminal Persuasion,' and Rogers and Smith, 'Public Perceptions of Subliminal Advertising.' The second source noted a similar finding in a 1985 survey and reported its own study, which showed that nearly 75 per cent of respondents were familiar with the concept after it was explained to them.

20 Don Schultz, a professor of advertising at the Medill School of Journalism at Northwestern University. Cited in Levine, 'Search and Find.'

21 Key, *Subliminal Seduction: Ad Media's Manipulation of a Not-So-Innocent America*. The page references in the text of this section are to that edition of the book.

22 That introduction was strange, however. McLuhan took the opportunity to express his views of the moment about advertising, T.S. Eliot, and Sigmund Freud, even mentioning Michel Foucault, as much as to discuss the book itself. Indeed one could read McLuhan's comments – for example 'the world of the subliminal is greatly reduced' (vii) – as expressing a certain doubt about the validity of Key's conclusions. In a letter to D. Carlton Williams of 8 July 1974, however, McLuhan extolled the virtues of Key's research and the courage of his convictions, in the face of hostility from the

advertising and media industries. See Molinaro, McLuhan, and Toye, eds, *Letters of Marshall McLuhan*, 501–2.

23 Key, *Media Sexploitation*, 10.

24 See Freud's essay 'Repression.' The editor notes that elsewhere Freud had claimed that, 'the theory of repression is the corner-stone on which the whole structure of psychoanalysis rests' (141).

25 Rogers and Seiler, 'The Answer Is No.'

26 Cited in Levine, 'Search and Find.'

27 Cited in 'Advertising Industry Sees Hidden-Message Ads as Fiction.' This had been occasioned by yet another scare resulting from the brief appearance of the word 'RATS' in a Republican ad attacking the Democratic hopefuls during the presidential campaign of 2000.

28 See, for example, Moore, 'Subliminal Advertising: What You See Is What You Get'; Gable, Wilkens, Harris, and Feinberg, 'An Evaluation of Subliminally Embedded Sexual Stimuli in Graphics'; and Beatty and Hawkins, 'Subliminal Stimulation: Some New Data and Interpretation.' There was also a very informative outline of experiments and discussions available on the web in January 2002 at www.csic.cornell.edu/201/subliminal, authored by one researcher, Nick Epley, in the Department of Psychology at Cornell University: 'Science or Science Fiction?: Investigating the Possibility (and Plausibility) of Subliminal Persuasion.'

29 These are discussed in Pratkanis, 'The Cargo-Cult Science of Subliminal Persuasion.' Pratkanis was one of the researchers in these studies.

30 Cited in Moore, 'Subliminal Perception: Facts and Fallacies.' The trial involved a suit against Judas Priest and CBS Records over alleged subliminal messages in rock music, which, it was claimed, had programmed the suicide of two teenagers.

31 Cited in Levine, 'Search and Find.'

32 See, for example, Freud's 1915 essay 'The Unconscious,' especially 190–1.

33 Freud, 'On Transformations of Instinct as Exemplified in Anal Eroticism,' 296.

34 There is, of course, now an enormous literature critical of Freud. I have found especially persuasive a brief dissection of Freud's theories written by the philosopher Colin McGinn: 'Freud under Analysis.'

35 Eysenck, ed., *The Blackwell Dictionary of Cognitive Psychology.*

36 See, for example, Carpenter, 'Stalking the Unconscious,' and Bower, 'The Mental Butler Did It.'

37 The speaker was John O'Toole, then president of the American Association of Advertising Agencies. He had written a review in 1989 of one of Key's later works. Cited in Moore, 'Subliminal Perception: Facts and Fallacies.'

38 Cited in Levine, 'Search and Find.'
39 Key, *The Age of Manipulation*, 18. Key also reproduces the ad as figure 8.
40 Mittal, 'Public Assessment of TV Advertising.'
41 There were a few: see Shavitt, Lowrey, and Haefner, 'Public Attitudes toward Advertising.'
42 Friedan, *The Feminine Mystique* (New York: W.W. Norton 2001). The page references in the text are to this Norton edition.
43 The 'creative revolution' refers to the apparent transformation or rebirth of American advertising in the late 1960s as a result of an influx of younger people (women as well as men, many from non-Anglo backgrounds) plus an effort to make advertising more entertaining, more like pop culture, especially suited to the age of television. The most extensive treatment of this revolution is contained in Thomas Frank's *The Conquest of Cool*, although Frank does not deal much with the rise in erotic appeals.
44 She discusses her background in Kilbourne, *Deadly Persuasion*, 17–25. The book was released as a paperback a year later by Simon and Schuster under the title *Can't Buy My Love*.
45 The 1987 version was more talky and preachy than the original. The 2000 version conformed better to the initial style of the documentary. Some of the examples she discussed persisted in the different videos, and Kilbourne was careful to identify those ads that dated from an earlier period.
46 This problem becomes clearer if you compare Kilbourne's selection of ads with that of another critic who published a book at roughly the same time: Williamson, *Decoding Advertisements*, initially published in London in 1978. Williamson offers, for example, two perfume ads, one for Babe and the other for Chanel No. 19, which sought to capture the attention of 'liberated' women by presenting women as aggressive and controlling figures.
47 The charge that 'images of female beauty' were employed as 'a political weapon' against feminism was explored at great length by Naomi Wolfe in *The Beauty Myth*, 10.
48 In 1968 Philip Morris introduced to America a cigarette designed for the new woman. The campaign featured images of attractive and active young women who lived a life of liberation, so it seemed, by comparison with their sisters in times past. The campaign also made notorious the slogan 'You've come a long way, baby.'
49 Kilbourne did actually use the term 'subliminal.' She was particularly taken with an advertisement for a Minolta camera in which a girl sat outside on a 'seat' made by the branching of a tree trunk – it looked as though she was emerging from a vagina, so it became an image that evoked childbirth. Kil-

bourne saw this as a fine example of subliminal advertising: the picture would register on the unconscious, where it would suggest to men how they too could be creative – by taking a picture.

50 Kilbourne also repeated the charge in *Deadly Persuasion*. 'Sex in advertising is pornographic because it dehumanizes and objectifies people, especially women, and because it fetishizes products, imbues them with an erotic charge – which dooms us to disappointment since products never can fulfill our sexual desires or meet our emotional needs. The poses and postures of advertising are often borrowed from pornography, as are many of the themes, such as bondage, sadomasochism, and the sexual exploitation of children' (271). The 1987 version was slightly less explicit, arguing that, 'Sex in advertising is pornographic in lots of ways ...' and referring to 'the culture's pornographic attitude toward sex ...' apparently 'both created by and reflected in the advertising.'

51 This does not mean that Kilbourne was anti-sex; rather, she opposed how eroticism was practised by advertisers. She tried to make this clear in the 1987 version of the documentary.

52 A survey of *Ms.* in the 1970s found occasional anti-fashion pieces, such as Germaine Greer's 'Down with Panties' (July 1972), Maria Josephy Schoolman's 'T-shirts for Tea' (February 1973), or Judith Thurman's 'How to Get Dressed and Still Be You!' (April 1979). See also the chapter on fashion in Faludi, *Backlash*, 169–99.

53 Davis, *Fashion, Culture, and Identity*, 81–99.

54 Hollander, *Feeding the Eye*, 147.

55 See, for example, the anthology of articles by Debbie Stoller, *The Bust Guide to the New Girl Order*, or the argument that women should reclaim fashion and beauty rituals in Naomi Wolfe, *Promiscuities*. One popular author, not an obvious feminist, concluded that in fact consumers now had the power in the fashion business: Agins, *The End of Fashion*.

56 In 2002 the address was www.jeankilbourne.com.

5 The Erotics of Power

1 Paglia, 'Madonna II: Venus of the Radio Waves,' 12–13. The essay was first published in *The Independent Sunday Review*, London, 21 July 1991.

2 The claim is derived from Jean Baudrillard's essay 'The Precession of Simulacra.' It was not only the mass media that produced simulacra – Baudrillard wrote about, for example, Disneyland and Watergate in this article. But the media played a crucial role in the whole process of hyperreality: see, for example, 'Absolute Advertising, Ground-Zero Advertising,' ibid., 87–94.

See also chapter 2 'Baudrillard and TV Ads: The Language of the Economy,' in Poster, *The Mode of Information*, 43–68.

3 Freud, *New Introductory Lectures on Psychoanalysis*, 137–8.

4 Edward Shorter has noted how recent is the history of S/M and how it, and its relative, fetish, have flourished in the twentieth century. See Shorter, *Written in the Flesh*, 200–36.

5 This is derived from an interview Foucault gave in Toronto in 1982 for a gay publication, *The Advocate*: 'Sex, Power and the Politics of Identity.' Carolyn Dean has talked of 'a sadomasochistic logic of desire in Foucault's work' that conditioned his views on power and sexuality. See her fascinating article 'The Productive Hypothesis,' 276.

6 The citation was available at People.com (people.aol.com/people/special/0,11859, 184308,00.html) in April 2002.

7 There is a particularly fine discussion of one genre of action heroes in James William Gibson, *Warrior Dreams*. Also on the American scene, see Stephen Prince, *Visions of Empire: Political Imagery in Contemporary American Film*; Jeffords, *Hard Bodies: Hollywood Masculinity in the Reagan Era*; Engelhardt, *The End of Victory Culture: Cold War America and the Disillusioning of a Generation*; King, *Heroes in Hard Times: Cop Action Movies in the U.S.*; and Hall, 'A Soldier's Body: GI Joe, Hasbro's Great American Hero, and the Symptoms of Empire.'

8 But not unique: there were other examples of erotic thrillers featuring sexy action heroes. Witness, for example, the Bride in *Kill Bill*, volume 1 (2003) and volume 2 (2004), played by Uma Thurman.

9 Though other writers, including Kingsley Amis, would write Bond novels later.

10 *New Statesman*, 5 April 1958, 430. Cited in Alexis Albion, 'Wanting to Be James Bond,' 215, n7.

11 This quotation from one of Fleming's essays, 'How to Write a Thriller,' is cited in Bennett and Woollacott, *Bond and Beyond*, 88.

12 This claim is made by Michael Denning in 'Licensed to Look: James Bond and the Heroism of Consumption,' 212.

13 On the connection between Fleming and Kennedy, see Skip Willman, 'The Kennedys, Fleming, and Cuba.'

14 Bennett and Woollacott, *Bond and Beyond*, 12.

15 Cited in an announcement about the re-release online at www.ianfleming.org, one of the major sites devoted to the Bond cult, in May 2002.

16 Chapman, *Licence to Thrill*, 14.

17 Bennett and Woollacott, *Bond and Beyond*, 16.

18 Albion, 'Wanting to Be James Bond,' 215, n3, and Chapman, *Licence to Thrill*, 112.

19 On the imitations, see Britton, *Beyond Bond*, 106–22.

20 For a lengthy discussion of the linkages among the books, the films, and domestic and international politics, see Black, *The Politics of James Bond*.

21 Connery had been replaced by George Lazenby in *On Her Majesty's Secret Service* (1969), but Lazenby proved hopelessly wooden in the role of Bond. Moore held the role for seven movies during the 1970s and 1980s, so far the record for one actor. Chapman has claimed that Moore's Bond was 'the English gentleman hero,' which proved less popular in America than Connery's Bond. See Chapman, 'Bond and Britishness,' 139.

22 Business data from the Internet Movie Database (us.imdb.com). In fact *Live and Let Die*, a much cheaper film to make, budgeted at $7 million, brought an even higher return on investment, since it earned around $160 million worldwide.

23 The film had an estimated budget of $40 million, according to imdb.com. That site estimated the American take at $35 million and the worldwide box office at $156 million.

24 Production remained in the hands of the Broccoli family (which had bought out Saltzman in the mid-1970s).

25 Garbage: *The World Is Not Enough*. Madonna: *Die Another Day*. Duran Duran had produced the theme song for *A View to a Kill*, and Paul and Lynda McCartney had sung the theme song for *Live and Let Die*. So, in fact, the choice of significant pop singers and/or groups was a feature of the Bond franchise.

26 Cited in *Newsweek*, 22 November 1999.

27 Variously, Chapman, *Licence to Thrill*, 251; *Newsweek*, 22 November 1999; and *New Marketing*, 28 March 1996.

28 The figures from Chapman, *Licence to Thrill*, 260; *Business Wire*, 7 May 1998; *Video Store*, 30 April – 6 May 2000; Chronicle Publishing Co., 5 December 1997; and imdb.com.

29 On an ironic note, Diesel starred as a secret agent in *xXx* (2002), a movie in which a clearly outclassed Bond character was killed off very quickly.

30 Cited in 'DAD DVD Sales Surpass Expectations.'

31 In 2004 MGM, and so Bond, was purchased by Sony.

32 *Secret Agent* (1984) and *Ice* (1987) won awards in the annual Cannes festival of cinema and television commercials.

33 Albany *Times Union*, 22 December 1997.

34 Grover, 'MGM Can Bank on Bonds.' I was, however, unable to verify that enormous figure at another source.

35 Jaffe, 'James Bond, Meta-Brand,' 96.

36 *Marketing* (London), 4 April 2002.

37 Bennett and Woollacott, *Bond and Beyond*, 213. This source notes statistics from Britain's IBA and America's Home Box Office, though without a date, and cites another source as the origin of the report. More surprising is the argument of Jaime Hovey, 'Lesbian Bondage, or Why Dykes Like 007,' where it is suggested that the Connery films had considerable appeal to lesbian viewers.

38 Bennett and Woollacott, *Bond and Beyond*, 246.

39 Reported in the *Washington Post*, 21 December 1998.

40 Listed amongst those fans were academics. Fleming's books and the Bond movies had always attracted some interest in the universities. But near the turn of the century they became something of a hot property in cultural studies. Two monographs were published, Chapman's *Licence to Thrill* and Black's *The Politics of James Bond*. Other scholars wrote chapters on Bond in broader surveys of the spy genre, such as Britton's *Beyond Bond* and Toby Miller's *Spyscreen*. In the latter book Miller published a version of his hypothesis about 'James Bond's penis' (a bit strange, perhaps, since that penis was always missing, never on display) a theory that captured the fancy of some, though likely not all, of the participants at a conference on 'The Cultural Politics of Ian Fleming and 007' held at Indiana University in 2003. That conference, some of whose papers were published later in Comentale, Watt, and Willman, eds, *Ian Fleming and James Bond*, apparently split between scholars who focused on history (like Chapman and Black, both British professors) and scholars who were consumed by theory, subjecting Fleming and/or Bond to various forms of textual analysis. There was reference to the heated disputes over approach and methodology in the introduction to the collection of papers, xiv–xvii, and in a paper Black gave entitled 'What We Can Learn from James Bond,' published by the History News Network (available online at hnn.us in October 2005).

41 I use the adjective 'masculine' to denote the fact that this is a result of social construction rather than biology.

42 McInerney, 'How Bond Saved America – and Me,' 13, 32.

43 See Chapman, *Licence to Thrill*, 36, 2.

44 Cited in Brosnan, *James Bond in the Cinema*, 15. Cubby Broccoli, the other producer, referred to the sex as 'lightweight.' 'We knew how far we could go, should go, with Bond in this area, and would never exceed it.' Broccoli censored the underwater scene that had captured McInerney's attention: in the initial sequence Auger's bikini floated to the surface 'in a burst of air bubbles from the lovers down below,' but that seemed just 'too suggestive' and was cut out of the film. Cubby Broccoli with Donald Zec, *When the Snow Melts*, 203.

45 'An idea of the film is widely circulated and promoted, an idea which can be called the "narrative image" of the film, the cinema industry's anticipatory reply to the question "What is the film like?" If anything is bought at the box office that is already known by the audience, it is this narrative image. Payment for a ticket is not an endorsement of a film ... It is an endorsement of the narrative image of the film, together with the general sense of the cinematic experience.' Ellis, *Visible Fictions*, 30.

46 The posters and the trailers were available on the web from a variety of different sites, in itself a sign of the significance of the Bond phenomenon. The chief source of trailers was www.jamesbond.com. There was also a collection of German trailers, unfortunately not complete, at a German site that shortly thereafter disappeared. Trailers and sometimes posters were also included in the DVD collection of Bond movies published after the appearance of *Die Another Day.*

47 Cited in Rebello, 'Selling Bond.'

48 *The Guardian* (Manchester), 30 March 2002.

49 By the 1990s there were both trailers and teasers. The teasers were shortened trailers, often completed before the whole of the movie was filmed, appearing as much as six months before the release of the movie, and sometimes run on television as a commercial.

50 Except in the movie *The World Is Not Enough*, where the walls of the church were, briefly, breached by the forces of chaos.

51 Wolfe made a distinction. 'In the new pornography, the theme is not sex. The new pornography depicts practitioners acting out another murkier drive: people staving teeth in, ripping guts open, blowing brains out and getting even with all those bastards.' Cited in Petersen, *The Century of Sex*, 310. Petersen's discussion of his sources suggests that the quotation came from a 1967 article by Tom Wolfe in *Esquire*.

52 Taking a different tack on this attribute of the Bond character, Patrick O'Donnell has referred to him as a 'cyborg-aristocrat.' See his article 'James Bond, Cyborg-Aristocrat.'

53 Michael Denning has argued that the imperative of looking, most especially the gazes of the tourist and the voyeur, was embedded in the Fleming novels. See 'Licensed to Look,' 219–27.

54 For the record, this cliché was not present in all the trailers and teasers made for *Licence to Kill, GoldenEye*, and *The World Is Not Enough*.

55 All four of Brosnan's Bonds secured a PG13 rating in the United States, which ensured that they were deemed suitable for the eyes of children.

56 Rees-Mogg in *The Times* (London), 29 December 1997, cited in Black, *The Politics of James Bond*, 201.

57 See, for instance, the lengthy article in *The Guardian*, 17 April 2005, by Jason Solomons, entitled 'My Kingdom for a Bond.'

58 Cited in an 'MTV Biorhythm' on Madonna, available at the Museum of Television and Radio, in New York. The program was produced by MTV in 1998.

59 Cited in the 'Marilyn Monroe Kodak Showcase 1999,' available at the Museum of Television and Radio.

60 Madonna made reference to the distinction between herself and past sex symbols. 'I take the preconceived notion of what a sex goddess is and throw it back in your face and say I can be a sex symbol, but I don't have to be a victim.' Cited in Pamela Robertson, 'Guilty Pleasures,' a 1996 essay from her book of the same title, republished in Benson and Metz, eds, *The Madonna Companion*, 278.

61 Steve Allen wrote a fine, though very critical, contemporary discussion of Madonna and vulgarity: 'Madonna,' which first appeared in the *Journal of Popular Culture*, vol. 27 no. 1 (Summer 1993), reprinted in Benson and Metz, *The Madonna Companion*, 144–57.

62 See Robertson, *Guilty Pleasures*.

63 'West's acts transgressed numerous boundaries of respectability: sexually aggressive in the manner of prostitutes, informed by black musical and dance styles, redolent of the working-class concert saloons she knew from her own childhood.' Turner, 'Sodom on the Hudson, 70.

64 Fiske, *Television Culture*, 250. Fiske was, however, a British import who had made his name initially in the 1970s in association with the originating British school of cultural studies.

65 'The main force of MTV as a cable channel is consumption on a whole variety of levels, ranging from the literal (i.e. selling the sponsor's goods, the rock stars' records, and MTV itself) to the psychological (i.e. selling the image, the "look," the style). MTV is more obviously than other programs one nearly continuous advertisement, the flow being merely broken down into different *kinds* of ads.' E. Anne Kaplan, *Rocking around the Clock*, 143

66 Ibid., 1–2.

67 *Les Brown's Encyclopedia of Television*, 368.

68 Burns, 'Music Television.'

69 The event was discussed, briefly, in Andrew Morton, *Madonna*, 165.

70 The description is from E. Anne Kaplan, *Rocking around the Clock*, 126.

71 Kathleen Hanna in *Bust* (Winter/January 2000), 53.

72 For a discussion of the fashion craze, see Rourke, 'A Mad, Mad World of "Madonnas"' (1985), reprinted in Benson and Metz, *The Madonna Companion*.

73 The fifth edition of *The Billboard Book of Top 40 Hits*, 288–9, listed between 1983 and 1991 twenty-four hits, seven of these 'gold' or million sellers and three 'platinum' or 2-million sellers (*Like a Prayer*, *Vogue*, and *Justify My Love*).

74 Taraborrelli, *Madonna*, 129.

75 Fiske, *Television Culture*, 321.

76 Andrew Morton, *Madonna*, 218.

77 Guilbert, *Madonna as Postmodern Myth*, 29.

78 See Faith, *Madonna, Bawdy and Soul*, 55. The first quotation is apparently from the magazine, the second is the author's paraphrase.

79 The ranking comes from *Bowker's Annual/Publisher's Weekly*, available online at http://www.engl.virginia.edu/ courses/bestsellers/best90.cgi in July 2002. The estimated earning comes from Faith, *Madonna*, 114.

80 There is a fine critique of the rise of Madonna scholars by Daniel Harris, called 'Make My Rainy Day,' which first appeared in *The Nation* (8 June 1992), reprinted in Benson and Metz, *The Madonna Companion*. The terms 'mass culture' and 'popular culture' both cover the same kinds of symbolic material – books, magazines, comics, exhibitions, newspapers, songs, movies, television programs, and the like. But mass culture is what 'they' make: it focuses attention on the goods and meanings the producers manufacture. Popular culture is what 'we' do with all of these symbolic goods: it focuses attention on what people make popular as well as what the consumers determine are the meanings of entertainment, news, or advertising.

81 The aforementioned John Fiske was one of the earliest Madonna scholars. He discussed her appeal during the mid-1980s not only in *Television Culture* but also in a chapter of *Reading the Popular*, a primer on how to do cultural studies, and in an article entitled 'British Cultural Studies and Television.' Cathy Schwichtenberg edited a collection of severely academic pieces entitled *The Madonna Connection: Representational Politics, Subcultural Identities, and Cultural Theory*, which thoroughly explored Madonna's music videos and boldly played with all kinds of theory. Fran Lloyd edited another collection of essays, these British rather than American, and less overtly theoretical, because they were supposed to introduce students to cultural studies: *Deconstructing Madonna*. A third compilation, much of this written by lesbian or gay specialists, was devoted to the study of Madonna's *Sex*: Frank and Smith, eds, *Madonnarama*. Then, also in 1993, there appeared a collection of dreams about Madonna gathered by a folklorist: Turner, ed., *I Dream of Madonna*. Later came Karlene Faith's *Madonna, Bawdy and Soul*, a very sympathetic account that endeavoured to sum up Madonna's cultural import. Equally sympathetic was Georges-Claude Guilbert's *Madonna as*

Postmodern Myth. Benson and Metz's *Madonna Companion* (1999) collected a range of pieces by journalists and academics on the performer's history. Madonna, apparently, was quite taken with all this academic attention, if only because it was just a further sign of her fame and significance.

82 There is an interesting discussion of the problems with this attitude in Frank and Smith's introduction to *Madonnarama*, especially 12–17.

83 Paglia, 'Madonna I: Animality and Artifice,' 5. The article had originally appeared in the *New York Times*, 14 December 1990.

84 Horkheimer and Adorno, *Dialectic of Enlightenment*, 120–67.

85 Jane D. Brown and Schulze, 'The Effects of Race, Gender, and Fandom on Audience Interpretations of Madonna's Music Videos.' An extended version of this article was published in the *Journal of Communication*, 40, no. 2 (1990). See also Schulze, White, and Brown, '"A Sacred Monster in Her Prime": Audience Construction of Madonna as Low-Other.'

86 Cited in Guilbert, *Madonna as Postmodern Myth*, 50.

87 '"People have always had this obsession with me, about my reinvention of myself," Madonna said. "I just feel like I'm shedding layers. I'm slowly revealing who I am."' Cited in Powers, 'New Tune for the Material Girl,' 81.

88 Cited in Mandziuk, 'Feminist Politics and Postmodern Seductions,' 167.

89 Andrew Morton, *Madonna*, 51.

90 Paglia, 'Madonna I,' 5.

91 *Rolling Stone:* 'If it isn't a fix then God clearly likes bad Catholic girls.' Cited in Andrew Morton, *Madonna*, 181.

92 Frank and Smith, 'Introduction: How to Use Your New Madonna,' in Frank and Smith, *Madonnarama*, 7–9.

93 From 1991. Cited in Pribram, 'Seduction, Control, and the Search for Authenticity,' 204.

94 Lloyd, 'The Changing Faces of Madonna,' 43.

95 Or perhaps she was implementing the idea of 'punctum' made famous in the work of Roland Barthes on photography. See Watts, 'Electrifying Fragments: Madonna and Postmodern Performance,' first published in the *New Theater Quarterly*, 12, no. 46 (May 1996), reprinted in Benson and Metz, *The Madonna Companion*.

96 On the cover of *US* magazine, 13 June 1991. Cited in David Tetzlaff, 'Metatextual Girl: → patriarchy → postmodernism → power → money→ Madonna,' in Schwichtenberg, ed., *The Madonna Connection*, 242.

97 The phrase appears in Kay Turner's introduction to *I Dream of Madonna*, 19.

98 Cited in Susan Bordo, '"Material Girl,"' 283, using material from John Snow, 'Madonna Rocks the Land,' *Time*, 27 May 1985, 77.

99 Cited in Fiske, *Reading the Popular*, 98. The woman was responding to a poster of Madonna.

100 Cited in Beverley Skeggs, 'A Good Time for Women Only,' 73. The rest of the quotation, though, explained how her brother swiftly used mockery to destroy such self-esteem.

101 Given the circumstances, the pun was presumably unintended. The young man was fifteen years old at the time. See Fiske, 'British Cultural Studies,' 306–7.

102 Paglia, 'Madonna II,' 6. This essay was initially published in *The Independent Sunday Review*, London, 21 July 1991.

103 Susan Bordo, by contrast, has described the streamlining of Madonna's body, and the videos that followed, as evidence of a betrayal of her earlier rebellion and a submission to what she calls 'the objectifying gaze.' See the finished version of her article ' "Material Girl," ' in Bordo, *Unbearable Weight*, 245–75.

104 He had done this most obviously in *Discipline and Punish: The Birth of the Prison*.

105 Lloyd, 'The Changing Faces of Madonna,' 43.

106 E. Anne Kaplan has a lengthy and very interesting discussion of who looks and how in this video: *Rocking around the Clock*, 119–27. Her book is more oriented to cinema theory and its roots in psychoanalysis than to Foucault's work, however.

107 Which was why 'I don't need to have one between my legs.' Madonna, *Sex*, np.

108 This comment reflects the arguments of Stallybrass and White in *The Politics and Poetics of Transgression*, especially 4–5.

109 Fiske, 'British Cultural Studies,' 309.

110 All of these quotations from Madonna haters appear in Schulze, White, and Brown, ' "A Sacred Monster in Her Prime," ' 26, 22.

111 These incidents were mentioned in the documentary *Truth or Dare*.

112 The program was available at the Museum of Television and Radio in New York city.

113 The quotation is cited in Melanie Morton, 'Don't Go for Second Sex, Baby!,' 220.

114 The quotation from *Newsweek* is cited in Metzstein, 'SEX: Signed, Sealed, Delivered ...' 94, and the quotation from the BBC program is cited in Skeggs, 'A Good Time for Women Only,' 59.

115 'Madonna was given the green light from Warner as long as she refrained from including pictures with penetration, explicit genitalia, sex with animals, and sex with children.' Bright, 'A Pornographic Girl,' 84.

116 Faith, in *Madonna, Bawdy and Soul*, 127–31 provides an interesting run-down of the views anonymous individuals expressed regarding Madonna in October 1992. They responded to a hotline set up by the Montreal *Gazette* to chart the public response to *Sex*. Of 200 people who called during the week, 65 per cent reacted favourably. The responses were similar to the comments that had always been made about Madonna, by both fans and haters.

117 Andrew Morton, *Madonna*, 245.

118 Reported in the *Toronto Star*, 21 September 1994, F7.

119 Cited in Faith, *Madonna, Bawdy and Soul*, 138.

6 A Theatre of the Libido

1 The channel was listed as Assmannshausen RTL in the Rhineland; the date was 30 July 1994.

2 No wonder a later review of this kind of dessert was titled 'Better than sex? Well ...' Posted at www.ciao.co.uk in June 2005. Long ago, however, ice cream had been identified by market researchers as a pleasure food. See the discussion of a psychoanalytic investigation of ice cream conducted around 1950 at the Tavistock Institute of Human Relations in London: Miller and Rose, 'Mobilizing the Consumer: Assembling the Subject of Consumption,' 7–11.

3 The surveys of London and Madrid occurred in December 1993, those of Cologne, Paris, and Stockholm in July 1994.

4 A survey of commercials in the United Kingdom and the Czech Republic from the summer of 1998 found that roughly one-quarter in each country used some form of sex appeal: Koudelova and Whitelock, 'A Cross-Cultural Analysis of Television Advertising in the UK and the Czech Republic,' 297.

5 Cited in Lambiase and Reichert, 'Future Questions and Challenges: Advertising Research in the Midst of Sex Noise,' 273.

6 *Advertising Age*, 18 June 2002. The ads showed beautiful people caught up in a bacchanal: the men and women were cleverly placed so that their body language suggested anal and oral sex, groping, spanking, peeing, and so on.

7 Shorter, *Written in the Flesh*, especially 167–236.

8 McNair, *Striptease Culture*, especially 35–108. See also McNair's earlier work, *Mediated Sex*.

9 The study is based on a database of 1,000 commercials, selected from many thousands of ads, originating around the world, though mostly western

Europe and America, and over the course of the last fifty years, though concentrated in the 1990s. These have been supplemented by roughly 200
other, less explicit commercials. The examples have been drawn from a
wide range of sources. Only the major sources are listed here. (1) Tapes of
award-winning ads: the Cannes festivals, a worldwide competition, 1972–
95; the International Broadcasting or IBA Awards (also called the Hollywood Awards), 1976–94; AdFilms, a Canadian firm that supplied a compilation of award winners, especially British ads, 1996–8; and the Bessies, an
English-Canadian festival, in the 1990s. (2) Tapes of interesting commercials, available for purchase, notably the International Showcase, 1986–
2000. (3) Research tapes: collections I assembled from various trips to
Europe and work at the National Museum of Photography, Film and Television in Bradford, England (1993). (4) Internet sites that allow users to
download the commercials collected there: the most significant of these is
Jean-Marie Boursicot's film library at www.adeater.com, which has an
enormous range of commercials from everywhere and throughout the
twentieth century (in June 2005 it claimed 700,000 films), though it special-
izes in European ads; the official site of the Clios, the most famous award
competition in the United States, at www.clioawards.com, which once
upon a time allowed the free download of award winners from the mid-
1990s; AdCritic, at www.adcritic.com, which was especially valuable for
American commercials in the late 1990s (the site became subscriber-only
after it was taken over by the magazine *Advertising Age*); the Commercial
Archive, also useful for American ads in the 1990s, which has been folded
into a new site called Adland at ad-rag.com; and www. advertisementave
.com, which contained a sample of ads made in the United States since
2000. Where necessary these sources are referenced directly in the text.
10 Cited in McCann-Erickson World Group, Bob Coen's Insiders' Report
2000–2001. Available on the McCann-Erickson website (www.mccann.com)
in April 2003. That represented close to one-quarter of all the ad expenditures of $247 billion.
11 In Baudrillard's seminal article 'The Precession of Simulacra,' 2 – first published in French in 1981. Recognizing the force of simulation meant accepting 'the knowledge that truth, reference, objective cause have ceased to
exist' (3). Ironically, later in the article (29), Baudrillard also declared the
end of the era of persuasion.
12 See also Poster, *The Mode of Information*, 43–68, for an extended discussion of
Baudrillard and TV ads.
13 The worldwide history of sex in advertising, never mind erotic commercials, has not yet been written. The American history of erotic ads, however,

has been done. Tom Reichert's *The Erotic History of Advertising* surveys the history of sex in advertising in the United States, dealing mostly with print campaigns. There is also a recent article, again on the American experience, by Juliann Sivulka, 'Historical and Psychological Perspectives of the Erotic Appeal in Advertising.' Much of this summarizes material from Sivulka's book *Soap, Sex, and Cigarettes.*

14 Each of these was available online in 1999 from the Boursicot Film Library. One woman exercised in a gymnasium (which allowed the camera to focus on her breasts), another frolicked in a swimming pool (and here the camera highlighted her bottom), and yet a third, an elegant woman, posed in a boudoir (where the camera admired her slim lines and displayed her nipples).

15 The First Clios were sixty-eight ads, mostly of the 1950s, judged excellent by a group of admakers at the end of the decade. They were available as the Celia Nachatovitz Diamant Memorial Library of Classic Television Commercials from the Television Center of Brooklyn College, City University of New York. The commercials were also written up in Diamant, *Television's Classic Commercials: The Golden Years 1948–58.*

16 The answer was that only her hairdresser knew for sure. Shirley Polykoff, a copywriter for Foote Cone and Belding, designed the slogan to suggest that not even other women could tell if she used hair colouring. At first the agency, at least the male managers, thought the slogan too provocative. But it worked: Clairol's sales apparently increased 400 per cent in six years. The campaign was more famous for its magazine ads than for its television commercials. Sivulka, *Soap, Sex, and Cigarettes,* 268.

17 I have discussed some of these aspects at much greater length in *The New Icons?: The Art of Television Advertising,* 59–87.

18 See Korinek, *Roughing It in the Suburbs: Reading Chatelaine Magazine in the Fifties and Sixties,* 152–7, 161, 162.

19 The ad was entitled *Flasher* and sponsored by West cigarettes (IS 1991).

20 Entitled *Sauna,* the ad was a Cannes winner in 1987. It did provide a brief shot of a man's testicles, though usually these were covered by hands.

21 A Cannes winner in 1988, entitled *Mother and Daughter,* made for Phebo, a body lotion. The ad cut between shots of a naked mother stroking her body with the lotion and shots of her naked daughter mimicking the mother's actions.

22 The Bessies were English Canada's awards competition, and I have surveyed these from 1973 onwards. There were some exceptions, of course. And rumour had it that French-Canadian admakers were much less restrained, although I did not locate a comparable collection of commercials that enabled me to evaluate the boast.

23 Cited in Lin, 'Uses of Sex Appeals in Prime-Time Commercials.' The samples were drawn from the big three networks, CBS, ABC, and NBC.

24 Cited in Reichert, Lambiase, Morgan, Carstaphen, and Zavoina, 'Cheesecake and Beefcake.' The researchers had looked at six consumer magazines, including *Time, Cosmopolitan*, and *Playboy*.

25 Cited in a story on the making of these commercials on the Schick website (in May 1996 at www.schick .com/shavingwoman.html).

26 For instance, an ad called *Remember* (U.S.A. 1972) that touted the virtues of Southwest Airlines: the spot featured a sexy spokeswoman, representing a stewardess, dressed in a tight-fitting orange tunic, hot pants (very short), and boots, who recounted the virtues of the airline.

27 The history of the commercial may be a bit more murky, however. It is not clear exactly what country, never mind what agency, entered the commercial. The ad was also available in the Boursicot Film Library, where it was listed as made in 1970 (two years before the award) and labelled 'International,' which in this context likely means European.

28 The ad won a Cannes award. I am indebted to a student of mine, Dorothy Noronha, for the identification of the song.

29 The ad had such an impact that it was remembered by young people in a survey in Edinburgh done in 1991. See O'Donohoe and Tynan, 'Beyond the Semiotic Strait-Jacket: Everyday Experiences of Advertising Involvement,' 240.

30 Cited in Cook, *The Discourse of Advertising*, 191.

31 See Simpson, 'Advertising Art or Obscenity? The Calvin Klein Jeans Ads.'

32 See Sivulka, 'Historical and Psychological Perspectives ...' 60.

33 See Reichert, *The Erotic History of Advertising*, 178.

34 The story of Dim's publicity was available online in a company history at the Musée de la Publicité website (www.ucad.fr) in February 2003.

35 Discussed in Gunter, *Media Sex*, 208–9. Apparently this was the signature of the Neutralia campaign: I witnessed a French ad, also in 1994, in which there were brief displays of a woman's bare breast and nipple.

36 That happy bunch refers to the actors featured in the 'Smiling' campaign for Labatt's Blue, a brand of beer that, in the early 1980s, was the country's favourite.

37 So, for example, a report of 30 April 1998 on *Mr. Showbiz News*, an online site, listed these estimates in U.S. dollars: Elle Macpherson at $40.3 million; Cindy Crawford, $37.7 million; Claudia Schiffer, $36 million; Linda Evangelista, $28.9 million; Naomi Campbell, $28.9 million; and Christy Turlington, $23.7 million.

38 From a documentary called *Queens of the Catwalk: Supermodels Uncovered*,

aired on the Learning Channel; the clip was available online at djuna.ninko
.com/christy/ multimedia in August 2005.

39 *Time*, 16 September 1991, 46.

40 Cited in the *Houston Chronicle*, 8 July 1993.

41 The reference here is to the vocabulary of Actor-Network Theory. Indeed
    the supermodels were an example of what are called 'immutable mobiles,'
    entities as signs transformed by a network that can be located in different
    settings to articulate particular sets of meanings. See the description of
    inscription in Latour, *Pandora's Hope*, 306–7.

42 Harris, 'Some Reflections on the Facial Expressions of Fashion Models,'
    138.

43 Collin Brooke argues that it made Crawford 'a household name.' See
    Brooke, 'Sex(haustion) Sells,' 141.

44 *Time*, among other news outlets, signalled the decline of the supermodels in
    a report by Joel Stein, 'The Fall of the Supermodel.' See also 'Could Super-
    models Be Losing Their Sizzle?,' *Salt Lake Tribune*, 26 November 1995,
    online edition, and 'Bye-bye Supermodels,' *Globe and Mail* (Toronto), 8
    October 1998, online edition.

45 ' "The models were overtaking the clothes, and the designers realized
    nobody was focusing on the collection," said Anny Kazanjian, director of
    public relations for Chanel Canada.' Cited in Delap, 'Out with the Super, in
    with the New.'

46 *Time*, 11 December 2000, 79.

47 The claim was made that sex in advertising no longer worked as well, espe-
    cially in the post-9/11 world, as it had before. See, for example, 'Racy Sales
    Pitch Losing Appeal,' and 'The Thrill Is Gone – or Is It?'

48 No advertising could show a woman veiled, or unveiling, in Saudi Arabia
    in the early 1990s. A 1986 law forbade the 'indecent representation of
    women' in India. In Malaysia a government-mandated code prohibited ads
    that featured women as 'the principal object,' unless the product was for
    women. For a brief overview of ad regulations at that time, see Boddewyn,
    'Controlling Sex and Decency in Advertising around the World'

49 There were exceptions, of course. In 1992 Hong Kong's Committee on Edu-
    cation and Publicity on AIDS sponsored a particularly sensual ad that was
    meant to reach the most promiscuous of residents (cited in *Marketing*, 1
    June 1992, 30). It was possible to go farther when the cause was just.

50 See Reichert, *The Erotic History of Advertising*, 188–97, for a discussion of the
    rapid rise of Victoria's Secret. There is also an extended discussion of Victo-
    ria's Secret in Juffer, *At Home with Pornography*, 145–66.

51 The study asked subjects (American, Danish, and Turkish) to assemble col-

lages of images that expressed their views of desire. Belk, Ger, and Askegaard, 'The Fire of Desire.'

52 'Calvin's World,' 63 and James Kaplan, 'The Triumph of Calvinism,' 50.

53 Steele, *Fifty Years of Fashion*, 126. Steele rightly suggests that these were
much more revolutionary than the Brooke Shields ads.

54 This image appeared in *Vogue*, June 1984, though it was used in a wide
variety of settings.

55 Cited in Steitmatter, *Sex Sells!*, 120.

56 James Martin, 'Calvinism,'23.

57 See Tucker, 'The Framing of Calvin Klein: A Frame Analysis of Media
Discourse about the August 1995 Calvin Klein Jeans Advertising Campaign.'

58 Kaplan, 'The Triumph of Calvinism,' 47.

59 See note 9 of this chapter.

60 This approach draws upon the methodology of semiotics, particularly the
technique employed by Roland Barthes in his study of the fashion system:
'The semiological project requires the constitution of a corpus reasonably
saturated with all the possible *differences* in clothing signs. On the other
hand, it matters far less that these differences are more or less often
repeated, for it is difference that makes meaning, not repetition. Structurally, a rare feature of Fashion is as important as a common one, a gardenia
as important as a long skirt: the objective here is to *distinguish* units, not to
count them.' Barthes, 'Written Clothing,' 438.

61 The numbers in parentheses refer to the particular example in table 6.1.

62 Such a designation, however, can only be subjective because it is based on a
personal assessment of body language, music and sound, and the sequence
of actions.

63 Of course such symbols appeared in non-erotic advertising as well. The
exaggerated nose of the notorious Joe Camel was widely regarded as a
phallic symbol, even within the industry. See Eckman and Goldberg, *The
Viability of the Marlboro Man among the 18–24 Segment.*

64 For a discussion of the style of lesbian chic in advertising, see Reichert,
'"Lesbian Chic" Imagery in Advertising.' In the print ads he used, Reichert
concluded that '"lesbians" in these ads dress, look, and for the most part
behave as stereotypically heterosexual women' (9), apparently a finding in
other similar surveys.

65 Such an image conformed to the type of male bodies prevalent in male lifestyle magazines during the 1990s. See Patterson and Elliott, 'Negotiating
Masculinities.' 236.

66 The ad nonetheless sparked some controversy because of the suggestion

that a person suffering a disability was likely to use his condition, in this
case blindness, to excuse harassment.

67 Berger, *Ways of Seeing*, 54.

68 From 1992 to 1999, Diesel normally produced at least two ads each year,
and these were available on its website.

69 In one issue at least, the magazine did run a feature called 'Death Becomes
You,' featuring models who played dead people. That issue also included
articles on 'drag queens and skin trade workers.' There was a brief critique
online in June 2005 at www.andelman.com/mrmedia/95/11.6.95.html.

70 The notion that advertising created networks had won increasing favour
among consumer researchers by the 1990s. Hence this comment: 'advertising is a quasi-fictional, culturally constituted system of symbols in which
products are strategically synchronized with scenes, props, people, and
actions.' Mick and Buhl, 'A Meaning-based Model of Advertising Experiences,' 318.

71 Many commercials did employ a story format, but certainly not all. One
content analysis of American commercials aired in 1997 found that roughly
a quarter employed this format. Escalas, 'Advertising Narratives,' 267.

72 These fables are identified by special letter (a, b, to some borrowings from
the Greek alphabet) for easy reference as well as the numbers used in table
6.1, to avoid any confusion when citing the commercials in the text. Note
that most of the original 100 also count as fables of lust.

73 In fact, the year before, Levi's 501s had run a very similar kind of commercial (Boursicot 1991) in which a macho man rides a motorcycle into the brokerage to steal away his girl from such a pedestrian life.

74 This idea of assembling a new partner or a new you appealed to all sorts of
admakers: a woman makes herself over in an Israeli spot for Helena Rubinstein (Cannes 1987); another woman dreams of customizing her man in a
Canadian ad for Lever Brothers Salon Selectives (Bessies 1999); and yet a
third woman proves she is out of the ordinary when, dressed to kill, she
handles the ball like a soccer pro in a Greek commercial for Diana Nylons
(Boursicot 1993).

75 Marx found his analogy in what he called 'the misty realm of religion.
There the products of the human brain appear as autonomous figures
endowed with a life of their own, which enter into relations both with each
other and with the human race. So it is in the world of commodities with
the products of men's hands. I call this the fetishism which attaches itself to
the products of labour as soon as they are produced as commodities ...'
Marx, *Capital*, 1:165.

76 Freud talked about fetishism in a number of different ways over the course

of his long career. But at one point he claimed that 'the fetish is a substitute for the woman's (the mother's) penis that the little boy once believed in and – for reasons familiar to us – does not want to give up.' Freud, 'Fetishism,' 352. A standard definition in psychoanalysis describes the fetish as 'an object which a fetishist endows with sexual significance and in the absence of which he is incapable of sexual excitement.' Rycroft, *A Critical Dictionary of Psychoanalysis*, 57.

77 The many other objects in these fables of lust may also play a part in the action. So, in the Chiemsee ad, the woman attaches the earphones of her portable music player to the head of the hapless professor, blasting his brain with rock, a further sign of his helplessness – as is the discarded pen, a symbol of authority, with which he had been marking papers before her arrival.

78 See Marx, *Capital*, 209, 1054.

79 The reference is to Deleuze and Guattari, *Anti-Oedipus*. See, in particular, 1–8, 24–7, 55, 222–62.

80 Cited in LaTour and Henthorne, 'Nudity and Sexual Appeals,' 91–2. A much earlier article by the two scholars had been the object of the ridicule.

81 So: 'various practitioners and academics have argued that research should address what consumers do with advertising, rather than what advertising does to them.' O'Donohoe, 'Advertising Uses and Gratifications,' 52.

82 Which led to this kind of concluding comment: 'What do consumers do with advertising? The apparent answer, for better or worse, is they negotiate their lives.' Mick and Buhl, 'A Meaning-Based Model of Advertising Experiences,' 336.

83 See O'Donohoe, 'Living with Ambivalence: Attitudes to Advertising in Postmodern Times.'

84 McQuarrie and Mick, 'Visual Rhetoric in Advertising,' 52.

85 Note these two different findings on American attitudes: 'Consumers generally credited only a small proportion of commercials with honesty and enjoyability and characterized much of the advertising as being misleading, boring, irritating, offensive, silly and trivial.' Mittal, 'Public Assessment of TV Advertising,' 35. 'More Americans say that they like rather than dislike advertising overall. They tend to report that they enjoy the advertisements they see, and they tend to find advertising generally informative and useful in guiding their own decision making. Also, although Americans report that they do not generally trust advertising, they tend to feel more confidence in advertising claims when focused on their actual purchase decisions.' Shavitt, Lowrey, and Haefner, 'Public Attitudes toward Advertising,' 7.

86 Haley, Staffaroni, and Fox, 'The Missing Measures of Copy Testing,' 48.

87 In one study of viewing in the United States, it was found that 'viewers are visually oriented to programming 62% of the time and to commercials 33% of the time.' Krugman, Cameron, and White, 'Visual Attention to Programming and Commercials,' 1. In a study of viewing in the Netherlands, program ratings dropped almost 29 per cent during the commercial break, though that was countered by an average of a 7 per cent increase in ratings caused by channel switchers from elsewhere chancing upon the commercial break. Van Meurs, 'Zapp!,' 51.

88 So O'Donohoe and Tynan noted how some of their informants had actually 'turned on the television at a particular (advertised!) time to see the next instalment of the Gold Blend campaign.' 'Beyond the Semiotic Strait-Jacket,' 239. The research was done on a small collection of young adults in Edinburgh, Scotland, in 1991. On the importance of the unexpected, see Ang and Low, 'Exploring the Dimensions of Ad Creativity.'

89 Neil Alperstein, working on the American scene in the 1980s, noted how the verbal content of ads worked its way into ordinary conversation, citing among many other examples the famous 'Where's the beef?' from a Wendy's commercial that, briefly in the mid-1980s, seemed to be everywhere. 'The Verbal Content of TV Advertising and Its Circulation in Everyday Life.'

90 See Ritson and Elliott, 'The Social Uses of Advertising.'

91 For discussions of the literature, see Smith, Haugtvedt, Jadrich, and Anton, 'Understanding Responses to Sex Appeals in Advertising,' and Reichert, Heckler, and Jackson, 'The Effects of Sexual Social Marketing Appeals on Cognitive Processing and Persuasion.'

92 Elliott, Jones, Banfield, and Barlow, 'Overt Sexuality in Advertising,' 189. Right after, however, they cited Foucault rather than Freud, referring to Foucault's description of sexuality as 'an especially dense transfer point for relations of power.'

93 Witness this comment on a survey of college students: 'Subjects reacted more favourably to the sexually-oriented ads, rating them as more entertaining, favourable, interesting, and original, though also rating them as more offensive.' Severn, Belch, and Belch, 'The Effects of Sexual and Non-Sexual Advertising Appeals and Information Level on Cognitive Processing and Communication Effectiveness,' 21. See also Dahl, Frankenburger, and Manchanda, 'Does It Pay to Shock?' The article examined responses to anti-AIDS print ads, one of which featured sexual imagery.

94 So Elliott and colleagues noted how a study confirmed that women found ads with nude women 'less interesting, less appealing and more offensive'

than did men. 'Overt Sexuality in Advertising,' 188. See also LaTour, Pitts, and Snook-Luther, 'Female Nudity, Arousal, and Ad Response;' Aylesworth, Goodstein, and Kalra, 'Effect of Archetypal Embeds on Feelings'; and Amanda B. Bower, 'Highly Attractive Models in Advertising and the Women Who Loathe Them.'

95 Indeed one scholar has claimed that romances function as a kind of softcore pornography for women, though her analysis was not based on any ethnographic or survey findings: Barbara B. Stern, 'Two Pornographies.' Some evidence for this view, however, was contained in one ethnographic project that probed the attitudes of three women towards a small sample of ads: Patti Williams, 'Female Role Portrayals in Print Advertising.'

96 Mittal and Lassar, 'Sexual Liberalism as a Determinant of Consumer Response to Sex in Advertising.' Reichert, '"Lesbian Chic" Imagery in Advertising.' Maciejewski, 'Is the Use of Sexual and Fear Appeals Ethical?'

97 O'Donohoe and Tynan, 'Beyond the Semiotic Strait-Jacket,' 239.

98 'Thus, the message for advertisers is that companionate love is approximately equally effective for young and mature consumers, but sexually explicit ads are more effective for young consumers.' Huang, 'Romantic Love and Sex,' 70. In a slightly different vein, Mittal and Lassar found that gender did not influence the ad evaluations of any of their student informants. 'Sexual Liberalism as a Determinant of Consumer Response to Sex in Advertising,' 124.

99 Elliott et al., 'Overt Sexuality in Advertising,' 201.

100 Belgian males liked erotic ads, Belgian females were less likely to do so, though Poles of both sexes responded more favourably to sex in advertising. See De Pelsmacker and Geuens, 'Reactions to Different Types of Ads in Belgium and Poland.' People in Hong Kong were more exercised by sexist portrayals, while the informants in Singapore were upset by sexual connotations in ads. See Prendergast and Ho, 'A Hong Kong View of Offensive Advertising.'

101 Seventy-two per cent of respondents in one study: Mittal, 'Public Assessment of TV Advertising,' 35.

102 In the mid-1990s an extensive survey of British attitudes was carried out by the Independent Television Commission. The findings are summarized in Gunter, Media Sex, 208–12.

103 Person, The Sexual Century, 215, and more broadly 211–29.

104 Kimmel, The Gender of Desire, 45–64.

105 The story of the origins of the campaign comes from an online article by Patrick Scullin, then a creative director at Hal Riney. The article was

available at www.ozonline.tv/Georgia/Oz/Oz10–5/allisglitter.html in August 2005. The site was Kevin McKelvey's 'All That Glitters Is Not Sold.'

106 Cooper, 'Sexual Harassment and the Swedish Bikini Team,' 389.

107 Cited in a brief online report at multinationalmonitor.org/hyper/issues/ 1991/12/mm1291_11.html \par in August 2005 that dealt with the Stroh cases.

108 Anderson, 'Top 100 Ad Campaigns of the 20th Century.'

109 The settlement was not disclosed. The court ruled that the commercials could not be used as evidence in the trial, though posters and promotional material available in the factory could be. See an AP story available online at www.mndaily.com/daily/gopher-archives/1993/12/02/ Stroh's_suit_settle.txt in August 2005.

110 Joe Celko, 'Ah, Swede Memories.' Or again, when asked about his fantasies, a man replied, 'The entire Swedish Bikini Team – big breasts, blonde, unbelievably curvy asses.' Cited in Kimmel, *The Gender of Desire*, 56.

111 From a story by Bob Cook in *Flakmagazine* online at flakmag.com/tv/ catfight.html in August 2005.

112 Elliott and Ritson, 'Practicing Existential Consumption.' The authors do suggest that this group of women had a reputation that others, presumably on campus, were aware of.

113 Elliott et al., 'Overt Sexuality in Advertising,' 206.

114 The term appears in Letiche, 'Viagra(ization) or Technoromanticism,' 254. See Haraway, 'A Cyborg Manifesto: Science, Technology, and Socialist-Feminism in the Late Twentieth Century,' in *Simians, Cyborgs and Women*. The discussion of the Viagra case is based on two academic articles – Mamo and Fishman, 'Potency in All the Right Places,' and Marshall, '"Hard Science"' – and a wide variety of items, ads, and promotional matter as well as news items and jokes, culled from the World Wide Web, including the Viagra website in 2002.

115 Annie Potts has talked about a 'Viagra-machine,' working off the notion of the 'desiring machine.' However, she defines her assemblage differently: 'I propose the existence of the Viagra-machine as an assemblage that comprises the drug itself, the biomedicalized (and non-biomedicalized) bodies of those linked to it (e.g. the user and others – such as his sexual partners, the medical professional prescribing Viagra, etc.), the Viagra-assisted erect penis and its various actions and effects (as well as the extra-penile effects), the lines that traverse these various connections and presume to dictate the impacts and outcomes of any experience associated with Viagra use, as well as those more disruptive lines that travel between, pro-

ducing unanticipated effects.' Potts, 'Deleuze on Viagra (Or, What Can a "Viagra-Body" Do?),' 22.

116 'Your brain sort of fills in the blanks.' In 2005 Pfizer began running a new series of commercials in Canada where users prepared to tell all to friends when suddenly they were silenced by an enlarged blue pill (Viagra of course) covering their mouths. *National Post* (Toronto), 11 April 2005.

117 Friedman, *A Mind of Its Own: A Cultural History of the Penis.*

118 See, for example, Morrow, 'Old Goats and Their Libidos.'

119 The average age of the thirty-three men was sixty, the average age of the twenty-seven women was fifty-three. The project has been written up in Potts, 'Deleuze on Viagra,' 17–36, and Potts, Grace, Gavey, and Vares, '"Viagra stories."'

120 See, for example, chapter 4 in Maines, *The Technology of Orgasm*, 67–110.

121 These 'permit individuals to effect by their own means, or with the help of others, a certain number of operations on their own bodies and souls, thoughts, conduct, and way of being, so as to transform themselves in order to attain a certain state of happiness, purity, wisdom, perfection, or immortality.' Foucault, 'Technologies of the Self,' 225.

122 The refugee was Tatiana Mamanova, her questioner Susan Cole. Reported in Susan Cole, *Pornography and the Sex Crisis*, 7.

123 I visited Beijing in April 2002.

124 Not that all the ads were erotic, of course. Most were not. Both KFC and Starbucks, for example, simply put up their names. A romantic couple, Westerners once again, performed on a billboard for Hengfusheng Jewellery. A colourful young woman, seemingly caught up in the excitement of a rave, fronted for the electronic devices of Kenwood.

125 The Sydney *Morning Herald* (20 May 2000) reported that Beijing had 'banned billboards where women show too much breast or thigh 15 centimetres above the knee ...'

126 Baudrillard, 'The Precession of Simulacra,' 6.

127 Pomian, *Collectors and Curiosities*, 5, 24–5, 30.

128 Barthes, 'Myth Today,' in *Mythologies*, 109–58. The book was first published in France in 1957. Barthes later came to think that the work lacked sophistication. But in retrospect, the most problematic notion in the essay was Barthes's claim that 'myth today' could only really be bourgeois. He thought that nothing revolutionary, by which he presumably meant thoroughly Marxist, could become myth or use myth. So any myths evident on the Left were really an indication of how the movement had surrendered to the bourgeois order.

129 More specifically, it said 'that France is a great Empire, that all her sons,

without any colour discrimination, faithfully serve under her flag, and that there is no better answer to the detractors of an alleged colonialism than the zeal shown by this Negro in serving his so-called oppressors.' Ibid., 116.

130 'In general myth prefers to work with poor, incomplete images, where the meaning is already relieved of its fat, and ready for a signification, such as caricatures, pastiches, symbols, etc.' Ibid., 127. In a later reflection on this essay, Barthes used the terms 'denote' (the overt meaning) and 'connote' (the ideological meaning) to describe the semiotic processes he analysed. See his 'Change the Object Itself. Mythology Today,' 166.

131 *Mythologies*, 124.

132 'It abolishes the complexity of human acts, it gives them the simplicity of essences, it does away with all dialectics, with any going back beyond what is immediately visible, it organizes a world which is without contra-dictions because it is without depth ...' Ibid., 143.

133 'The hypothesis of this essay is that the word "modern" designates two sets of entirely different practices which must remain distinct if they are to remain effective ... The first set of practices, by "translation," creates mix-tures between entirely new types of beings, hybrids of nature and culture. The second, by "purification," creates two entirely distinct ontological zones: that of human beings on the one hand; that of nonhumans on the other.' Latour, *We Have Never Been Modern*, 10–11.

Conclusion

1 My extension of Foucault is only partial. The Eros project is just one of a number of stories that can be told about sex in the twentieth century, sto-ries like that of the 'sexual revolution' itself or the AIDS tragedy. So Caro-lyn Dean has outlined a different story regarding the significance of 'derepression' and the issue of manhood in France after the First World War: Dean, 'The Productive Hypothesis.' Recently, Todd May has offered some useful guidelines on applying and extending Foucault, with particu-lar reference to the drama of sexuality: May, 'Foucault Now?'

2 The term serves as the title for part two of Foucault, *The History of Sexual-ity*, vol.1: *An Introduction*. Although Foucault took Reich and Marcuse to task, mostly in interviews, he was otherwise clearly impressed by the achievements of the Frankfurt School, of which Marcuse was a member: see Foucault, 'Interview with Michel Foucault.'

3 Foucault could be very ambiguous about the existence of repression. In one paper in 1975, for example, he claimed that he had initially intended

to write 'something like a history of sexual repression, a history of sexual anomaly' but then discovered that 'the necessary documents' did not exist: 'what I was looking for was not there to be deciphered in terms of the body of mechanisms that we call repression.' Yet almost immediately after that comment, he referred to the 'schema of analysis' originated by Wilhelm Reich, 'whose validity I admit'! Liberation theory just didn't suit his objectives. Foucault, 'Schizo-Culture: Infantile Sexuality,' 154. Some years later, in 1982, he stated, 'Indeed, it is not a question of denying the existence of repression. It's one of showing that repression is always a part of a much more complex political strategy regarding sexuality.' Foucault, 'An Ethics of Pleasure,' 375.

4 Foucault, *The History of Sexuality*, 136–59. Here he explained that the term 'biopower' served 'to designate what brought life and its mechanisms into the realm of explicit calculations and made knowledge-power an agent of transformation of human life' (143). Foucault later specified that by the related term 'biopolitics' 'I meant the endeavour, begun in the eighteenth century, to rationalize the problems presented to governmental practice by the phenomena characteristic of a group of living human beings constituted as a population: health, sanitation, birthrate, longevity, race ...' That definition appeared in his summary of the lectures he delivered at the Collège de France in 1977–8, entitled 'The Birth of Biopolitics,' 73. Foucault also discussed biopower and biopolitics in a lecture published in '*Society Must Be Defended*,' 239–63. The paradigm has been developed further by later scholars, sometimes as part of the discussion of governmentality. See, for example, Dean, *Governmentality*, 98–112; Rose, *Powers of Freedom*; Gunn, 'From Hegemony to Governmentality'; Culp, 'Rethinking Governmentality'; Dickinson, 'Biopolitics, Fascism, Democracy'; Lemke, 'The Birth of Biopolitics'; Rabinow and Rose, 'Thoughts on the Concept of Biopower Today'; Rose, 'The Politics of Life Itself'; and Genel, 'The Question of Biopower.'

5 'Power induces and produces desire, power gives desire its objects, power, indeed, is desirable ... Power produces the very form of the subject, it produces what makes up the subject.' 'Schizo-Culture,' 158. But in *The History of Sexuality*, 152, he explicitly denied any attempt to efface the body: 'the biological and the historical are not consecutive to one another ... but are bound together in an increasingly complex fashion in accordance with the development of the modern technologies of power that take life as their objective.'

6 'The emphasis on the body should undoubtedly be linked to the process of growth and establishment of bourgeois hegemony: not, however, because of the market value assumed by labor capacity, but because of what the

"cultivation" of its own body could represent politically, economically, and historically for the present and the future of the bourgeoisie.' Foucault, *The History of Sexuality*, 125.

7 'It is through sex – in fact, an imaginary point determined by the deployment of sexuality – that each individual has to pass in order to have access to his own intelligibility (seeing that it is both the hidden aspect and the generative principle of meaning), to the whole of his body (since it is a real and threatened part of it, while symbolically constituting the whole), to his identity (since it joins the force of a drive to the singularity of a history).' Foucault, *The History of Sexuality*, 155–6. Foucault employs the term 'desiring subject' in the introduction to vol. 2 of *The History of Sexuality, The Use of Pleasure*, 5–6.

8 'I believe the so-called "sexual liberation" movements must be understood as movements of affirmation "beginning with" sexuality. Which means two things: these are movements which take off from sexuality, from the apparatus of sexuality within which we're trapped, which make it function to the limit; but at the same time, these movements are displaced in relation to sexuality, disengaging themselves from it and going beyond it.' Foucault, 'The End of the Monarchy of Sex,' 217. The interview was given in 1977, a year after the French publication of *The History of Sexuality*.

9 Near the end of his book, Foucault made this intriguing, and slightly mysterious, comment: 'It is the agency of sex that we must break away from, if we aim – through a tactical reversal of the various mechanisms of sexuality – to counter the grips of power with the claims of bodies, pleasures, and knowledges, in their multiplicity and their possibility of resistance. The rallying point for the counterattack against the deployment of sexuality ought not to be sex-desire, but bodies and pleasures.' *The History of Sexuality*, 157. This was hardly a blueprint for liberation.

10 In 1983, on the eve of the publication of his last two books on sexuality, which dealt with sex in ancient Europe, contrary to what had been suggested in the introductory volume, Foucault told an interviewer, 'I must confess that I am much more interested in problems about techniques of the self and things like that than sex ... sex is boring.' 'On the Genealogy of Ethics,' 253.

11 One of the most revealing expressions of his later thoughts on power is contained in a paper, first published in English in 1982, entitled 'The Subject and Power.'

12 This he outlined in his course summary of 1977–8, 'The Birth of Biopolitics.' There is further discussion of the issue of liberalism in Colin Gordon's introduction to *The Foucault Effect: Studies in Governmentality*, edited by Gra-

ham Burchall, Colin Gordon, and Peter Miller, 1–51. The introduction is entitled 'Governmental Rationality: An Introduction.'

13 Foucault defined technologies of the self in a lecture given in English and first published in 1981: 'Techniques that permit individuals to effect, by their own means, a certain number of operations on their own bodies, their own souls, their own thoughts, their own conduct, and this in a manner so as to transform themselves, modify themselves, and to attain a certain state of perfection, happiness, purity, supernatural power.' He had added this to a list he claimed was inspired by the work of Jürgen Habermas: 'techniques of production, techniques of signification or communication, and techniques of domination.' Foucault, 'Sexuality and Solitude,' 177.

14 On 'the S&M phenomenon,' in which Foucault was a happy participant, he once said: 'This mixture of rules and openness has the effect of intensifying sexual relations by introducing a perpetual novelty, a perpetual tension and a perpetual uncertainty which the simple consummation of the act lacks. The idea is also to make use of every part of the body as a sexual instrument.' Foucault, 'Sexual Choice, Sexual Act,' 331. This interview occurred in 1982.

15 Foucault had this to say about liberation in a 1984 interview: 'I have always been somewhat suspicious of the notion of liberation, because if it is not treated with precautions and within certain limits, one runs the risk of falling back on the idea that there exists a human nature or base that, as a consequence of certain historical, economic and social processes, has been concealed, alienated or imprisoned in and by mechanisms of repression.' 'The Ethics of the Concern for Self as a Practice of Freedom,' 433. Yet in a 1982 interview where he talked about the gay movement, he said, 'It's quite true that there was a real liberation process in the early 70s.' 'Sex, Power and the Politics of Identity,' 381.

16 The case for Foucault as a champion of the active self, an individual seeking freedom and seeking to avoid control, has been well argued by T.J. Berard in a reconsideration of the whole corpus of Foucault's work, though especially his project on sexuality. T.J. Berard, 'Michel Foucault, *The History of Sexuality*, and the Reformulation of Social Theory.'

17 Freud and Foucault were not always so far apart as it might seem. That has been pointed out by Ann Laura Stoler in her analysis of sex and colonialism: 'But saying "yes" to Foucault has not always meant saying "no" to Freud, not even for Foucault himself. Despite Foucault's rejection of the repressive hypothesis, there are surprising ways in which their projects can and do converge ... Both were concerned with boundary formation, with the "internal enemy" within ... [W]e might look to Edward Said's supremely Foucauldian analysis of Orientalist discourse and Western dom-

ination where Freud's notion of projection, of the Orient as the West's "sur-
rogate self" is a crucial but buried part of his argument.' Stoler, *Race and the
Education of Desire*, 168–9. For a much stronger claim that Foucault and
Freud were partners rather than rivals in their approach to sexuality, see
Teresa de Lauretis, 'The Stubborn Drive.'

18 'We're really going to have to rid ourselves of the "Marcuseries" and "Reichianisms" which encumber us and which would have us believe that of all
things sexuality is the most obstinately "repressed" and "overrepressed"
by our "bourgeois," "capitalist," "hypocritical" and "Victorian" society.'
Foucault, 'Sorcery and Madness,' 201.

19 Foucault, *The History of Sexuality*, 12.

20 Ibid., 4.

21 'A great sexual sermon – which has had its subtle theologians and its popular voices – has swept through our societies over the last decades; it has
chastised the old order, denounced hypocrisy, and praised the rights of the
immediate and the real; it has made people dream of a New City.' Ibid., 7–8.

22 Although Foucault occasionally made reference to economic factors as
causing or shaping change, he did not pay much attention to consumption.
In fact in a short comment on the altered strategies of sexuality and the
changed nature of capitalism in the twentieth century, he admitted that 'the
exploitation of wage labour does not demand the same violent and physical constraints as in the nineteeth century.' But this he considered of slight
consequence for his drama, a matter of correspondence rather than cause.
Ibid., 114.

23 Foucault was careful to distinguish the different mechanisms at play but
also to emphasize how in practice they worked together to produce effects.
'Power relations, relations of communication, objective capacities should
not therefore be confused. This is not to say that there is a question of three
separate domains. Nor that there is, on the one hand, the field of things, of
perfected technique, work, and the transformation of the real, and, on the
other, that of signs, communication, reciprocity, and the production of
meaning; finally that of the domination of the means of constraint, of inequality and the action of men upon other men. It is a question of three types
of relationships that in fact always overlap one another, support one
another reciprocally, and use each other mutually as means to an end.' Foucault, 'The Subject and Power,' 337–8.

24 Marcuse, *One-Dimensional Man*, 84–104.

25 Foucault's first major work directly on the question of power was *Discipline
and Punish: The Birth of the Prison*, where he explicitly denied that we lived in
a society of the spectacle and instead argued the centrality of surveillance.

26 See Debord, *The Society of the Spectacle*, where he outlined how capitalism has made spectacle its main instrument of authority over humanity.

27 Foucault, 'Body/Power,' 57.

28 Consumers could become 'entrepreneurs of themselves, seeking to maximize their "quality of life" through the artful assembly of a "life-style" put together through the world of goods.' Miller and Rose, 'Governing Economic Life,' 99. Miller and Rose were not speaking about eroticism in particular. Rather their article is a thoughtful and detailed attempt to apply Foucault's ideas about governmentality and the like to the ways in which economic life was administered, mostly in postwar Britain.

29 Foucault, *The History of Sexuality*, 105.

30 So he noted how doctors, educators, and eventually psychiatrists came to worry about 'the nervous woman, the frigid wife, the indifferent mother – or worse, the mother beset by murderous obsessions – the impotent, sadistic, perverse husband, the hysterical or neurasthenic girl, the precocious and already exhausted child, and the young homosexual who rejects marriage or neglects his wife.' Ibid., 110.

31 Ibid., 44.

32 Ibid., 154.

33 'Today's novel feature is the flattening-out of the antagonism between culture and social reality through the obliteration of the oppositional, alien, and transcendent elements in the higher culture by virtue of which it constituted *another dimension* of reality.' Marcuse, *One-Dimensional Man*, 57

34 Ibid., 75.

35 True, Foucault only mentioned 'what has been called hyper-repressive desublimation,' and then just to dismiss it as of no particular significance to his drama. Foucault, *The History of Sexuality*, 114. Still Douglas Kellner has argued that Marcuse's view of the self and its desires 'anticipates the poststructuralist critique of the subject,' including the views of Foucault: Kellner, 'Marcuse and the Quest for Radical Subjectivity.' And Joel Whitebook has pointed out that both Foucault and Marcuse '*insist on the overwhelming weight of the constructed factor in determining the nature of our sexual lives.*' Whitebook, 'Michel Foucault: A Structuralist in Marcusean Clothing,' 64.

36 Marcuse, *One-Dimensional Man*, 73.

37 That kind of limit was true of other forms of biopower. 'It is not that life has been totally integrated into techniques that govern and administer it; it constantly escapes them.' Foucault, *The History of Sexuality*, 143.

38 Contrary to what seemed the thrust of his earlier work on prisons, Foucault now insisted not just on the possibility of resistance but on its constant existence and significance. 'Where there is power, there is resistance, and

yet, or rather consequently, this resistance is never in a position of exterior-
ity in relation to power ... Their [power relationships'] existence depends on
a multiplicity of points of resistance: these play the role of adversary, target,
support, or handle in power relations.' Foucault, *The History of Sexuality*, 95.

39 Foucault, 'The Subject and Power,' 546.

40 Norwegian Cruise Line: the ad *Constitution* won a Clio in 1995.

41 Jay, *The Dialectical Imagination*, 216.

42 To which Marcuse might have answered, that didn't matter. Indeed it was
proof that people had been colonized. Sex (something he thought lesser)
had triumphed over Eros (the 'Life Instincts').

43 Foucault did not usually describe particular arrangements of these technologies in so many words, although in 'The Subject and Power' (337–9) he
did briefly sketch the example of an educational institution as one of the
'regulated and concerted systems' composed of 'the adjustments of abili-
ties, the resources of communication, and power relations' (338). Usually he
theorized, and in slightly different ways, at a more abstract level. He said,
on one occasion, late in his life (1982) that he had devoted most of his attention to only two of these technologies, domination and the self, citing as an
example his first study of madness. He added, bringing this concern up to
date, 'The encounter between the technologies of domination of others and
those of the self I call "governmentality."' Foucault, 'Technologies of the
Self,' 225.

44 See Dickinson, 'Biopolitics, Fascism, Democracy,' 4, for a brief discussion of
the dual process of normalization and pathologization in biopolitical enterprises. Foucault dealt at some length with the issue of normalizing in his
discussion of disciplinary power, *Discipline and Punish*, especially 170–94.

45 Foucault used the term 'knowing subject' (201) in the first 'Preface to *The
History of Sexuality*, Volume Two,' published as a separate essay, and republished in *Ethics*. The phrase referring to self-formation (282) appeared in an
interview from 1984, 'The Ethics of the Concern for Self as a Practice of
Freedom,' also in *Ethics*. There is also some comment on the need to 'know
oneself' and 'govern oneself' in 'Subjectivity and Truth,' a course summary,
also in *Ethics*.

46 See Rose, *Powers of Freedom*.

47 I have dealt at length with the character of this brand of advertising, in
Rutherford, *Endless Propaganda: The Advertising of Public Goods*. Broadly
speaking, such advertising worked to warn and cajole, sometimes urging
sacrifices, often preaching right conduct.

48 That last borrowing from slang is also a play on a comment by Marcuse
where he despaired over the victory of a 'Happy Consciousness.' 'It reflects

the belief that the real is rational, and that the established system, in spite of everything, delivers the goods. The people are led to find in the productive apparatus the effective agent of thought and action to which their personal thought and action can and must be surrendered. And in this transfer, the apparatus assumes the role of a moral agent. Conscience is absolved by reification, by the general necessity of things.' Marcuse, *One-Dimensional Man*, 79.

Research Sources and Sites

(i) Advertising Collections

Ad*Access database of Duke University

AdCritic, at www.adcritic.com, late 1990s

AdFilms, a Canadian firm that supplied a compilation of award winners, especially British ads, 1996–8

advertisementave.com, post-2000 ads

Amalfi, window ads, September 1999

Barcelona, June 2002

Beijing, Wangfujing street, April 2002

Bessies, The. An English-Canadian award festival of advertising, 1990s

Boursicot Film Library, Jean-Marie, at www.adeater.com.

Cannes Lions (International Advertising Film Festival) festivals, 1972–95

Clios, 1990s, at www.clioawards.com

Commercial Archive, 1990s, at ad-rag.com

Diesel ads, 1992–9, diesel.com

First Clios, The. Celia Nachatovitz Diamant Memorial Library of Classic Television Commercials, the Television Center of Brooklyn College, City University of New York

ianfleming.org

International Broadcasting or IBA Awards (also called the Hollywood Awards), 1976–94

jamesbond.com

John W. Hartman Center for Sales, Advertising and Marketing History of Duke University, scriptorium.lib.duke.edu/hartman/

Kevin McKelvey's 'All That Glitters Is Not Sold' at www.ozonline.tv/Georgia/Oz/Oz10–5/allisglitter.html (Swedish Bikini Team)

Kodak International Showcase, 1986–2000

National Museum of Photography, Film and Television, Bradford, England
New York, Times Square, October 2000
Nice, May 2001
Reeperbahn, Hamburg, September 1999
schick.com/shavingwoman.html
Television ad survey: London and Madrid, December 1993; Cologne, Paris,
    and Stockholm, 1994; Assmannshausen RTL in the Rhineland, July 1994

(ii) Magazines

Advertising Age
Harper's Bazaar, 1950s and 1960s (Maidenform ads)
Ladies Home Journal, 1950s and 1960s (Maidenform ads)
MS., 1970s and 1980s (fashion articles)
Playboy, 1950s and 1960s
Vogue, 1950s (Maidenform ads)
Woman's Day, 1950s (Maidenform ads)

(iii) Museums and Exhibitions

Beate Uhse Erotik-Museum, Berlin
Brooklyn's Museum of Art (*Exposed: The Victorian Nude*)
Centro Cultural Estación Mapoche, Santiago, Chile (*Tres Grandes De España*)
Erotic Art Museum, Hamburg
Erotisch Museum, Amsterdam
Guggenheim Museum, New York (*Giorgio Armani*)
Metropolitan Museum of Art, New York (*Surrealism: Desire Unbound*)
Montreal Museum of Fine Arts (*Picasso Erotique*)
Musée de la publicité, Paris
Musée de l'érotisme, Paris
Museo Erótico de Madrid
Museu de l'Eròtica, Barcelona
Museum Erotica, Copenhagen
Museum of Ancient Chinese Sex Culture, Shanghai
Museum of Sex, New York
Museum of Television and Radio, New York
Palau de la Virriena, Barcelona (*jardín de eros*)
Seksmuseum (and Venustempel), Amsterdam
Textile Museum of Canada, Toronto (*Moral Fibre*)
Thyssen Museum, Madrid (*Die Brücke*)

Bibliography

Adams, Simon, and Raelene Francis. 'Lifting the Veil: The Sex Industry, Museums and Galleries.' *Labour History* 85 (2003). Online through the historycooperative.com.

Ades, Dawn. *Dalí*. London: Thames and Hudson, 1995.

Agins, Teri. *The End of Fashion: How Marketing Changed the Clothing Business Forever*. New York: HarperCollins, 2000.

Albion, Alexis. 'Wanting to Be James Bond.' In Edward P. Comentale, Stephen Watt, and Skip Willman, eds. *Ian Fleming and James Bond: The Cultural Politics of 007*, 202–20. Bloomington and Indianapolis: Indiana University Press, 2005.

Allen, Amy. 'Pornography and Power.' *Journal of Social Philosophy*. 34, no. 4 (Winter 2001): 512–31.

Allen, Steve. 'Madonna.' In Carol Benson and Allan Metz, eds, *The Madonna Companion: Two Decades of Commentary*, 144–57. New York: Schirmer Books, 1999.

Allyn, David. *Make Love, Not War. The Sexual Revolution: An Unfettered History*. Boston: Little Brown, 2000.

Alperstein, Neil. 'The Verbal Content of TV Advertising and Its Circulation in Everyday Life.' *Journal of Advertising* 19, no. 2 (Spring 1990): 15–22.

Anderson, Mark. 'Top 100 Ad Campaigns of the 20th Century.' Online at medialit.med. sc.edu/topcenturyads.htm in August 2003.

Anderson, Patricia. *Passion Lost: Public Sex, Private Desire in the Twentieth Century*. Toronto: Thomas Allen, 2001.

Ang, Swee Hoon, and Sharon Y.M. Low. 'Exploring the Dimensions of Ad Creativity.' *Psychology and Marketing* 17 (October 2000): 835–54.

Arcand, Bernard. *The Jaguar and the Anteater: Pornography and the Modern World*. Translated by Wayne Grady. Toronto: McClelland and Stewart, 1993.

Attwood, Feona. 'Reading Porn: The Paradigm Shift in Pornography Research.' *Sexualities* 5, no. 1 (2002): 91–105.

Aylesworth, Andrew B., Ronald C. Goodstein, and Ajay Kalra. 'Effect of Archetypal Embeds on Feelings: An Indirect Route to Affecting Attitudes?' *Journal of Advertising* 28, no. 3 (Fall 1999): 73–81.

Bakhtin, Mikhail. *Rabelais and His World.* Translated by Hélène Iswolsky. Bloomington: Indiana University Press, 1984.

Baltera, Lorraine. 'Maidenform Goes on Stage for Dream Theme Revival.' *Advertising Age,* 26 April 1976, 39.

Barthes, Roland. 'Change the Object Itself. Mythology Today.' In *Image – Music – Text*, translated by Stephen Heath, 165–9. New York: Hill and Wang, 1977.

– 'Myth Today.' In *Mythologies*, translated by Annette Lavers, 109–58. London: Granada, 1973.

– 'Written Clothing.' In Chandra Mukerji and Michael Schudson, eds, *Rethinking Popular Culture: Contemporary Perspectives in Cultural Studies*, 432–45. Berkeley and Oxford: University of California Press, 1991.

Bataille, Georges. *Erotism: Death and Sensuality.* Translated by Mary Dalwood. San Francisco: City Lights Books, 1986.

Baudrillard, Jean. 'Absolute Advertising, Ground-Zero Advertising.' In *Simulacra and Simulation*, translated by Sheila Faria Glaser, 87–94. Ann Arbor: University of Michigan Press, 1994.

– 'The Precession of Simulacra.' In *Simulacra and Simulation.* Translated by Sheila Faria Glaser, 1–42. Ann Arbor: University of Michigan Press, 1994.

– *The System of Objects.* Translated by James Benedict. London: Verso, 1996.

Bauman, Zygmunt. 'On Postmodern Uses of Sex.' *Theory, Culture and Society* 15, no. 3–4 (1998): 19–33.

Baumgardner, Jennifer, and Amy Richards. *Manifesta.* New York: Farrar Straus Giroux, 2000.

Beatty, Sharon, and Del Hawkins.'Subliminal Stimulation: Some New Data and Interpretation.' *Journal of Advertising* 18, issue 3 (1989): 4+.

Bech, Ulrich, Wolfgang Bonss, and Christoph Lau. 'The Theory of Reflexive Modernization: Problematic, Hypotheses and Research Programme.' *Theory, Culture and Society* 20, no. 2 (2003): 1–33.

Beck, Marianna, and Jack Hafferkamp. 'The Era of Sex Museums.' *Libido, The Journal of Sex and Sensibility.* Available online in January 2002.

– 'Sex Please, We're Tourists.' Online at CANOE TRAVEL as 'Europe's Sex Museums.'

Belk, Russell W. 'Possessions and the Extended Self.' *Journal of Consumer Research* 15 (September 1988): 139–68.

Belk, Russell, Güliz Ger, and Søren Askegaard. 'The Fire of Desire: A Multi-sited Inquiry into Consumer Passion.' *Journal of Consumer Research* 30 (December 2003): 326–51.

Bennett, Tony. *The Birth of the Museum: History, Theory, Politics*. London and New York: Routledge, 1995.

Bennett, Tony, and Janet Woollacott. *Bond and Beyond: The Political Career of a Popular Hero*. Houndmills and London: Macmillan Education, 1987.

Benson, Carol, and Allan Metz, ed. *The Madonna Companion: Two Decades of Commentary*. New York: Schirmer Books, 1999.

Berard, T.J. 'Michel Foucault, *The History of Sexuality*, and the Reformulation of Social Theory.' *Journal for the Theory of Social Behaviour* 29, no. 3 (1999): 203–27.

Berger, John. *Ways of Seeing*. London: British Broadcasting Corporation and Penguin Books, 1972.

Billboard Book of Top 40 Hits, The. 5th ed. New York: Watson-Guptill Publications, 1992.

Black, Jeremy. *The Politics of James Bond: From Fleming's Novels to the Big Screen*, Westport, CT: Praeger, 2001.

– 'What We Can Learn from James Bond.' Published by the History News Network. Available online at hnn.us in October 2005.

Boadella, David. *Wilhelm Reich: The Evolution of His Work*. London: Vision Press, 1973.

Boddewyn, Jean. 'Controlling Sex and Decency in Advertising around the World.' *Journal of Advertising* 20, no. 4 (December 1991): 25–35.

Bordo, Susan. '"Material Girl": The Effacements of Postmodern Culture.' In Cathy Schwichtenberg, ed., *The Madonna Connection: Representational Politics, Subcultural Identities, and Cultural Theory*, 265–90. Boulder, CO: Westview Press, 1993.

– *Unbearable Weight: Feminism, Western Culture, and the Body*. Berkeley and London: University of California Press, 2003.

Bower, Amanda B. 'Highly Attractive Models in Advertising and the Women Who Loathe Them: The Implications of Negative Affect for Spokesperson Effectiveness.' *Journal of Advertising* 28, no. 3 (Fall 2001): 73–81.

Bower, Bruce. 'The Mental Butler Did It.' *Science News* (30 October 1999): 280+.

Bowker's Annual/Publisher's Weekly. Available online at http://www.engl. virginia.edu/ courses/bestsellers/best90.cgi in July 2002.

'Bra Battle Centers on New Ads, New Angles, New Users.' *Printers' Ink*, 17 November 1961.

Braddock, A.P. *Psychology and Advertising*. London: Butterworth, 1932.

Brandt, Pamela. 'Barbie Buys a Bra.' In Yona Zeldis McDonough, ed., *The Barbie Chronicles: A Living Doll Turns Forty*, 53–8. New York: Simon and Schuster, 1999.

Bright, Susie. 'A Pornographic Girl.' In Lisa Frank and Paul Smith, eds, *Madonnarama: Essays on Sex and Popular Culture*, 81–6. Pittsburgh: Cleis Press, 1993.

Britton, Wesley. *Beyond Bond: Spies in Fiction and Film*. Westport, CT: Praeger, 2005.

Broccoli, Cubby, with Donald Zec. *When the Snow Melts: The Autobiography of Cubby Broccoli*. London: Boxtree, 1998.

Brooke, Collin. 'Sex(haustion) Sells: Marketing in a Saturated Mediascape.' In Tom Reichert and Jacqueline Lambiase, eds, *Sex in Advertising: Perspectives on the Erotic Appeal*, 133–50. Mahwah, NJ: Lawrence Erlbaum Associates, 2003.

Brosnan, John. *James Bond in the Cinema*. 2nd ed. San Diego: A.S. Barnes and Co., 1981.

Brown, Jane D., and Laurie Schulze. 'The Effects of Race, Gender, and Fandom on Audience Interpretations of Madonna's Music Videos.' In Gail Dines and Jean M. Humez, eds, *Gender, Race and Class in Media: A Text-Reader*, 508–17. Thousand Oaks, CA: Sage Publications, 1995.

Brown, Stephen, Pauline Maclaren, and Lorna Stevens. 'Marcadia Postponed: Marketing, Utopia and the Millennium.' *Journal of Marketing Management* 12 (1996): 671–83.

Buckley, Kerry. *Mechanical Man: John Broadus Watson and the Beginnings of Behaviorism*. New York: Guilford Press, 1989.

Burchall, Graham, Colin Gordon, and Peter Miller, eds. *The Foucault Effect: Studies in Governmentality*. Chicago: University of Chicago Press, 1991.

Burns, Gary. 'Music Television.' *The Encyclopedia of Television*. Online at the Museum of Broadcast Communications in Chicago (http://www.museum.tv/archives/ etv/index.html) in July 2002.

Burtt, Harold. *Psychology of Advertising*. Boston: Houghton Mifflin, 1938.

'Bye-bye Supermodels.' *Globe and Mail* (Toronto), 8 October 1998. Online edition.

Calt, Ray. 'Advertising's Debt to Dr. Freud.' *Advertising Age* (July 1952): 67, 98.

'Calvin's World.' *Newsweek*, 11 September 1995.

Carpenter, Betsy. 'Stalking the Unconscious.' *U.S. News and World Report*, 22 October 1990, 60+.

Celant, Germano, and Harold Koda (with Susan Cross and Karole Vail), organizers. *Giorgio Armani*. New York: Solomon R. Guggenheim Foundation/ Harry N. Abrams, 2000.

Celko, Joe. 'Ah, Swede Memories.' Online at www.intelligententerprise.com/ db_area/archives/1999/ 992004/celko.jhtml in August 2005.

Chamberlain, Kathy. 'Idolatry: Barbie Dolls and Feminism.' *Tikkun*, March-April 1995. Online copy: Infotrac, August 1999.

Chapman, James. 'Bond and Britishness.' In Edward P. Comentale, Stephen Watt, and Skip Willman, eds, *Ian Fleming and James Bond: The Cultural Politics of 007*, 123–43. Bloomington and Indianapolis: Indiana University Press, 2005.

– *Licence to Thrill: A Cultural History of the James Bond Films*. London and New York: I.B. Taurus, 1999.

Cocks, H.G. 'Saucy Stories: Pornography, Sexology and the Marketing of Sexual Knowledge in Britain, c. 1918–70.' *Social History* 29, no. 4 (November 2004): 465–84.

Cole, Susan. *Pornography and the Sex Crisis*. Toronto: Amanita Enterprises, 1989.

Coleman, Barbara J. 'Maidenform(ed): Images of American Women in the 1950s.' In Carol Siegel and Ann Kibbey, eds, *Forming and Reforming Identity*, 3–29. New York: New York University Press, 1995.

Combalía, Victoria, and Jean-Jacques Lebel, eds. *Jardín de Eros*. Barcelona: Institut de Cultura de Barcelona, 1999.

Comentale, Edward P., Stephen Watt, and Skip Willman, eds, *Ian Fleming and James Bond: The Cultural Politics of 007*. Bloomington and Indianapolis: Indiana University Press, 2005.

Cook, Guy. *The Discourse of Advertising*. London and New York: Routledge, 1992.

Cooper, Stacey J. 'Sexual Harassment and the Swedish Bikini Team: A Reevaluation of the "Hostile Environment" Doctrine.' *Columbia Journal of Law and Social Problems* 26 (Spring 1993): 387–434.

'Could Supermodels Be Losing Their Sizzle?' *Salt Lake Tribune*, 26 November 1995. Online edition.

Cox, Don Richard. 'Barbie and Her Playmates.' *Journal of Popular Culture* 11, no. 2 (Fall 1977): 303–7.

Cross, Gary. 'Toy.' *American Heritage*, May 1999. Online copy: Infotrac.

Culp, Robert. 'Rethinking Governmentality: Training, Cultivation, and Cultural Citizenship in Nationalist China.' *The Journal of Asian Studies* 65, no. 3 (August 2006): 529–54.

Curti, Merle. 'The Changing Concept of "Human Nature" in the Literature of American Advertising.' *Business History Review* 41, no. 4 (Winter 1967): 333–57.

'DAD DVD Sales Surpass Expectations.' 6 June 2003. Online at MI6.co.uk (available October 2005).

Dahl, Darren, Kristina Frankenburger, and Rajesh Manchanda. 'Does It Pay to Shock? Reactions to Shocking and Nonshocking Advertising Content among University Students.' *Journal of Advertising Research* (September 2003): 268–80.

Dalí, Salvador. *The Secret Life of Salvador Dalí*. Translated by Haakon Chevalier. New York: Dover, 1993.

Davis, Fred. *Fashion, Culture, and Identity*. Chicago and London: University of Chicago Press, 1992.

Dean, Carolyn J. *The Frail Social Body: Pornography, Homosexuality, and Other Fantasies in Interwar France*. Berkeley and London: University of California Press, 2000.

– 'History, Pornography and the Social Body.' In Jennifer Mundy, ed., *Surrealism: Desire Unbound*, 227–43. London: Tate Publishing, 2001.

– 'The Productive Hypothesis: Foucault, Gender, and the History of Sexuality.' *History and Theory* 33, no. 3 (October 1994): 271–96.

– *The Self and Its Pleasures: Bataille, Lacan, and the History of the Decentered Subject*. Ithaca and London: Cornell University Press, 1992.

Dean, Mitchell. *Governmentality: Power and Rule in Modern Society*. London and Thousand Oaks: Sage, 1999.

Debord, Guy. *The Society of the Spectacle*. Translated by Donald Nicholson-Smith. New York: Zone Books, 1995.

Decker, Andrew. 'Pop Goes the Easel.' *Cigar Aficionado* (March/April 1998). Online at www.cigaraficionado.com/Cigar/Aficionado/goodlife/fm398.html in December 2001.

Delap, Leanne. 'Out with the Super, in with the New.' *Globe and Mail* (Toronto), 10 March 1999. Online edition.

de Lauretis, Teresa. 'The Stubborn Drive.' *Critical Inquiry* 24, no. 4 (Summer 1998): 851–78.

Deleuze, Gilles, and Félix Guattari. *Anti-Oedipus: Capitalism and Schizophrenia*. Translated by Robert Hurley, Mark Seem, and Helen Lane. Minneapolis: University of Minnesota Press, 1983.

– *A Thousand Plateaus: Capitalism and Schizophrenia*. Translated by Brian Massumi. Minneapolis and London: University of Minnesota Press, 1987.

D'Emilio, John, and Estelle B. Freedman. *Intimate Matters: A History of Sexuality in America*. New York: Harper and Row 1988.

De Mott, Benjamin. 'The Anatomy of "Playboy."' *Commentary* 34, no. 2 (August 1962): 111–19.

Denning, Michael. 'Licensed to Look: James Bond and the Heroism of Consumption.' In Francis Mulhern, ed., *Contemporary Marxist Literary Criticism*, 211–29. New York and London: Longman, 1992.

De Pelsmacker, Patrick, and M. Geuens. 'Reactions to Different Types of Ads in Belgium and Poland.' *International Marketing Review* 15, no. 4 (1998): 277–90.

Descharnes, Robert, and Gilles Néret. *Salvador Dalí 1904–1989*. Köln: Taschen, 1997.

Diamant, Lincoln. *Television's Classic Commercials: The Golden Years 1948–58.* New York: Hastings House, 1971.

Dichter, Ernest. *Handbook of Consumer Motivations: The Psychology of the World of Objects.* New York: McGraw-Hill, 1964.

– *The Strategy of Desire.* Garden City, NY: Doubleday, 1960.

Dicke, Tom. 'Review of *Disaster in Dearborn: The Story of the Edsel,* by Thomas E. Bonsall.' *Business History Review* (Summer 2003), www.hbs.edu/bhr/archives/bookreviews/77/2003summertdicke.pdf.

Dickinson, Edward Ross. 'Biopolitics, Fascism, Democracy: Some Reflections on Our Discourse about "Modernity."' *Central European History* 37, no. 1 (2004): 1–48.

Dines, Gail. 'Dirty Business: *Playboy* Magazine and the Mainstreaming of Pornography.' In Gail Dines, Robert Jensen, and Ann Russo, *Pornography: The Production and Consumption of Inequality,* 37–63. New York: Routledge 1998.

– '"I Buy It for the Articles": *Playboy* Magazine and the Sexualization of Consumerism.' In Gail Dines and Jean Humez, eds, *Gender, Race and Class in Media: A Text-Reader,* 254–62. Thousand Oaks, CA: Sage, 1995.

Dines, Gail, Robert Jensen, and Ann Russo. *Pornography: The Production and Consumption of Inequality.* New York and London: Routledge, 1998.

Donovan, Bess. 'The Menace of Barbie Dolls.' *Ramparts,* 25 January 1965, 25–8.

Dubin, Steven C. *Arresting Images: Impolitic Art and Uncivil Actions.* London and New York: Routledge, 1992.

– 'How "Sensation" Became a Scandal.' *Art in America,* January 2000. Online at www.findarticles.com in August 2001.

– 'Who's That Girl? The World of Barbie Deconstructed.' In Yona Zeldis McDonough, ed., *The Barbie Chronicles: A Living Doll Turns Forty,* 19–40. New York: Simon and Schuster, 1999.

Ducille, Ann. 'Dyes and Dolls: Multicultural Barbie and the Merchandising of Difference.' *Difference: A Journal of Feminist Cultural Studies* 6, no. 1 (Spring 1994). Online copy, Infotrac, August 1999.

Eagleton, Terry. *Ideology: An Introduction.* London: Verso, 1991.

Easton, John. 'Consuming Interests.' *University of Chicago Magazine* 93, no. 6 (August 2001). Online in January 2002.

Eckman, B., and S. Goldberg. *The Viability of the Marlboro Man among the 18–24 Segment.* Tobacco Documents Online, dated 03/02/1992, taken from the Minnesota Trial Exhibits Set.

Ehrenreich, Barbara. *The Hearts of Men: American Dreams and the Flight from Commitment.* Garden City, NY: Anchor Press, 1983.

Elias, Norbert. *The Civilizing Process: Sociogenetic and Psychogenetic Investigations.* Rev. ed. Translated by Edmund Jephcott. Edited by Eric Dunning,

Johan Goudsblom, and Stephen Mennell. Oxford: Blackwell Publishers, 2000.

Elkins, James. *The Object Stares Back: On the Nature of Seeing*. San Diego: Harcourt, 1996.

Elliott, Richard, Abigail Jones, Andrew Banfield, and Matt Barlow. 'Overt Sexuality in Advertising: A Discourse Analysis of Gender Responses.' *Journal of Consumer Policy* 18 (June 1995): 187–217.

Elliott, Richard, and Mark Ritson. 'Practicing Existential Consumption: The Lived Meaning of Sexuality in Advertising.' *Advances in Consumer Research* 22 (1995): 740–5.

Ellis, John. *Visible Fictions. Cinema:Television:Video*. London: Routledge and Kegan Paul, 1982.

Engelhardt, Tom. *The End of Victory Culture: Cold War America and the Disillusioning of a Generation*. Amherst: University of Massachusetts Press, 1998.

Epley, Nick. 'Science or Science Fiction?: Investigating the Possibility (and Plausibility) of Subliminal Persuasion.' January 2002, www.csic.cornell.edu/201/subliminal.

Escalas, Jennifer Edson. 'Advertising Narratives: What Are They and How Do They Work?' In Barbara B. Stern, ed., *Representing Consumers: Voices, Views and Visions*, 267–89. London and New York: Routledge, 1998.

Ewen, Stuart. *All Consuming Images: The Politics of Style in Contemporary Culture*. New York: Basic Books, 1988.

Eysenck, Michael, ed. *The Blackwell Dictionary of Cognitive Psychology*. Oxford: Blackwell, 1990.

Faith, Karlene. *Madonna, Bawdy and Soul*. Toronto: University of Toronto Press, 1997.

Faludi, Susan. *Backlash: The Undeclared War against American Women*. New York and London: Doubleday, 1991.

Finkelstein, Haim. *Salvador Dalí's Art and Writing, 1927–1942: The Metamorphosis of Narcissus*. New York: Cambridge University Press, 1996.

Fiske, John. 'British Cultural Studies and Television.' In Robert Allen, ed., *Channels of Discourse, Reassembled: Television and Contemporary Criticism*, 2nd ed., 284–326. Chapel Hill: University of North Carolina Press, 1992.

– *Reading the Popular*. Boston: Unwin Hyman, 1989.

– *Television Culture*. London: Methuen, 1987.

Forrester, John. *Dispatches from the Freud Wars: Psychoanalysis and Its Passions*. Cambridge, MA: Harvard University Press, 1997.

Foster, Hal. 'Hey, That's Me.' Review of Bruce Mau's *Life Style*. *London Review of Books*, 5 April 2001, 13, 14.

Foucault, Michel. 'The Birth of Biopolitics.' In *Essential Works of Foucault 1954–*

1984, vol. 1: *Ethics: Subjectivity and Truth*, edited by Paul Rabinow, translated by Robert Hurley, et al., 73–9. New York: New Press, 1997.

– *The Birth of the Clinic: An Archaeology of Medical Perception*. Translated by A.M. Sheridan Smith. New York: Vintage Books, 1994.

– 'Body/Power.' In *Power/Knowledge: Selected Interviews and Other Writings 1972–1977*, edited by Colin Gordon, 57–8. New York: Pantheon Books, 1980.

– 'The Confession of the Flesh.' In *Power/Knowledge: Selected Interviews and Other Writings 1972–1977*, edited by Colin Gordon, 194–228. New York: Pantheon Books, 1980.

– 'Different Spaces.' In *Essential Works of Foucault, 1954–1984*, vol. 2: *Aesthetics, Method and Epistemology*, edited by James D. Faubion, translated by Robert Hurley, 175–85. New York: New Press, 1998.

– *Discipline and Punish: The Birth of the Prison*. Translated by Alan Sheridan. New York: Vintage Books, 1979.

– 'The End of the Monarchy of Sex.' In *Foucault Live (Interviews, 1961–1984)*, edited by Sylvère Lotringer, translated by Lysa Hochroth and John Johnston, 214–25. New York: Semiotext[e], 1996.

– 'The Ethics of the Concern for Self as a Practice of Freedom.' In *Essential Works of Foucault 1954–1984*, vol. 1: *Ethics: Subjectivity and Truth*, edited by Paul Rabinow, translated by Robert Hurley, et al., 281–301. New York: New Press, 1997.

– 'An Ethics of Pleasure.' In *Foucault Live (Interviews, 1961–1984)*, edited by Sylvère Lotringer, translated by Lysa Hochroth and John Johnston, 371–81. New York: Semiotext[e], 1996.

– *The History of Sexuality*, vol. 1: *An Introduction*. Translated by Robert Hurley. New York: Vintage Books, 1990.

– 'Interview with Michel Foucault.' In *Essential Works of Foucault 1954–1984*, vol. 3: *Power*, edited by James D. Faubion, translated by Robert Hurley, et al., 272–8. New York: New Press, 2000.

– 'On the Genealogy of Ethics: An Overview of Work in Progress.' In *Essential Works of Foucault 1954–1984*, vol. 1: *Ethics: Subjectivity and Truth*, edited by Paul Rabinow, translated by Robert Hurley, et al., 253–80. New York: New Press, 1997.

– *The Order of Things: An Archaeology of the Human Sciences*. New York: Vintage Books 1994.

– [First] 'Preface to *The History of Sexuality*, Volume Two.' In *Essential Works of Foucault 1954–1984*, vol. 1: *Ethics: Subjectivity and Truth*, edited by Paul Rabinow, translated by Robert Hurley, et al., 199–205. New York: New Press, 1997.

– 'Schizo-Culture: Infantile Sexuality.' In *Foucault Live (Interviews, 1961–1984)*.

edited by Sylvère Lotringer, translated by Lysa Hochroth and John Johnston, 154–67. New York: Semiotext[e], 1996.

- 'Sex, Power and the Politics of Identity.' In *Foucault Live (Interviews, 1961–1984)*, edited by Sylvère Lotringer, translated by Lysa Hochroth and John Johnston, 384–8. New York: Semiotext[e], 1996.
- 'Sexual Choice, Sexual Act.' In *Foucault Live (Interviews, 1961–1984)*, edited by Sylvère Lotringer, translated by Lysa Hochroth and John Johnston, 322–34. New York: Semiotext[e], 1996.
- 'Sexuality and Solitude.' In *Essential Works of Foucault 1954–1984*, vol. 1: *Ethics: Subjectivity and Truth*, edited by Paul Rabinow, translated by Robert Hurley, et al., 175–84. New York: New Press, 1997.
- *'Society Must Be Defended': Lectures at the Collège de France 1975–1976*. Edited by Mauro Bertani and Alessandro Fontana. Translated by David Macey. New York: Picador, 2003.
- 'Sorcery and Madness.' In *Foucault Live (Interviews, 1961–1984)*, edited by Sylvère Lotringer, translated by Lysa Hochroth and John Johnston, 200–2. New York: Semiotext[e], 1996.
- 'The Subject and Power.' In *Essential Works of Foucault 1954–1984*, vol. 3: *Power*, edited by James D. Faubion, translated by Robert Hurley, et al., 326–48. New York: New Press, 2000.
- 'Subjectivity and Truth,' In *Essential Works of Foucault 1954–1984*, vol. 1: *Ethics: Subjectivity and Truth*, edited by Paul Rabinow, translated by Robert Hurley, et al., 87–92. New York: New Press, 1997.
- 'Technologies of the Self.' In *Essential Works of Foucault 1954–1984*, vol. 1: *Ethics: Subjectivity and Truth*, edited by Paul Rabinow, translated by Robert Hurley, et al., 223–51. New York: New Press, 1997.
- *The History of Sexuality*, vol. 2: *The Use of Pleasure*. Translated by Robert Hurley. New York: Vintage Books, 1990.

Fox, Stephen. *The Mirror Makers: A History of American Advertising and Its Creators*. New York: Vintage Books, 1985.

Frank, Lisa, and Paul Smith, eds. *Madonnarama: Essays on Sex and Popular Culture*. Pittsburgh: Cleis Press, 1993.

Frank, Thomas. *The Conquest of Cool: Business Culture, Counterculture, and the Rise of Hip Consumerism*. Chicago and London: University of Chicago Press, 1997.

Freedberg, David. *The Power of Images: Studies in the History and Theory of Response*. Chicago: University of Chicago Press, 1989.

Freud, Sigmund. *Civilization and Its Discontents*. New York: Dover Publications, 1994.

- 'Creative Writers and Day-Dreaming.' In *The Standard Edition of the Complete*

Psychological Works of Sigmund Freud, vol. 9. General editor James Strachey. London: Hogarth Press and the Institute of Psycho-Analysis, 1959.

– 'Fetishism.' In *The Penguin Freud Library*, vol. 7: *On Sexuality*, edited by Angela Richards, 345–57. London: Penguin Books, 1991.

– *The Interpretation of Dreams*. In *The Penguin Freud Library*, vol. 4. Edited by James Strachey. London: Penguin Books, 1991.

– *New Introductory Lectures on Psychoanalysis*. In *The Penguin Freud Library*. vol. 2. Edited by James Strachey. London: Penguin Books, 1991.

– 'On Transformations of Instinct as Exemplified in Anal Eroticism.' In *The Penguin Freud Library*, vol. 7: *On Sexuality*, edited by Angela Richards, 293–302. London: Penguin Books, 1977.

– 'Repression.' In *The Penguin Freud Library*, vol. 11: *On Metapsychology: The Theory of Psychoanalysis*, edited by Angela Richards, 145–58. London: Penguin Books, 1991.

– 'Three Essays on the Theory of Sexuality.' In *The Penguin Freud Library*, vol. 7: *On Sexuality*, edited by Angela Richards, 33–169. London: Penguin Books, 1991.

– 'The Unconscious.' In *The Penguin Freud Library*, vol. 11: *On Metapsychology: The Theory of Psychoanalysis*, edited by Angela Richards, 159–222. London: Penguin Books, 1984.

Friedan, Betty. *The Feminine Mystique*. New York: W.W. Norton, 1997.

Friedman, David. *A Mind of Its Own: A Cultural History of the Penis*. New York: Free Press, 2001.

Fromm, Erich. 'The Method and Function of an Analytic Social Psychology: Notes on Psychoanalysis and Historical Materialism.' In *The Crisis of Psychoanalysis*, 110–34. New York: Holt, Rinehart and Winston, 1970.

– 'Psychoanalytic Characterology and Its Relevance for Social Psychology.' In *The Crisis of Psychoanalysis*, 135–58. New York: Holt, Rinehart and Winston, 1970.

Gable, Myron, Henry Wilkens, Lynn Harris, and Richard Feinberg. 'An Evaluation of Subliminally Embedded Sexual Stimuli in Graphics.' *Journal of Advertising* 16, issue 1 (1987): 26+.

Garfield, Bob. 'Barbie Becomes More Than Just a Pretty Face.' *Advertising Age*, 15 February 1999.

Gay, Peter. *Freud: A Life for Our Times*. New York: W.W. Norton, 1998.

Genel, Katia. 'The Question of Biopower: Foucault and Agamben.' Translated by Craig Carson. *Rethinking Marxism* 18, no. 1 (January 2006): 43–62.

Gerson, Walter, and Sander Lund. '*Playboy* Magazine: Sophisticated Smut or Social Revolution?' *Journal of Popular Culture* 1, no. 3 (Winter 1969): 218–27.

Gibson, Ian. *The Shameful Life of Salvador Dalí*. London: Faber and Faber, 1997.

Gibson, James William. *Warrior Dreams: Paramilitary Culture in Post-Vietnam America.* New York: Hill and Wang, 1994.

Gibson, Pamela Church, and Roma Gibson, eds. *Dirty Looks: Women, Pornography, Power.* London: British Film Institute, 1993.

Gilbert, Sylvie, ed. *Arousing Sensation: A Case Study of Controversy Surrounding Art and the Erotic.* Banff: Banff Centre Press, 1999.

Goodman, Ralph. 'Freud and the Hucksters.' *The Nation*, 14 February 1953.

Grossman, Atina. *Reforming Sex: The German Movement for Birth Control and Abortion Reform, 1920–1950.* New York: Oxford University Press, 1995.

Grover, Ronald. 'MGM Can Bank on Bonds.' *BusinessWeek Online*, 18 November 2002. Available at businessweek.com.

Guilbert, Georges-Claude. *Madonna as Postmodern Myth.* Jefferson, NC: McFarland and Co., 2002.

Gunn, Simon. 'From Hegemony to Governmentality: Changing Conceptions of Power in Social History.' *Journal of Social History*, 39, no. 3 (Spring 2006): 705–20.

Gunter, Barrie. *Media Sex: What Are the Issues?* Mahwah, NJ: Lawrence Erlbaum Associates, 2002.

Habermas, Jürgen. 'Modernity: An Unfinished Project.' In Maurizio Passerin d'Entrèves and Seyla Benhabib, eds, *Habermas and the Unfinished Project of Modernity: Critical Essays on the Philosophical Discourse of Modernity*, 38–58. Cambridge, MA: MIT Press, 1997.

Hale Jr, Nathan G. *The Rise and Crisis of Psychoanalysis in the United States: Freud and the Americans, 1917–1985.* New York: Oxford University Press, 1995.

Haley, Russell, James Staffaroni, and Arthur Fox. 'The Missing Measures of Copy Testing.' *Journal of Advertising Research* 34, no. 3 (May/June 1994): 46+. Online edition.

Hall, Karen J. 'A Soldier's Body: GI Joe, Hasbro's Great American Hero, and the Symptoms of Empire.' *Journal of Popular Culture* 38, no. 1 (August 2004): 34–54.

Halttunen, Karen. 'Humanitarianism and the Pornography of Pain in Anglo-American Culture.' *American Historical Review* 100, no. 2 (April 1995): 303–34.

Hamilton, Richard. *Collected Words 1953–1982.* London: Thames and Hudson, 1982.

Hamilton, William. 'In a New Museum, a Blue Period.' *New York Times*, 11 March 1999.

Haraway, Donna. *Simians, Cyborgs and Women: The Reinvention of Nature.* New York: Routledge, 1991.

Harris, Daniel. 'Make My Rainy Day.' In Carol Benson and Allan Metz, eds,

The Madonna Companion: Two Decades of Commentary, 219–225. New York: Schirmer Books, 1999.

– 'Some Reflections on the Facial Expressions of Fashion Models: 100 Years of *Vogue.' Salmagundi* 98–9 (1993): 129–40.

Harvey, David. 'The Body as an Accumulation Strategy.' *Environment and Planning D: Society and Space* 16 (1998): 401–21.

Haug, W.F. *Critique of Commodity Aesthetics: Appearance, Sexuality and Advertising in Capitalist Society.* Translated by Robert Bock. Minneapolis: University of Minnesota Press, 1986.

Hedger, Leigh. 'Kinsey Collections Reveal the Value of Variety.' Paper on the Indiana University website, July 2000. Available at http://www.indiana.edu/~rcapub/v20n2/p28.html.

Henry, Harry. *Motivation Research: Its Practice and Uses for Advertising, Marketing, and Other Business Purposes.* London: Crosby Lockwood, 1958.

Hetherington, Kevin. 'From Blindness to Blindness: Museums, Heterogeneity and the Subject.' In John Law and John Hassard, eds, *Actor Network Theory and After,* 51–73. Oxford: Blackwell/The Sociological Review, 1999.

Hewitt, Duncan. 'China Sex Museum Goes Public.' *BBC News,* 8 February 2001.

Hickman, Tom. *The Sexual Century: How Private Passion Became a Public Obsession.* London: Carlton Books, 1999.

Hollander, Anne. *Feeding the Eye: Essays.* Berkeley and London: University of California Press, 1999.

Hollows, Joanne. 'The Bachelor Dinner: Masculinity, Class, and Cooking in *Playboy,* 1953–1961.' *Continuum: Journal of Media and Cultural Studies* 16, no. 2 (2002): 143–55.

Hook, Melissa. 'Material Girl.' In Yona Zeldis McDonough, ed., *The Barbie Chronicles: A Living Doll Turns Forty,* 169–76. New York: Simon and Schuster, 1999.

Horkheimer, Max, and Theodor Adorno. *Dialectic of Enlightenment.* Translated by John Cumming. New York: Continuum, 1995.

Horowitz, Daniel. 'The Emigré as Celebrant of American Consumer Culture: George Katona and Ernest Dichter.' In Susan Strasser, Charles McGovern, and Matthias Judt, eds, *Getting and Spending: European and American Consumer Societies in the Twentieth Century,* 149–66. Cambridge: Cambridge University Press, 1998.

– *Vance Packard and American Social Criticism.* Chapel Hill: University of North Carolina Press, 1994.

Hovey, Jaime. 'Lesbian Bondage, or Why Dykes Like 007.' In Edward P. Comentale, Stephen Watt, and Skip Willman, eds, *Ian Fleming and James Bond: The Cultural Politics of 007,* 42–54. Bloomington and Indianapolis: Indiana University Press, 2005.

Howard, Vicki. '"At the Curve Exchange": Postwar Beauty Culture and Working Women at Maidenform.' *Enterprise and Society* 1 (September 2000): 591–618.

Huang, Ming-Hui. 'Romantic Love and Sex: Their Relationship and Impacts on Ad Attitudes.' *Psychology and Marketing* 21, no. 1 (January 2004): 53–73.

Hughes, Lawrence. 'Maidenform Dreams Big.' *Sales Management*, 5 April 1963, 35–9, 118–24.

Hunt, Lynn, ed. *The Invention of Pornography.* New York: Zone Books, 1993.

Huxley, Aldous. *Brave New World.* Harmondsworth: Penguin Books, 1955.

'Ida Rosenthal.' *Time*, 24 October 1960.

Infante, Guillermo Cabrera. *La Habana Para un Infante Difento.* Barcelona: Seix Barral Bibloteca Brave, 2000.

Ingham, John, and Lynne Feldman. 'Hefner, Hugh Marston.' In *Contemporary American Business Leaders: A Biographical Dictionary*, 217–26. New York: Greenwood Press, 1990.

'It's Not the Doll, It's the Clothes.' *Business Week*, 16 December 1961.

Jaffe, Aaron. 'James Bond, Meta-Brand.' In Edward P. Comentale, Stephen Watt, and Skip Willman, eds, *Ian Fleming and James Bond: The Cultural Politics of 007*, 87–106. Bloomington and Indianapolis: Indiana University Press, 2005.

James Bond Collection, The. Vols 1–3. MGM Home Entertainment, 2002.

Jancovich, Mark. 'Placing Sex: Sexuality, Taste and Middlebrow Culture in the Reception of *Playboy* Magazine.' *The Journal of Cult Media* Issue 2 (Autumn/Winter 2001). Online at http://www.cult-media.com/issue2/Ajanc.htm, September 2005.

Jay, Martin. *The Dialectical Imagination: A History of the Frankfurt School and the Institute of Social Research, 1923–1950.* Berkeley: The University of California Press, 1973.

– *Downcast Eyes: The Denigration of Vision in Twentieth-Century French Thought.* Berkeley: University of California Press, 1993.

Jeffords, Susan. *Hard Bodies: Hollywood Masculinity in the Reagan Era.* New Brunswick, NJ: Rutgers University Press, 1994.

Johnson, Christopher. 'Great Wall of Sex Silence.' *NOW Magazine* (Toronto), 23–9 August 2001. Online edition.

Juffer, Jane. *At Home with Pornography: Women, Sex, and Everyday Life.* New York and London: New York University Press, 1998.

Kallan, Richard, and Robert Brooks. 'The Playmate of the Month: Naked but Nice.' *Journal of Popular Culture* 8, no. 2 (Fall 1974): 328–37.

Kaplan, E. Anne. *Rocking around the Clock: Music Television, Postmodernism, and Consumer Culture.* New York: Routledge, 1987.

Kaplan, James. 'The Triumph of Calvinism.' *New York,* 18 September 1995.

Katz, Barry. *Herbert Marcuse and the Art of Liberation: An Intellectual Biography.* London: NLB, 1982.

Kellner, Douglas. *Herbert Marcuse and the Crisis of Marxism.* Berkeley: University of California Press, 1984.

– 'Marcuse and the Quest for Radical Subjectivity.' February 2000. Online (April 2006) at dogma.free.fr/txt/Kellner-Marcuse01.htm.

Kendrick, Walter. *The Secret Museum: Pornography in Modern Culture.* New York: Penguin Books, 1987.

Key, Wilson Bryan. *The Age of Manipulation.* New York: Henry Holt, 1989.

– *Media Sexploitation.* Englewood Cliffs, NJ: Prentice-Hall, 1976.

– *Subliminal Seduction: Ad Media's Manipulation of a Not-So-Innocent America.* Englewood Cliffs, NJ: Prentice-Hall, 1973.

Kilbourne, Jean. *Deadly Persuasion: Why Women and Girls Must Fight the Addictive Power of Advertising.* New York: Free Press, 1999.

– *Killing Us Softly: Advertising's Image of Women.* Video documentary. Three editions (1979, 1987, 2000).

Kimmel, Michael. *The Gender of Desire: Essays on Male Sexuality.* Albany: State University of New York Press, 2005.

King, Neal. *Heroes in Hard Times: Cop Action Movies in the U.S.* Philadelphia: Temple University Press, 1999.

Koldeweij, Jos, Paul Vandenbroeck, and Bernard Vermet, eds. *Hieronymus Bosch: The Complete Paintings and Drawings.* Museum Boijmans Van Beuningen, Rotterdam. Rotterdam and Amsterdam: NAi Publishers and Ludion Ghent, 2001.

Korinek, Valerie. *Roughing It in the Suburbs: Reading* Chatelaine *Magazine in the Fifties and Sixties.* Toronto: University of Toronto Press, 2000.

Koudelova, Rady, and Jeryl Whitelock. 'A Cross-Cultural Analysis of Television Advertising in the UK and the Czech Republic.' *International Marketing Review* 18, no. 3 (2001): 286–300.

Krugman, Dean, Glen Cameron, and Candace White. 'Visual Attention to Programming and Commercials: The Use of In-Home Observations.' *Journal of Advertising* 24, no. 1 (Spring 1995). Online edition.

Kuspit, Donald. 'The Uses of Irony: Popularity and Beauty in Mel Ramos's Painting.' In Donald Kuspit with Louis K. Meisel, *Mel Ramos Pop Art Fantasies: The Complete Paintings,* 12–32. New York: Watson-Guptill Publications, 2004.

Lakshmanan, Indira. 'China Gets Officially Hot and Bothered.' *San Francisco Chronicle,* 31 December 2000. Online at www.sfgate.com, January 2002.

Lambiase, Jacqueline, and Tom Reichert. 'Future Questions and Challenges:

Advertising Research in the Midst of Sex Noise.' In Tom Reichert and Jacqueline Lambiase, eds, *Sex in Advertising: Perspectives on the Erotic Appeal*, 273–8. Mahwah, NJ: Lawrence Erlbaum Associates, 2003.

Laqueur, Thomas W. *Solitary Sex: A Cultural History of Masturbation*. New York: Zone Books, 2004.

Larsen, David. 'South Park's Solar Anus, or, Rabelais Returns: Cultures of Consumption and the Contemporary Aesthetic of Obscenity.' *Theory, Culture and Society* 18, no. 4 (2001): 65–82.

Latour, Bruno. 'Is *Re*-Modernization Occurring – and If So, How to Prove It? A Commentary on Ulrich Bech.' *Theory, Culture and Society* 20 no. 2 (2003): 35–48.

– *Pandora's Hope: Essays on the Reality of Science Studies*. Cambridge, MA: Harvard University Press, 1999.

– *We Have Never Been Modern*. Translated by Catherine Porter. Cambridge, MA: Harvard University Press, 1993.

LaTour, Michael, and Tony Henthorne. 'Nudity and Sexual Appeals: Understanding the Arousal Process and Advertising Response.' In Tom Reichert and Jacqueline Lambiase, eds, *Sex in Advertising: Perspectives on the Erotic Appeal*, 91–106. Mahwah, NJ: Lawrence Erlbaum Associates, 2003.

LaTour, Michael S., Robert E. Pitts, and David C. Snook-Luther. 'Female Nudity, Arousal, and Ad Response: An Experimental Investigation.' *Journal of Advertising* 19, no. 4 (1990): 51–62.

Law, John, and John Hassard, eds. *Actor Network Theory and After*. Oxford: Blackwell Publishers/The Sociological Review, 1999.

Lears, Jackson. *Fables of Abundance: A Cultural History of Advertising in America*. New York: Basic Books, 1994.

Leavy, Jane. 'Is There a Barbie Doll in Your Past?' *Ms.*, September 1979, 102.

Lemke, Thomas. '"The Birth of Bio-Politics": Michel Foucault's Lecture at the Collège de France on Neo-Liberal Governmentality.' *Economy and Society* 30 no. 2 (May 2001): 190–207.

Les Brown's Encyclopedia of Television. 3rd ed. Detroit: Visible Ink Press, 1992.

Letiche, Hugo. 'Viagra(ization) or Technoromanticism.' *Consumption, Markets and Culture* 5, no. 3, (2002): 247–60.

Levine, Joshua. 'Search and Find: Subliminal Advertising Theoretician Wilson Bryan Key Survives Ridicule.' *Forbes* 148, no. 5 (2 September 1991).

Levinson, Jerrold. 'Erotic Art and Pornographic Pictures.' *Philosophy and Literature* 29 (2005): 228–40.

Lin, Carolyn. 'Uses of Sex Appeals in Prime-Time Commercials.' *Sex Roles: A Journal of Research* 38, no. 5–6(March 1998): 461–76.

Livingstone, Marco. *Pop Art: A Continuing History*. New York: Thames and Hudson, 2000.

Lloyd, Fran. 'The Changing Faces of Madonna.' In Fran Lloyd, ed., *Deconstructing Madonna*, 9–15. London: Batsford, 1993.

Lloyd, Fran, ed. *Deconstructing Madonna*. London: Batsford, 1993.

Loeb, Lori Anne. *Consuming Angels: Advertising and Victorian Women*. New York: Oxford, 1994.

Lord, M.G. *Forever Barbie: The Unauthorized Biography of a Real Doll*. New York: William Morrow and Company, 1994.

– 'Pornutopia: How Feminist Scholars Learned to Love Dirty Pictures.' In the now defunct online journal *Lingua Franca* of 1997.

Lucas, D.H. *Psychology for Advertisers*. New York and London: Harper and Brothers, 1930.

Lucie-Smith, Edward. *Movements in Art since 1945*. New rev. ed. London: Thames and Hudson, 1984.

Luke, Timothy W. *Museum Politics: Power Plays at the Exhibition*. Minneapolis and London: University of Minnesota Press, 2002.

Lyotard, J.-F. *Libidinal Economy*. Translated by Iain Hamilton Grant. Bloomington and Indianapolis: Indiana University Press, 1993.

Maciejewski, Jeffrey J. 'Is the Use of Sexual and Fear Appeals Ethical? A Moral Evaluation by Generation Y College Students.' *Journal of Current Issues and Research in Advertising* 26, no. 2 (Fall 2004): 97–105.

Madonna. *The Girlie Show*. Warner Reprise Video, 1993.

– *The Immaculate Collection*. Warner Reprise Video, 1990.

– *Justify My Love*. Warner Reprise Video, 1990.

– *Sex*. New York: Warner Books, 1992.

– *Truth or Dare*. Miramax Films, Alliance Video, 1998.

– *The Video Collection 93:99*. Warner Reprise Video, 1999.

'Maidenform's Mrs. R.' *Fortune*, July 1950, 75.

Maines, Rachel P. *The Technology of Orgasm: 'Hysteria,' the Vibrator, and Women's Sexual Satisfaction*. Baltimore and London: Johns Hopkins University Press, 1999.

Mamiya, Christin J. *Pop Art and Consumer Culture: American Super Market*. Austin: University of Texas Press, 1992.

Mamo, Laura, and Jennifer R. Fishman. 'Potency in All the Right Places: Viagra as a Technology of the Gendered Body.' *Body and Society* 7, no. 4 (2001): 13–35.

Mandziuk, Roseann. 'Feminist Politics and Postmodern Seductions: Madonna and the Struggle for Political Articulation.' In Cathy Schwichtenberg, ed., *The Madonna Connection: Representational Politics, Subcultural Identities, and Cultural Theory*, 167–87. Boulder, CO: Westview Press, 1993.

Manuel, Frank E., and Fritzie P. Manuel. *Utopian Thought in the Western World*. Cambridge, MA: Harvard University Press, 1979.

Marchand, Philip. *Marshall McLuhan: The Medium and the Messenger.* Toronto: Random House Canada, 1989.

Marchand, Roland. *Advertising the American Dream: Making Way for Modernity 1920–1940.* Berkeley: University of California Press, 1985.

Marcuse, Herbert. *Eros and Civilization: A Philosophical Inquiry into Freud.* Boston: Beacon Press, 1974.

– *An Essay on Liberation.* London: Allen Lane, 1969.

– *One-Dimensional Man: Studies in the Ideology of Advanced Industrial Society.* Boston: Beacon Press, 1991.

Marshall, Barbara L. "'Hard Science": Gendered Constructions of Sexual Dysfunction in the "Viagra Age."' *Sexualities* 5, no. 2 (2002): 131–58.

Martin, Denis-Constant. 'Politics behind the Mask: Studying Contemporary Carnivals in Political Perspective, Theoretical and Methodological Suggestions.' *Questions de Recherche/Research in Question* no. 2 (November 2001): 1–34.

Martin, James. 'Calvinism.' *America,* 23 September 1995.

Martin, Richard. *Fashion and Surrealism.* New York: Rizzoli, 1987.

Marx, Karl. *Capital: A Critique of Political Economy.* Vol. 1. Translated by Ben Fowkes. London: Penguin Classics, 1990.

May, Todd. 'Foucault Now?' *Foucault Studies* no. 3 (November 2005): 65–76.

Mayer, Martin. *Madison Avenue, USA.* New York: Pocket Books, 1959.

Maynard, Joyce. 'Looking Back at Barbie.' *Across the Board,* December 1976, 17–20.

McCann-Erickson World Group. 'Bob Coen's Insiders Report 2000–2001.' Online at www.mccann.com in April 2003.

McCarthy, David. *Pop Art.* London: Tate Gallery, 2000.

McDonald, Joe. 'Chinese Sexual Museum Has High-Minded Goals.' Associated Press report in *Post-Intelligencer* (Seattle), 11 November 1999.

McDowell, Colin. *Fashion Today.* London: Phaidon Press, 2000.

McGinn, Colin. 'Freud under Analysis.' *New York Review of Books,* 4 November 1999, 20–4.

McInerney, Jay. 'How Bond Saved America – and Me.' In Jay McInery et al., *Dressed to Kill: James Bond: The Suited Hero,* 13–37. Paris and New York: Flammarion, 1996.

McLuhan, Marshall. *The Mechanical Bride: Folklore of Industrial Man.* Boston: Beacon Press, 1967.

– 'Sight, Sound, and the Fury.' In Bernard Rosenberg and David Manning White, eds, *Mass Culture: The Popular Arts in America,* 489–95. New York: Free Press, 1964.

– *Understanding Media.* 2nd ed. New York: New American Library, 1964.

McNair, Brian. *Mediated Sex: Pornography and Postmodern Culture*. London and New York: Arnold, 1996.
– *Striptease Culture: Sex, Media and the Democratization of Desire*. London: Routledge, 2002.
McQuarrie, Edward F., and David Glen Mick. 'Visual Rhetoric in Advertising: Text-Interpretive, Experimental, and Reader-Response Analyses.' *Journal of Consumer Research* 26 (June 1999): 37–54.
Mendelson, Jordana. 'Of Politics, Postcards and Pornography: Salvador Dalí's *Le Mythe tragique de l'Angélus de Millet.*' In Raymond Spiteri and Donald LaCoss, eds, *Surrealism, Politics and Culture*, 169–78. Aldershot: Ashgate, 2003.
Metzstein, Margery. 'SEX: Signed, Sealed, Delivered ...' In Fran Lloyd, ed., *Deconstructing Madonna*, 91–8. London: Batsford, 1993.
Mick, David Glen, and Claus Buhl. 'A Meaning-Based Model of Advertising Experiences.' *Journal of Consumer Research* 19 (December 1992): 317–38.
Miller, G. Wayne. *Toy Wars: The Epic Struggle between G.I. Joe, Barbie and the Companies That Made Them*. New York: Time Books, 1998.
Miller, Jonathan. *McLuhan*. London: Fontana/Collins, 1971.
Miller, Peter, and Nikolas Rose. 'Governing Economic Life.' In Mike Gane and Terry Johnson, eds, *Foucault's New Domains*, 75–105. London and New York: Routledge, 1993.
– 'Mobilizing the Consumer: Assembling the Subject of Consumption.' *Theory, Culture and Society* 14, no. 1 (1997): 1–36.
Miller, Russell. *Bunny: The Real Story of Playboy*. London: Michael Joseph, 1984.
Miller, Toby. *Spyscreen: Espionage on Film and TV from the 1930s to the 1960s*. Oxford: Oxford University Press, 2003.
Mittal, Banwari. 'Public Assessment of TV Advertising: Faint Praise and Harsh Criticism.' *Journal of Advertising Research* 34, no. 1 (January/February 1994). Online from ProQuest.
Mittal, Banwari, and Walfried M. Lassar. 'Sexual Liberalism as a Determinant of Consumer Response to Sex in Advertising.' *Journal of Business and Psychology* 15, no. 1 (Fall 2000): 111–27.
Molinaro, Matie, Corinne McLuhan, and William Toye, eds, *Letters of Marshall McLuhan*. Toronto: Oxford University Press, 1987.
Montgomery, Sara Teasdale. 'Norman, Craig and Kummel, Inc.' In John McDonough and Karen Egolf, eds, *The Advertising Age Encyclopedia of Advertising*, vol. 2: 1153–1156. New York: Fitzroy Dearborn, 2003.
Moog, Carol. *'Are They Selling Her Lips?': Advertising and Identity*. New York: William Morrow, 1990.
Moore, Timothy. 'Subliminal Advertising: What You See Is What You Get.' *Journal of Marketing* 46 (March 1982): 6+.

- 'Subliminal Perception: Facts and Fallacies.' *Skeptical Inquirer*, Spring 1992. Available online at www.esicop.org/si/9204/subliminal-perception.html.

Morrow, Lance. 'Old Goats and Their Libidos.' *Time*, 18 October 1999. Online edition.

Morton, Andrew. *Madonna*. New York: St Martin's Paperbacks, 2002.

Morton, Melanie. 'Don't Go for Second Sex, Baby!' In Cathy Schwichtenberg, ed., *The Madonna Connection: Representational Politics, Subcultural Identities, and Cultural Theory*, 213–35. Boulder, CO: Westview Press, 1993.

Mundy, Jennifer, ed. *Surrealism: Desire Unbound*. London: Tate Publishing, 2001.

Myrone, Martin. 'Prudery, Pornography and the Victorian Nude (Or, What Do We Think the Butler Saw?).' In Allison Smith, ed., *Exposed: The Victorian Nude*, 23–36. New York: Watson-Guptill Publications, 2001.

Nelson, Sara. 'Dream Lovers.' *Madison Avenue*, January 1985, 80.

Néret, Gilles. *Dessous: Lingerie as Erotic Weapon*. Köln: Taschen, 2001.

Ni, Ching-Ching. 'This Museum Won't Give Up.' *Los Angeles Times* Service. Online at the *International Herald Tribune*, January 2002.

Norton, Kevin, Timothy Olds, Scott Olive, and Stephen Dank. 'Ken and Barbie at Life Size.' *Sex Roles: A Journal of Research* 34, no. 3–4 (February 1996). Online copy: Infotrac, August 1999.

Ochs, Elinor, and Lisa Capps. 'Narrating the Self.' *Annual Review of Anthropology* 25 (1996): 19–43.

O'Donnell, Patrick. 'James Bond, Cyborg-Aristocrat.' In Edward P. Comentale, Stephen Watt, and Skip Willman, eds, *Ian Fleming and James Bond: The Cultural Politics of 007*, 55–68. Bloomington and Indianapolis: Indiana University Press, 2005.

O'Donohoe, Stephanie. 'Advertising Uses and Gratifications.' *European Journal of Marketing* 28, no. 8/9 (1994): 52–75.

- 'Living with Ambivalence: Attitudes to Advertising in Postmodern Times.' *Marketing Theory* 1, no. 1 (September 2001): 91–108.

O'Donohoe, Stephanie, and Caroline Tynan. 'Beyond the Semiotic Strait-Jacket: Everyday Experiences of Advertising Involvement.' In Stephen Brown and Darach Turley, eds, *Consumer Research: Postcards from the Edge*, 220–48. London and New York: Routledge, 1997.

'On Erotic Art.' In *The Routledge Encyclopedia of Philosophy*. Online, Version 1.0, August 2002. London: Routledge, 2002.

Orwell, George. 'Benefit of Clergy: Some Notes on Salvador Dali.' In *Dickens, Dali and Others*, 170–84. New York: Harcourt, Brace and World, 1946.

O'Sickey, Ingeborg. 'Barbie Magazine and the Aesthetic Commodification of Girls' Bodies.' In Shari Benstock and Suzanne Ferriss, eds, *On Fashion*, 21–40. New Brunswick, NJ: Rutgers University Press, 1994.

Owen, David. 'Where Toys Come From.' *Atlantic Monthly,* October 1986. Online from Infotrac.

Packard, Vance. *The Hidden Persuaders.* New York: Pocket Books, 1975.

Paglia, Camille. 'Madonna I: Animality and Artifice.' In *Sex, Art, and American Culture: Essays,* 3–5. New York: Vintage Books, 1992.

– 'Madonna II: Venus of the Radio Waves.' In *Sex, Art, and American Culture: Essays,* 6–13. New York: Vintage Books, 1992.

– *Sexual Personae: Art and Decadence from Nefertiti to Emily Dickinson.* New York: Vintage Books, 1991.

Parkin, Katherine. 'The Sex of Food and Ernest Dichter: The Illusion of Inevitability.' *Advertising and Society Review* 5, no. 2 (2004). Online edition.

Patterson, Maurice, and Richard Elliott. 'Negotiating Masculinities: Advertising and the Inversion of the Male Gaze.' *Consumption, Markets and Culture* 5, no. 3 (2002): 231–46.

Person, Ethel Spector. *The Sexual Century.* New Haven and London: Yale University Press, 1999.

Peterson, James. *The Century of Sex:* Playboy's *History of the Sexual Revolution, 1900–1999.* New York: Grove Press, 1999.

Picasso Érotique. Munich and Montreal: Prestel-Verlag and Musée des Beaux-Arts, 2001.

Poffenberger, Albert. *Psychology in Advertising.* 2nd ed. New York and London: McGraw-Hill, 1932.

Pomian, Krzysztof. *Collectors and Curiosities: Paris and Venice, 1500–1800.* Translated by Elizabeth Wiles-Portier. Cambridge: Polity Press, 1990.

Poster, Mark. *The Mode of Information: Poststructuralism and Social Context.* Chicago: University of Chicago Press, 1990.

Potts, Annie. 'Deleuze on Viagra (Or, What Can a "Viagra-Body" Do?). *Body and Society* 10, no. 1 (2004): 17–36.

Potts, Annie, Victoria Grace, Nicola Gavey, and Tiina Vares. '"Viagra Stories": Challenging "Erectile Dysfunction."' *Social Science and Medicine* 59 (2004): 489–99.

Powers, Ann. 'New Tune for the Material Girl: I'm Neither.' In Carol Benson and Allan Metz, eds, *The Madonna Companion: Two Decades of Commentary,* 79–83. New York: Schirmer Books, 1999.

Pratkanis, Anthony. 'The Cargo-Cult Science of Subliminal Persuasion.' *Skeptical Inquirer,* Spring 1992. Online copy in January 2002 at http://www.csicop.org/si/.

Prendergast, Gerard, and Benny Ho. 'A Hong Kong View of Offensive Advertising.' *Journal of Marketing Communications* 8 (2002): 165–77.

Pribram, E. Deidre. 'Seduction, Control, and the Search for Authenticity:

Madonna's Truth or Dare.' In Cathy Schwichtenberg, ed., *The Madonna Connection: Representational Politics, Subcultural Identities, and Cultural Theory*, 189–212. Boulder, CO: Westview Press, 1993.

Prince, Stephen. *Visions of Empire: Political Imagery in Contemporary American Film*. New York: Praeger, 1992.

'Q&A: Liu Dalin and His Sex Museum.' Online at en1.chinabroadcast.cn. Posted 8 July 2004; available October 2005.

Quindlen, Anna. 'Barbie at 35.' In Yona Zeldis McDonough, ed., *The Barbie Chronicles: A Living Doll Turns Forty*, 117–20. New York: Simon and Schuster, 1999.

Rabinow, Paul, and Nikolas Rose. 'Thoughts on the Concept of Biopower Today.' Online at www.molsci.org/files/Rose_Rabinow_Biopower_Today.pdf on 18 May 2006.

'Racy Sales Pitch Losing Appeal.' *National Post* (Toronto), 30 August 2004, FP1, FP11.

Radforth, Robert. *Dalí*. London: Phaidon, 1997.

Rakstis, Ted. 'Debate in the Doll House.' *Today's Health*, December 1970, 28–31, 65–6.

Rand, Erica. *Barbie's Queer Accessories*. Durham, NC: Duke University Press, 1995.

Ratcliff, Carter. *Andy Warhol*. New York: Abbeville Press, 1983.

Rebello, Stephen. 'Selling Bond: The Artists behind the Outrageous Movie Poster Ideas That Convinced Us Nobody Did It Better.' Repr. from *Cinefantastique* 19, no. 5 (July 1989). Online at www.ianfleming.org in June 2002.

Reich, Wilhelm. 'Dialectical Materialism and Psychoanalysis.' In Lee Baxandall, ed., *Sex-Pol, Essays 1929–1934: Wilhelm Reich*, translated by Anna Bostock, Tom Dubose, and Lee Baxandall, 1–74. New York: Random House, 1966.

– *The Sexual Revolution: Toward a Self-Regulating Character Structure*. Translated by Therese Pol. New York: Farrar, Straus and Giroux, 1974.

– 'What Is Class Consciousness?' In Lee Baxandall, ed., *Sex-Pol, Essays 1929–1934: Wilhelm Reich*, translated by Anna Bostock, Tom Dubose, and Lee Baxandall, 275–358. New York: Random House, 1966.

Reiche, Reimut. *Sexuality and Class Struggle*. Translated by Susan Bennett. London: New Left Books, 1970.

Reichert, Tom. *The Erotic History of Advertising*. Amherst, NY: Prometheus Books, 2003.

– '"Lesbian Chic" Imagery in Advertising: Interpretations and Insights of Female Same-Sex Eroticism.' *Journal of Current Issues and Research in Advertising* 23, no. 2 (Fall 2001): 9–22.

Reichert, Tom, Susan Heckler, and Sally Jackson. 'The Effects of Sexual Social Marketing Appeals on Cognitive Processing and Persuasion.' *Journal of Advertising* 30, no. 1 (Spring 2001): 13–27.

Reichert, Tom, Jacqueline Lambiase, Susan Morgan, Meta Carstaphen, and Susan Zavoina. 'Cheesecake and Beefcake: No Matter How You Slice It, Sexual Explicitness in Advertising Continues to Increase.' *Journalism and Mass Communication Quarterly* 76, no. 1 (Spring 1999): 7–20.

Richardson, Michael. 'Seductions of the Impossible: Love, the Erotic and Sacrifice in Surrealist Discourse.' *Theory, Culture and Society* 15, no. 3–4 (1998): 375–92.

Ricoeur, Paul. *Lectures on Ideology and Utopia*. Edited by George H. Taylor. New York: Columbia University Press, 1986.

Rieff, Philip. *The Triumph of the Therapeutic: Uses of Faith after Freud*. New York: Harper and Row, 1966.

Ritson, Mark, and Richard Elliott. 'The Social Uses of Advertising: An Ethnographic Survey of Adolescent Advertising Audiences.' *Journal of Consumer Research* 26, no. 3 (December 1999): 260–77.

Robertson, Pamela. *Guilty Pleasures: Feminist Camp from Mae West to Madonna*. Durham, NC: Duke University Press, 1996.

– 'Guilty Pleasures.' In Carol Benson and Allan Metz, eds, *The Madonna Companion: Two Decades of Commentary*, 268–90. New York: Schirmer Books, 1999.

Robinson, Paul A. *The Freudian Left: Wilhelm Reich, Geza Roheim, Herbert Marcuse*. New York: Harper and Row, 1969.

Roegiers, Patrick. 'The Bobkin, the Vulva and the Eye-Popping Gaze of the Painter.' In *Picasso Érotique*, 68–75. Munich and Montreal: Prestel-Verlag and Musée des Beaux-Arts, 2001.

Rogers, Martha, and Christine Seiler. 'The Answer Is No: A National Survey of the Advertising Industry.' *Journal of Advertising Research*, March/April 1994. Available online from ProQuest.

Rogers, Martha, and Kirk Smith. 'Public Perceptions of Subliminal Advertising: Why Practitioners Shouldn't Ignore This Issue.' *Journal of Advertising Research*, March/April 1993. Available online from ProQuest.

Rose, Nikolas. *Inventing Our Selves: Psychology, Power, and Personhood*. Cambridge: Cambridge University Press, 1998.

– 'The Politics of Life Itself.' *Theory, Culture and Society* 18, no. 6 (2001): 1–30.

– *Powers of Freedom: Reframing Political Thought*. Cambridge: Cambridge University Press, 1999.

Roudinesco, Elisabeth. *Jacques Lacan*. Translated by Barbara Bray. New York: Columbia University Press, 1997.

Rourke, Mary. 'A Mad, Mad World of "Madonnas."' In Carol Benson and Allan

Metz, eds, *The Madonna Companion: Two Decades of Commentary*, 116–19. New York: Schirmer Books 1999.

Rutherford, Paul. *Endless Propaganda: The Advertising of Public Goods*. Toronto: University of Toronto Press. 2000.

– *The New Icons? The Art of Television Advertising*. Toronto: University of Toronto Press, 1994.

Rycroft, Charles. *A Critical Dictionary of Psychoanalysis*. 2nd ed. London: Penguin Books, 1995.

– *Wilhelm Reich*. New York: Viking Press, 1969.

Sacco, Joe. 'Dreams for Sale: How the One for Maidenform Came True.' *Advertising Age*, 12 September 1977, 63–4.

Schauble, John. 'Life's Basics Are Food and Sex: The Chinese Excel at One.' *The Age* (Melbourne, Australia), 19 May 2000.

Schiffman, Leon, and Leslie Kanuk. *Consumer Behavior*. 2nd ed. Englewood Cliffs, NJ: Prentice-Hall, 1983.

Schneider, Cy. *Children's Television: The Art, the Business, and How It Works*. Chicago: NTC Business Books, 1987.

Schulze, Laurie, Anne Barton White, and Jane D. Brown. '"A Sacred Monster in Her Prime": Audience Construction of Madonna as Low-Other.' In Cathy Schwichtenberg, ed., *The Madonna Connection: Representational Politics, Subcultural Identities, and Cultural Theory*, 15–37. Boulder, CO: Westview Press, 1993.

Schwichtenberg, Cathy, ed. *The Madonna Connection: Representational Politics, Subcultural Identities, and Cultural Theory*. Boulder, CO: Westview Press, 1993.

Secrest, Meryle. *Salvador Dalí*. New York: E.P. Dutton, 1986.

Seidman, Steven. *Romantic Longings: Love in America, 1830–1980*. New York and London: Routledge, 1991.

Seigel, Jerrold. 'Problematizing the Self.' In Victoria Bonnell and Lynn Hunt, eds, *Beyond the Cultural Turn: New Directions in the Study of Society and Culture*, 281–314. Berkeley: University of California Press, 1999.

Seitz, Philip. 'The Mattel Story: Success.' *Toys and Playthings*, February 1966, 70–3.

Severn, Jessica, George E. Belch, and Michael A. Belch. 'The Effects of Sexual and Non-Sexual Advertising Appeals and Information Level on Cognitive Processing and Communication Effectiveness.' *Journal of Advertising* 19, no. 1 (1990): 14–22.

Shalit, Ruth. 'The Return of the Hidden Persuaders.' *Salon Media*, 27 September 1999. Online.

Shavitt, Sharon, Pamela Lowrey, and James Haefner. 'Public Attitudes toward Advertising: More Favourable Than You Might Think.' *Journal of*

Advertising Research 38, no. 4 (July/August 1998). Available online from ProQuest.

Shaw, Susan M. 'Men's Leisure and Women's Lives: The Impact of Pornography on Women.' *Leisure Studies* 18 (1999): 197–212.

Shorter, Edward. *A History of Psychiatry: From the Era of the Asylum to the Age of Prozac*. New York: John Wiley, 1997.

– *Written in the Flesh: A History of Desire*. Toronto: University of Toronto Press, 2005.

Sigel, Lisa Z. 'Filth in the Wrong People's Hands: Postcards and the Expansion of Pornography in Britain and the Atlantic World, 1880–1914.' *Journal of Social History* 33, no. 4 (Summer 2003): 859–85.

Simpson, Maria. 'Advertising Art or Obscenity? The Calvin Klein Jeans Ads.' *Journal of Popular Culture* 17, no. 3 (Fall 1983): 146–52.

Sinclair, John. *Images Incorporated: Advertising as Industry and Ideology*. London: Croom Helm, 1987.

Sivulka, Juliann. 'Historical and Psychological Perspectives of the Erotic Appeal in Advertising.' In Tom Reichert and Jacqueline Lambiase, eds, *Sex in Advertising: Perspectives on the Erotic Appeal*, 39–63. Mahwah, NJ: Lawrence Erlbaum Associates, 2003.

– *Soap, Sex, and Cigarettes: A Cultural History of American Advertising*. Belmont, CA: Wadsworth, 1998.

'6,000 Years of Sex at Chinese Museums.' Online at msnbc.msn.com. Posted 15 December 2003; available in October 2005.

Skeggs, Beverley. 'A Good Time for Women Only.' In Fran Lloyd, ed., *Deconstructing Madonna*, 61–73. London: Batsford, 1993.

Smith, Alison, ed. *Exposed: The Victorian Nude*. New York: Watson-Guptill Publications, 2002.

Smith, Stephen, Curtis Haugtvedt, John Jadrich, and Mark Anton. 'Understanding Responses to Sex Appeals in Advertising: An Individual Difference Approach.' *Advances in Consumer Research* 22 (1995): 735–9.

Sobieszek, Robert A. *The Art of Persuasion: A History of Advertising Photography*. New York: Abrams, 1988.

Solomons, Jason. 'My Kingdom for a Bond.' *The Guardian*, 17 April 2005. Online at film.guardian.co.uk.

Somers, Margaret R. 'The Narrative Construction of Identity.' *Theory and Society* 23, no. 5 (October 1994): 605–49.

Stallybrass, Peter, and Allon White. *The Politics and Poetics of Transgression*. London: Methuen, 1986.

Stam, Robert. *Subversive Pleasures: Bakhtin, Cultural Criticism, and Film*. Baltimore, MD: Johns Hopkins University Press, 1992.

Starn, Randolph. 'A Historian's Brief Guide to New Museum Studies.'
   American Historical Review 110, no. 1 (February 2005). Online at www.
   historycooperative.org.
Steele, Valerie. *Fetish: Fashion, Sex and Power*. New York and Oxford: Oxford
   University Press, 1996.
– *Fifty Years of Fashion: New Look to Now*. New Haven, CT: Yale University
   Press, 1997.
Stein, Joel. 'The Fall of the Supermodel.' *Time*, 9 November 1998, 74–5.
Steinem, Gloria. 'I Was a Playboy Bunny.' In *Outrageous Acts and Everyday
   Rebellions*, 29–69. New York: Holt, Rinehart and Winston, 1983.
Steitmatter, Rodger. *Sex Sells! The Media's Journey from Repression to Obsession*.
   Cambridge, MA: Westview Press, 2004.
Stephens, Mariflo. 'Barbie Doesn't Live Here Anymore.' In Yona Zeldis
   McDonough, ed., *The Barbie Chronicles: A Living Doll Turns Forty*, 193–6. New
   York: Simon and Schuster, 1999.
Stern, Barbara B. 'The Importance of Being Ernest: Commemorating Dichter's
   Contribution to Advertising Research.' *Journal of Advertising Research*, June
   2004, 165–9.
– 'Literary Criticism and the History of Marketing Thought: A New Perspec-
   tive on "Reading" Marketing Theory.' *Journal of the Academy of Marketing Sci-
   ence* 18, no. 4 (Fall 1990): 334+.
– 'Two Pornographies: A Feminist View of Sex in Advertising.' *Advances in
   Consumer Research* 18 (1991): 384–91.
Stern, Susan (producer/director/narrator). *Barbie Nation: An Unauthorized Tour*.
   El Rio Productions, 1998.
Stoler, Laurie Ann. *Race and the Education of Desire: Foucault's History of Sexuality
   and the Colonial Order of Things*. Durham and London: Duke University Press,
   1995.
Stoller, Debbie. *The Bust Guide to the New Girl Order*. New York: Penguin Books,
   1999.
Talese, Gay. *Thy Neighbor's Wife*. Garden City, NY: Doubleday, 1980.
Taraborrelli, J. Randy. *Madonna: An Intimate Biography*. New York: Berkley
   Books, 2002.
Tarpley, J. Douglas. 'History: 1970s.' In John McDonough and Karen Egolf, eds,
   The Advertising Age Encylopedia of Advertising, vol. 2: 791–5. New York:
   Fitzroy Dearborn, 2003.
Tetzlaff, David. 'Metatextual Girl: → patriarchy→ postmodernism→ power →
   money → Madonna.' In Cathy Schwichtenberg, ed., *The Madonna Connection:
   Representational Politics, Subcultural Identities, and Cultural Theory*, 239–64.
   Boulder, CO: Westview Press, 1993.

'The Thrill Is Gone – or Is It?' *Toronto Star*, 13 November 2004, A3.

Theriault, Florence. *Theriault Presents Barbie: A Value Guide and Description of the Barbie Doll and Other Mattel Dolls*. Annapolis, MD: Gold Horse Publishing, 1985.

Tucker, Lauren. 'The Framing of Calvin Klein: A Frame Analysis of Media Discourse about the August 1995 Calvin Klein Jeans Advertising Campaign.' *Critical Studies in Mass Communication* 15 (1998): 141–57.

Turner, Grady T. 'Sodom on the Hudson: Innovation, Reaction and Spectacle on America's Sexual Frontier.' In Museum of Sex, *NYC Sex: How New York City Transformed Sex in America*, 11–77. New York: Scala Publishers, 2002.

Turner, Kay, ed. *I Dream of Madonna: Women's Dreams of the Goddess of Pop*. San Francisco: Collins Publishers, 1993.

Twitchell, James B. *Adcult USA: The Triumph of Advertising in American Culture*. New York: Columbia University Press, 1996.

Van Meurs, Lex. 'Zapp! A Study on Switching Behavior during Commercial Breaks.' *Journal of Advertising Research* 38, no. 1 (January/February 1998). Available online at Expanded Academic ASAP.

Varnedoe, Kirk, and Adam Gopnik. *High and Low: Modern Art and Popular Culture*. New York: Museum of Modern Art, 1990.

Vilaseca, David. *Dalí: The Apocryphal Subject: Masochism, Identification and Paranoia in Salvador Dalí's Autobiographical Writings*. Catalan Studies, vol. 17. New York: Peter Lang, 1995.

Wain, Martin. *Freud's Answers: The Social Origins of Our Psychoanalytic Century*. Chicago: Ivan R. Dee, 1998.

Watts, Mark. 'Electrifying Fragments: Madonna and Postmodern Performance.' In Carol Benson and Allan Metz, eds, *The Madonna Companion: Two Decades of Commentary*, 290–301. New York: Schirmer Books, 1999.

Westenhouser, Kitturah. *The Story of Barbie*. Paducah: Collector Books, 1994.

Whitebook, Joel. 'Michel Foucault: A Structuralist in Marcusean Clothing.' *Thesis Eleven* no. 71 (November 2002): 52–70.

– *Perversion and Utopia: A Study in Psychoanalysis and Critical Theory*. Cambridge, MA: MIT Press, 1996.

Williams, Linda. *Hard Core: Power, Pleasure, and the 'Frenzy of the Visible.'* Berkeley: University of California Press, 1992.

Williams, Patti. 'Female Role Portrayals in Print Advertising: Talking with Women about Their Perceptions and Their Preferences.' *Advances in Consumer Research* 22 (1995): 753–60.

Williamson, Judith. *Decoding Advertisements: Ideology and Meaning in Advertising*. London and New York: Marion Boyars, 1992.

Willman, Skip. 'The Kennedys, Fleming, and Cuba.' In Edward P. Comentale,

Stephen Watt, and Skip Willman, eds. *Ian Fleming and James Bond: The Cultural Politics of 007*, 178–201. Bloomington and Indianapolis: Indiana University Press, 2005.

Wolfe, Naomi. *The Beauty Myth*. Toronto: Vintage Books, 1991.

– *Promiscuities*. Toronto: Vintage Books 1998.

Wolitzer, Meg. 'Barbie as Boy Toy.' In Yona Zeldis McDonough, ed., *The Barbie Chronicles: A Living Doll Turns Forty*, 207–10. New York: Simon and Schuster 1999.

Xantha Miller, Allison. 'Sex in the City.' *Lingua Franca*, September 1998. A now-defunct online journal.

Yalom, Marilyn. *A History of the Breast*. New York: Knopf, 1997.

Young, Robert M. 'Darwin, Marx, Freud: The Foundations of the Human Sciences.' In newsletter of *Cheiron*, Spring 1988. Available online July 1999.

Zinsser, William. 'Barbie Is a Million-Dollar Doll.' *Saturday Evening Post*, 12 December 1964.

Index

Abbott Laboratories, 89

ABC (American Broadcasting Network), 161, 186, 302n23

Absolut vodka, 192, 254

Actor-Network Theory, 259n25, 303n41

Adams, Charles, 73

admakers, 93, 141, 301, 305; advocates of sin, 7, 77, 126, 193, 246; and fashion, 199–200; instruments of authority, 68, 140, 144; makers of fantasies, 53, 133, 136, 197, 213, 229, 232–3, 248; as manipulaters, 71, 80, 81, 130–1, 140, 144, 147, 228–9, 230, 274nn2–11; and pornography, 14, 81, 153, 204–5, 215; and sex, 96, 193, 194, 201, 204, 212, 247, 253; and violence, 220; and voyeurism, 45; and women, 150, 152. *See also* advertising

Adorno, Theodor, 63, 177, 260n33, 270n57, 297n84

ads (print), 101, 110, 118, 123, 127, 129, 131, 140, 142, 143, 144, 154, 273n1, 278nn63–72, 287nn17–18, 310nn124–5, 317n40; advocacy, 198; campaigns, 9, 69, 79, 80, 81, 91–9, 116, 117–18, 133, 151, 162–3, 165, 176, 193, 195–6, 198, 203–4, 213, 214, 217, 218, 232, 234–5, 236–7, 238–9, 252, 253, 256, 271n71, 274n2, 288n27, 289n48, 301n16, 302n39, 307n88, 308n105; causing controversies, 79, 204, 234–5, 216–17, 288n30; criticism of, 128, 142–3, 149–53; as cultural agents, 98, 137–8, 192, 239, 241–3, 249; as marketing tools, 73, 141, 164, 200, 295n65; and pornography, 20, 36, 91, 99, 110, 111; promise of, 45, 46, 95–6; responses to, 93–4, 97–8, 136, 137–9, 177, 231, 236–7, 307n93, 308nn100–101; and romance, 80, 117, 308n95; and sexual imagery, 79, 99, 111, 130, 141–2, 146, 152, 153, 191, 194, 204–5, 240–1, 277n48, 279n95, 299n6; styles of, 89, 94–7, 125, 131–3, 204, 276, 289n43, 304n65; and wants, 74. *See also* commercials and trailers

adultery, 55, 59, 60, 139, 142

advertising, 99, 100, 110, 144, 198, 203, 271n71, 272n82, 273nn93 and 96, 274nn2–11, 282n140, 284n167, 285n2, 286n14, 287nn15–22,

Hildebrandt (artist), 30, 33
Hilfiger fashions, 241
Hill, Anita, 234
Hintaus, Tom, 203
Hirschfeld, Magnus, 17, 23
History of Sexuality, The (Foucault), 244, 257n1, 264n56, 311n2, 312nn4–6, 313nn6–9, 314n16, 315nn19–22, 316nn29–32, 35, and 37, 317nn38 and 45
Hit 100.6 radio, 208, 212
Hitchcock, Alfred, 88
Hitler, Adolf, 56, 71, 83
Holiday Inn, 209, 218
Holland, 199, 211, 277n44
Hollander, Anne, 7, 154, 257n4, 258n15, 290n54
homosexuality, 27, 59, 67, 75, 84, 85, 119, 133, 176, 233, 316n30
Hopeless (painting), 125
Hopkins, Claude, 71, 272n84
Horkheimer, Max, 63, 177, 260n33, 270n57, 297n84
Horowitz, Daniel, 272nn81 and 82, 273n97
Hot Bods underwear, 209, 215
Hovey, Jaime, 293n37
Huang, Ming-Hui, 308n98
Hucksters, The (Wakeman), 127
Human Nature (music video), 179, 180, 184, 188
Hunt, Lynn, 126, 260n7, 264n52, 265n60
Hustler, 112
Hutton, Lauren, 199
Huxley, Aldous, 61, 270n52

I Love You with My Ford (painting), 125, 134
IBM, 163

Ice (ad), 142, 207, 224, 292n32
incest, 84, 189
Independent Television Commission, 308n102
Infante, Guillermo Cabrera, 39, 265n58
Institute for Advanced Study of Human Sexuality, 13
Institute for Motivational Research, 72
Institute of Psychoanalysis, 70
intercourse, 27, 29, 39, 59, 76, 86, 105, 152, 172, 185, 190, 205, 207, 239, 274n14. *See also* lovemaking
International Playtex, 98
International Psychoanalytical Association, 56
Interpretation of Dreams, The (Freud), 84, 278n57, 283n153
Isla Bonita, La (music video), 179, 180
Ivory soap, 72, 74, 130

J&B Scotch whisky, 110, 209, 224, 229
J. Walter Thompson (agency), 80, 111
Jackson, Michael, 174
Jade Man cologne, 208, 215
Jancovich, Mark, 279n95, 281n114
jardín de eros (exhibition), 14, 22, 24, 30, 34, 36, 40, 85, 265n64
Jaws, 169
Jaws (Bond villain), 159, 169
Jay, Martin, 164, 234, 266n77, 267n9, 269n38, 317n41
Jessica, 236, 237, 253
Jinx (Bond 'girl'), 159, 162
Johns, Jasper, 123
Johnson, Paul, 158, 172
Jones, Grace, 169
Jones, Samantha (TV character), 213
Jordache jeans, 196